Shojo Beat

# VAMPIRE KNIGHT

**Story & Art by**
**Matsuri**
**Hino**

**Vol. 1**

# VAMPIRE KNIGHT

## Contents

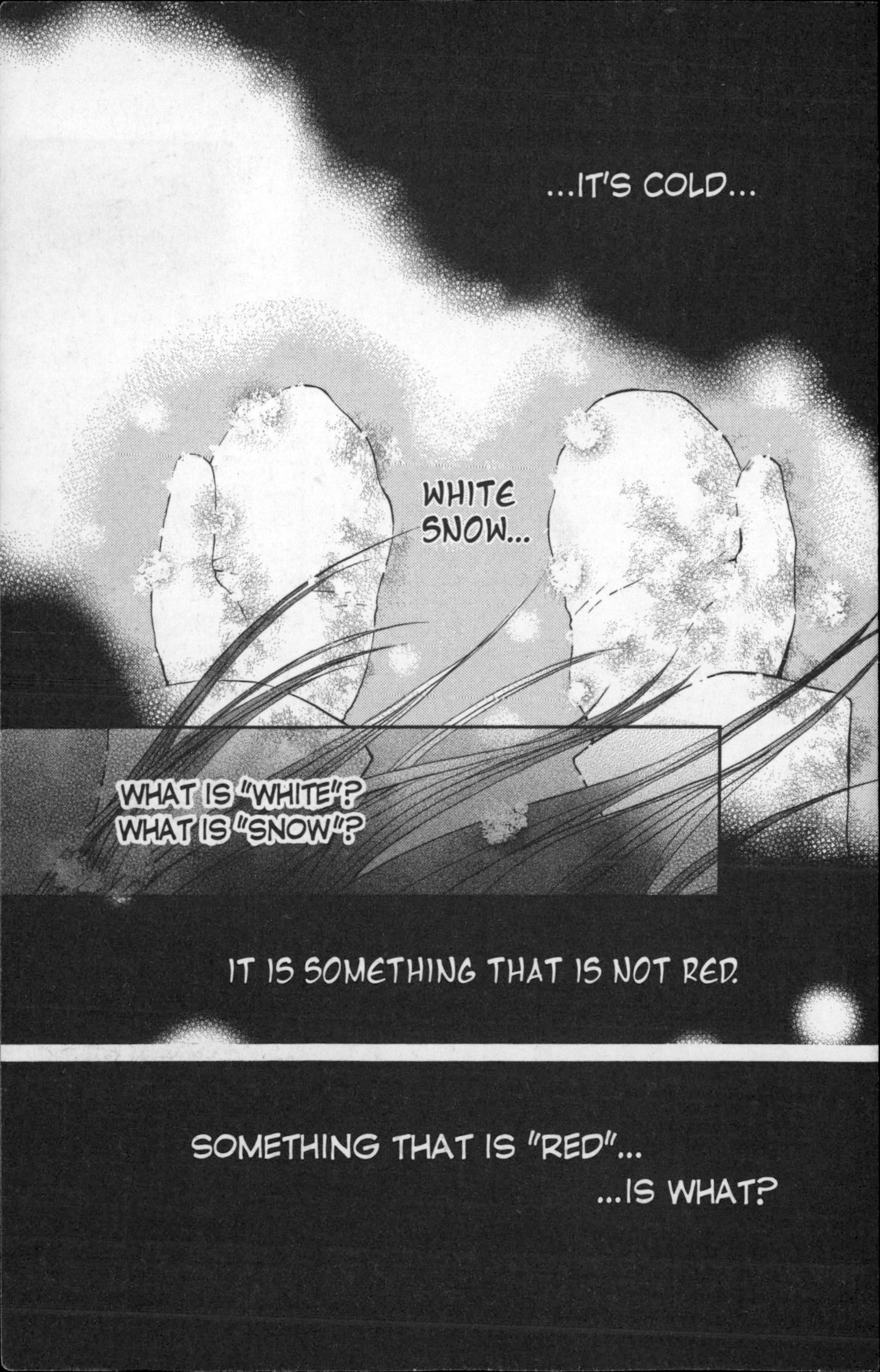

...IT'S COLD...
WHITE SNOW...
WHAT IS "WHITE"? WHAT IS "SNOW"?
IT IS SOMETHING THAT IS NOT RED.
SOMETHING THAT IS "RED"...
...IS WHAT?

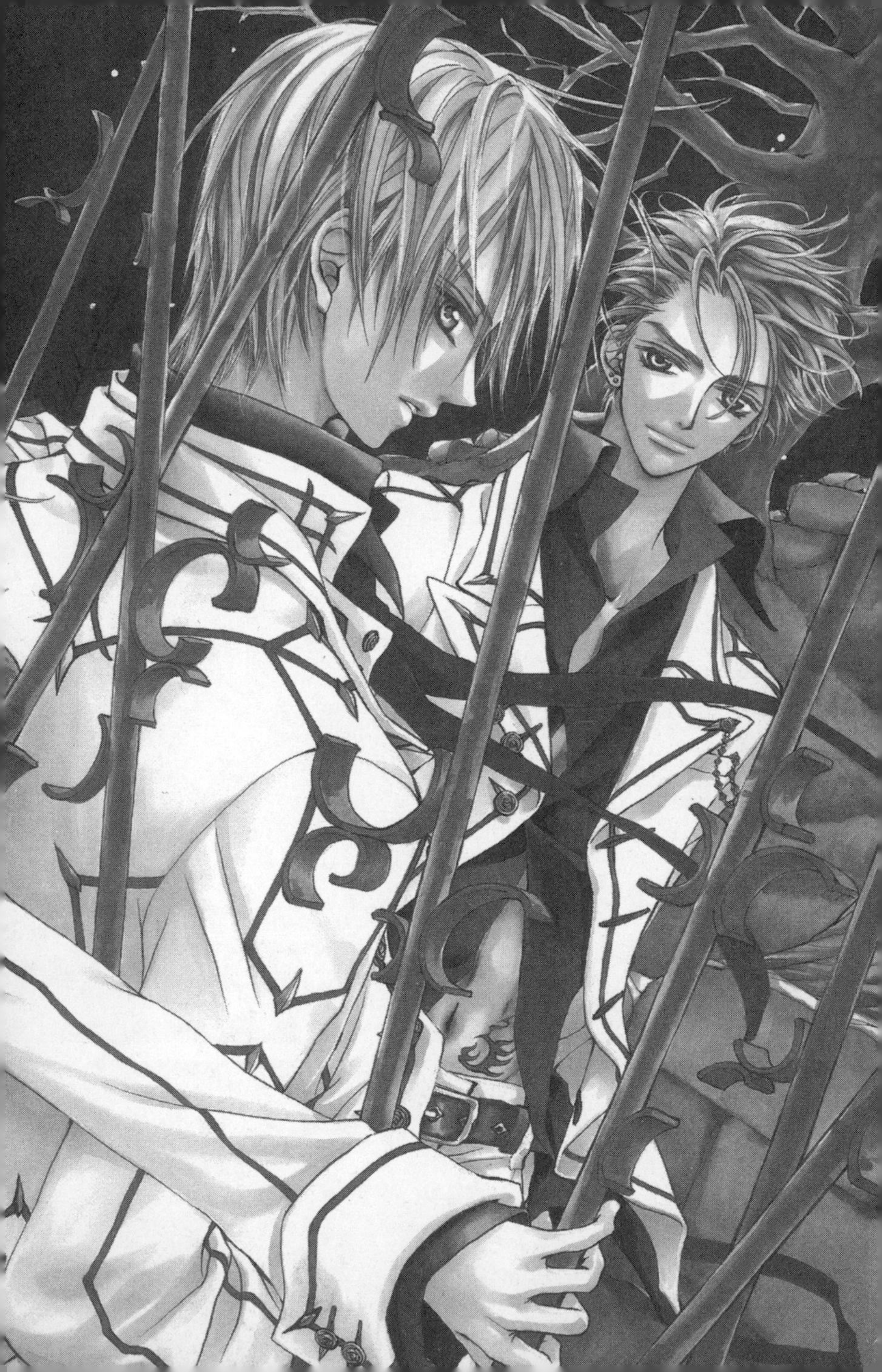

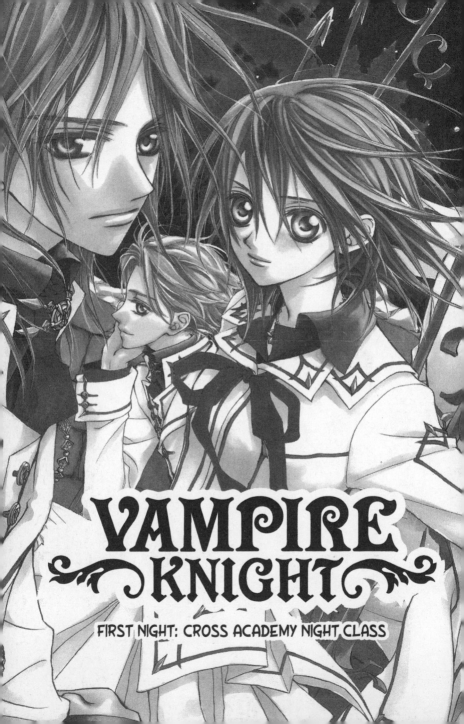

# VAMPIRE KNIGHT

## FIRST NIGHT: CROSS ACADEMY NIGHT CLASS

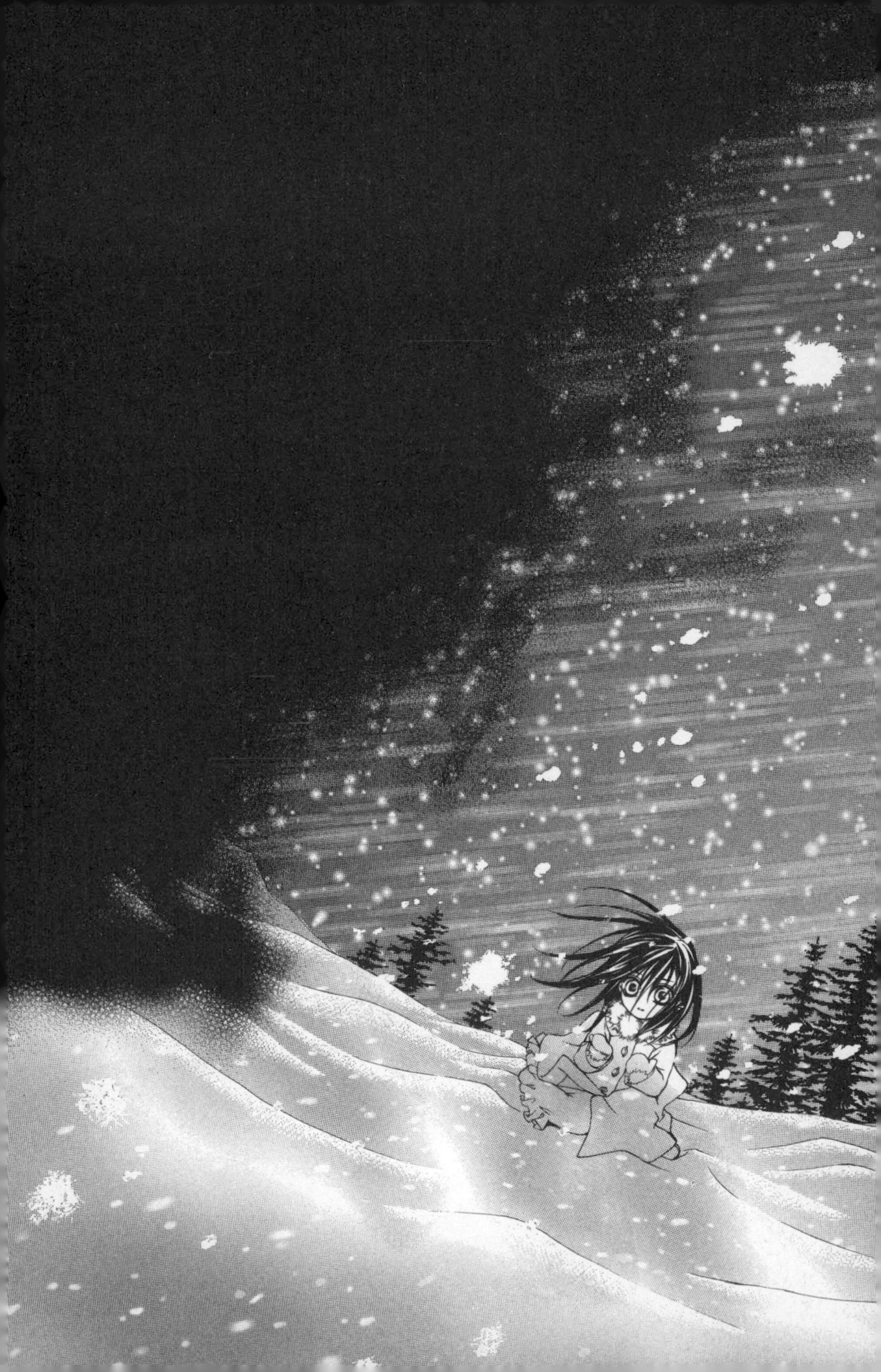

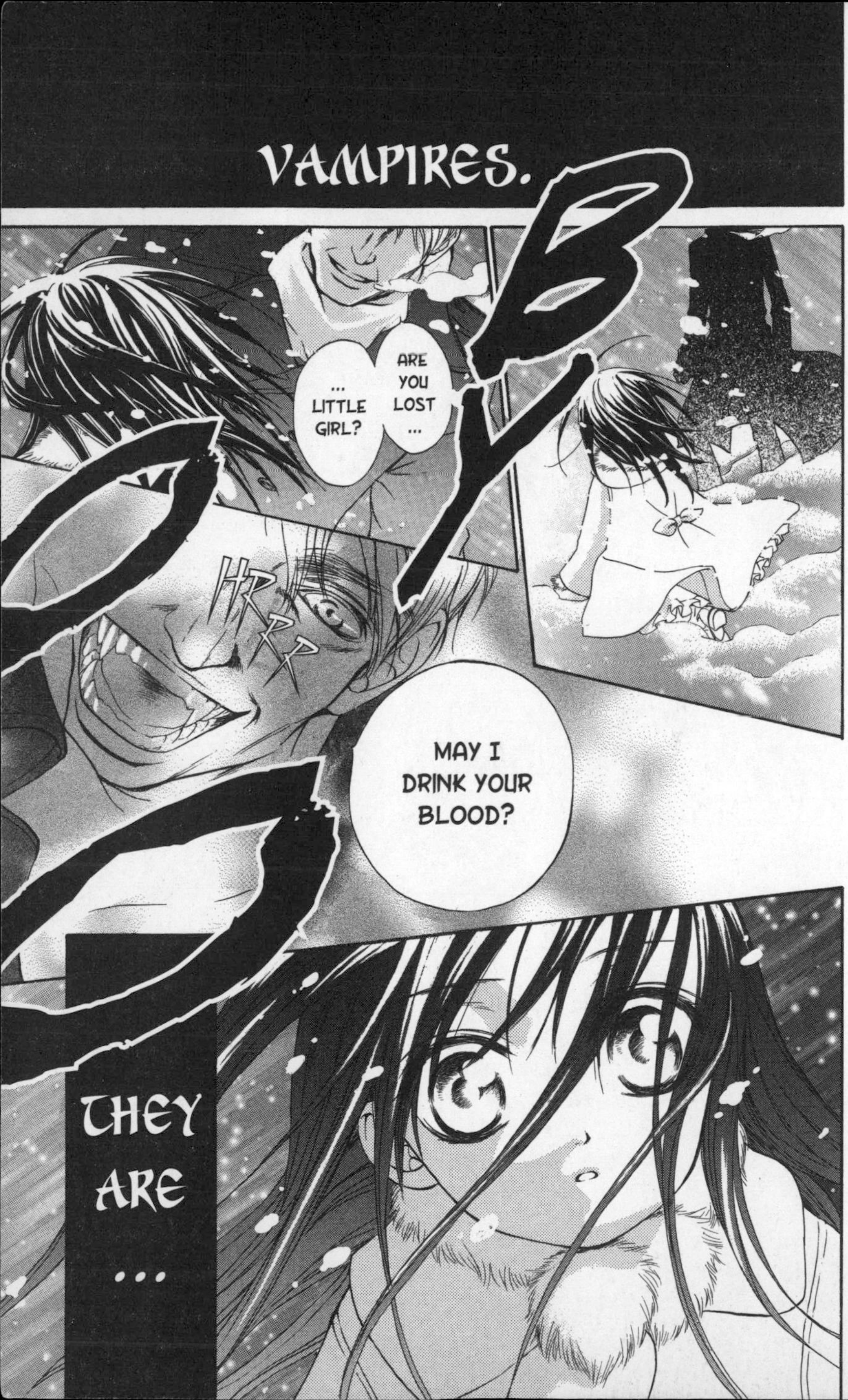
VAMPIRES.
ARE YOU LOST ...
... LITTLE GIRL?
HRRRR
MAY I DRINK YOUR BLOOD?
THEY ARE ...

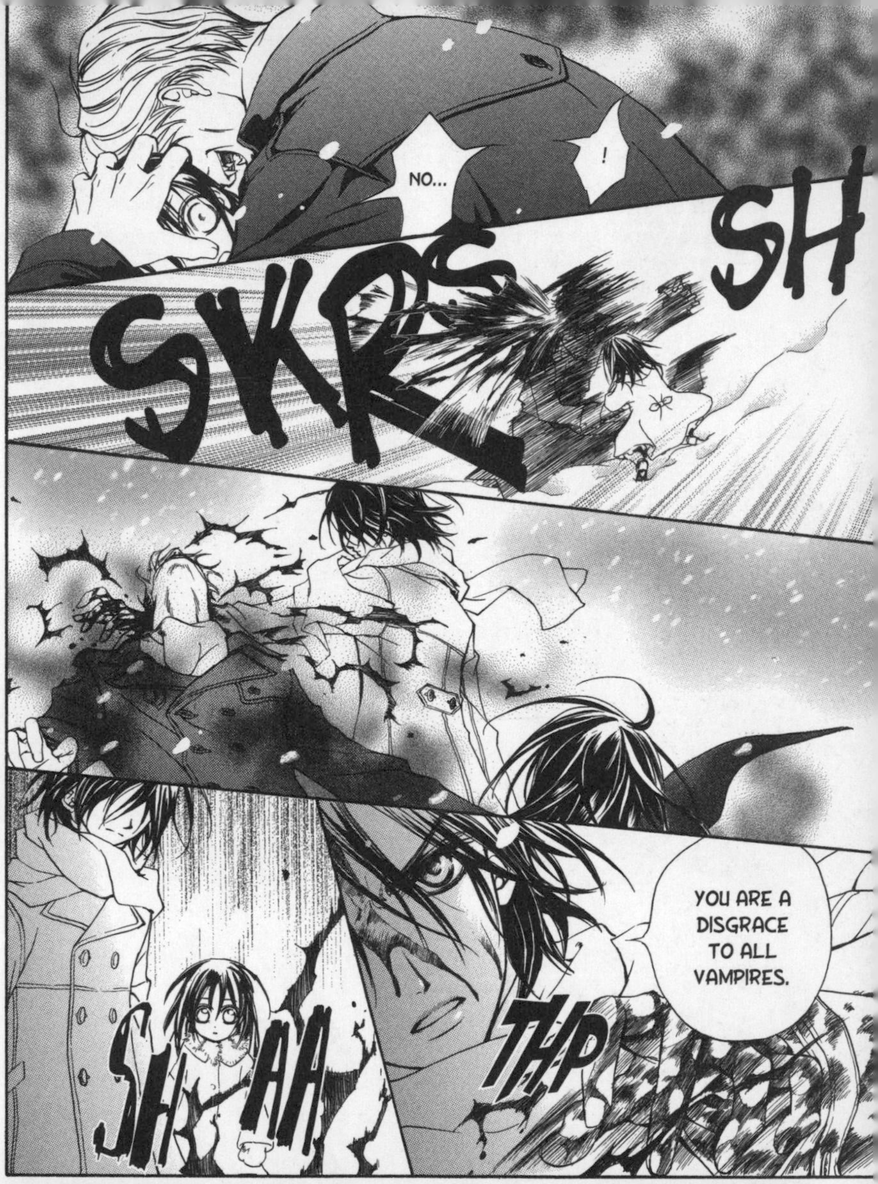
!
NO...
SKRSSH
YOU ARE A DISGRACE TO ALL VAMPIRES.
THP
SHAA

...BEASTS IN HUMAN FORM...

...WHO DRINK THE BLOOD FROM LIVING HUMANS.

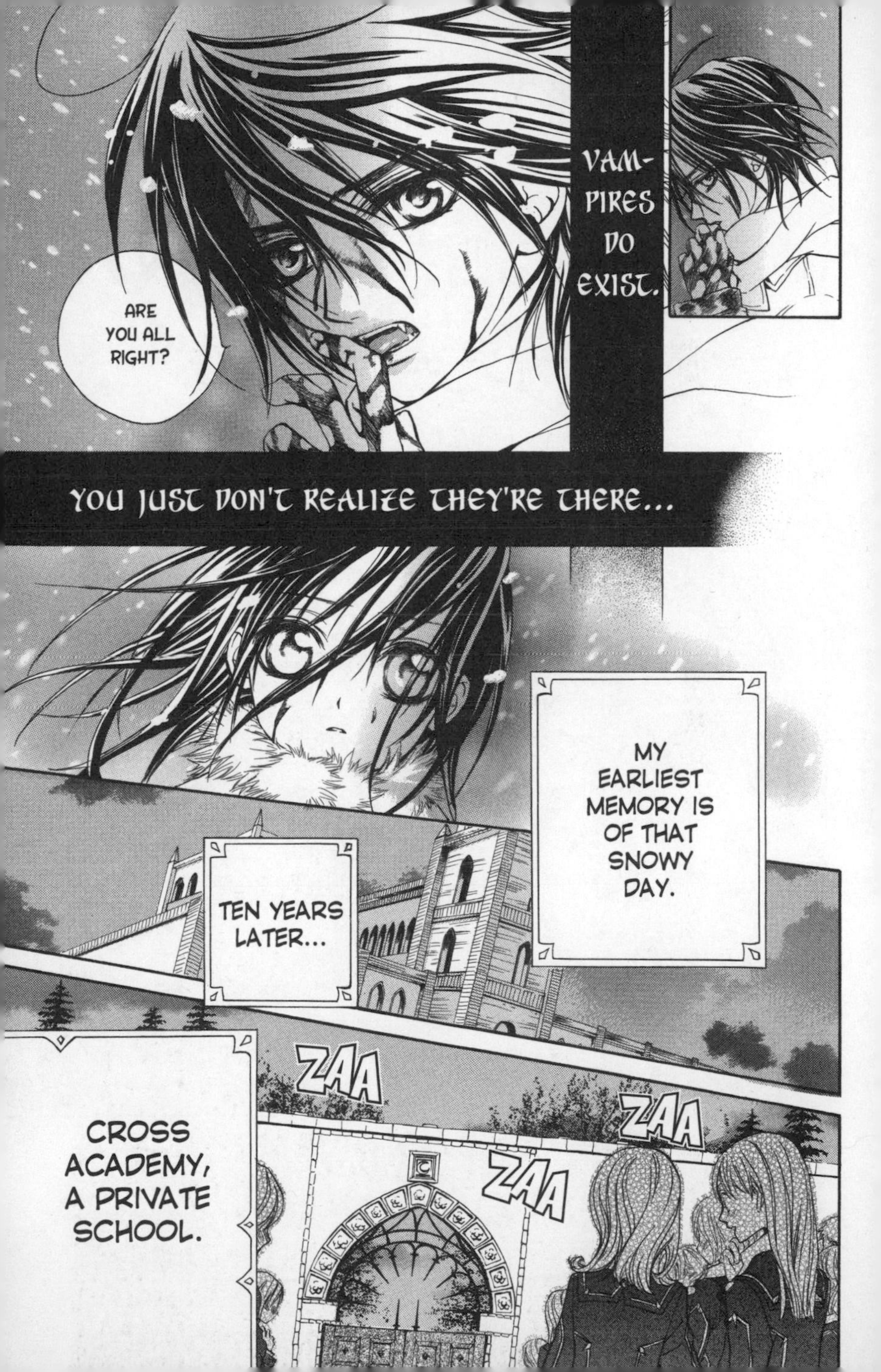
VAMPIRES DO EXIST.
ARE YOU ALL RIGHT?
YOU JUST DON'T REALIZE THEY'RE THERE...
MY EARLIEST MEMORY IS OF THAT SNOWY DAY.
TEN YEARS LATER...
ZAA
ZAA
ZAA
CROSS ACADEMY, A PRIVATE SCHOOL.

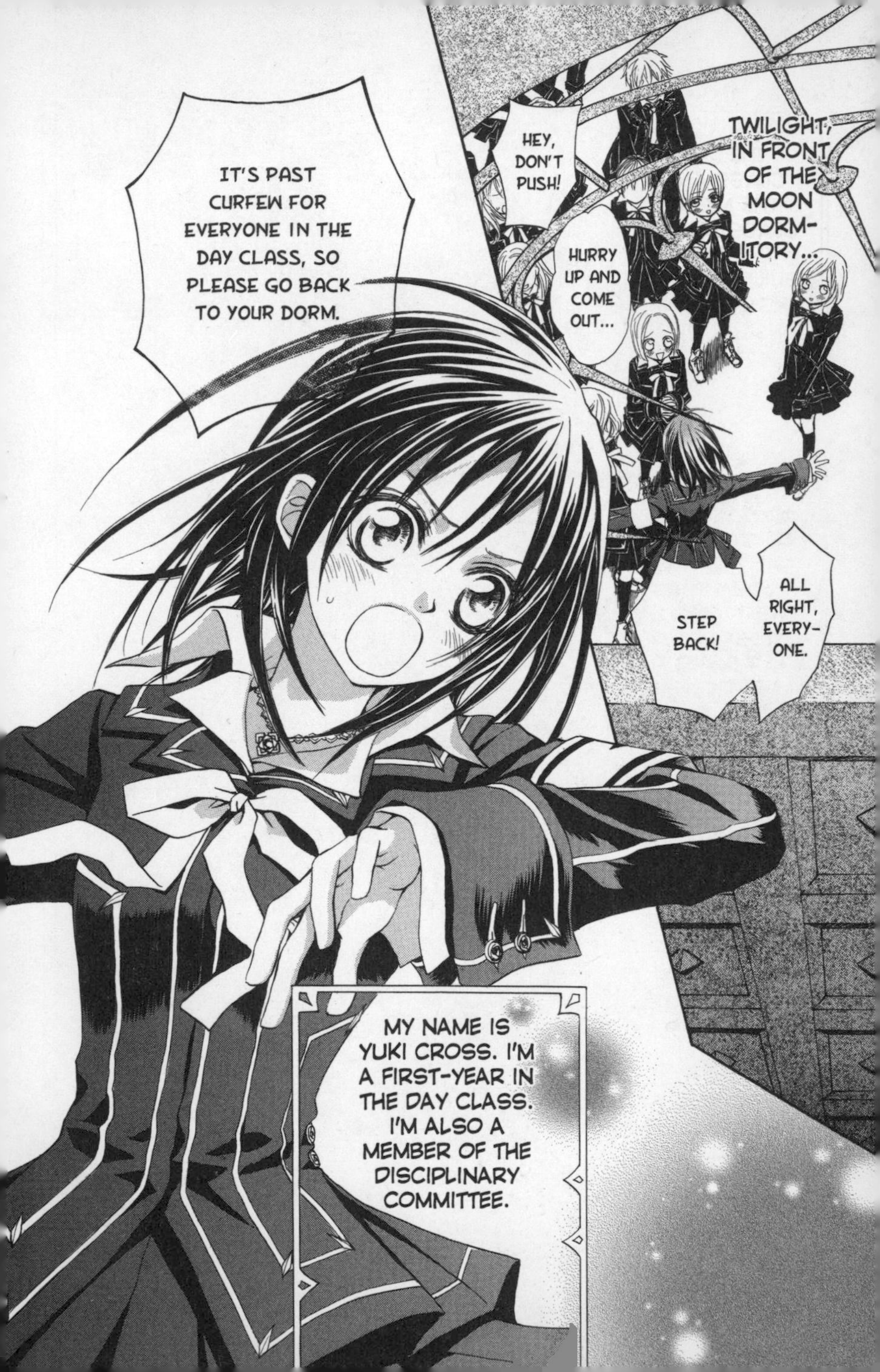
TWILIGHT, IN FRONT OF THE MOON DORMITORY...
HEY, DON'T PUSH!
HURRY UP AND COME OUT...
ALL RIGHT, EVERYONE.
STEP BACK!
IT'S PAST CURFEW FOR EVERYONE IN THE DAY CLASS, SO PLEASE GO BACK TO YOUR DORM.
MY NAME IS YUKI CROSS. I'M A FIRST-YEAR IN THE DAY CLASS. I'M ALSO A MEMBER OF THE DISCIPLINARY COMMITTEE.

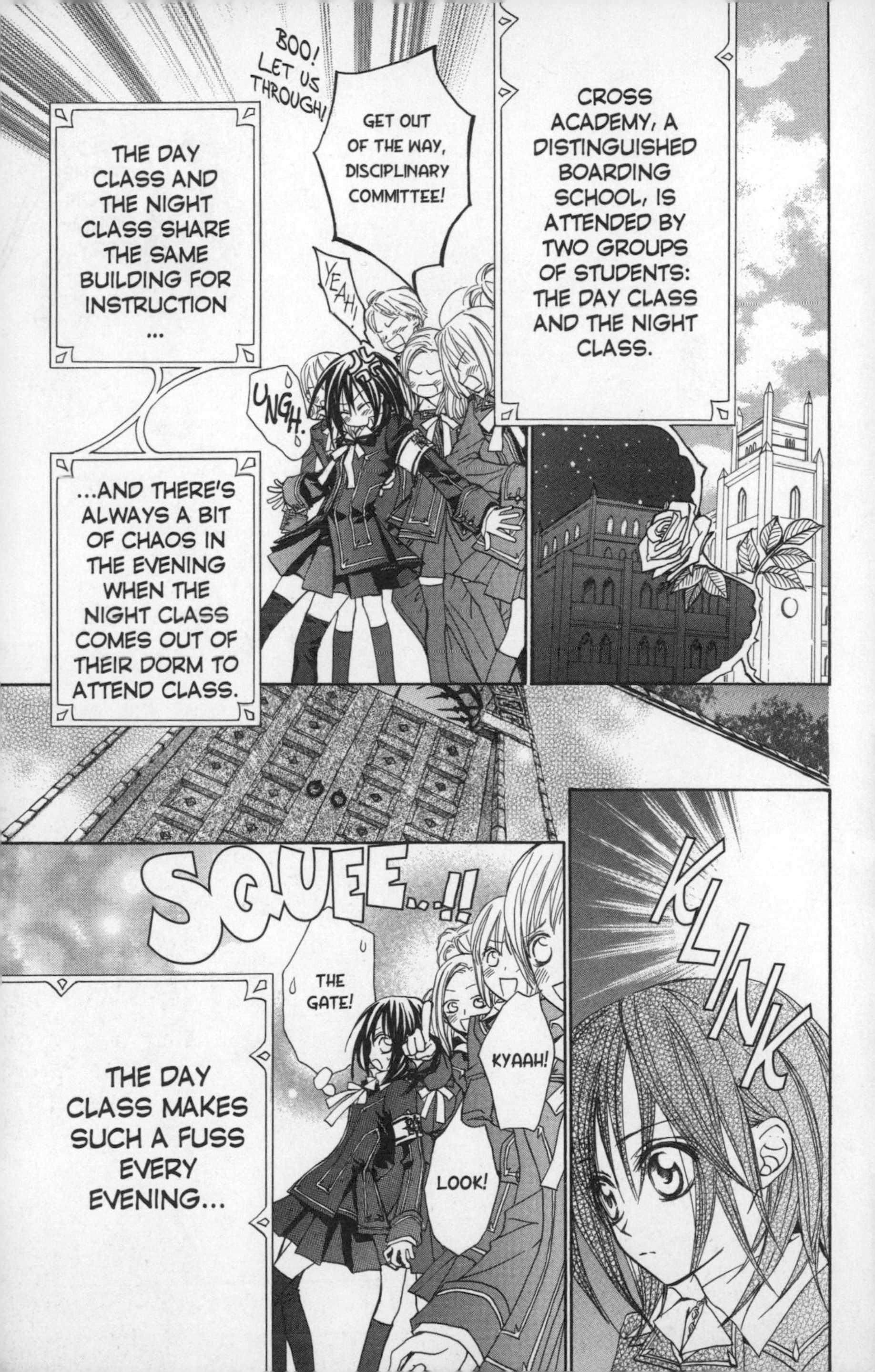
CROSS ACADEMY, A DISTINGUISHED BOARDING SCHOOL, IS ATTENDED BY TWO GROUPS OF STUDENTS: THE DAY CLASS AND THE NIGHT CLASS.
BOO! LET US THROUGH!
GET OUT OF THE WAY, DISCIPLINARY COMMITTEE!
YEAH!
UNGH.
THE DAY CLASS AND THE NIGHT CLASS SHARE THE SAME BUILDING FOR INSTRUCTION ...
...AND THERE'S ALWAYS A BIT OF CHAOS IN THE EVENING WHEN THE NIGHT CLASS COMES OUT OF THEIR DORM TO ATTEND CLASS.
KLINK
SQUEE...!!
KYAAH!
THE GATE!
LOOK!
THE DAY CLASS MAKES SUCH A FUSS EVERY EVENING...

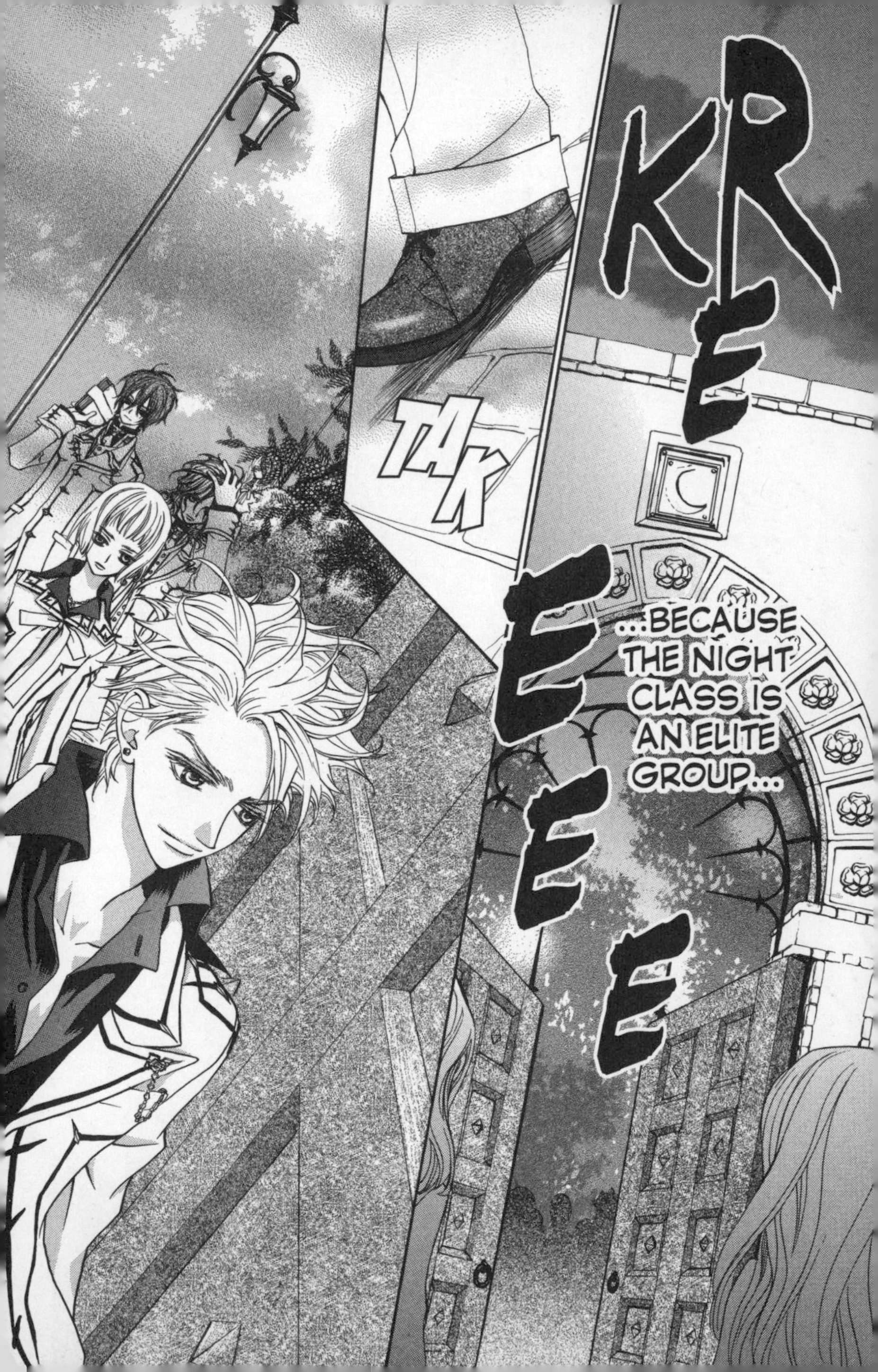
KREEEEE
TAK
...BECAUSE THE NIGHT CLASS IS AN ELITE GROUP...

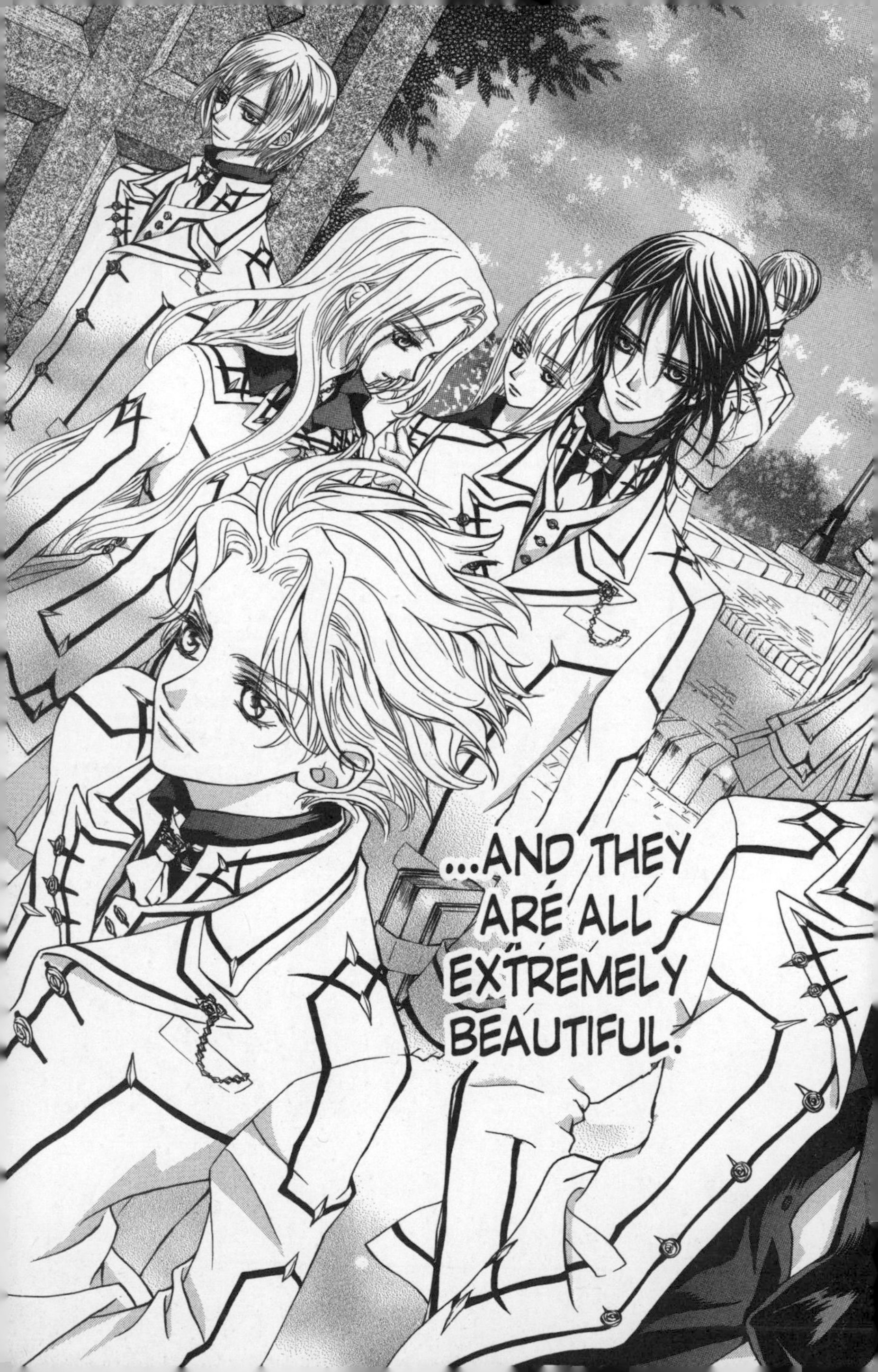
...AND THEY ARÉ ALL EXTREMELY BEAUTIFUL.

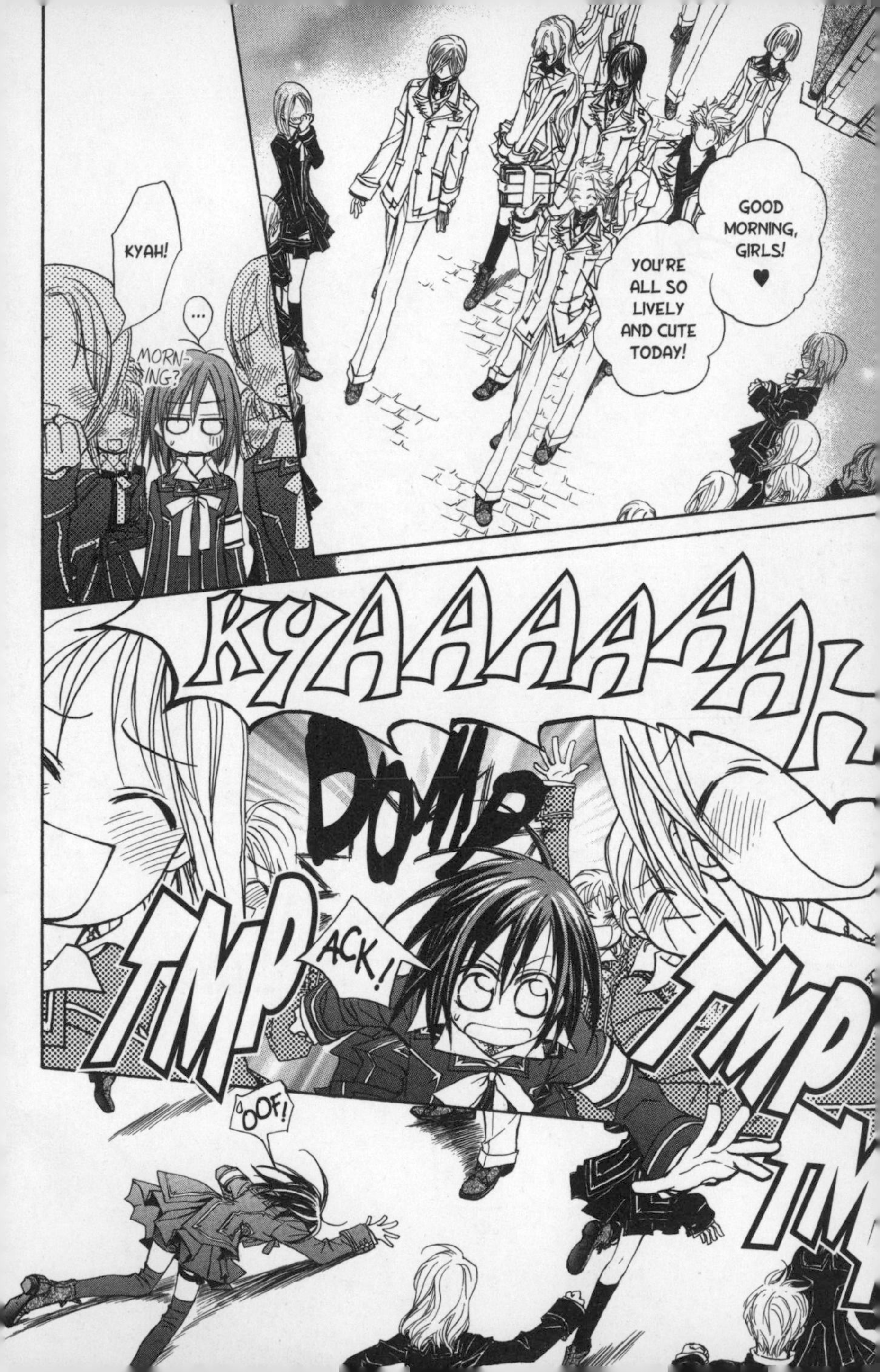
GOOD MORNING, GIRLS! ♥
YOU'RE ALL SO LIVELY AND CUTE TODAY!
KYAH!
...
MORNING?
KYAAAAAAAH
TMP
DOMP
ACK!
TMP
OOF!

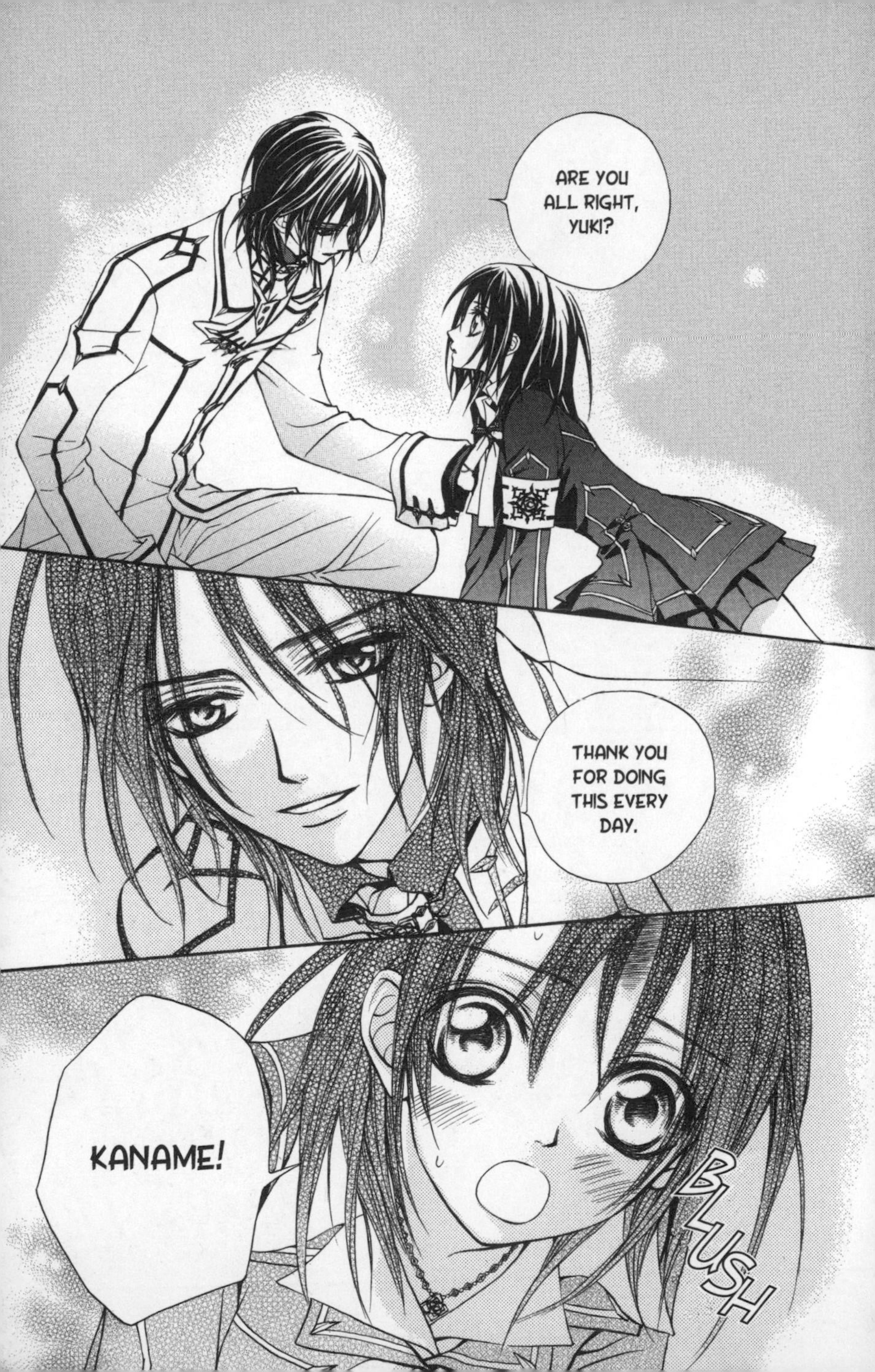
ARE YOU ALL RIGHT, YUKI?
THANK YOU FOR DOING THIS EVERY DAY.
KANAME!
BLUSH

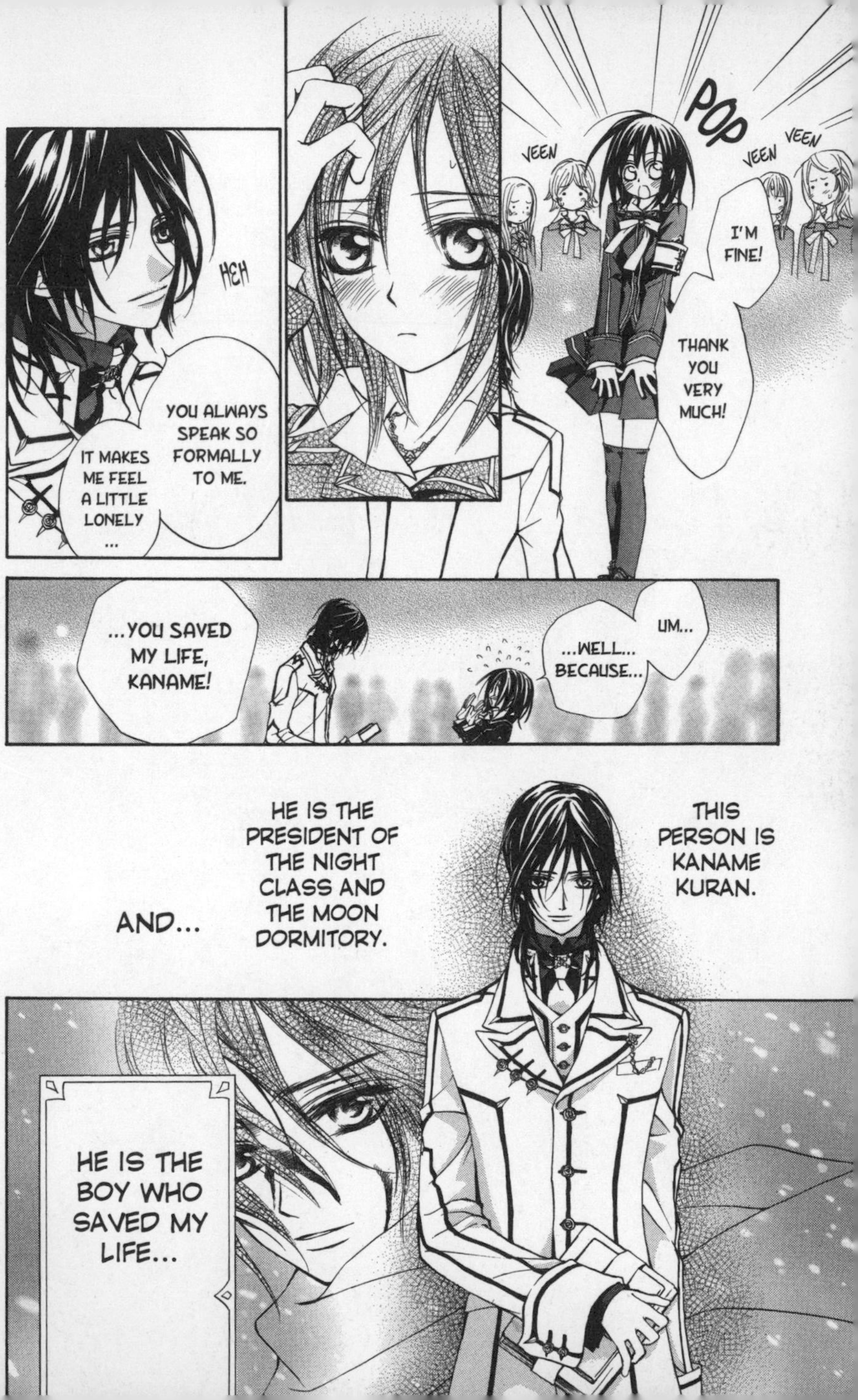
VEEN
VEEN
POP
VEEN
I'M FINE!
THANK YOU VERY MUCH!
HEH
YOU ALWAYS SPEAK SO FORMALLY TO ME.
IT MAKES ME FEEL A LITTLE LONELY ...
UM...
...WELL... BECAUSE...
...YOU SAVED MY LIFE, KANAME!
THIS PERSON IS KANAME KURAN.
HE IS THE PRESIDENT OF THE NIGHT CLASS AND THE MOON DORMITORY.
AND...
HE IS THE BOY WHO SAVED MY LIFE...

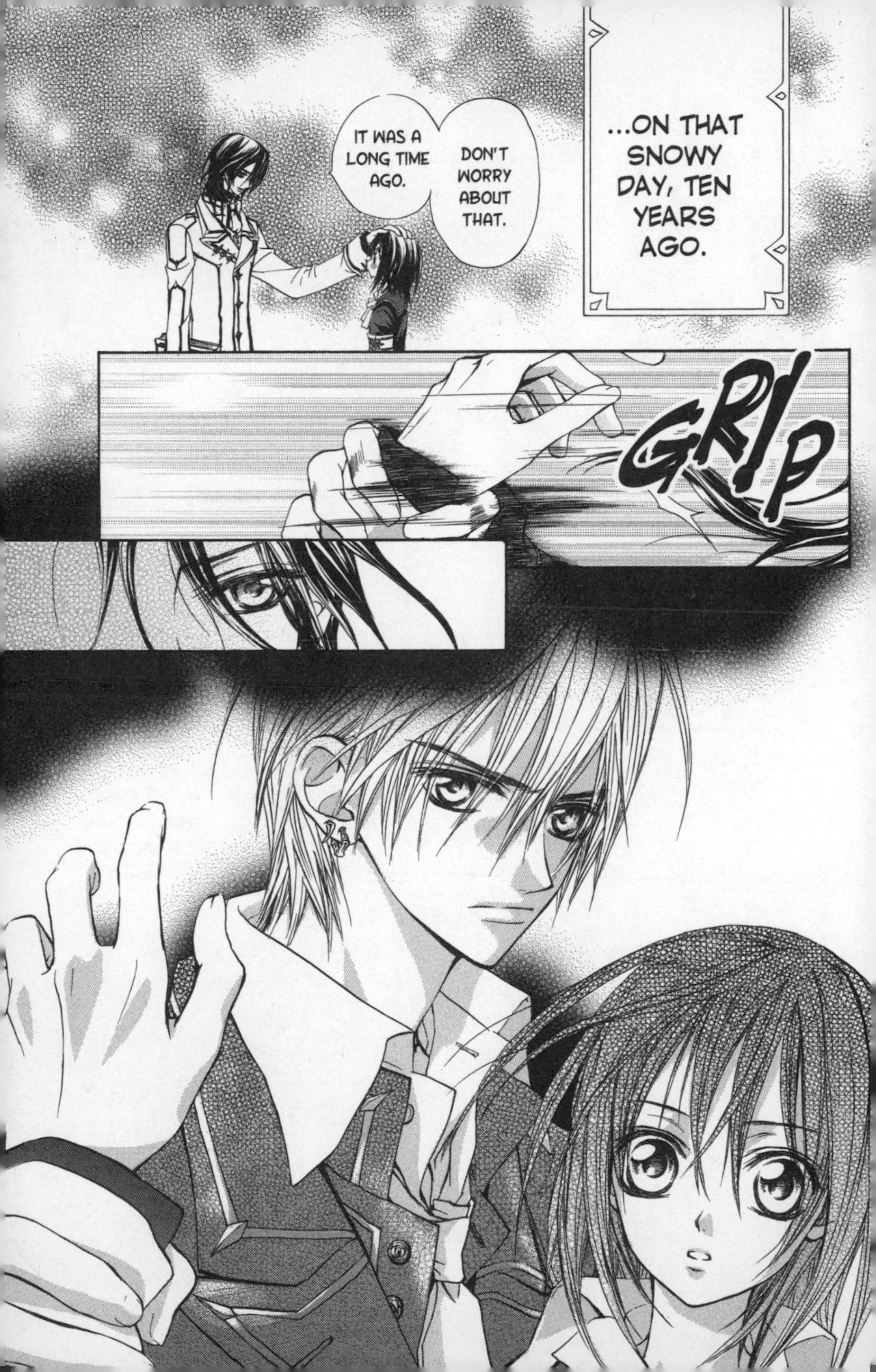
...ON THAT SNOWY DAY, TEN YEARS AGO.
DON'T WORRY ABOUT THAT.
IT WAS A LONG TIME AGO.
GRIP

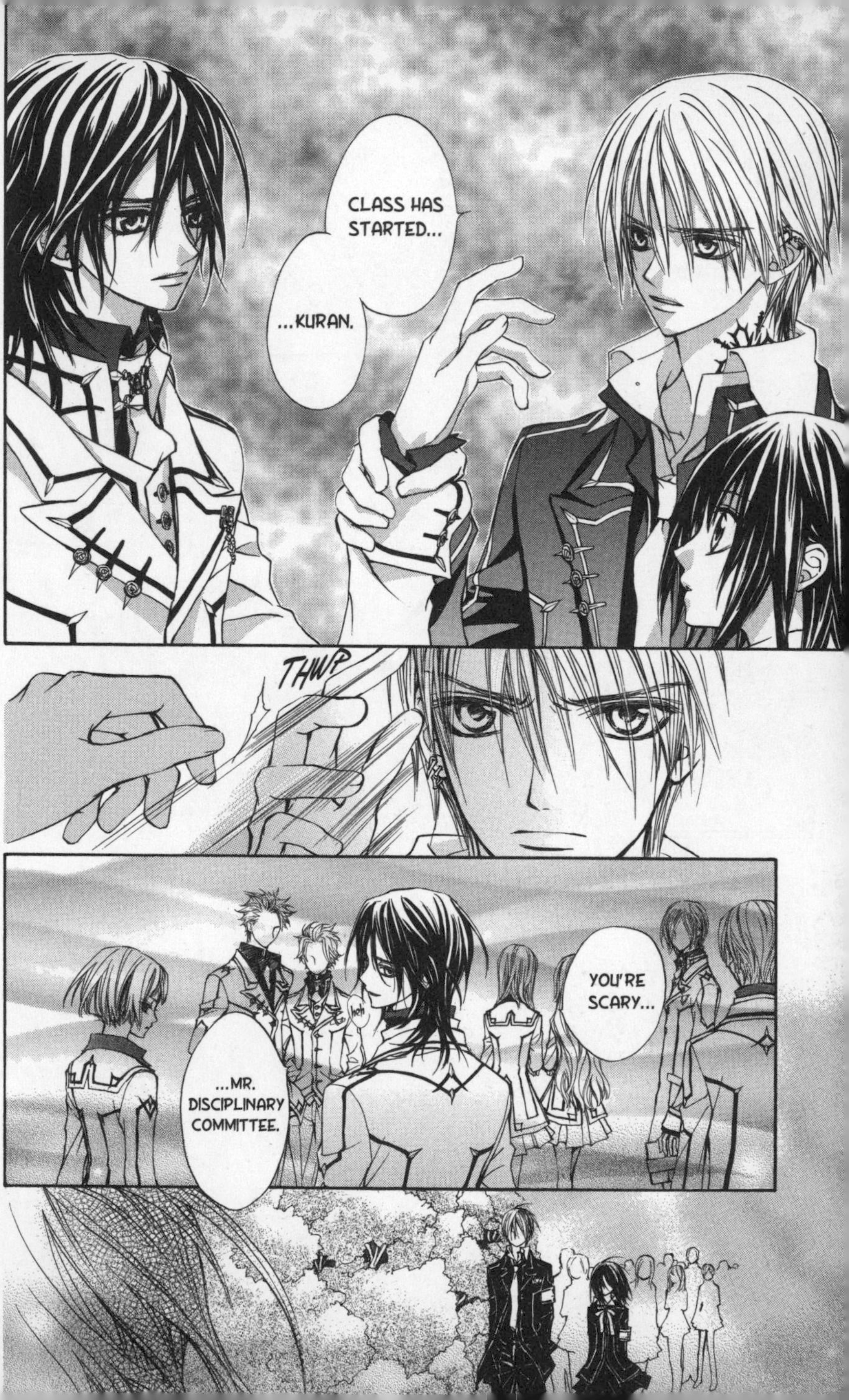
CLASS HAS STARTED...
...KURAN.
THWP
YOU'RE SCARY...
heh
...MR. DISCIPLINARY COMMITTEE.

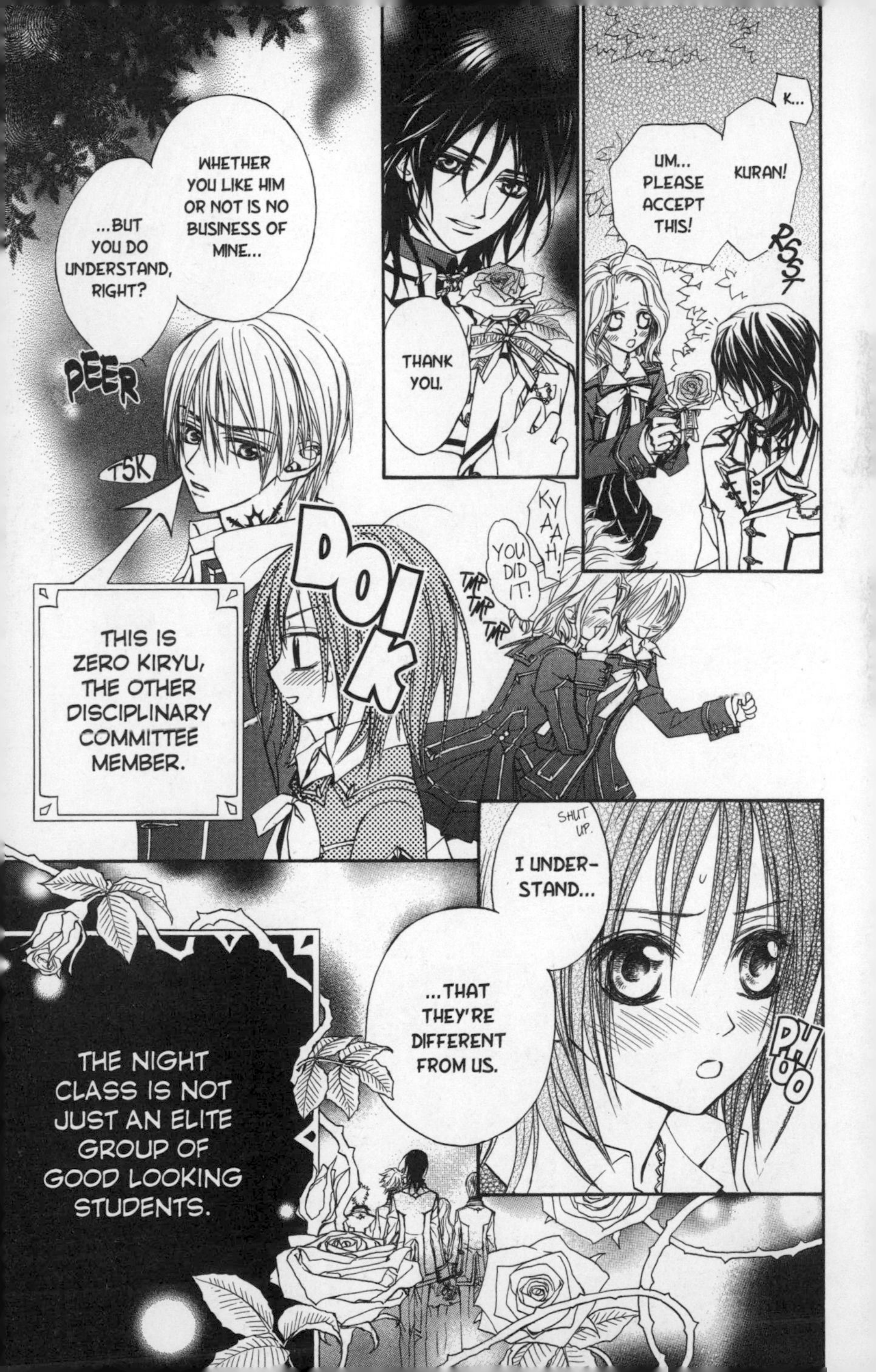
K...
KURAN!
UM... PLEASE ACCEPT THIS!
RSST
THANK YOU.
WHETHER YOU LIKE HIM OR NOT IS NO BUSINESS OF MINE...
...BUT YOU DO UNDERSTAND, RIGHT?
PEER
TSK
KYAAH!
YOU DID IT!
TMP TMP TMP
DOINK
THIS IS ZERO KIRYU, THE OTHER DISCIPLINARY COMMITTEE MEMBER.
SHUT UP.
I UNDER-STAND...
...THAT THEY'RE DIFFERENT FROM US.
PHOO
THE NIGHT CLASS IS NOT JUST AN ELITE GROUP OF GOOD LOOKING STUDENTS.

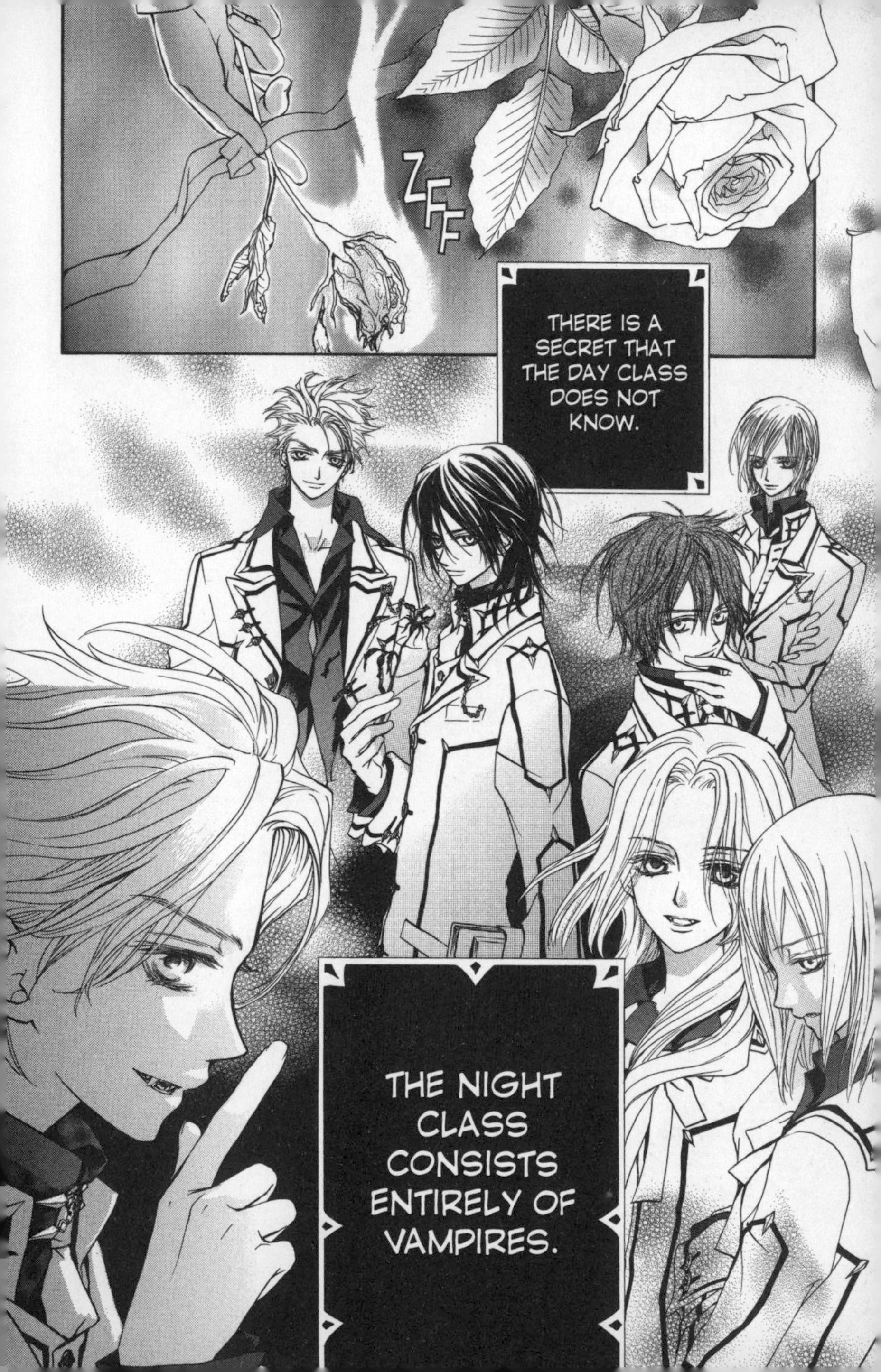
ZFF
THERE IS A SECRET THAT THE DAY CLASS DOES NOT KNOW.
THE NIGHT CLASS CONSISTS ENTIRELY OF VAMPIRES.

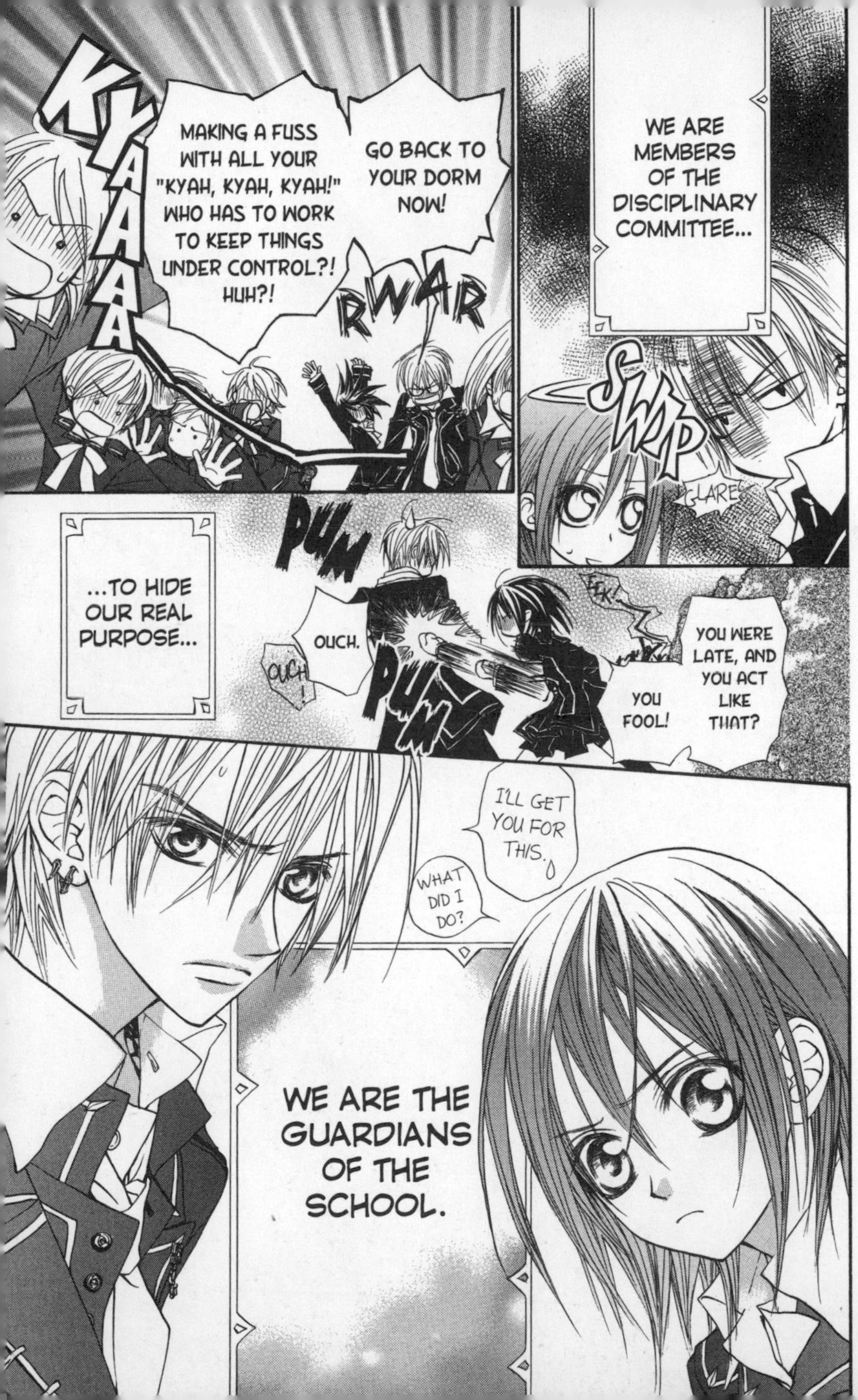
WE ARE MEMBERS OF THE DISCIPLINARY COMMITTEE...
SWIP
GLARE
GO BACK TO YOUR DORM NOW!
MAKING A FUSS WITH ALL YOUR "KYAH, KYAH, KYAH!" WHO HAS TO WORK TO KEEP THINGS UNDER CONTROL?! HUH?!
KYAAAAA
RWAR
YOU WERE LATE, AND YOU ACT LIKE THAT?
YOU FOOL!
EEK!
PUM
PUM
OUCH.
OUCH!
...TO HIDE OUR REAL PURPOSE...
I'LL GET YOU FOR THIS.
WHAT DID I DO?
WE ARE THE GUARDIANS OF THE SCHOOL.

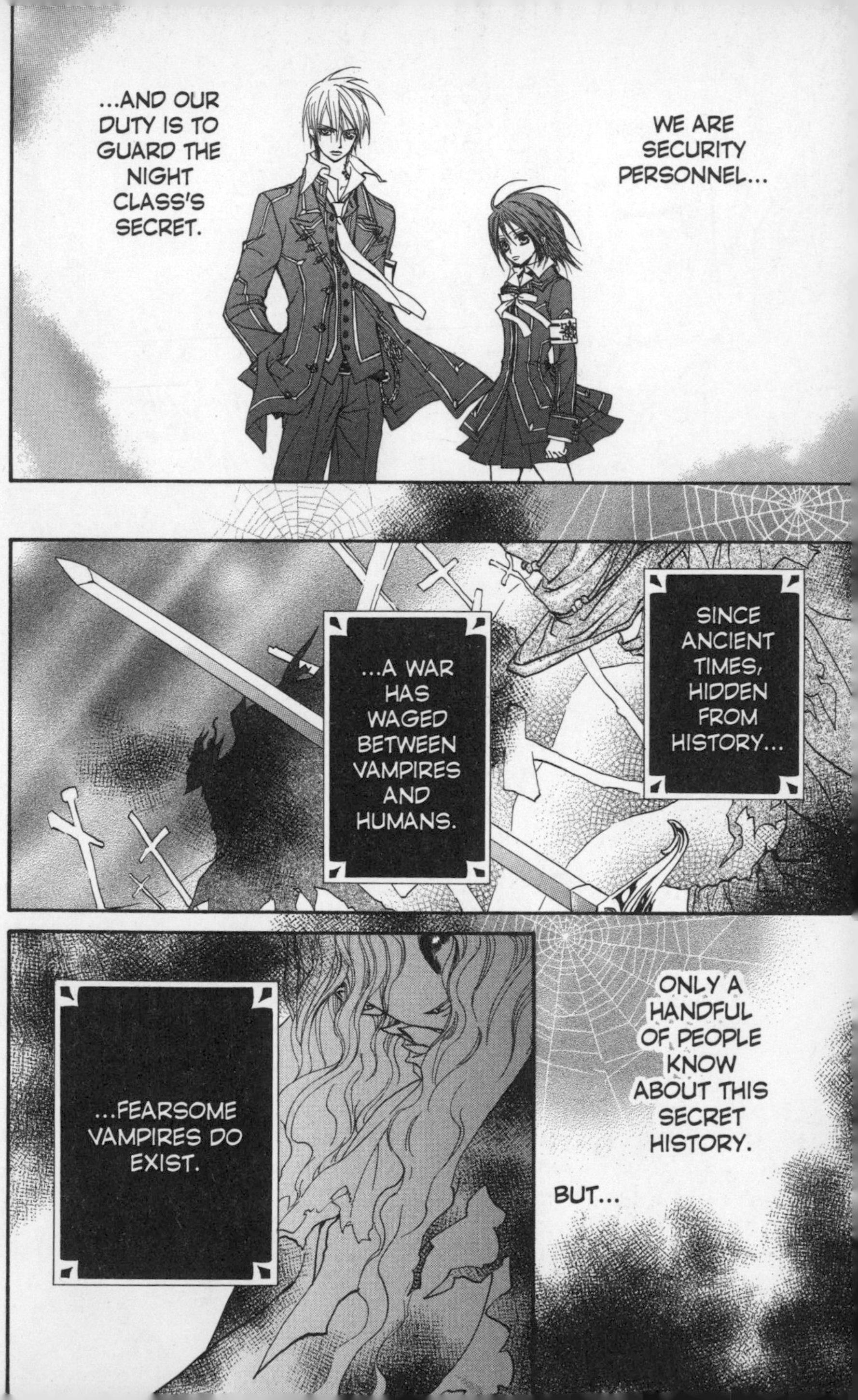
WE ARE SECURITY PERSONNEL...
...AND OUR DUTY IS TO GUARD THE NIGHT CLASS'S SECRET.
SINCE ANCIENT TIMES, HIDDEN FROM HISTORY...
...A WAR HAS WAGED BETWEEN VAMPIRES AND HUMANS.
ONLY A HANDFUL OF PEOPLE KNOW ABOUT THIS SECRET HISTORY.
BUT...
...FEARSOME VAMPIRES DO EXIST.

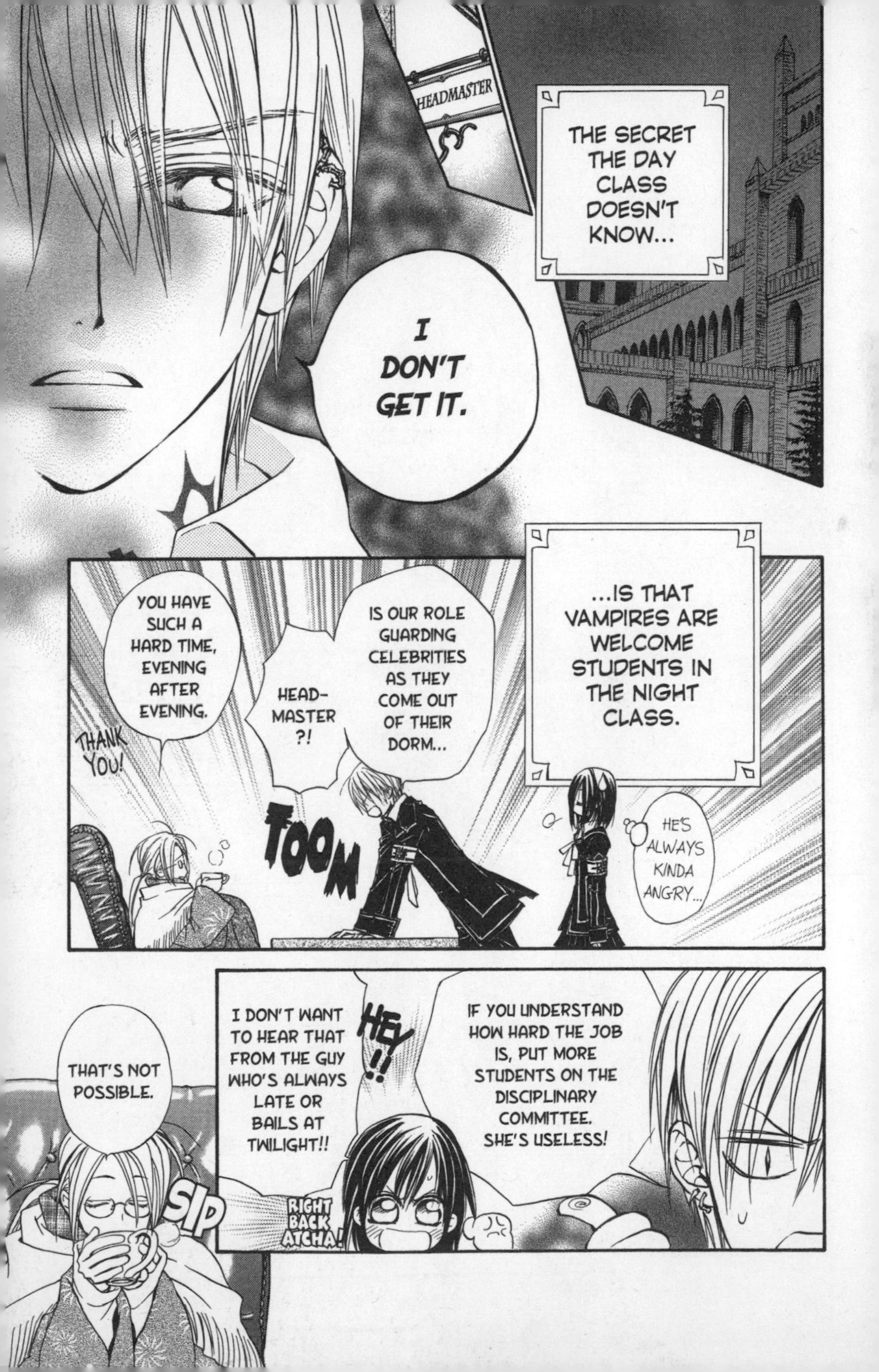

THE SECRET THE DAY CLASS DOESN'T KNOW...
HEADMASTER
I DON'T GET IT.
...IS THAT VAMPIRES ARE WELCOME STUDENTS IN THE NIGHT CLASS.
HE'S ALWAYS KINDA ANGRY...
IS OUR ROLE GUARDING CELEBRITIES AS THEY COME OUT OF THEIR DORM...
HEAD-MASTER?!
TOOM
YOU HAVE SUCH A HARD TIME, EVENING AFTER EVENING.
THANK YOU!
IF YOU UNDERSTAND HOW HARD THE JOB IS, PUT MORE STUDENTS ON THE DISCIPLINARY COMMITTEE. SHE'S USELESS!
HEY!!
I DON'T WANT TO HEAR THAT FROM THE GUY WHO'S ALWAYS LATE OR BAILS AT TWILIGHT!!
RIGHT BACK ATCHA!
THAT'S NOT POSSIBLE.
SIP

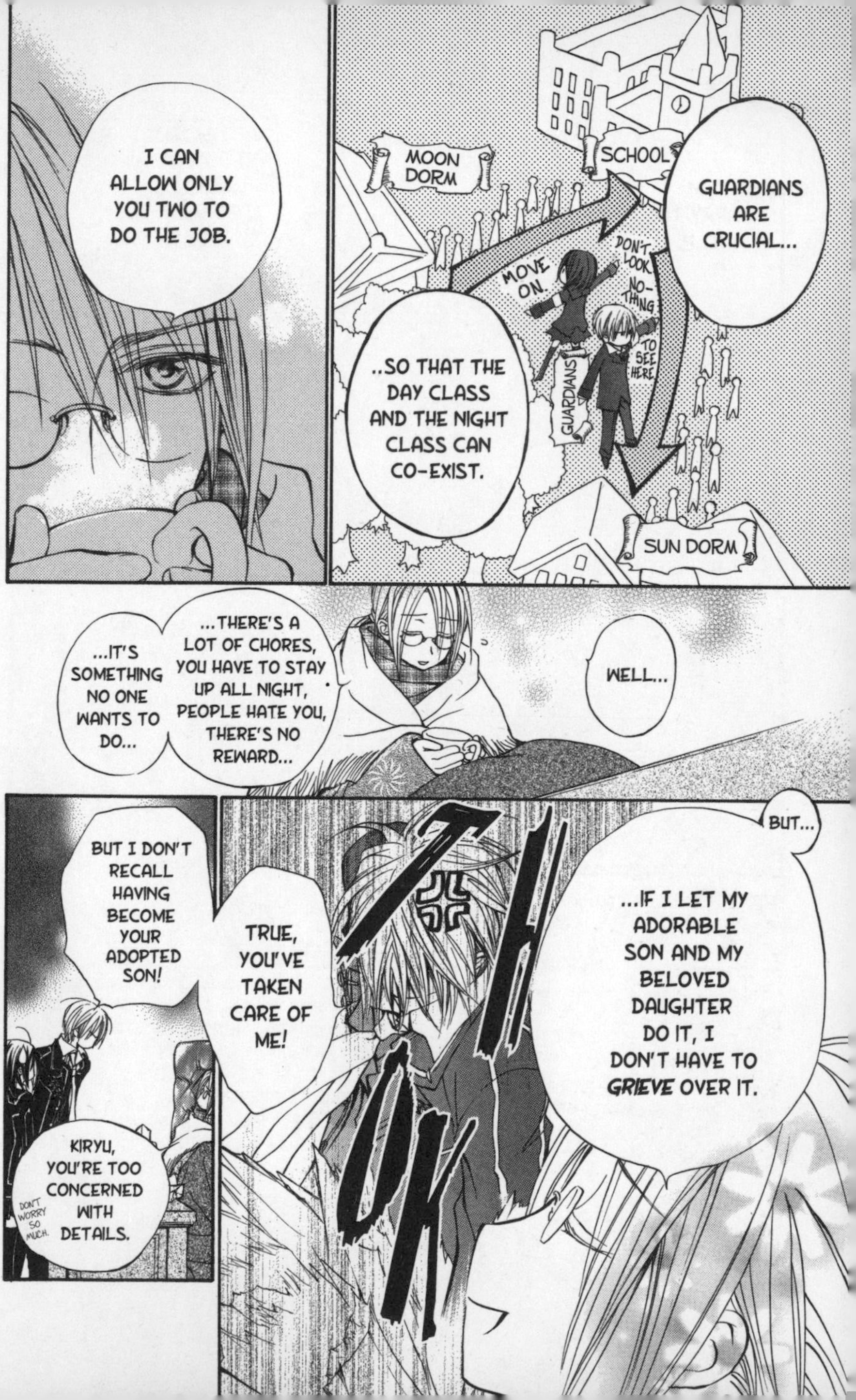
SCHOOL
MOON DORM
GUARDIANS ARE CRUCIAL...
DON'T LOOK. NO-THING TO SEE HERE
MOVE ON.
GUARDIANS
..SO THAT THE DAY CLASS AND THE NIGHT CLASS CAN CO-EXIST.
SUN DORM
I CAN ALLOW ONLY YOU TWO TO DO THE JOB.
WELL...
...THERE'S A LOT OF CHORES, YOU HAVE TO STAY UP ALL NIGHT, PEOPLE HATE YOU, THERE'S NO REWARD...
...IT'S SOMETHING NO ONE WANTS TO DO...
BUT...
...IF I LET MY ADORABLE SON AND MY BELOVED DAUGHTER DO IT, I DON'T HAVE TO GRIEVE OVER IT.
TRUE, YOU'VE TAKEN CARE OF ME!
BUT I DON'T RECALL HAVING BECOME YOUR ADOPTED SON!
KIRYU, YOU'RE TOO CONCERNED WITH DETAILS.
DON'T WORRY SO MUCH.

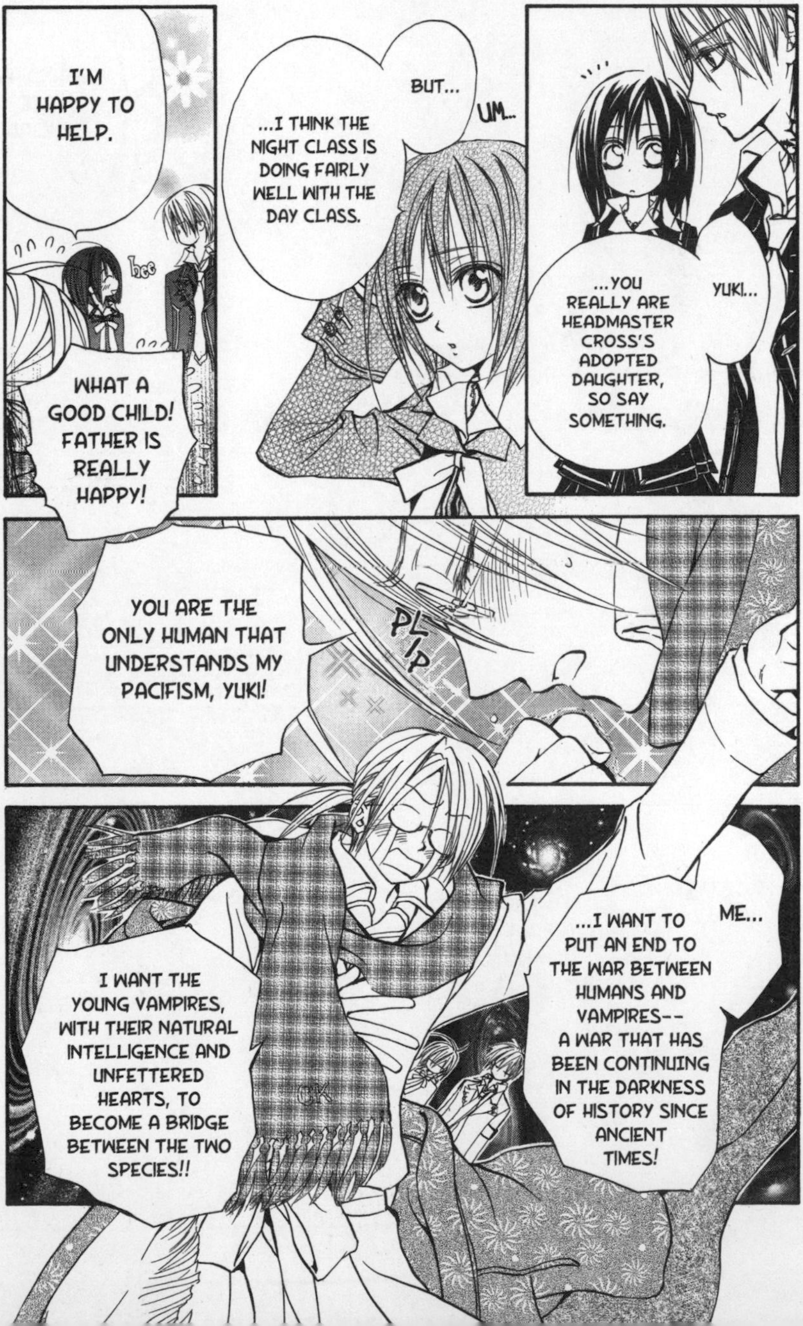
YUKI...
...YOU REALLY ARE HEADMASTER CROSS'S ADOPTED DAUGHTER, SO SAY SOMETHING.
UM...
BUT...
...I THINK THE NIGHT CLASS IS DOING FAIRLY WELL WITH THE DAY CLASS.
I'M HAPPY TO HELP.
hee
WHAT A GOOD CHILD! FATHER IS REALLY HAPPY!
YOU ARE THE ONLY HUMAN THAT UNDERSTANDS MY PACIFISM, YUKI!
PLIP
ME...
...I WANT TO PUT AN END TO THE WAR BETWEEN HUMANS AND VAMPIRES-- A WAR THAT HAS BEEN CONTINUING IN THE DARKNESS OF HISTORY SINCE ANCIENT TIMES!
I WANT THE YOUNG VAMPIRES, WITH THEIR NATURAL INTELLIGENCE AND UNFETTERED HEARTS, TO BECOME A BRIDGE BETWEEN THE TWO SPECIES!!

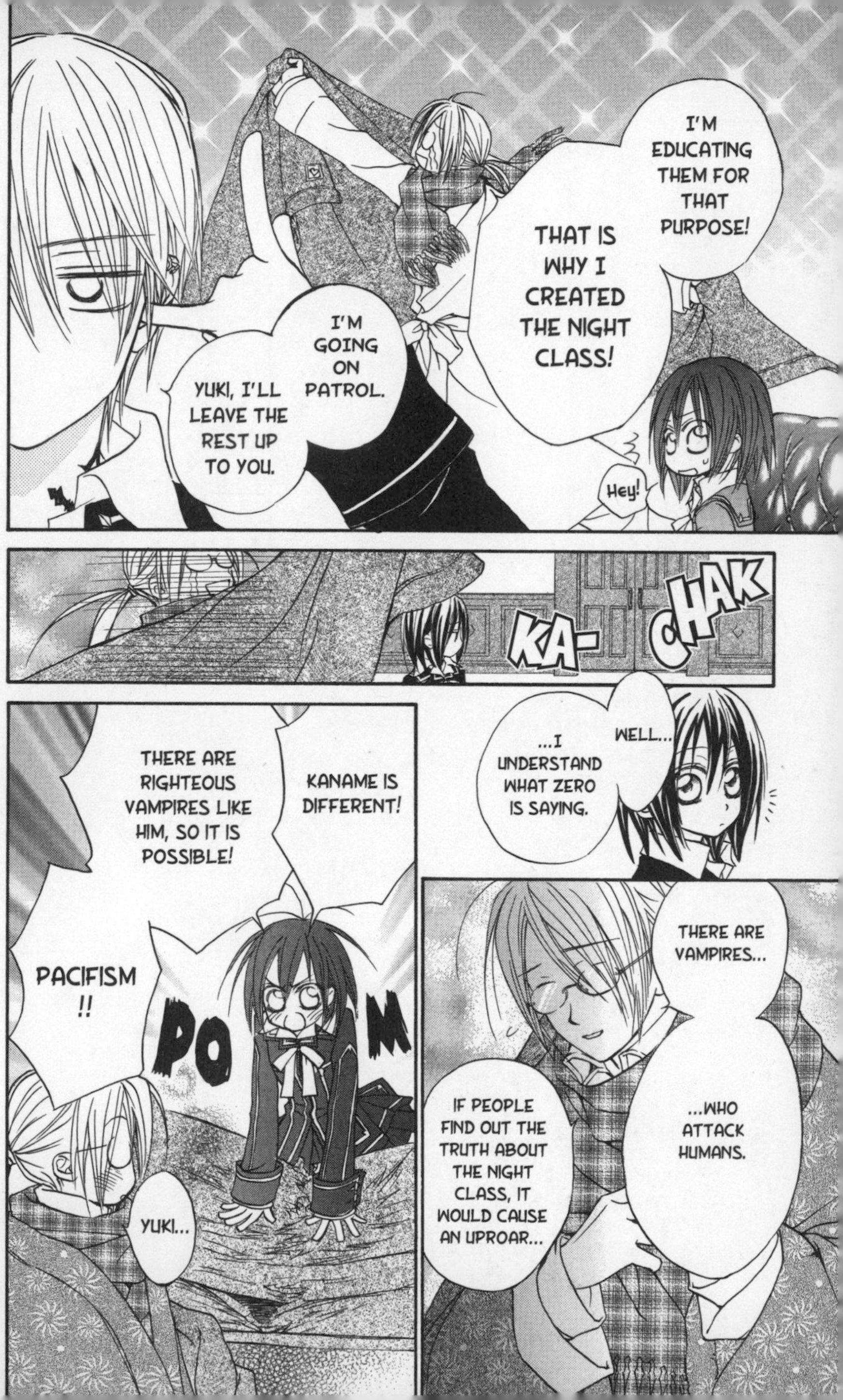
I'M EDUCATING THEM FOR THAT PURPOSE!
THAT IS WHY I CREATED THE NIGHT CLASS!
Hey!
I'M GOING ON PATROL.
YUKI, I'LL LEAVE THE REST UP TO YOU.
KA-CHAK
WELL...
...I UNDERSTAND WHAT ZERO IS SAYING.
THERE ARE VAMPIRES...
...WHO ATTACK HUMANS.
IF PEOPLE FIND OUT THE TRUTH ABOUT THE NIGHT CLASS, IT WOULD CAUSE AN UPROAR...
KANAME IS DIFFERENT!
THERE ARE RIGHTEOUS VAMPIRES LIKE HIM, SO IT IS POSSIBLE!
PACIFISM !!
POM
YUKI...

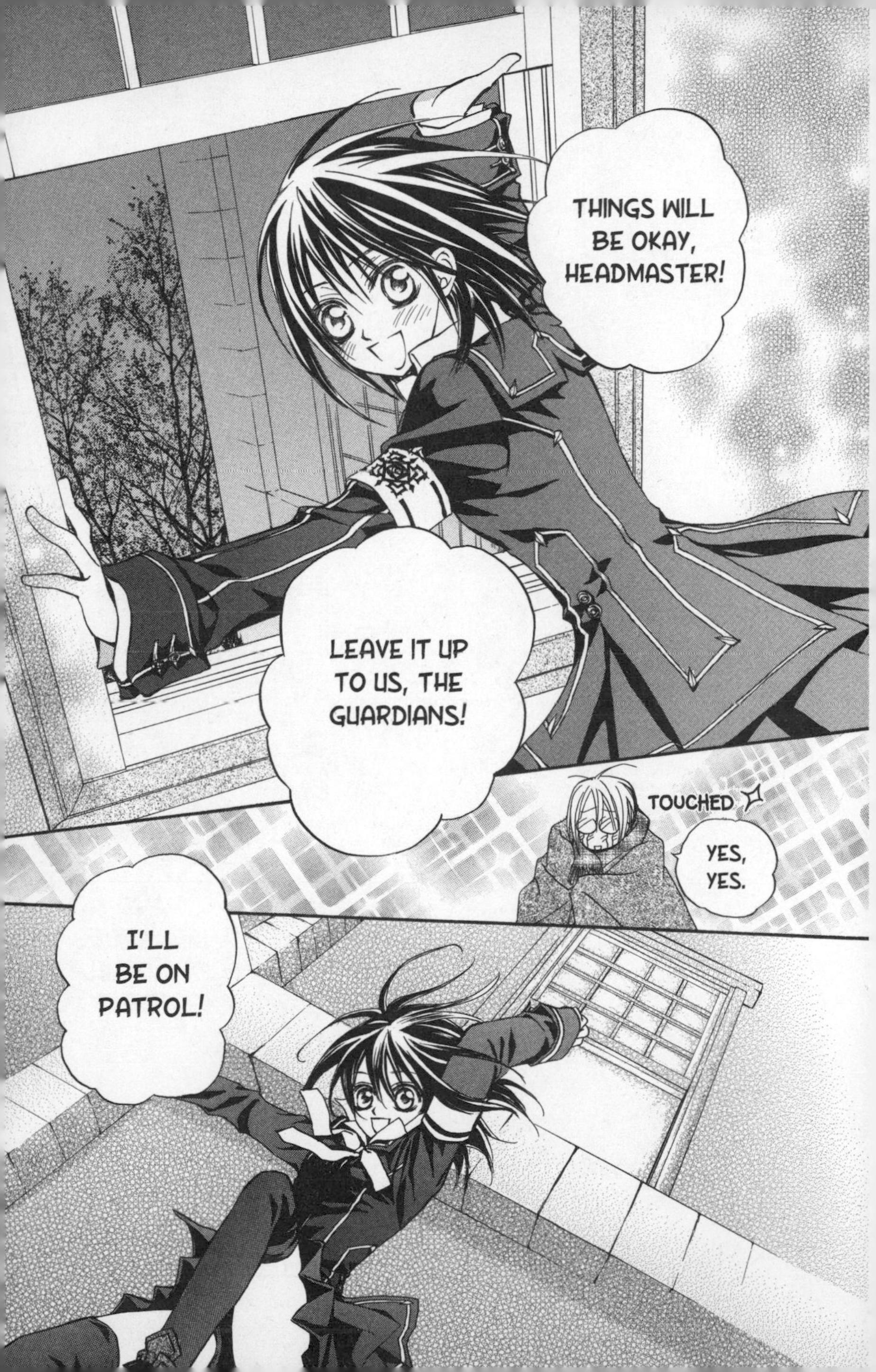
THINGS WILL BE OKAY, HEADMASTER!
LEAVE IT UP TO US, THE GUARDIANS!
TOUCHED
YES, YES.
I'LL BE ON PATROL!

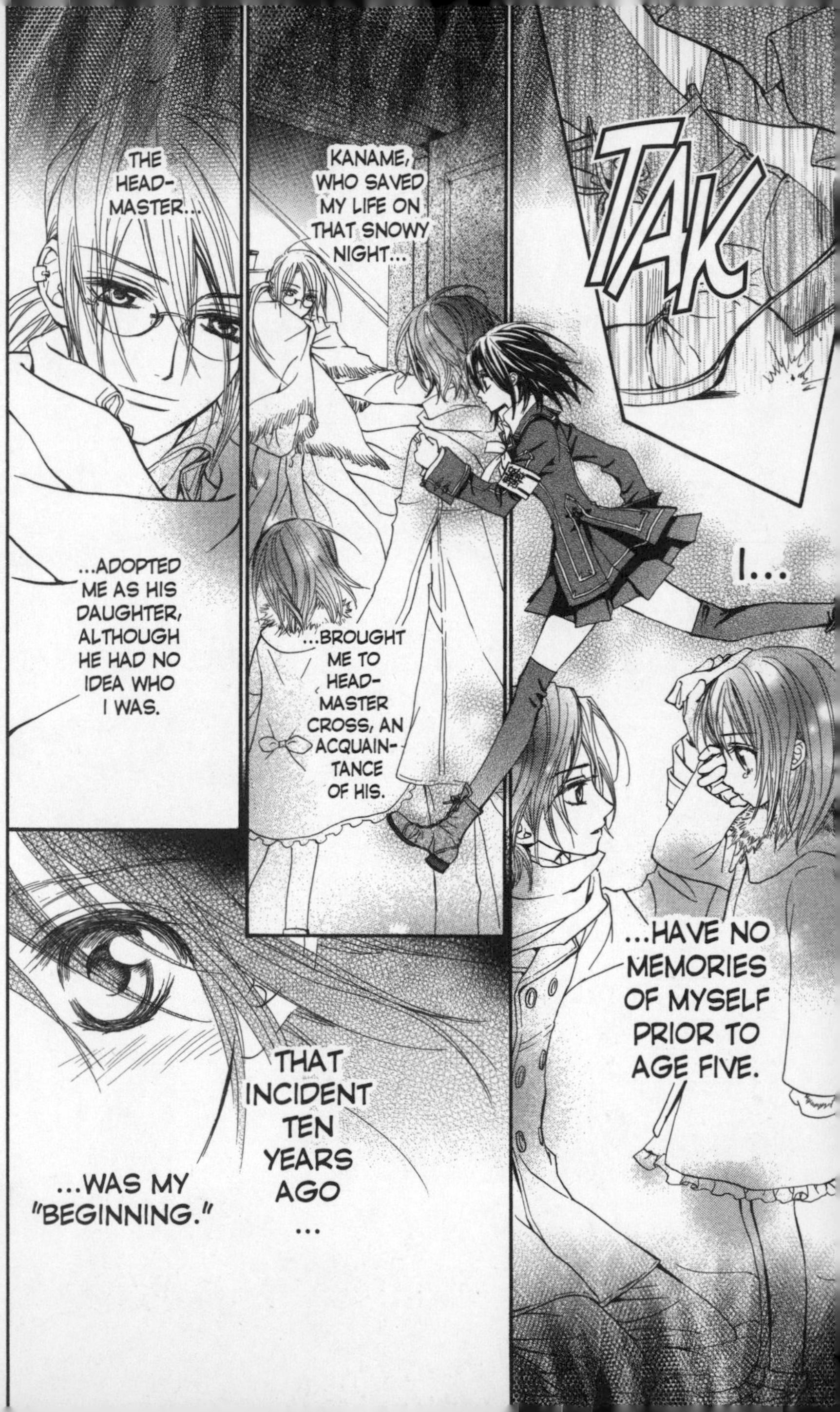
TAK
I...
...HAVE NO MEMORIES OF MYSELF PRIOR TO AGE FIVE.
KANAME, WHO SAVED MY LIFE ON THAT SNOWY NIGHT...
...BROUGHT ME TO HEAD-MASTER CROSS, AN ACQUAIN-TANCE OF HIS.
THE HEAD-MASTER...
...ADOPTED ME AS HIS DAUGHTER, ALTHOUGH HE HAD NO IDEA WHO I WAS.
THAT INCIDENT TEN YEARS AGO...
...WAS MY "BEGINNING."

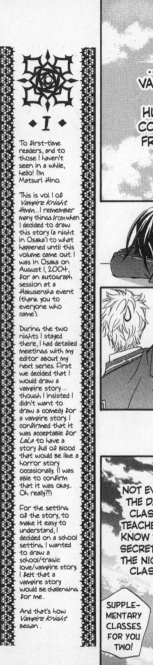

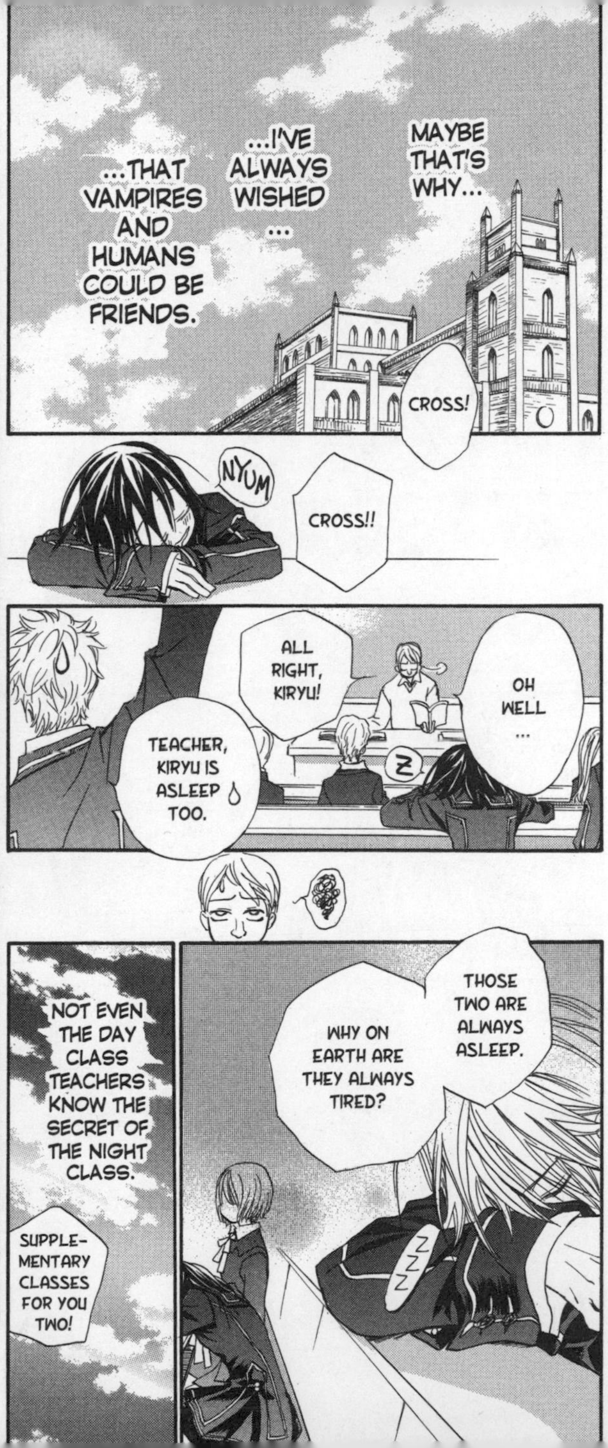
MAYBE THAT'S WHY...
...I'VE ALWAYS WISHED...
...THAT VAMPIRES AND HUMANS COULD BE FRIENDS.
CROSS!
CROSS!!
NYUM
OH WELL...
ALL RIGHT, KIRYU!
TEACHER, KIRYU IS ASLEEP TOO.
Z
THOSE TWO ARE ALWAYS ASLEEP.
WHY ON EARTH ARE THEY ALWAYS TIRED?
ZZZ
NOT EVEN THE DAY CLASS TEACHERS KNOW THE SECRET OF THE NIGHT CLASS.
SUPPLEMENTARY CLASSES FOR YOU TWO!

♦ I ♦

To first-time readers, and to those I haven't seen in a while, hello! I'm Matsuri Hino.

This is vol. 1 of *Vampire Knight*. Hmm... I remember many things from when I decided to draw this story (a night in Osaka) to what happened until this volume came out. I was in Osaka on August 1, 2004, for an autograph session at a Hakusensha event (thank you to everyone who came).

During the two nights I stayed there, I had detailed meetings with my editor about my next series. First we decided that I would draw a vampire story... though I insisted I didn't want to draw a comedy for a vampire story. I confirmed that it was acceptable for *LaLa* to have a story full of blood that would be like a horror story occasionally. (I was able to confirm that it was okay... Oh really?!)

For the setting of the story, to make it easy to understand, I decided on a school setting. I wanted to draw a school/tragic love/vampire story. I felt that a vampire story would be challenging for me.

And that's how *Vampire Knight* began.

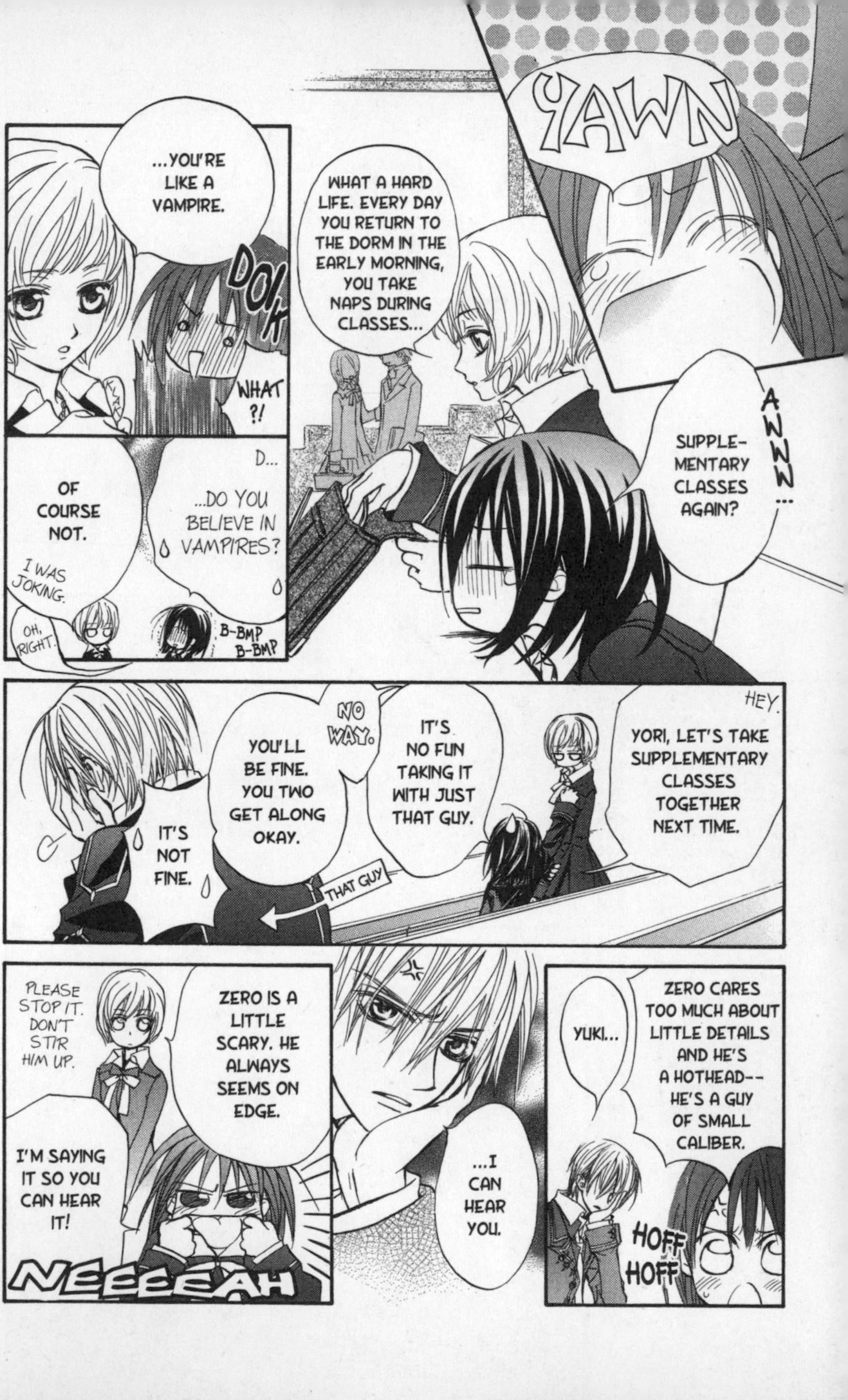
YAWN
AWWW...
SUPPLEMENTARY CLASSES AGAIN?
WHAT A HARD LIFE. EVERY DAY YOU RETURN TO THE DORM IN THE EARLY MORNING, YOU TAKE NAPS DURING CLASSES...
...YOU'RE LIKE A VAMPIRE.
DOK
WHAT ?!
D...
...DO YOU BELIEVE IN VAMPIRES?
OF COURSE NOT.
I WAS JOKING.
OH, RIGHT.
B-BMP B-BMP
HEY.
YORI, LET'S TAKE SUPPLEMENTARY CLASSES TOGETHER NEXT TIME.
IT'S NO FUN TAKING IT WITH JUST THAT GUY.
NO WAY.
YOU'LL BE FINE. YOU TWO GET ALONG OKAY.
IT'S NOT FINE.
THAT GUY
ZERO CARES TOO MUCH ABOUT LITTLE DETAILS AND HE'S A HOTHEAD--HE'S A GUY OF SMALL CALIBER.
YUKI...
HOFF HOFF
...I CAN HEAR YOU.
ZERO IS A LITTLE SCARY. HE ALWAYS SEEMS ON EDGE.
PLEASE STOP IT. DON'T STIR HIM UP.
I'M SAYING IT SO YOU CAN HEAR IT!
NEEEEAH

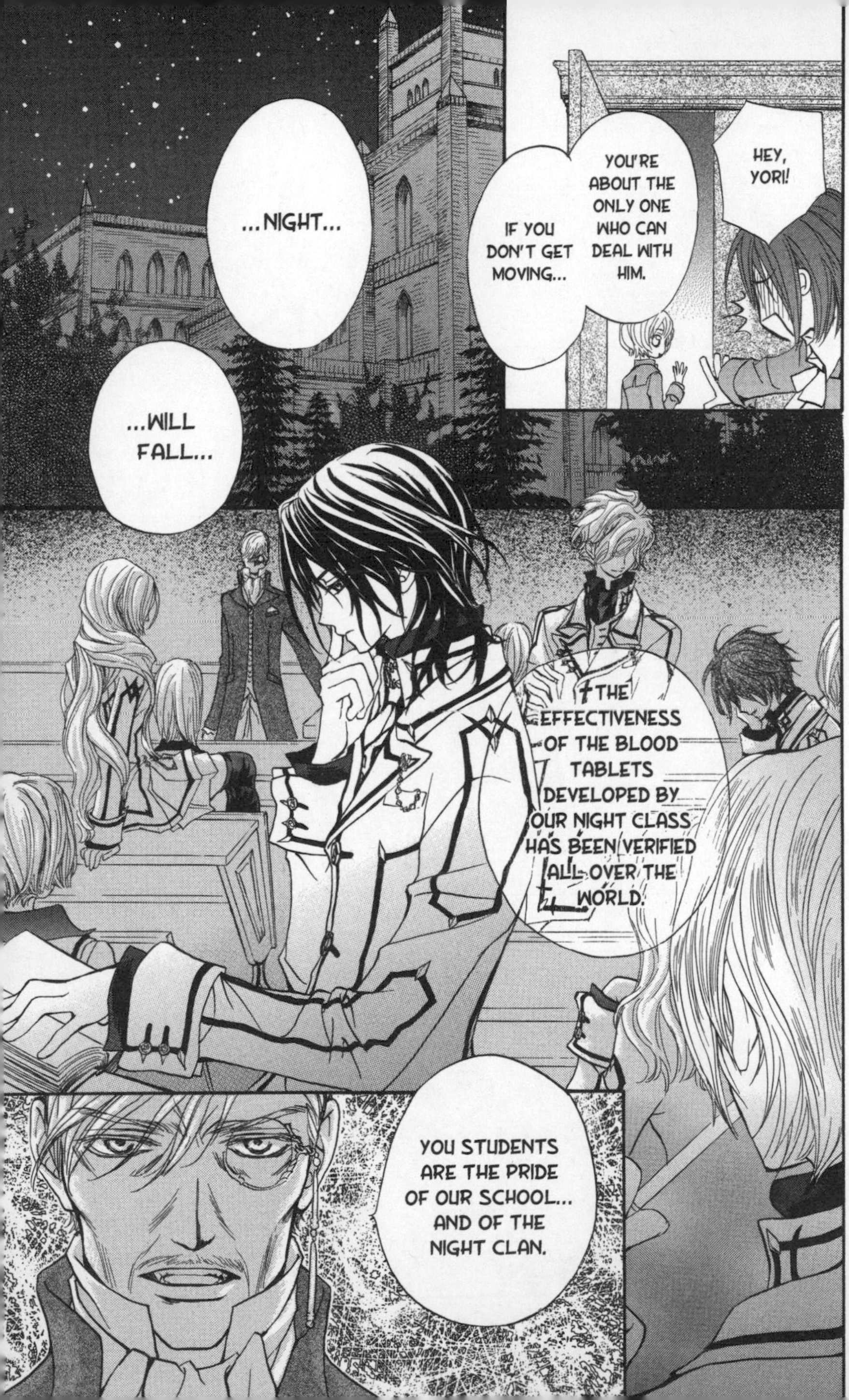
HEY, YORI!
YOU'RE ABOUT THE ONLY ONE WHO CAN DEAL WITH HIM.
IF YOU DON'T GET MOVING...
...NIGHT...
...WILL FALL...
THE EFFECTIVENESS OF THE BLOOD TABLETS DEVELOPED BY OUR NIGHT CLASS HAS BEEN VERIFIED ALL OVER THE WORLD.
YOU STUDENTS ARE THE PRIDE OF OUR SCHOOL... AND OF THE NIGHT CLAN.

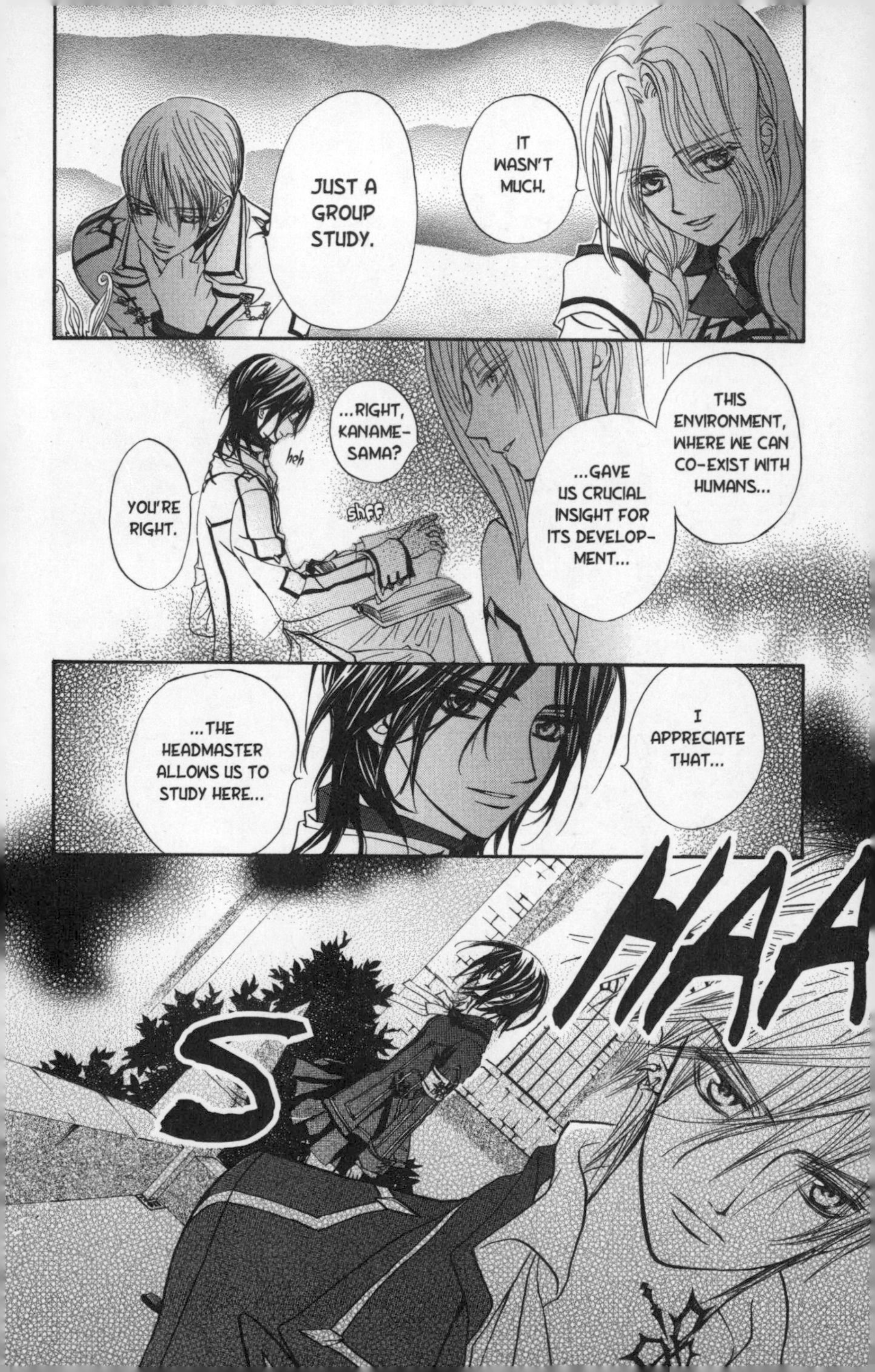
IT WASN'T MUCH.
JUST A GROUP STUDY.
THIS ENVIRONMENT, WHERE WE CAN CO-EXIST WITH HUMANS...
...GAVE US CRUCIAL INSIGHT FOR ITS DEVELOPMENT...
...RIGHT, KANAME-SAMA?
heh
shff
YOU'RE RIGHT.
I APPRECIATE THAT...
...THE HEADMASTER ALLOWS US TO STUDY HERE...
HAA
S

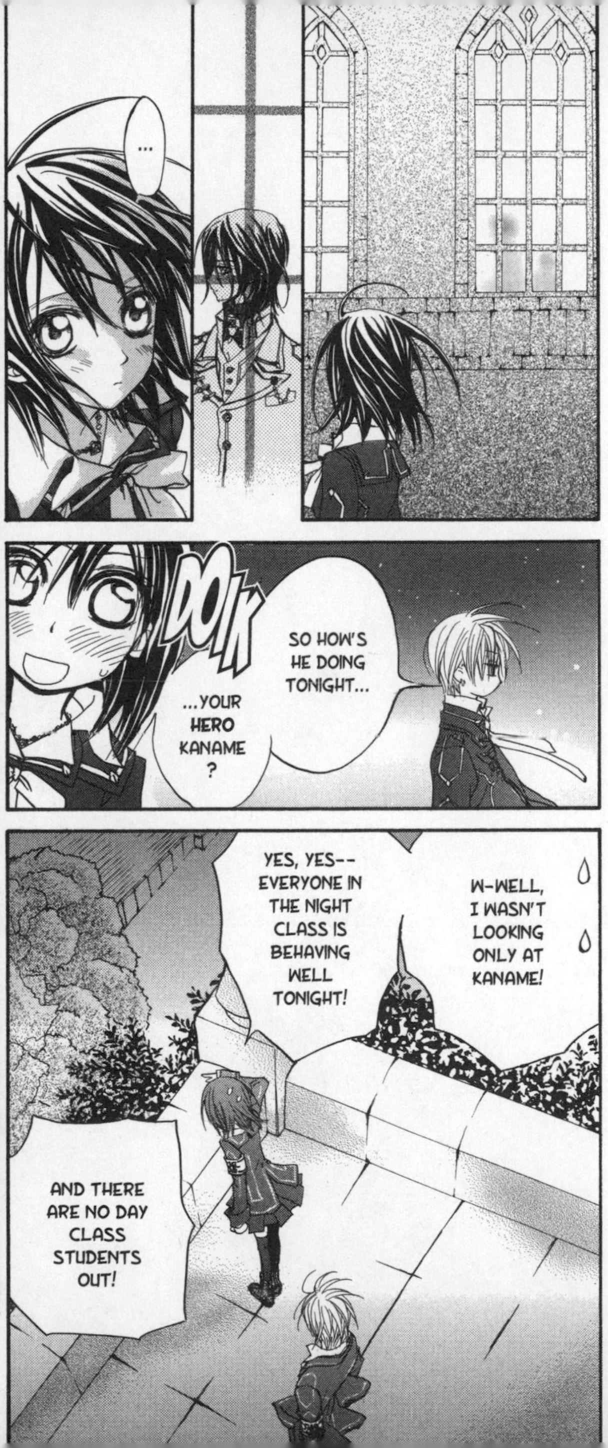
...
SO HOW'S HE DOING TONIGHT...
...YOUR HERO KANAME ?
DOIK
W-WELL, I WASN'T LOOKING ONLY AT KANAME!
YES, YES-- EVERYONE IN THE NIGHT CLASS IS BEHAVING WELL TONIGHT!
AND THERE ARE NO DAY CLASS STUDENTS OUT!

II

*Vampire Knight* is my first series with a serious twist. Considering that my previous *MeruPuri* had "cute and lovely♡" as its theme, this time it's "fresh blood, blood-covered school LOVE." They're quite different. (The "LOVE" portion becomes "If you want to hurry, go slow.")

I was apprehensive that a lot of readers would be surprised... But I'm looking forward to the kinds of responses I will receive. ^^ But in the end, the same person is drawing them: "The roots of all works are the same." I'd be happy if you don't get scared, but come with me.

I've always wanted to draw a vampire story, and because it's a "serious" story, I'm all fired up. Since I made my debut, I've been told that my drawings suit happy and bubbly stories (by all my editors...), and because I have fun drawing love comedies, I had avoided putting an emphasis on anything serious.

I'm really, really looking forward to how the serious *Vampire Knight* will turn out... Mu ha ha ha!

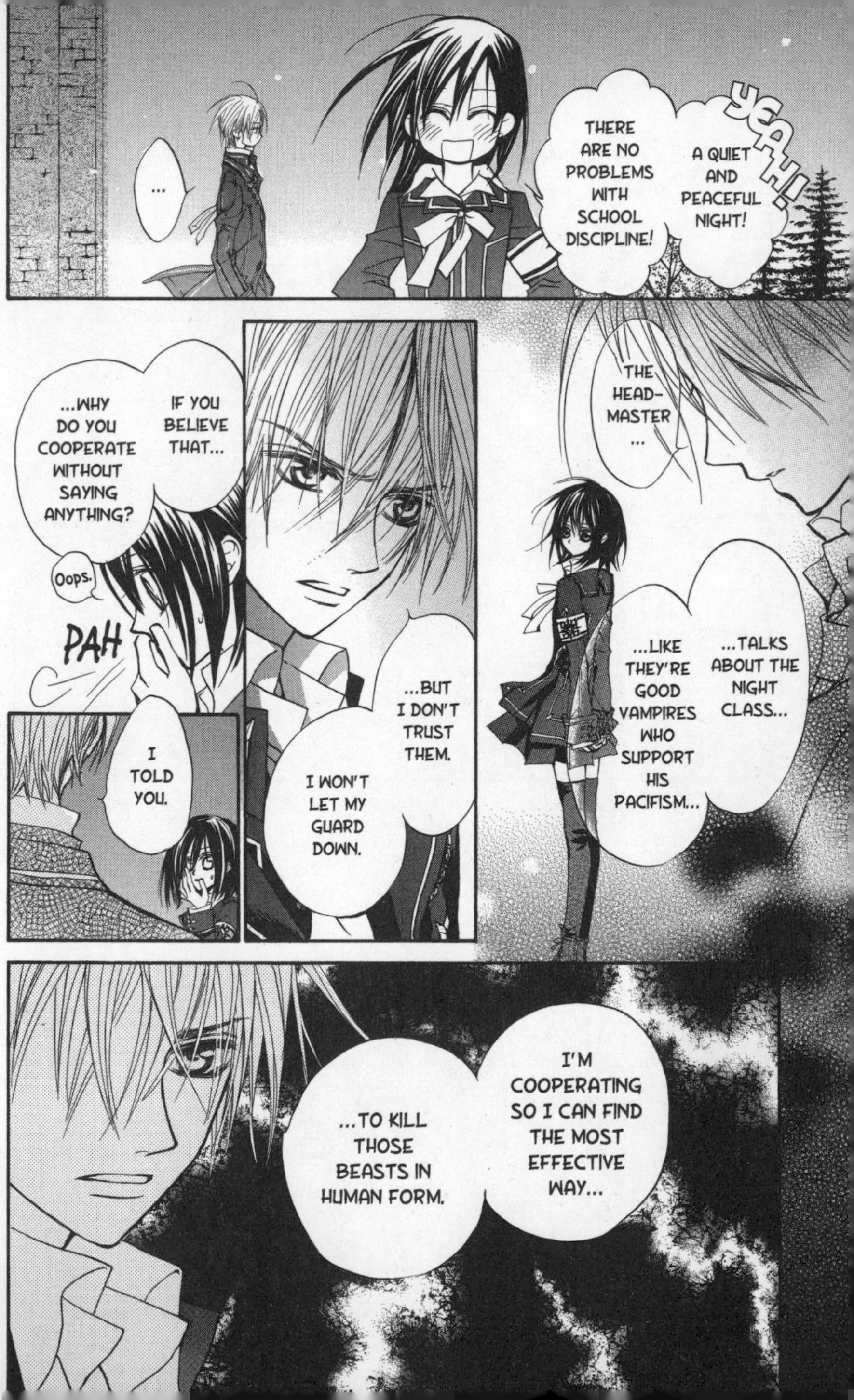
YEAH!
A QUIET AND PEACEFUL NIGHT!
THERE ARE NO PROBLEMS WITH SCHOOL DISCIPLINE!
...
THE HEAD-MASTER ...
...TALKS ABOUT THE NIGHT CLASS...
...LIKE THEY'RE GOOD VAMPIRES WHO SUPPORT HIS PACIFISM...
...BUT I DON'T TRUST THEM.
I WON'T LET MY GUARD DOWN.
IF YOU BELIEVE THAT...
...WHY DO YOU COOPERATE WITHOUT SAYING ANYTHING?
Oops.
PAH
I TOLD YOU.
I'M COOPERATING SO I CAN FIND THE MOST EFFECTIVE WAY...
...TO KILL THOSE BEASTS IN HUMAN FORM.

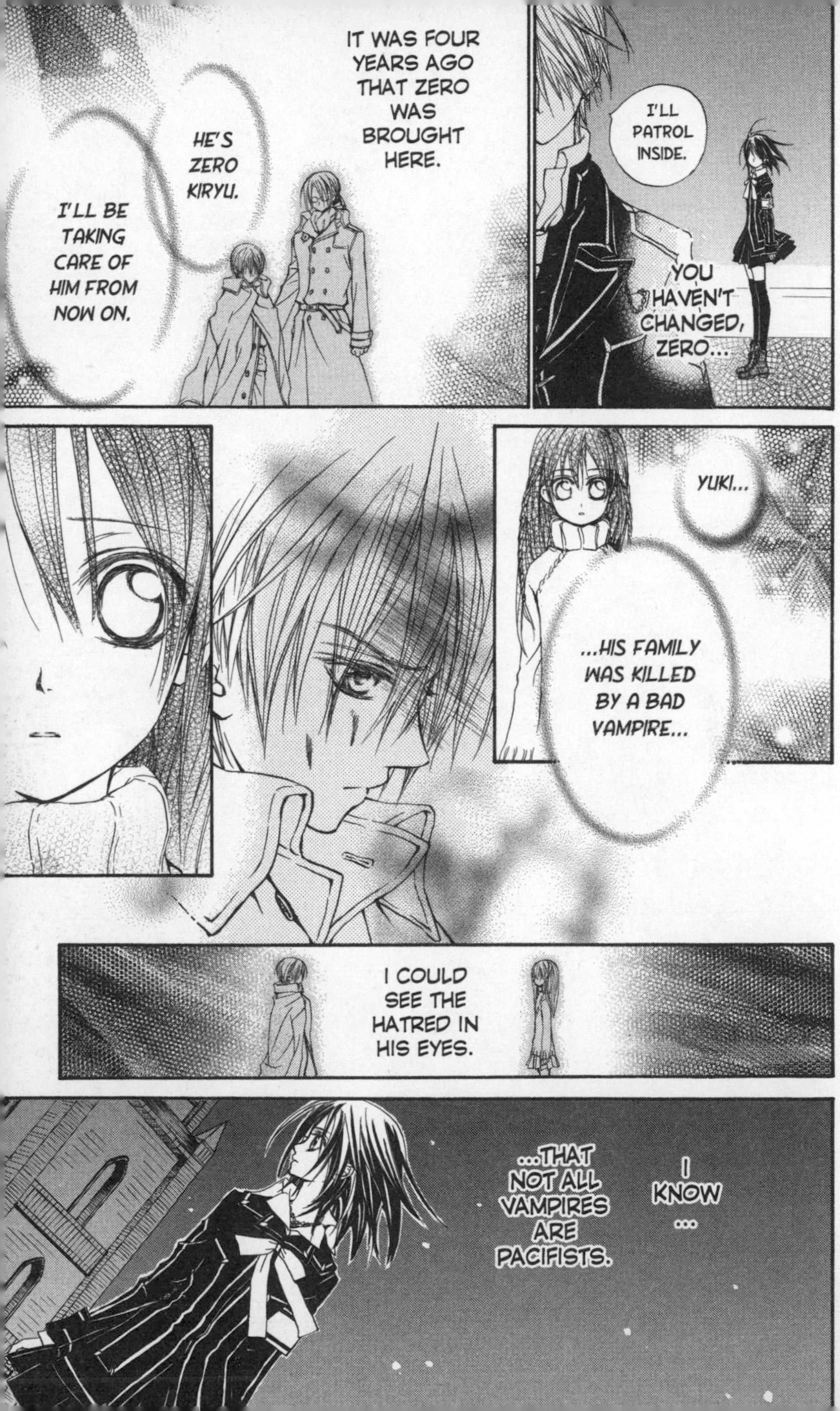
I'LL PATROL INSIDE.
YOU HAVEN'T CHANGED, ZERO...
IT WAS FOUR YEARS AGO THAT ZERO WAS BROUGHT HERE.
HE'S ZERO KIRYU.
I'LL BE TAKING CARE OF HIM FROM NOW ON.
YUKI...
...HIS FAMILY WAS KILLED BY A BAD VAMPIRE...
I COULD SEE THE HATRED IN HIS EYES.
I KNOW...
...THAT NOT ALL VAMPIRES ARE PACIFISTS.

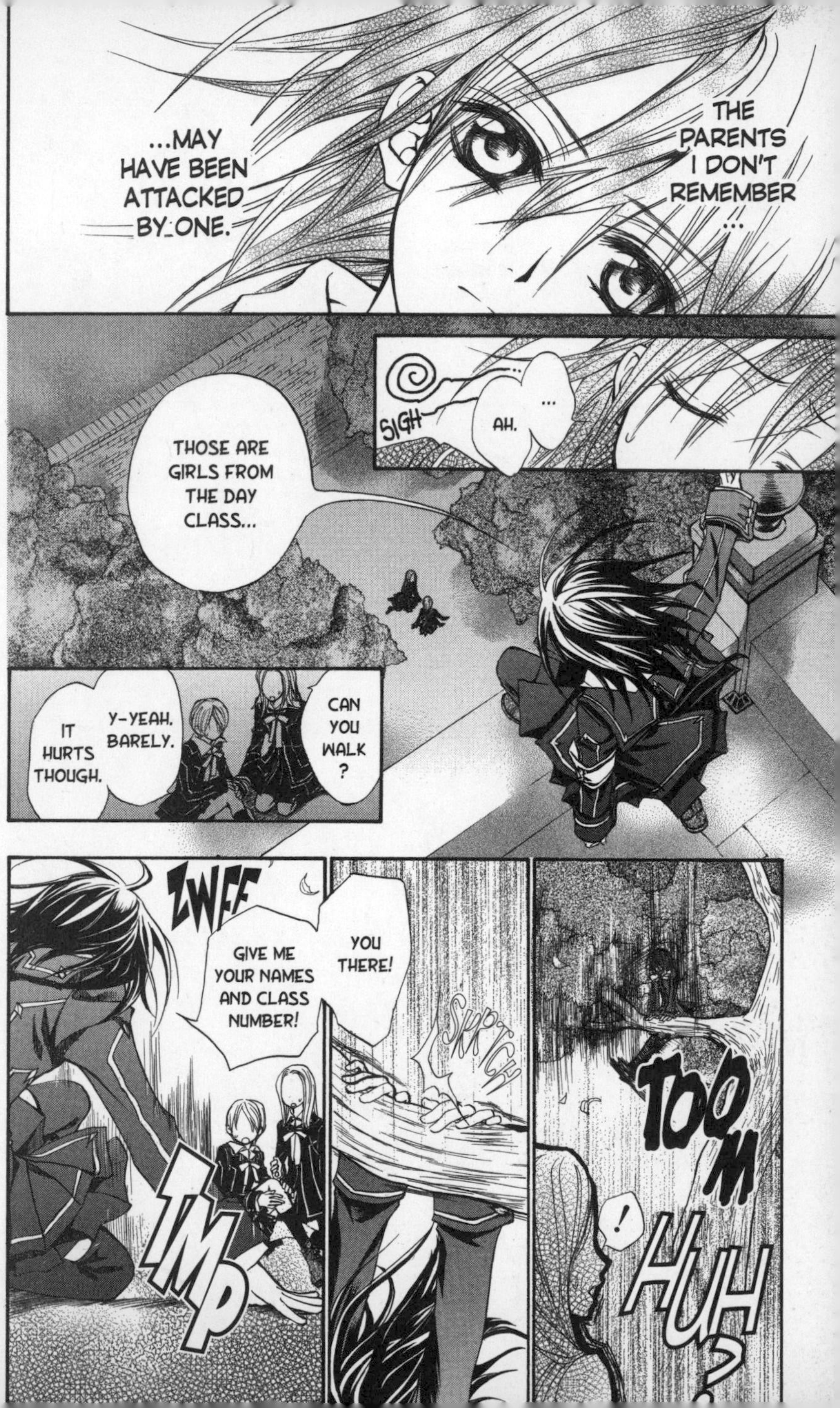
THE PARENTS I DON'T REMEMBER...
...MAY HAVE BEEN ATTACKED BY ONE.
SIGH
...
AH.
...
THOSE ARE GIRLS FROM THE DAY CLASS...
CAN YOU WALK?
Y-YEAH. BARELY.
IT HURTS THOUGH.
TOOM
!
HUH?
SKRTCH
YOU THERE!
GIVE ME YOUR NAMES AND CLASS NUMBER!
ZWFF
TMP

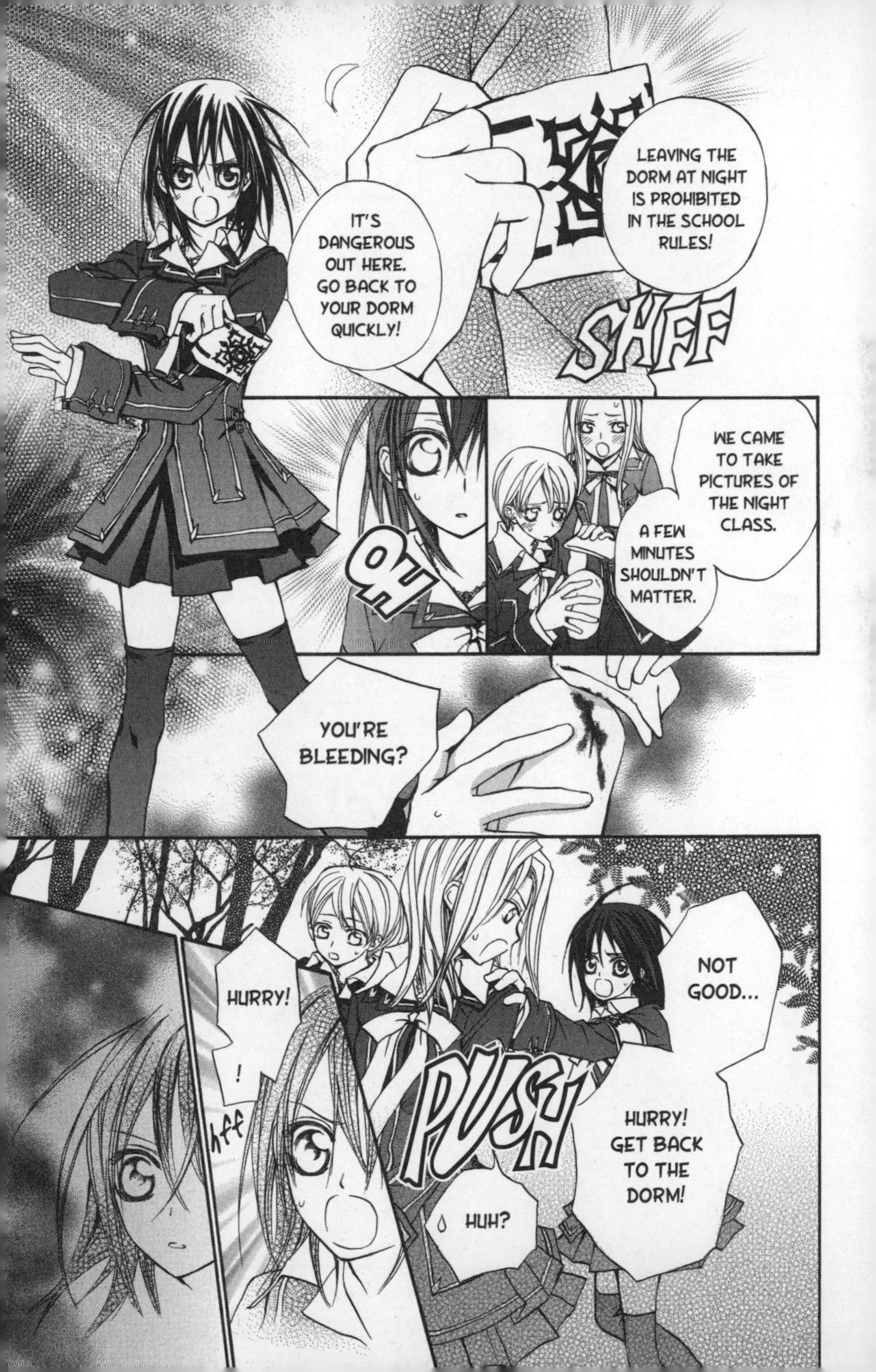
LEAVING THE DORM AT NIGHT IS PROHIBITED IN THE SCHOOL RULES!
IT'S DANGEROUS OUT HERE. GO BACK TO YOUR DORM QUICKLY!
SHFF
WE CAME TO TAKE PICTURES OF THE NIGHT CLASS.
A FEW MINUTES SHOULDN'T MATTER.
OH
YOU'RE BLEEDING?
NOT GOOD...
HURRY! GET BACK TO THE DORM!
PUSH
HUH?
HURRY!
!
hff

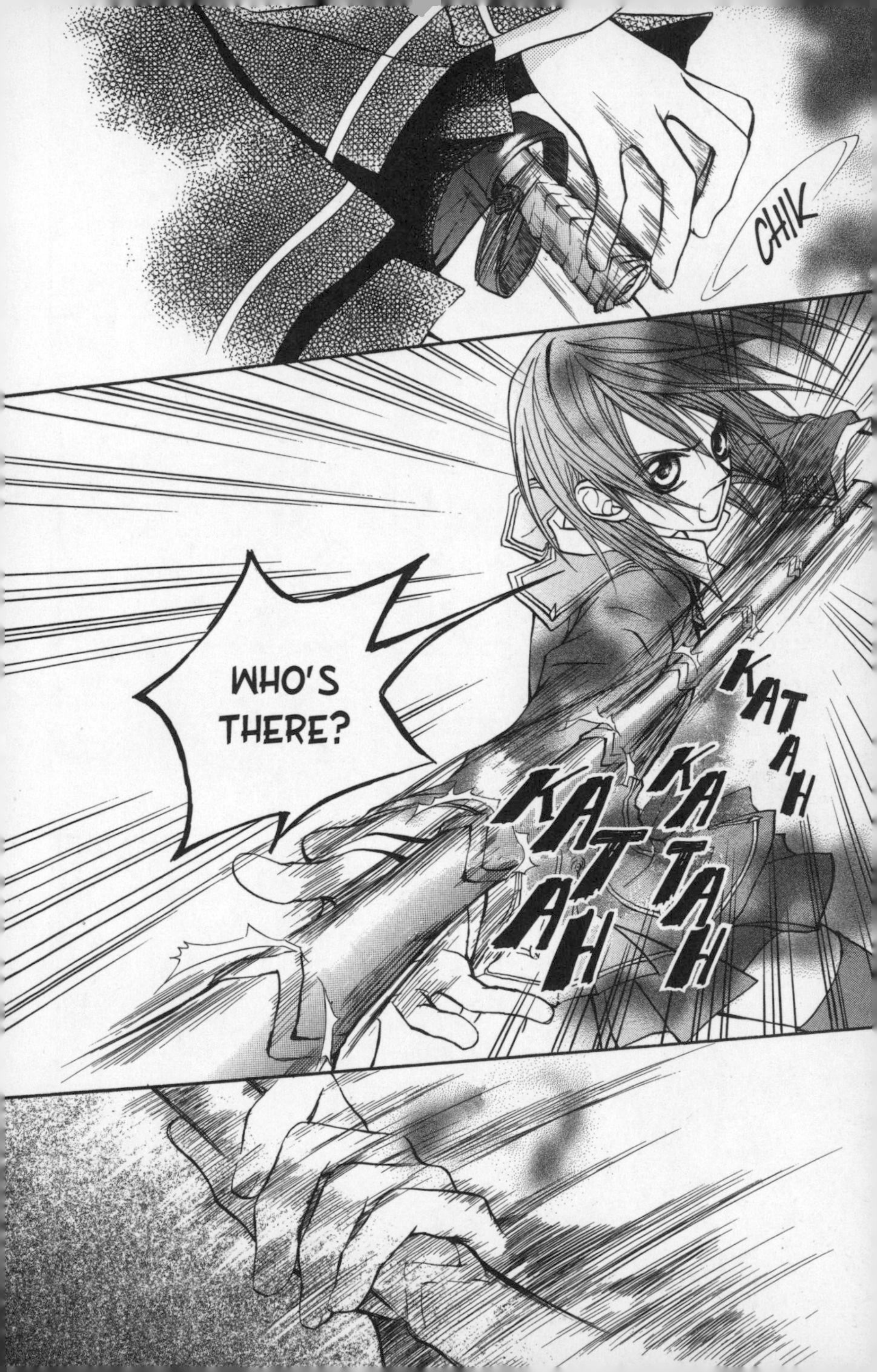
CHIK
KATAH
KATAH
KATAH
WHO'S THERE?

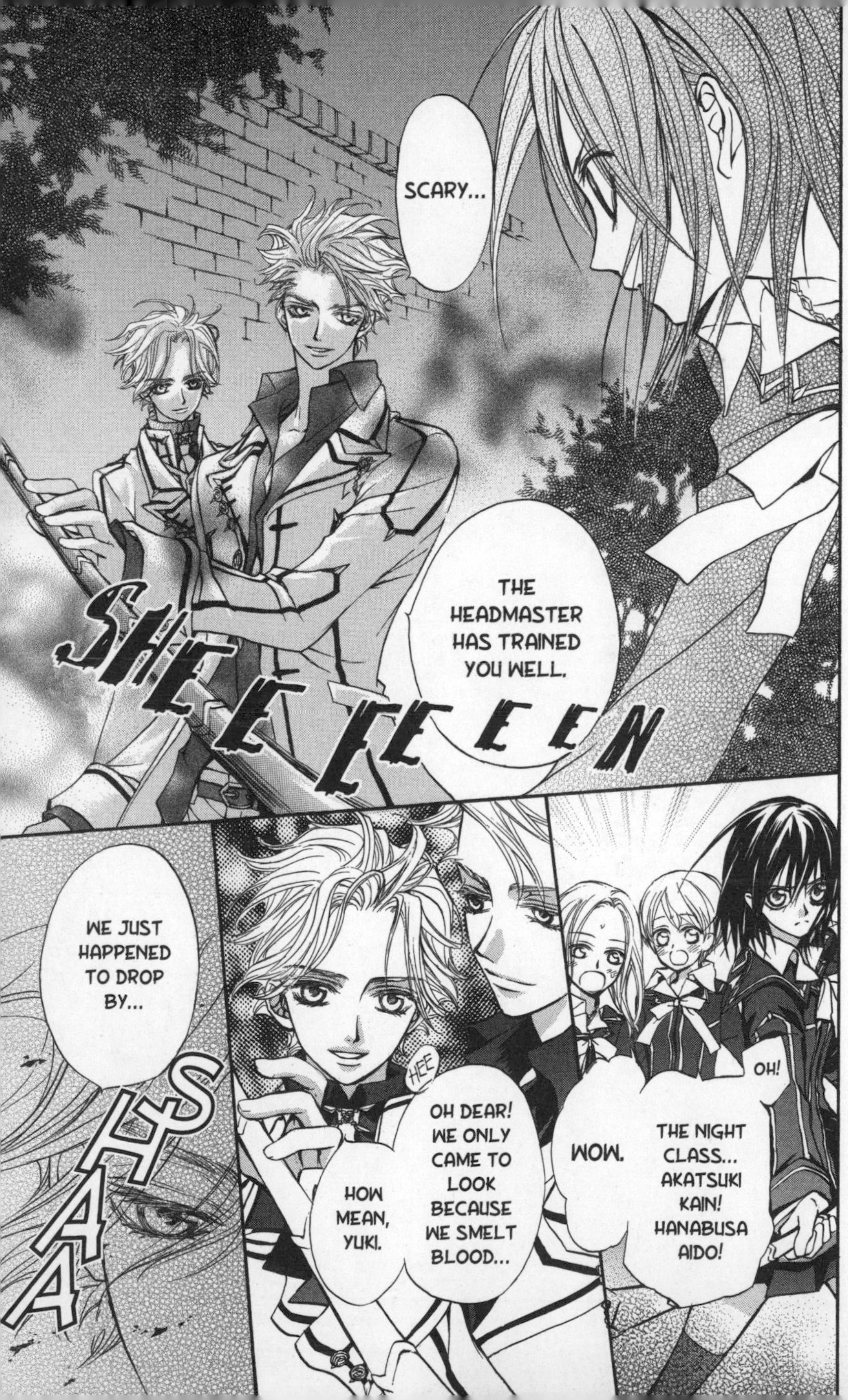
SCARY...
THE HEADMASTER HAS TRAINED YOU WELL.
SHEEEEEN
OH!
THE NIGHT CLASS... AKATSUKI KAIN! HANABUSA AIDO!
WOW.
HEE
OH DEAR! WE ONLY CAME TO LOOK BECAUSE WE SMELT BLOOD...
HOW MEAN, YUKI.
WE JUST HAPPENED TO DROP BY...
SHAA

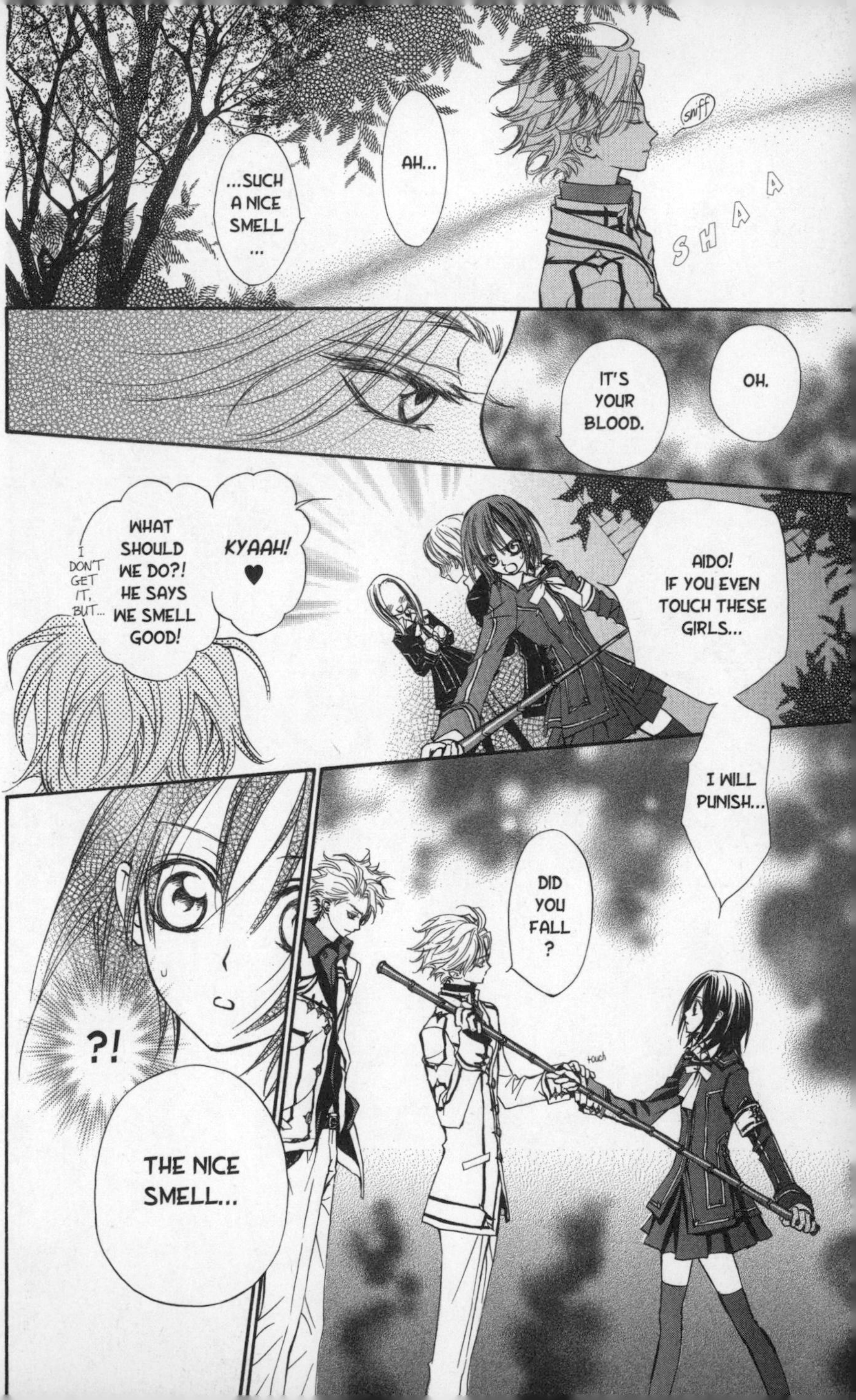
sniff
AH...
SHAA
...SUCH A NICE SMELL ...
OH.
IT'S YOUR BLOOD.
AIDO! IF YOU EVEN TOUCH THESE GIRLS...
KYAAH! ♥
WHAT SHOULD WE DO?! HE SAYS WE SMELL GOOD!
I DON'T GET IT, BUT...
I WILL PUNISH...
DID YOU FALL ?
touch
?!
THE NICE SMELL...

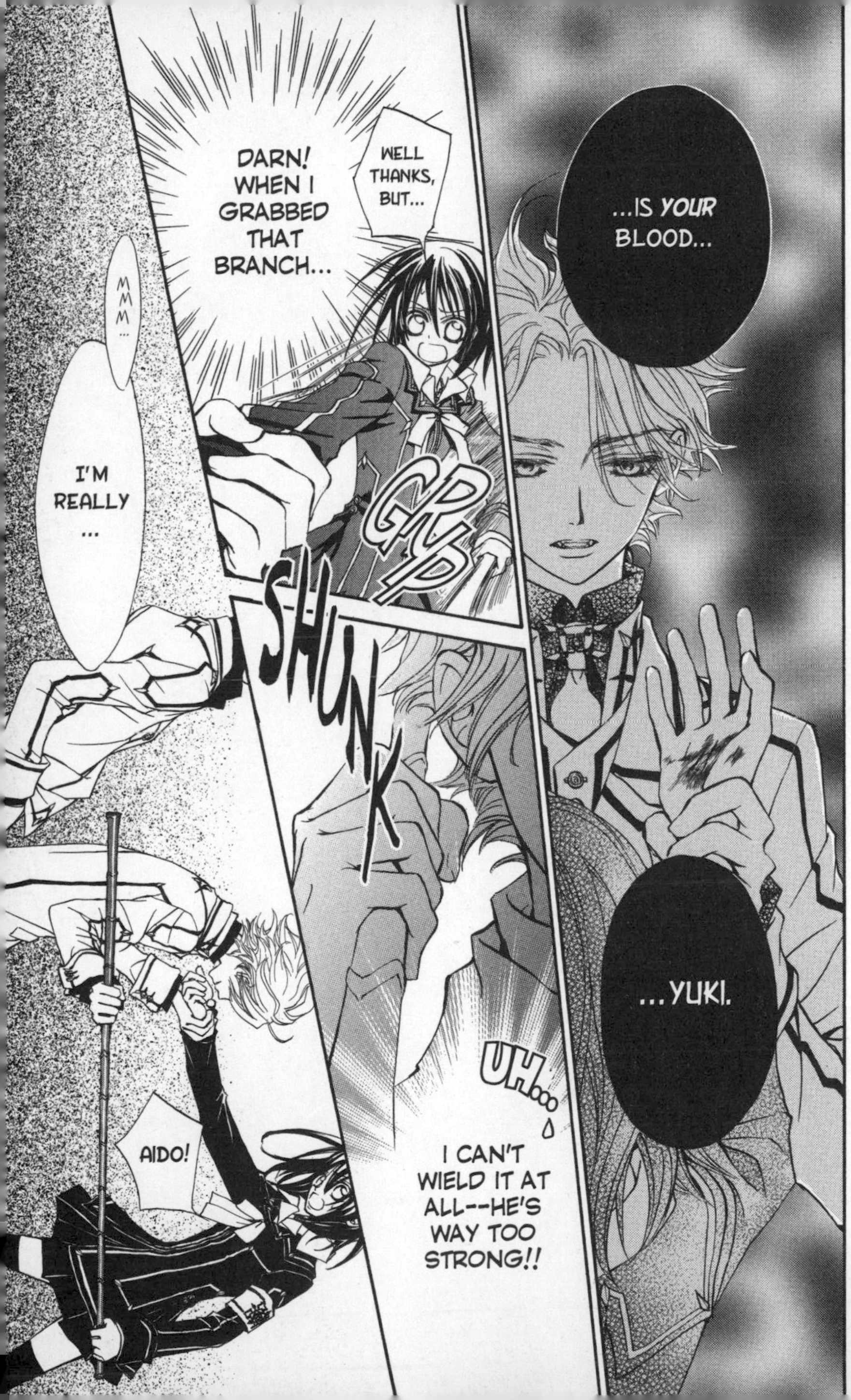
...IS *YOUR* BLOOD...
...YUKI.
WELL THANKS, BUT...
DARN! WHEN I GRABBED THAT BRANCH...
GRP
SHUNK
UH...
I CAN'T WIELD IT AT ALL--HE'S WAY TOO STRONG!!
MMM...
I'M REALLY ...
AIDO!

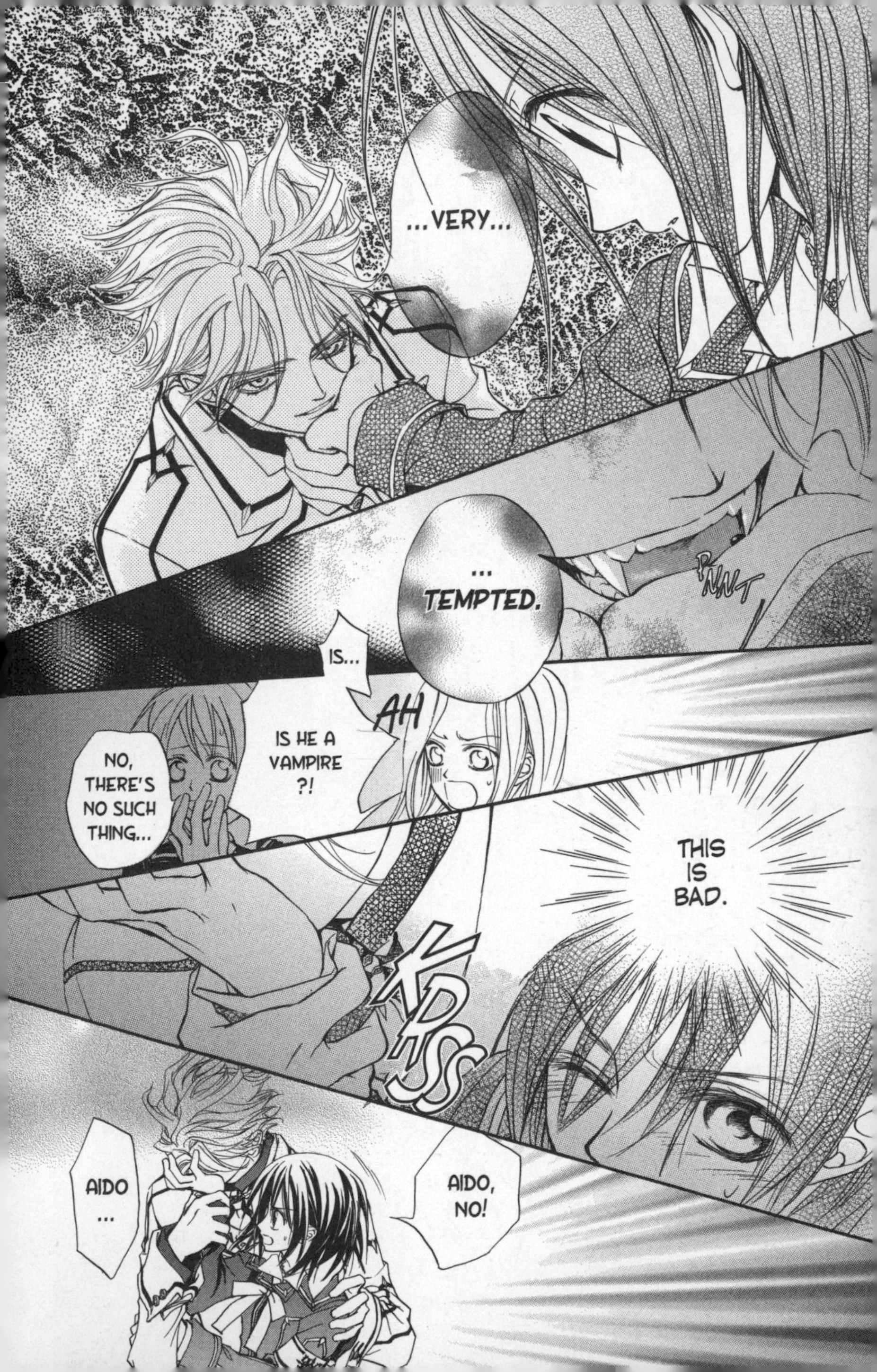
...VERY...
...
TEMPTED.
PNNT
IS...
AH
IS HE A VAMPIRE ?!
NO, THERE'S NO SUCH THING...
THIS IS BAD.
KRSS
AIDO, NO!
AIDO
...

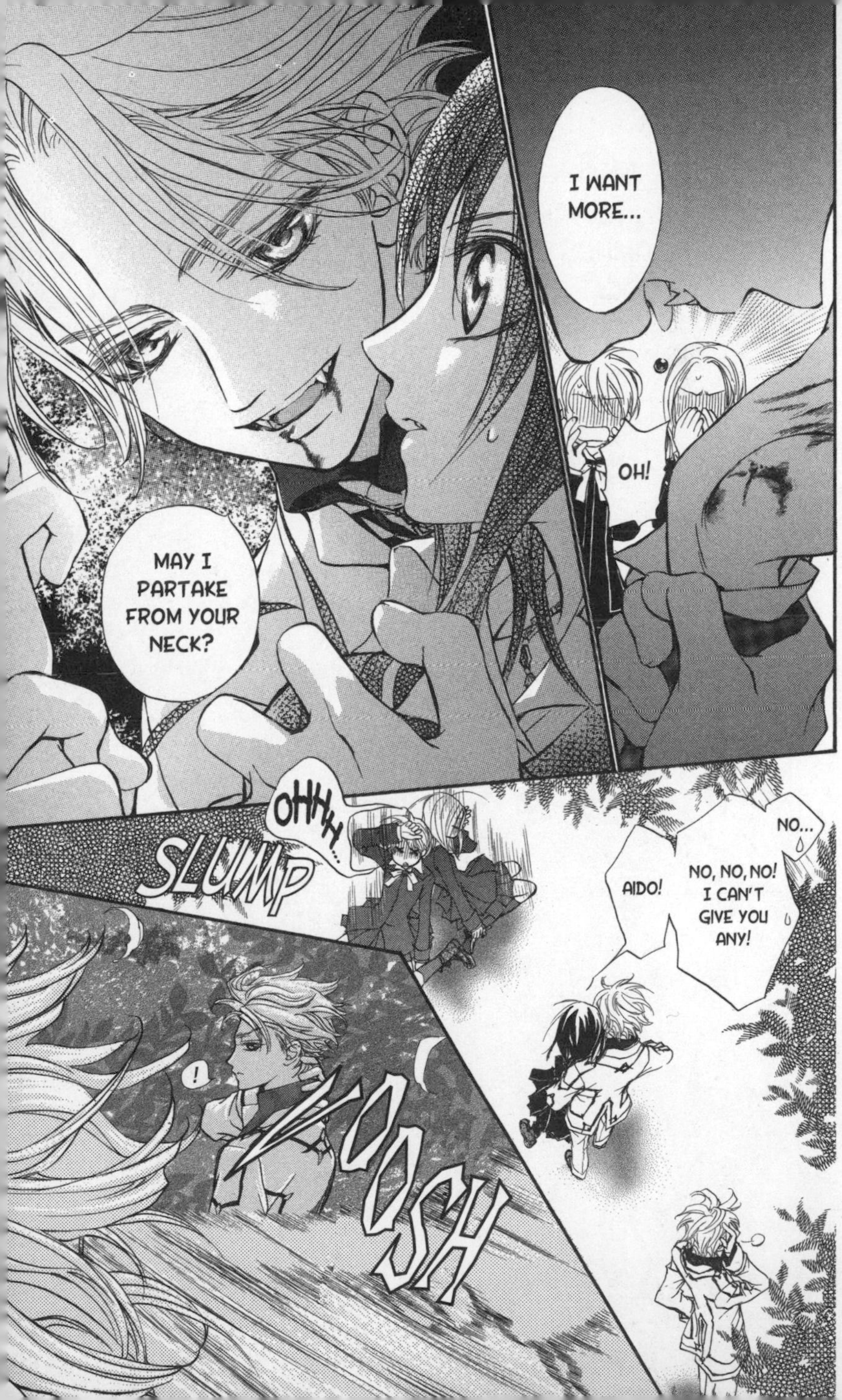
I WANT MORE...
OH!
MAY I PARTAKE FROM YOUR NECK?
NO...
NO, NO, NO! I CAN'T GIVE YOU ANY!
AIDO!
OHHH...
SLUMP
!
WOOSH

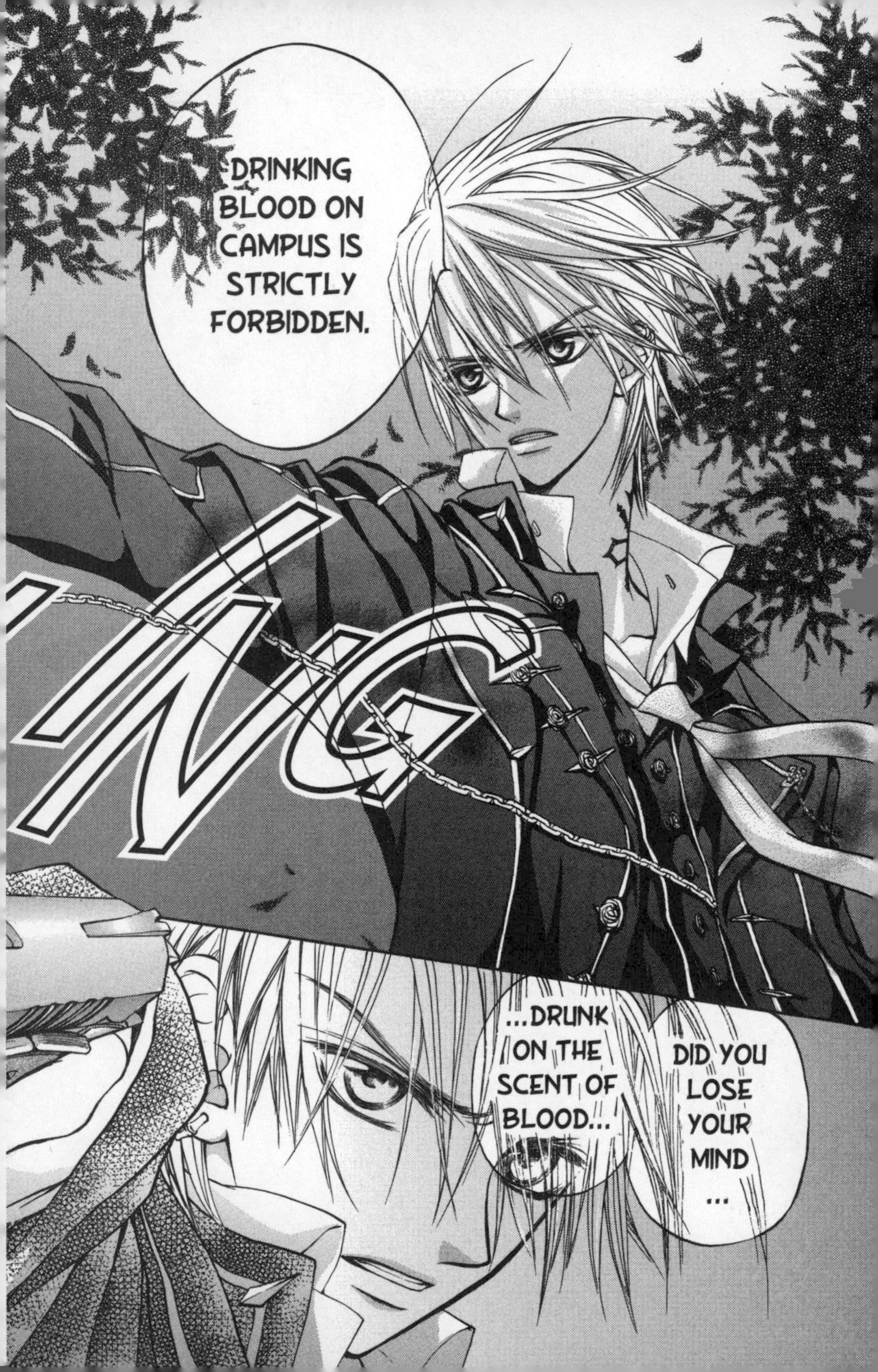
DRINKING BLOOD ON CAMPUS IS STRICTLY FORBIDDEN.
DID YOU LOSE YOUR MIND ...
...DRUNK ON THE SCENT OF BLOOD...

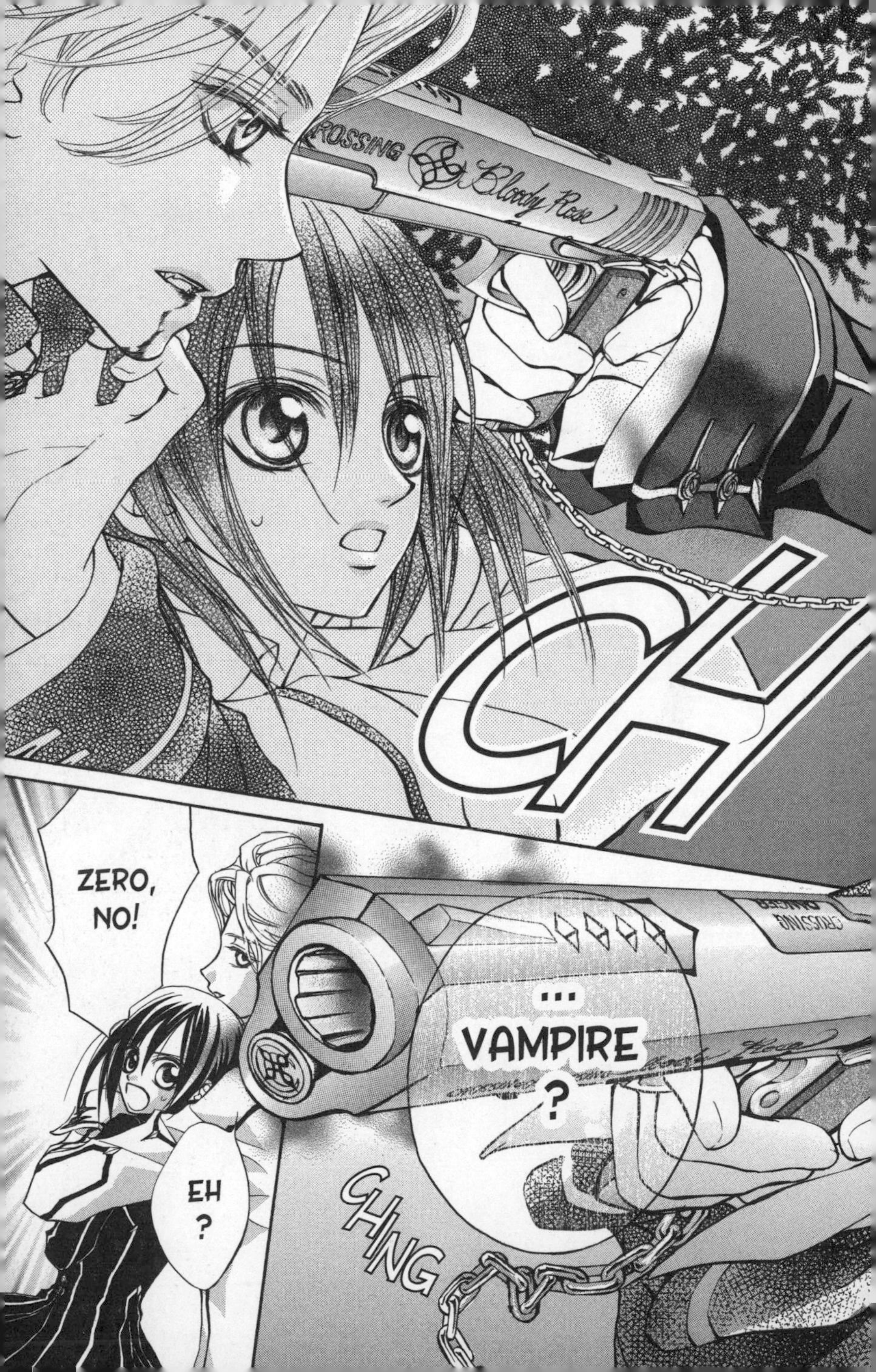
CROSSING
Bloody Rose
CH
...VAMPIRE?
EH?
ZERO, NO!
CHING

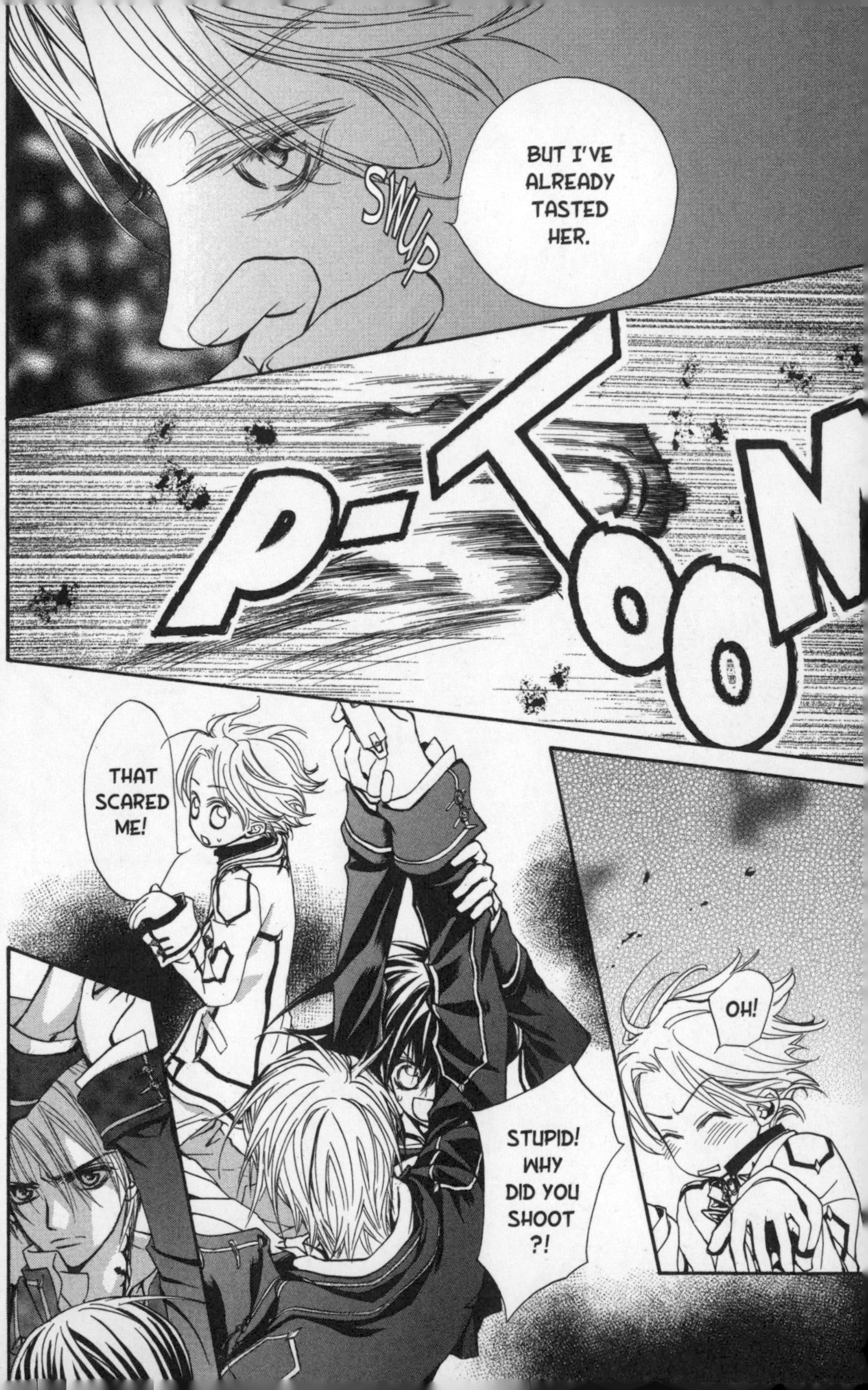
SWUP
BUT I'VE ALREADY TASTED HER.
P-TOOM
OH!
THAT SCARED ME!
STUPID! WHY DID YOU SHOOT ?!

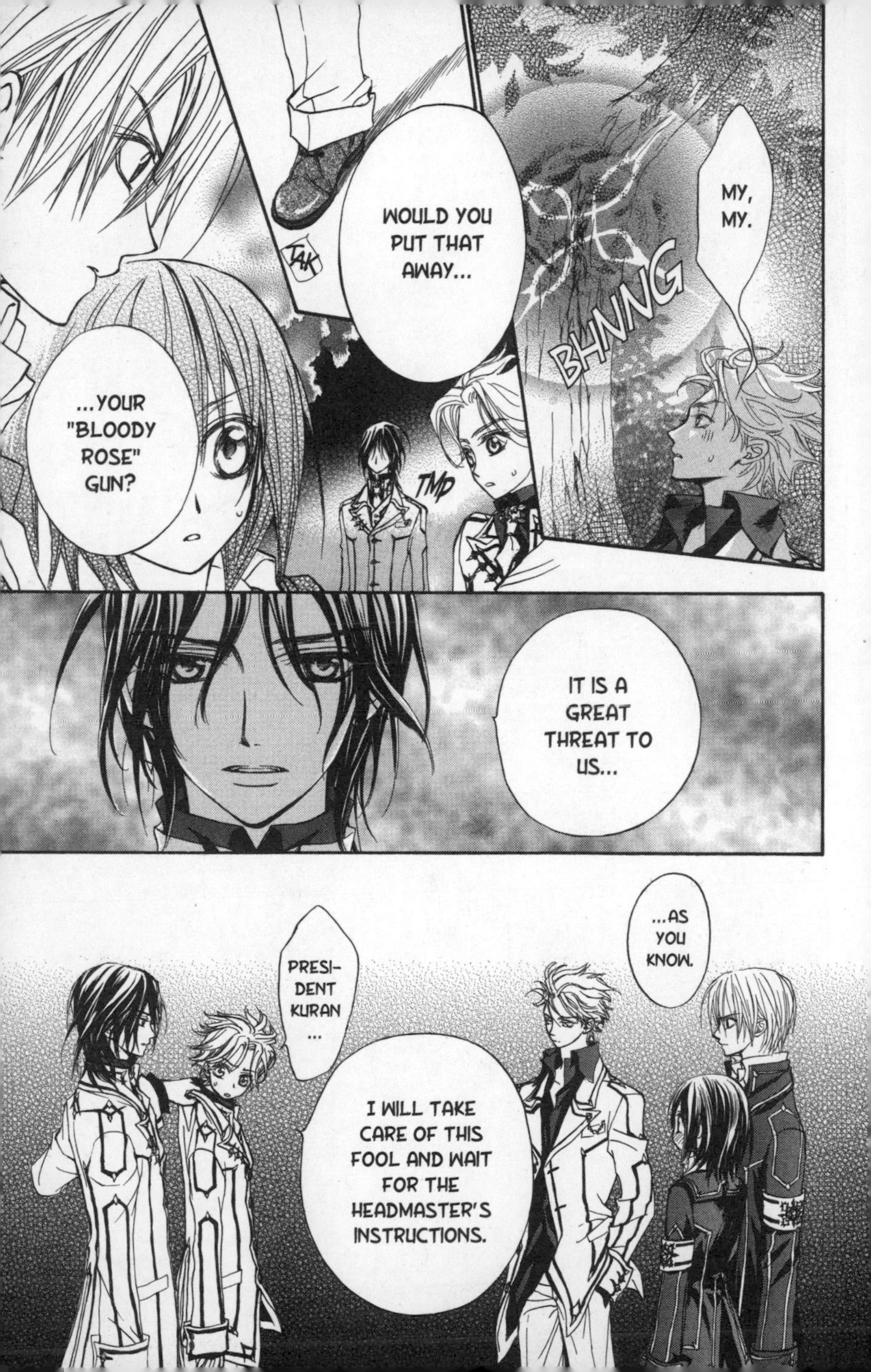
MY, MY.
BHNNG
WOULD YOU PUT THAT AWAY...
TAK
...YOUR "BLOODY ROSE" GUN?
TMP
IT IS A GREAT THREAT TO US...
...AS YOU KNOW.
PRESI-DENT KURAN...
I WILL TAKE CARE OF THIS FOOL AND WAIT FOR THE HEADMASTER'S INSTRUCTIONS.

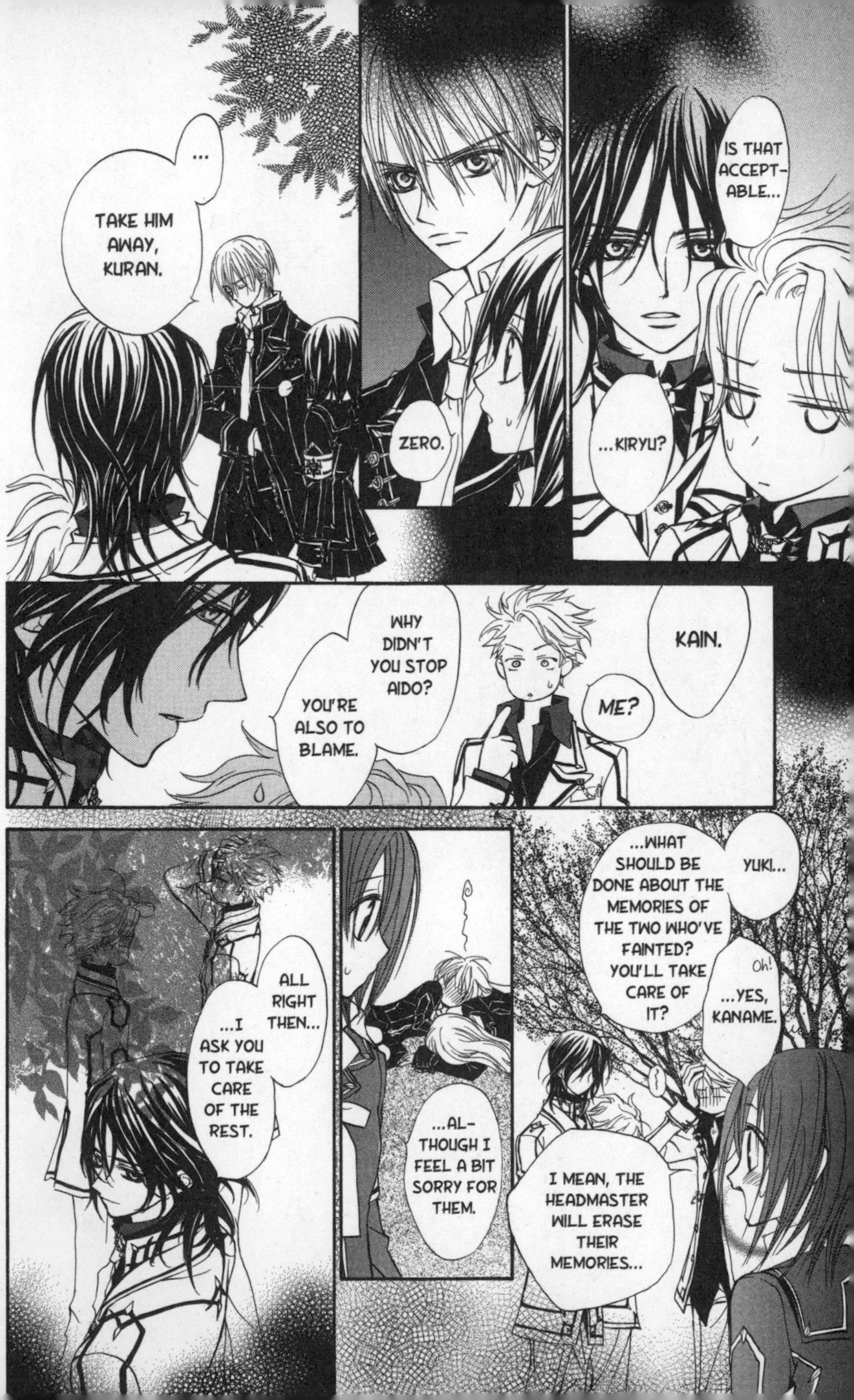
IS THAT ACCEPT-ABLE...
...KIRYU?
ZERO.
...
TAKE HIM AWAY, KURAN.
KAIN.
ME?
WHY DIDN'T YOU STOP AIDO?
YOU'RE ALSO TO BLAME.
YUKI...
...WHAT SHOULD BE DONE ABOUT THE MEMORIES OF THE TWO WHO'VE FAINTED? YOU'LL TAKE CARE OF IT?
Oh!
...YES, KANAME.
I MEAN, THE HEADMASTER WILL ERASE THEIR MEMORIES...
...AL-THOUGH I FEEL A BIT SORRY FOR THEM.
ALL RIGHT THEN...
...I ASK YOU TO TAKE CARE OF THE REST.

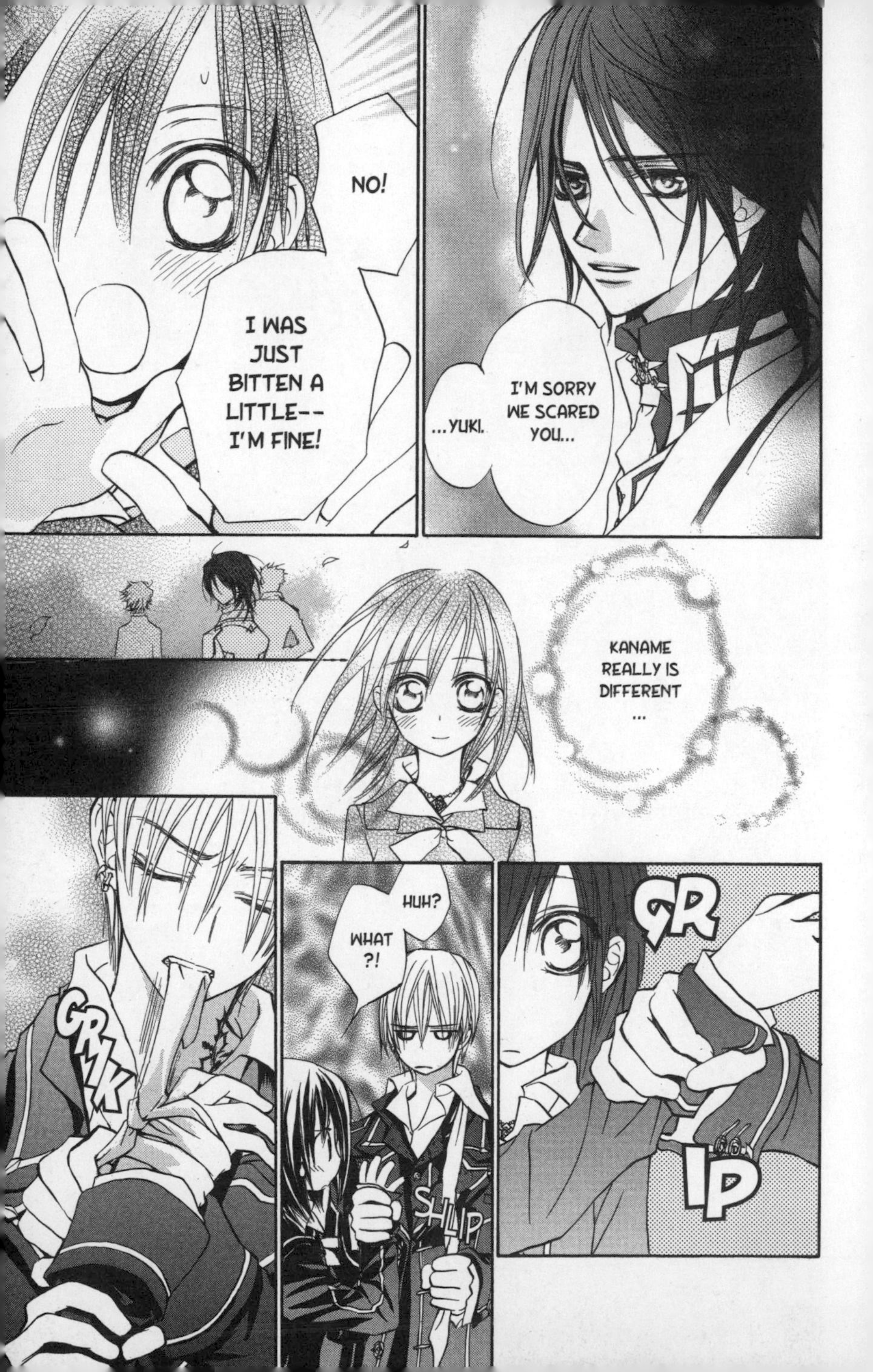
I'M SORRY WE SCARED YOU...
...YUKI.
NO!
I WAS JUST BITTEN A LITTLE-- I'M FINE!
KANAME REALLY IS DIFFERENT ...
GR
IP
HUH?
WHAT ?!
SHLIP
GRMK

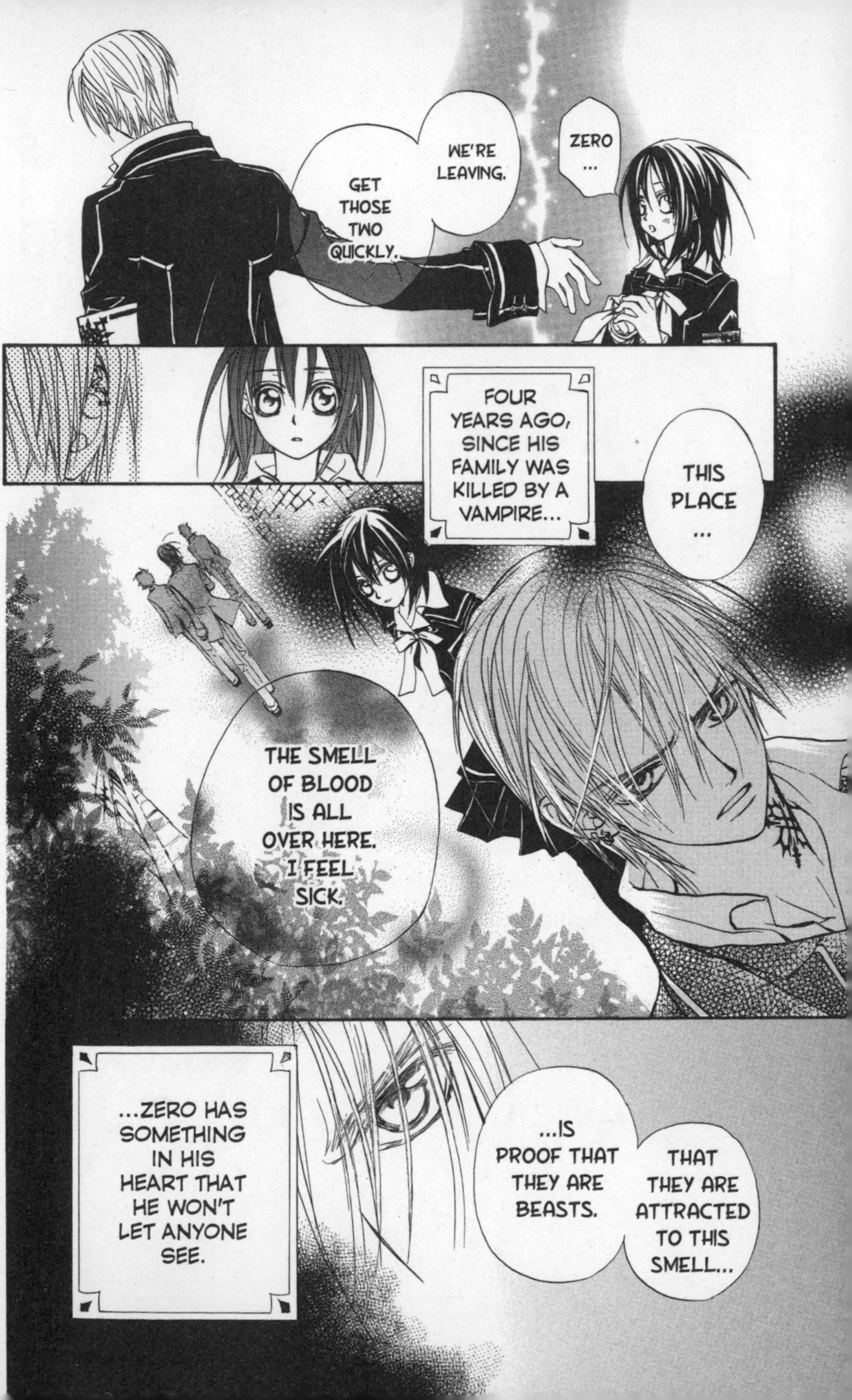
ZERO ...
WE'RE LEAVING. GET THOSE TWO QUICKLY.
FOUR YEARS AGO, SINCE HIS FAMILY WAS KILLED BY A VAMPIRE...
THIS PLACE ...
THE SMELL OF BLOOD IS ALL OVER HERE. I FEEL SICK.
THAT THEY ARE ATTRACTED TO THIS SMELL...
...IS PROOF THAT THEY ARE BEASTS.
...ZERO HAS SOMETHING IN HIS HEART THAT HE WON'T LET ANYONE SEE.

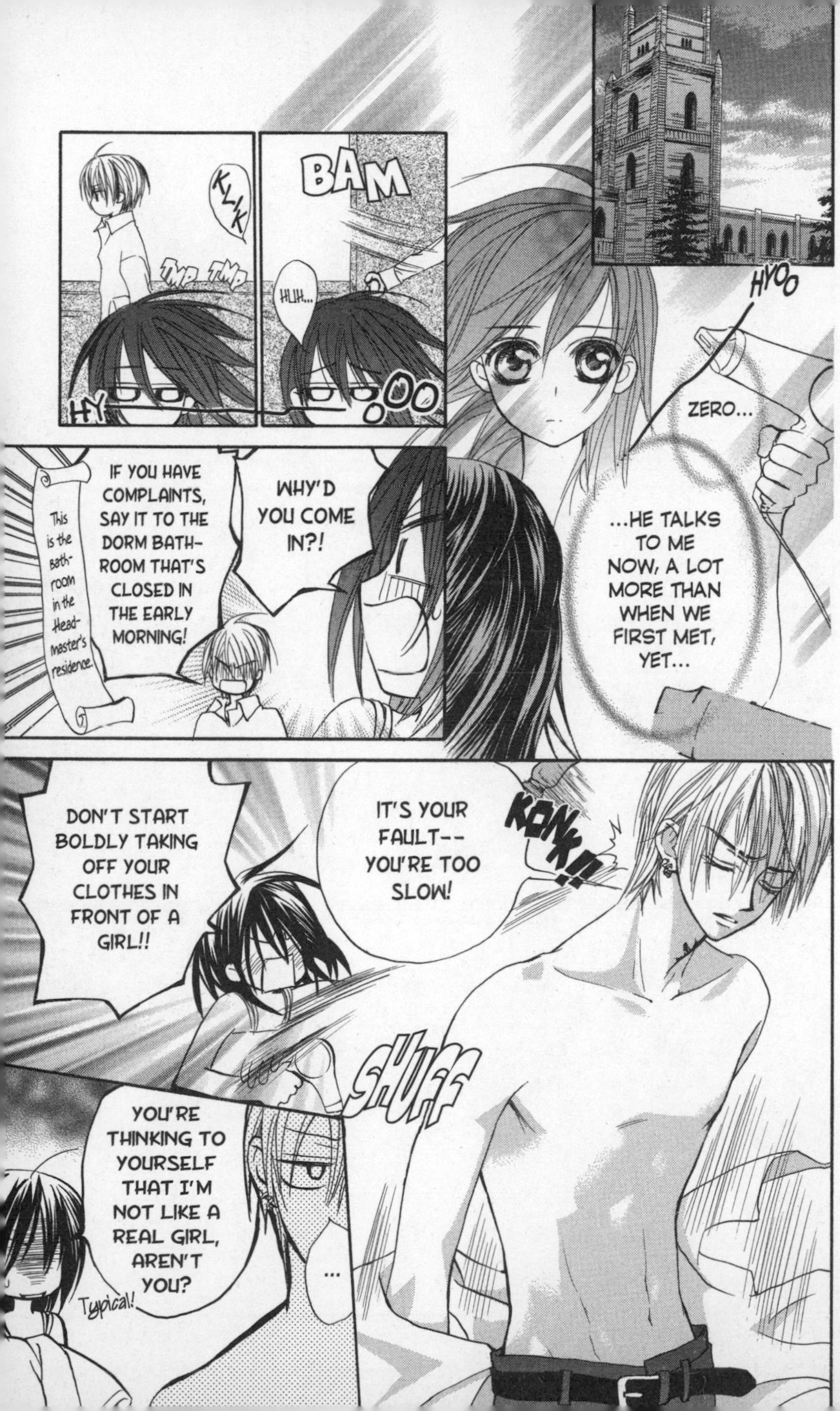
HYOO
ZERO...
...HE TALKS TO ME NOW, A LOT MORE THAN WHEN WE FIRST MET, YET...
BAM
HUH...
OOO
KLIK
TMP TMP
HY
WHY'D YOU COME IN?!
IF YOU HAVE COMPLAINTS, SAY IT TO THE DORM BATHROOM THAT'S CLOSED IN THE EARLY MORNING!
This is the bathroom in the Headmaster's residence.
KONK!!
IT'S YOUR FAULT-- YOU'RE TOO SLOW!
DON'T START BOLDLY TAKING OFF YOUR CLOTHES IN FRONT OF A GIRL!!
SHUFF
...
YOU'RE THINKING TO YOURSELF THAT I'M NOT LIKE A REAL GIRL, AREN'T YOU?
Typical!

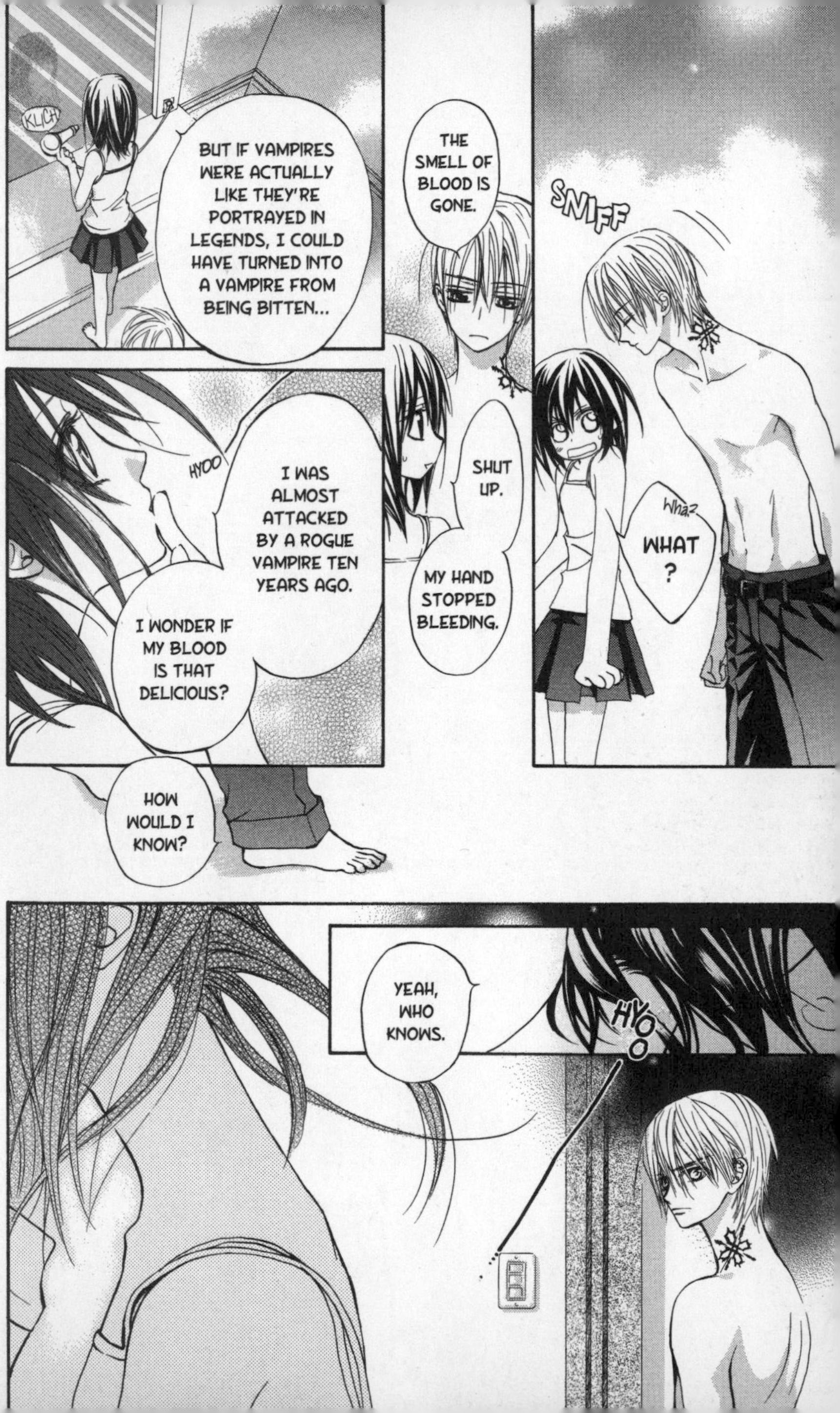
SNIFF
THE SMELL OF BLOOD IS GONE.
Wha?
WHAT?
SHUT UP.
MY HAND STOPPED BLEEDING.
KLICH
BUT IF VAMPIRES WERE ACTUALLY LIKE THEY'RE PORTRAYED IN LEGENDS, I COULD HAVE TURNED INTO A VAMPIRE FROM BEING BITTEN...
HYOO
I WAS ALMOST ATTACKED BY A ROGUE VAMPIRE TEN YEARS AGO.
I WONDER IF MY BLOOD IS THAT DELICIOUS?
HOW WOULD I KNOW?
HYOO
YEAH, WHO KNOWS.

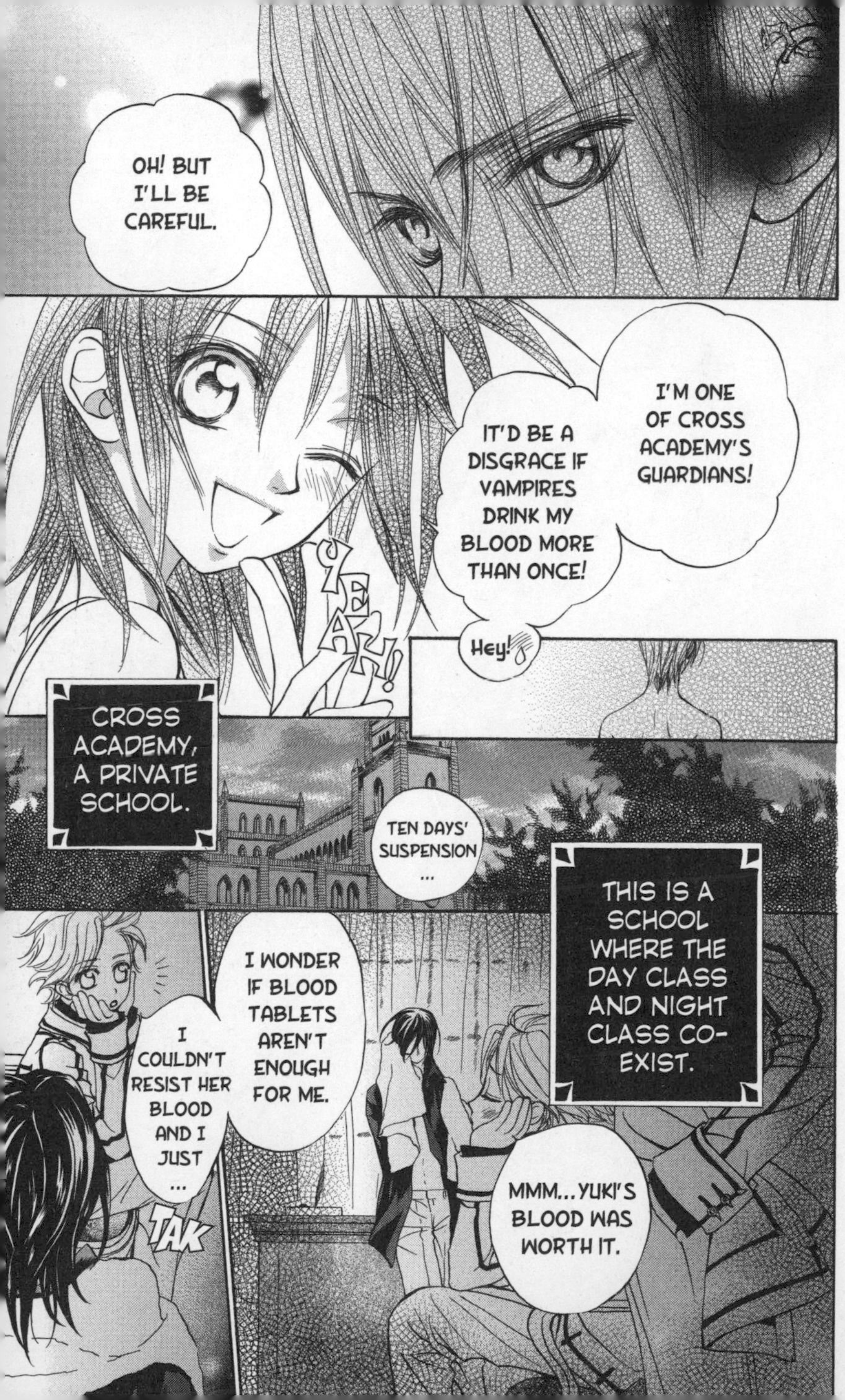
OH! BUT I'LL BE CAREFUL.
I'M ONE OF CROSS ACADEMY'S GUARDIANS!
IT'D BE A DISGRACE IF VAMPIRES DRINK MY BLOOD MORE THAN ONCE!
YEAH!
Hey!
CROSS ACADEMY, A PRIVATE SCHOOL.
TEN DAYS' SUSPENSION ...
THIS IS A SCHOOL WHERE THE DAY CLASS AND NIGHT CLASS CO-EXIST.
MMM...YUKI'S BLOOD WAS WORTH IT.
I WONDER IF BLOOD TABLETS AREN'T ENOUGH FOR ME.
I COULDN'T RESIST HER BLOOD AND I JUST ...
TAK

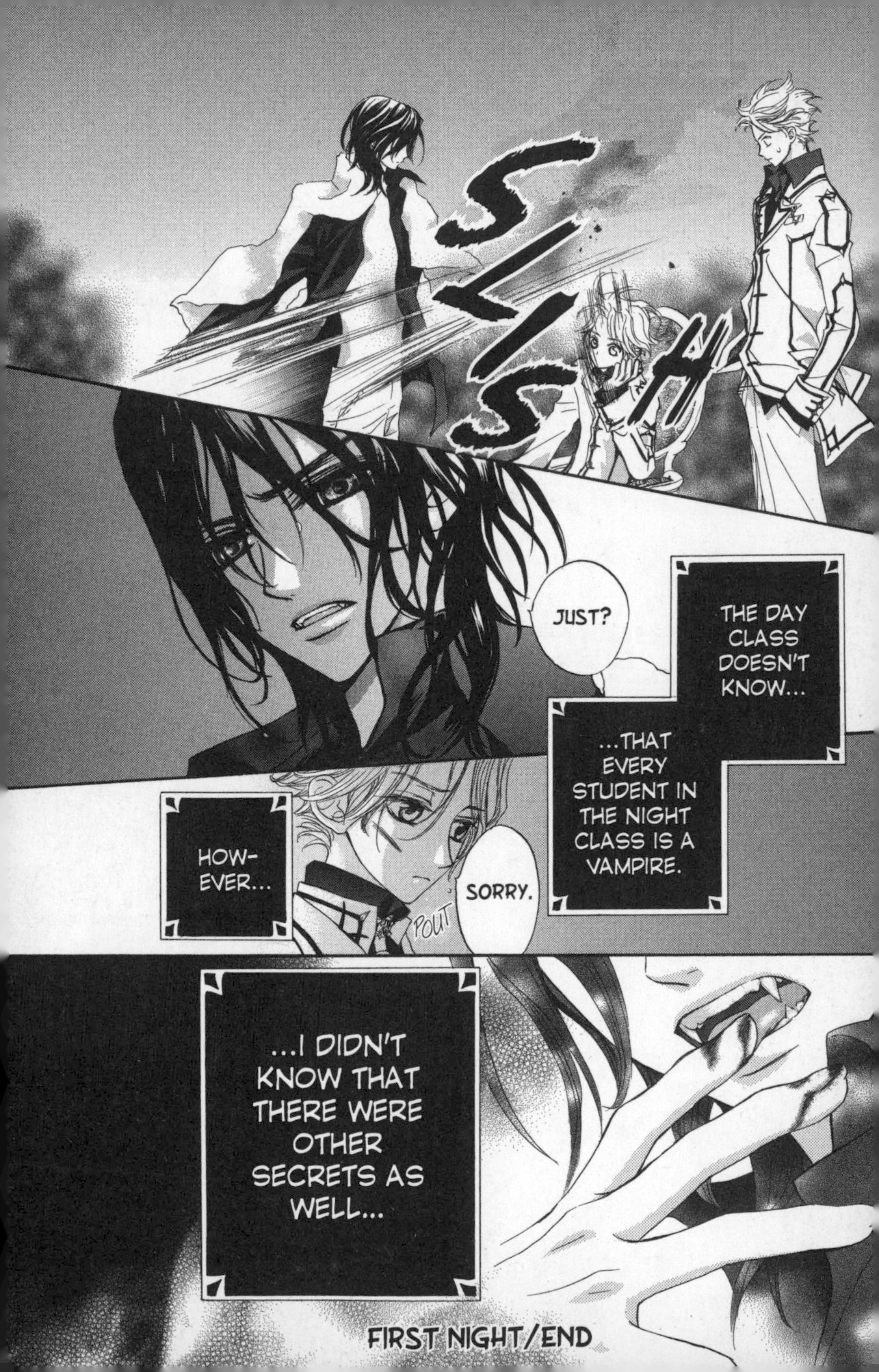
SLISH
THE DAY CLASS DOESN'T KNOW...
JUST?
...THAT EVERY STUDENT IN THE NIGHT CLASS IS A VAMPIRE.
SORRY.
POUT
HOW-EVER...
...I DIDN'T KNOW THAT THERE WERE OTHER SECRETS AS WELL...
FIRST NIGHT/END

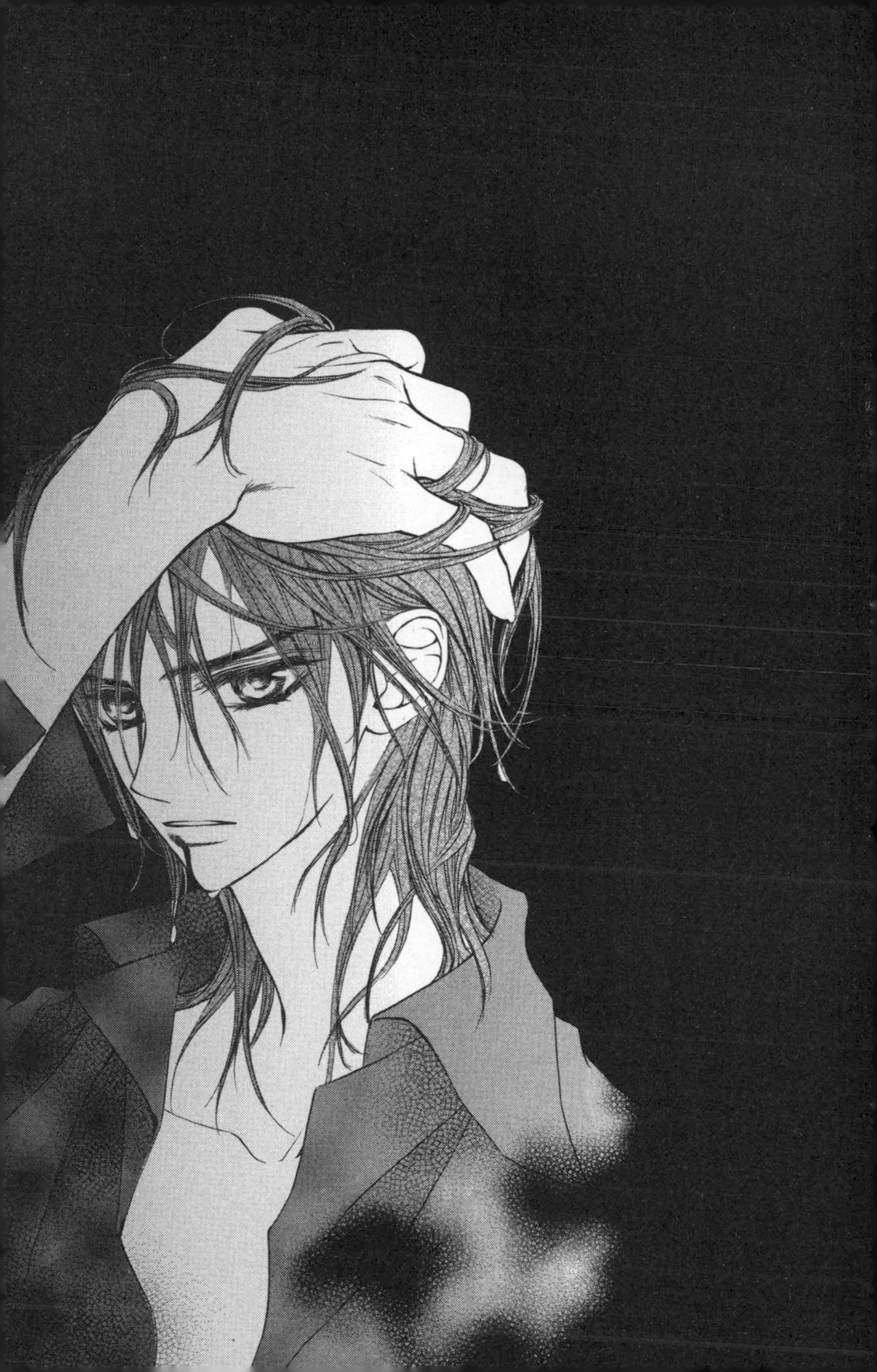

## WARNING: VAMPIRES COVERED IN BLOOD ARE PROHIBITED FROM ENTERING THIS PAGE!!

### Agony at My Desk

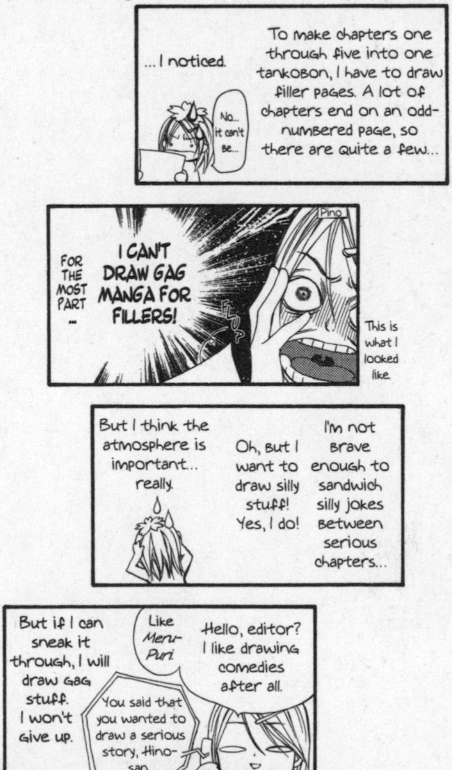
To make chapters one through five into one tankobon, I have to draw filler pages. A lot of chapters end on an odd-numbered page, so there are quite a few...
...I noticed.
No... it can't be...
Pino
I CAN'T DRAW GAG MANGA FOR FILLERS!
FLOP
FOR THE MOST PART...
This is what I looked like.
I'm not brave enough to sandwich silly jokes between serious chapters...
Oh, but I want to draw silly stuff! Yes, I do!
But I think the atmosphere is important... really.
Hello, editor? I like drawing comedies after all.
Like Meru-Puri.
You said that you wanted to draw a serious story, Hino-san.
But if I can sneak it through, I will draw gag stuff. I won't give up.

I thought I might get tired of comedies by doing two in a row, considering my personality...

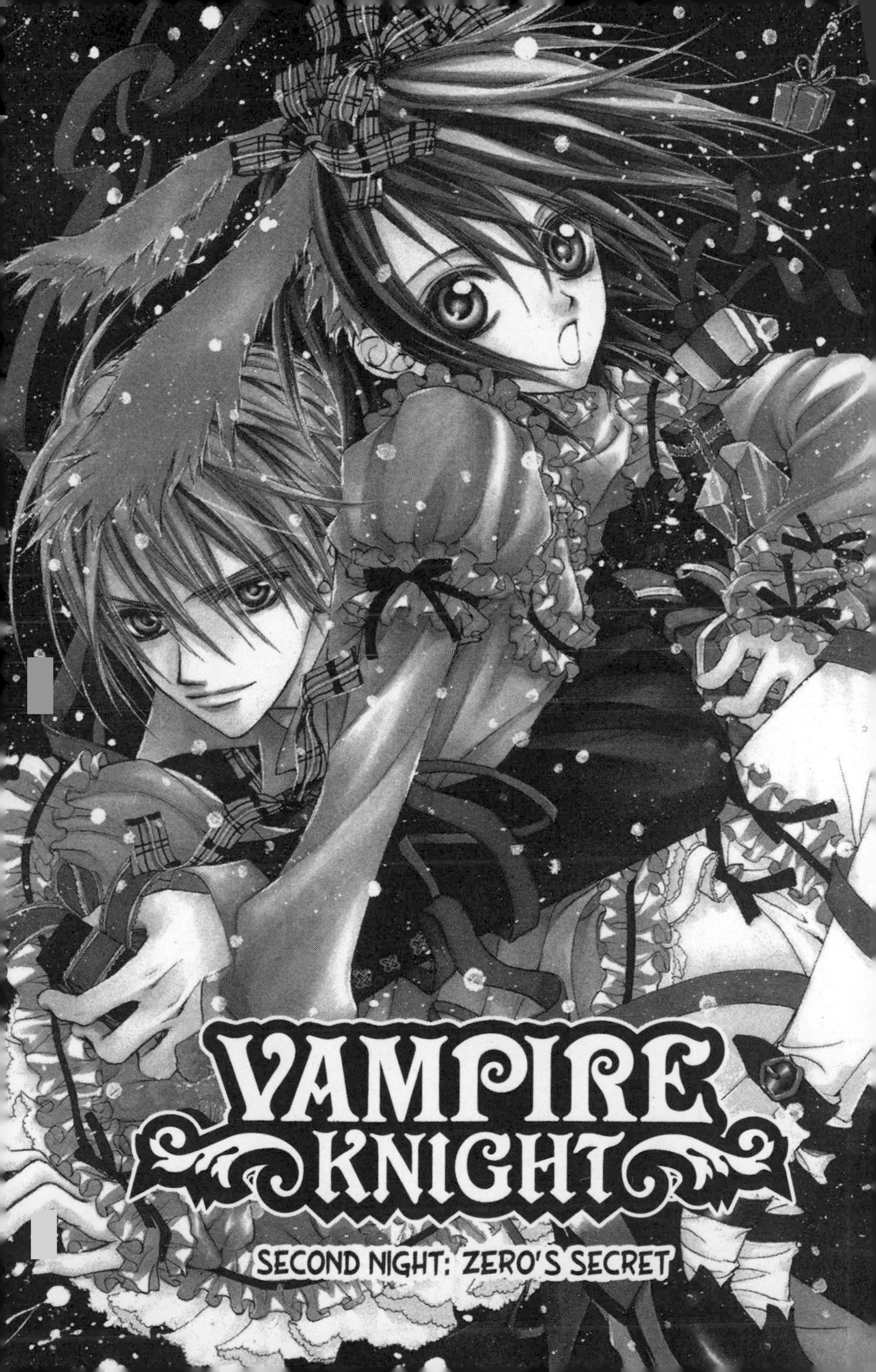
VAMPIRE KNIGHT
SECOND NIGHT: ZERO'S SECRET

**WARNING: VAMPIRES COVERED IN BLOOD ARE PROHIBITED FROM ENTERING THIS PAGE!!**

✿ My Cute Daughter... ✿

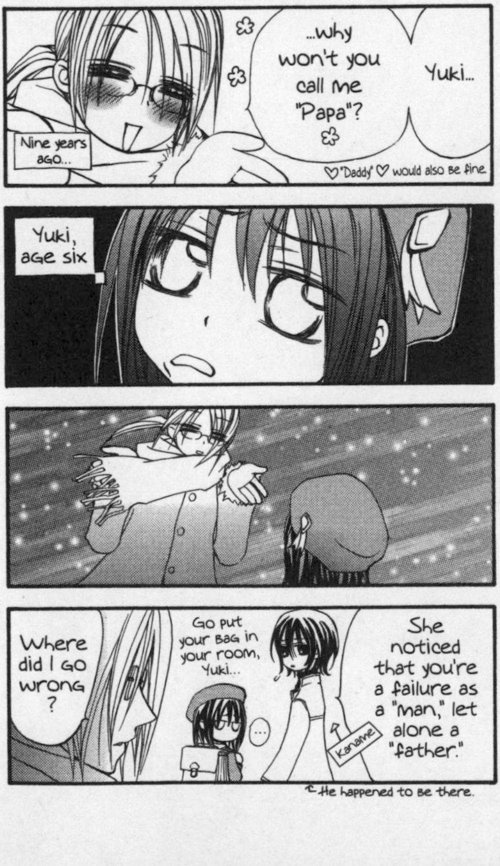
Yuki...
...why won't you call me "Papa"?
♡"Daddy"♡ would also be fine.
Nine years ago...
Yuki, age six
She noticed that you're a failure as a "man," let alone a "father."
Kaname
Go put your bag in your room, Yuki...
...
Where did I go wrong?
He happened to be there.

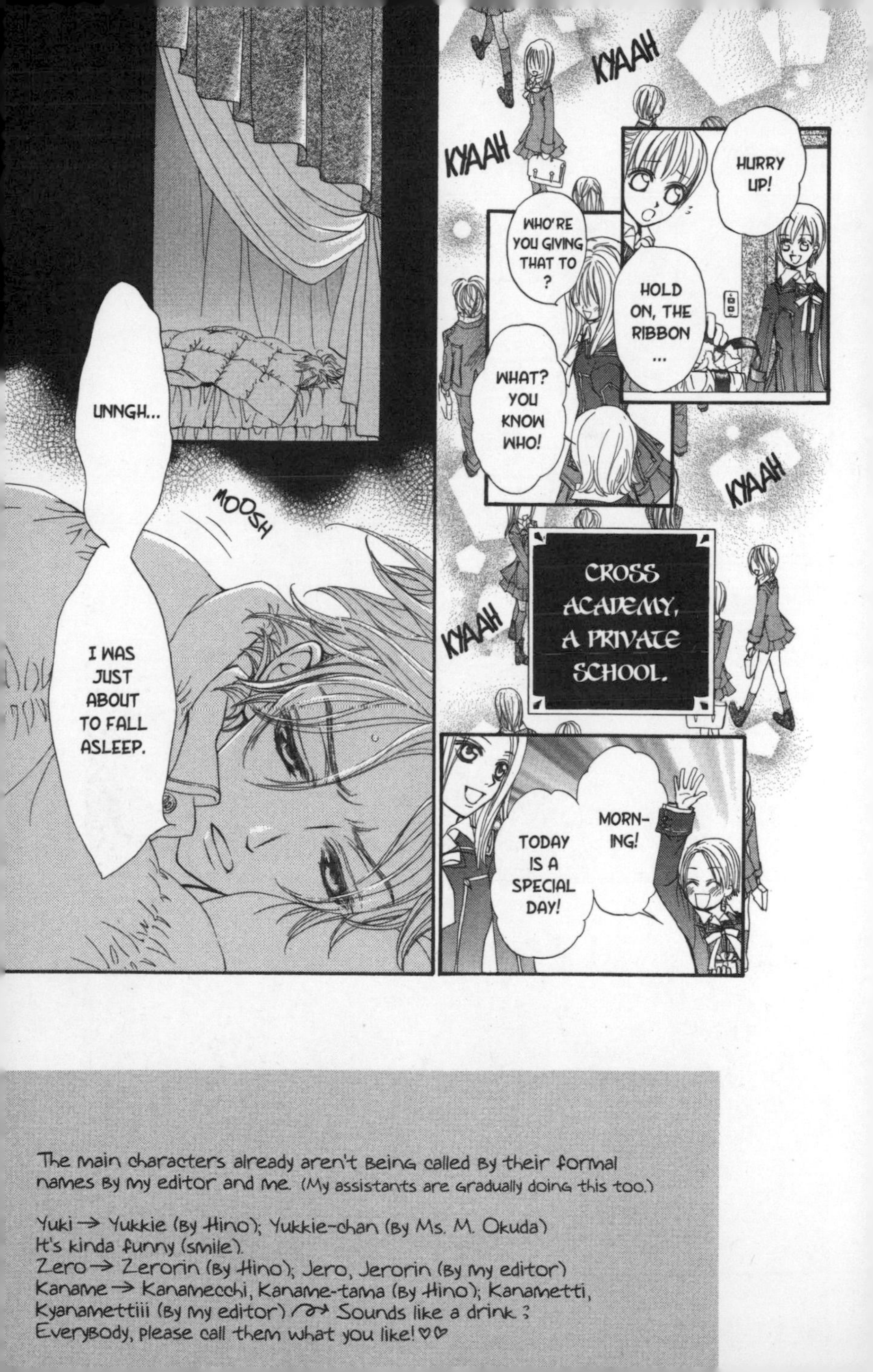
KYAAH
KYAAH
HURRY UP!
HOLD ON, THE RIBBON ...
WHO'RE YOU GIVING THAT TO ?
WHAT? YOU KNOW WHO!
KYAAH
CROSS ACADEMY, A PRIVATE SCHOOL.
KYAAH
MORN-ING!
TODAY IS A SPECIAL DAY!
UNNGH...
MOOSH
I WAS JUST ABOUT TO FALL ASLEEP.

The main characters already aren't being called by their formal names by my editor and me. (My assistants are gradually doing this too.)

Yuki → Yukkie (by Hino); Yukkie-chan (by Ms. M. Okuda)
It's kinda funny (smile).
Zero → Zerorin (by Hino); Jero, Jerorin (by my editor)
Kaname → Kanamecchi, Kaname-tama (by Hino); Kanametti, Kyanamettiii (by my editor) ↝ Sounds like a drink ?
Everybody, please call them what you like! ♡♡

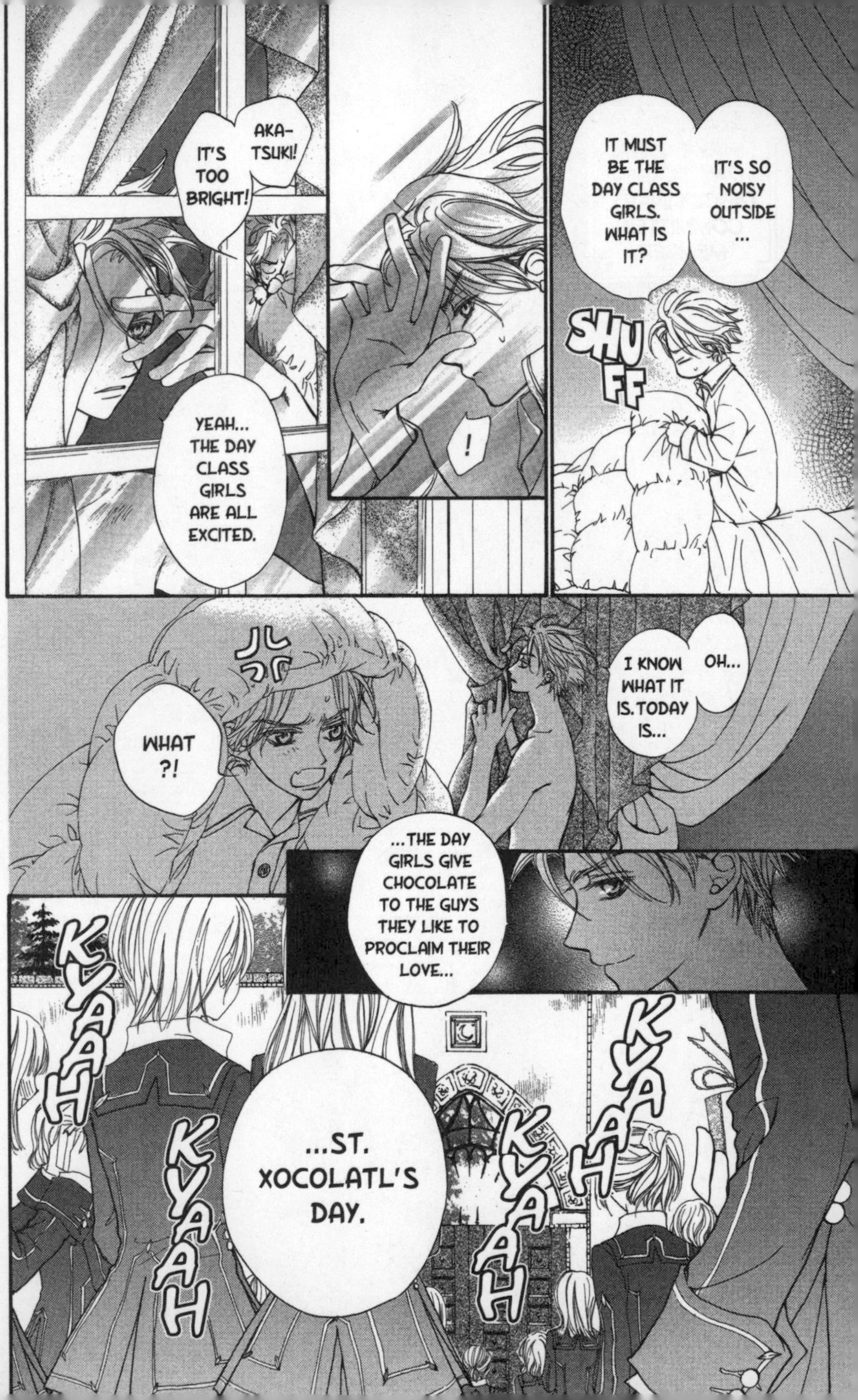
IT'S SO NOISY OUTSIDE ...
IT MUST BE THE DAY CLASS GIRLS. WHAT IS IT?
SHUFF
!
AKA-TSUKI!
IT'S TOO BRIGHT!
YEAH... THE DAY CLASS GIRLS ARE ALL EXCITED.
OH...
I KNOW WHAT IT IS. TODAY IS...
WHAT ?!
...THE DAY GIRLS GIVE CHOCOLATE TO THE GUYS THEY LIKE TO PROCLAIM THEIR LOVE...
KYAAH
KYAAH
...ST. XOCOLATL'S DAY.
KYAAH
KYAAH

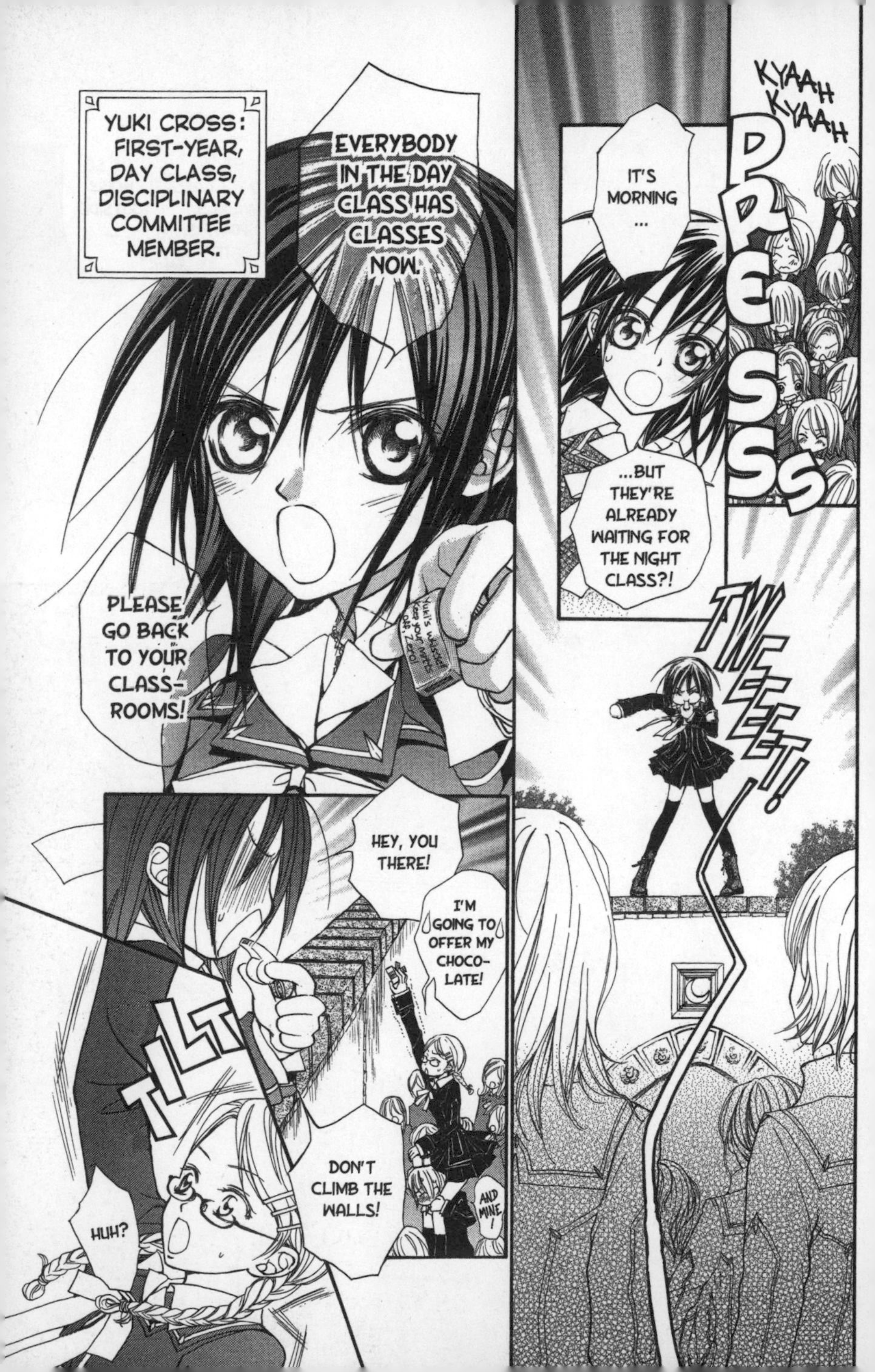
KYAAH KYAAH
PRESSS
IT'S MORNING...
...BUT THEY'RE ALREADY WAITING FOR THE NIGHT CLASS?!
TWEEEET!!
YUKI CROSS: FIRST-YEAR, DAY CLASS, DISCIPLINARY COMMITTEE MEMBER.
EVERYBODY IN THE DAY CLASS HAS CLASSES NOW.
Yuki's whistle! Keep your mitts off, Zero!
PLEASE GO BACK TO YOUR CLASSROOMS!
HEY, YOU THERE!
I'M GOING TO OFFER MY CHOCOLATE!
AND MINE!
DON'T CLIMB THE WALLS!
TILT
HUH?

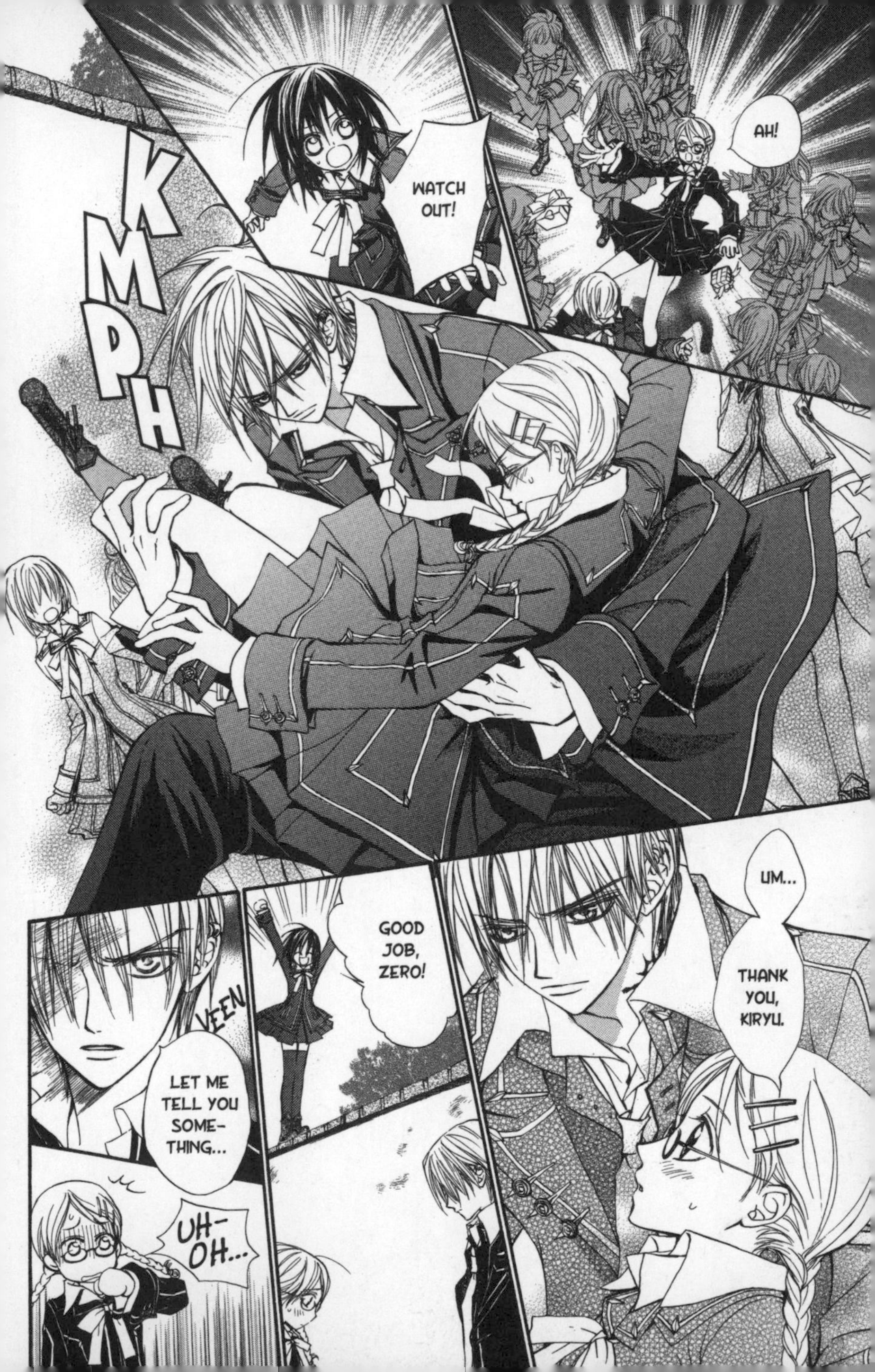
AH!
WATCH OUT!
KMPH
UM...
THANK YOU, KIRYU.
GOOD JOB, ZERO!
VEEN
LET ME TELL YOU SOME-THING...
UH-OH...

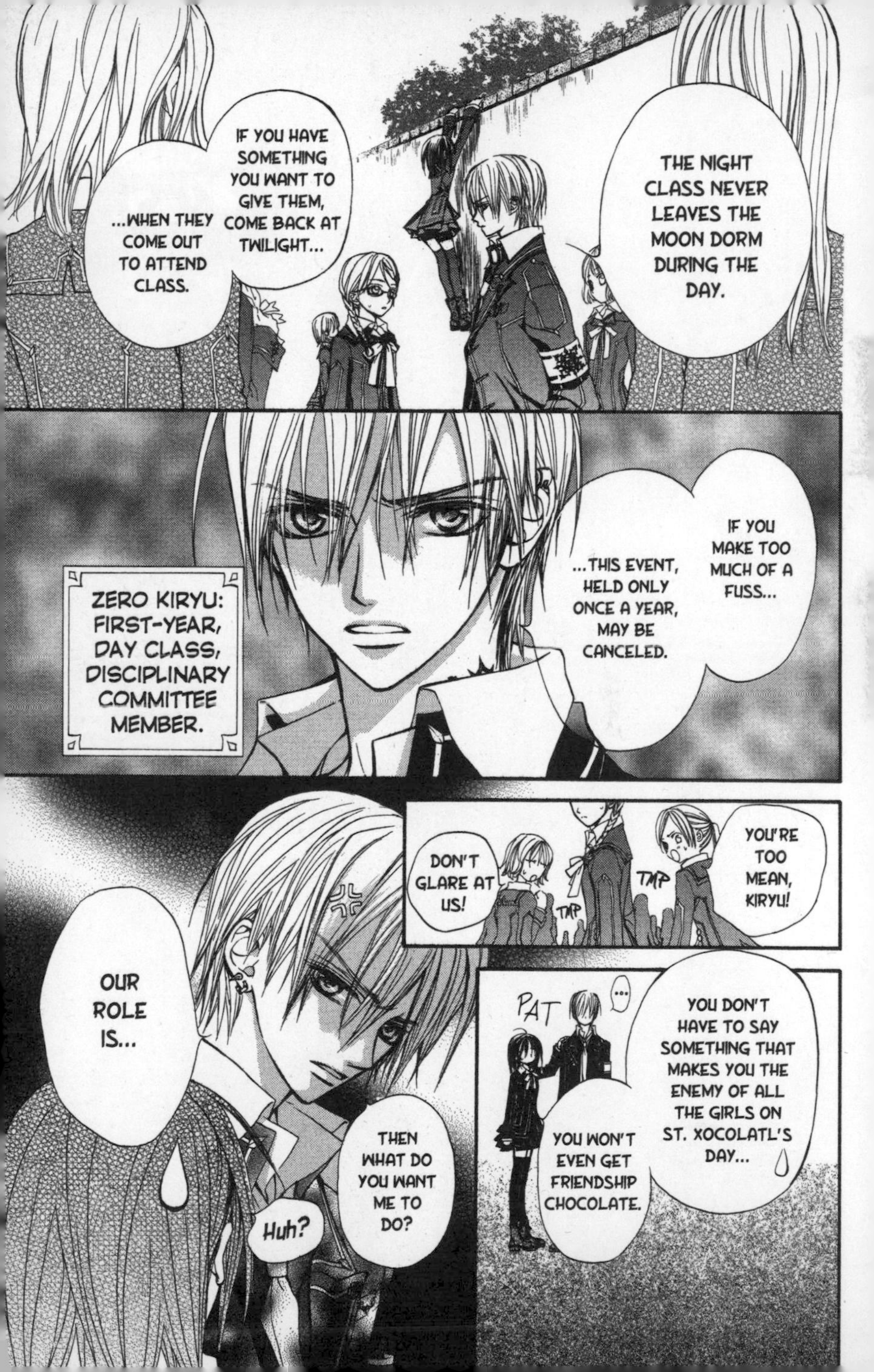
THE NIGHT CLASS NEVER LEAVES THE MOON DORM DURING THE DAY.
IF YOU HAVE SOMETHING YOU WANT TO GIVE THEM, COME BACK AT TWILIGHT...
...WHEN THEY COME OUT TO ATTEND CLASS.
IF YOU MAKE TOO MUCH OF A FUSS...
...THIS EVENT, HELD ONLY ONCE A YEAR, MAY BE CANCELED.
ZERO KIRYU: FIRST-YEAR, DAY CLASS, DISCIPLINARY COMMITTEE MEMBER.
YOU'RE TOO MEAN, KIRYU!
TMP
TMP
DON'T GLARE AT US!
YOU DON'T HAVE TO SAY SOMETHING THAT MAKES YOU THE ENEMY OF ALL THE GIRLS ON ST. XOCOLATL'S DAY...
...
PAT
YOU WON'T EVEN GET FRIENDSHIP CHOCOLATE.
THEN WHAT DO YOU WANT ME TO DO?
Huh?
OUR ROLE IS...

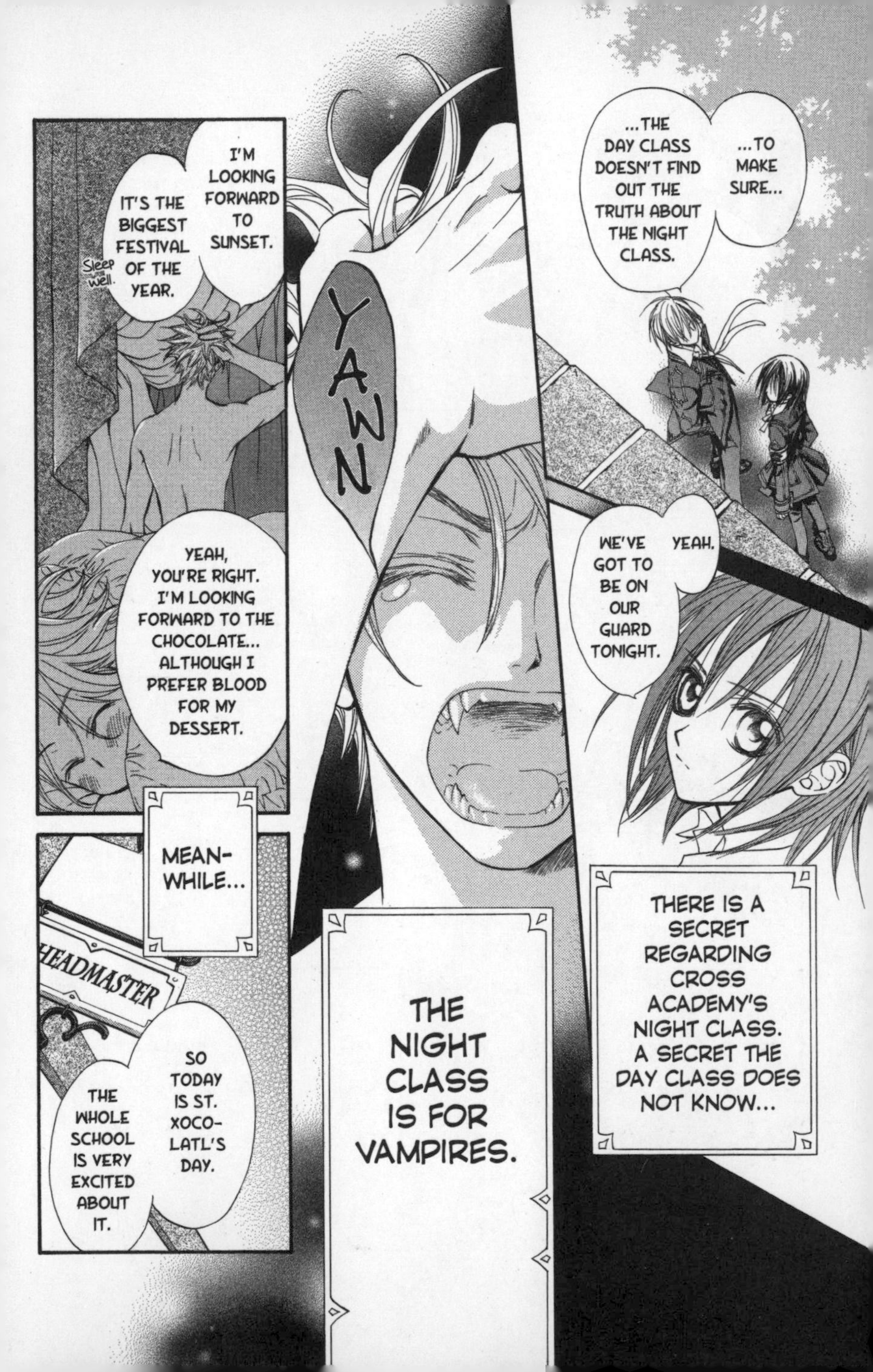
...TO MAKE SURE...
...THE DAY CLASS DOESN'T FIND OUT THE TRUTH ABOUT THE NIGHT CLASS.
YEAH.
WE'VE GOT TO BE ON OUR GUARD TONIGHT.
THERE IS A SECRET REGARDING CROSS ACADEMY'S NIGHT CLASS. A SECRET THE DAY CLASS DOES NOT KNOW...
YAWN
THE NIGHT CLASS IS FOR VAMPIRES.
I'M LOOKING FORWARD TO SUNSET.
IT'S THE BIGGEST FESTIVAL OF THE YEAR.
Sleep well.
YEAH, YOU'RE RIGHT. I'M LOOKING FORWARD TO THE CHOCOLATE... ALTHOUGH I PREFER BLOOD FOR MY DESSERT.
MEAN-WHILE...
HEADMASTER
SO TODAY IS ST. XOCO-LATL'S DAY.
THE WHOLE SCHOOL IS VERY EXCITED ABOUT IT.

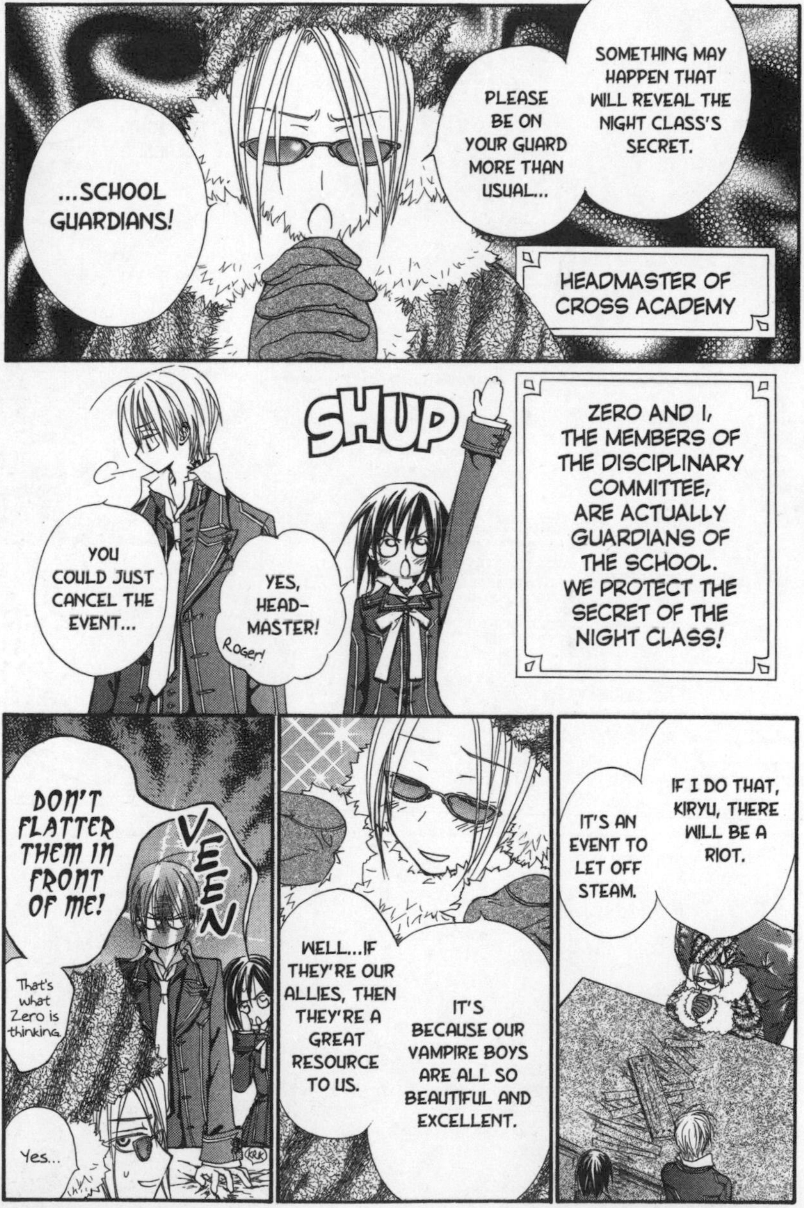
SOMETHING MAY HAPPEN THAT WILL REVEAL THE NIGHT CLASS'S SECRET.
PLEASE BE ON YOUR GUARD MORE THAN USUAL...
...SCHOOL GUARDIANS!
HEADMASTER OF CROSS ACADEMY
ZERO AND I, THE MEMBERS OF THE DISCIPLINARY COMMITTEE, ARE ACTUALLY GUARDIANS OF THE SCHOOL. WE PROTECT THE SECRET OF THE NIGHT CLASS!
SHUP
YES, HEAD-MASTER!
Roger!
YOU COULD JUST CANCEL THE EVENT...
IF I DO THAT, KIRYU, THERE WILL BE A RIOT.
IT'S AN EVENT TO LET OFF STEAM.
IT'S BECAUSE OUR VAMPIRE BOYS ARE ALL SO BEAUTIFUL AND EXCELLENT.
WELL...IF THEY'RE OUR ALLIES, THEN THEY'RE A GREAT RESOURCE TO US.
DON'T FLATTER THEM IN FRONT OF ME!
VEEN
That's what Zero is thinking.
Yes...

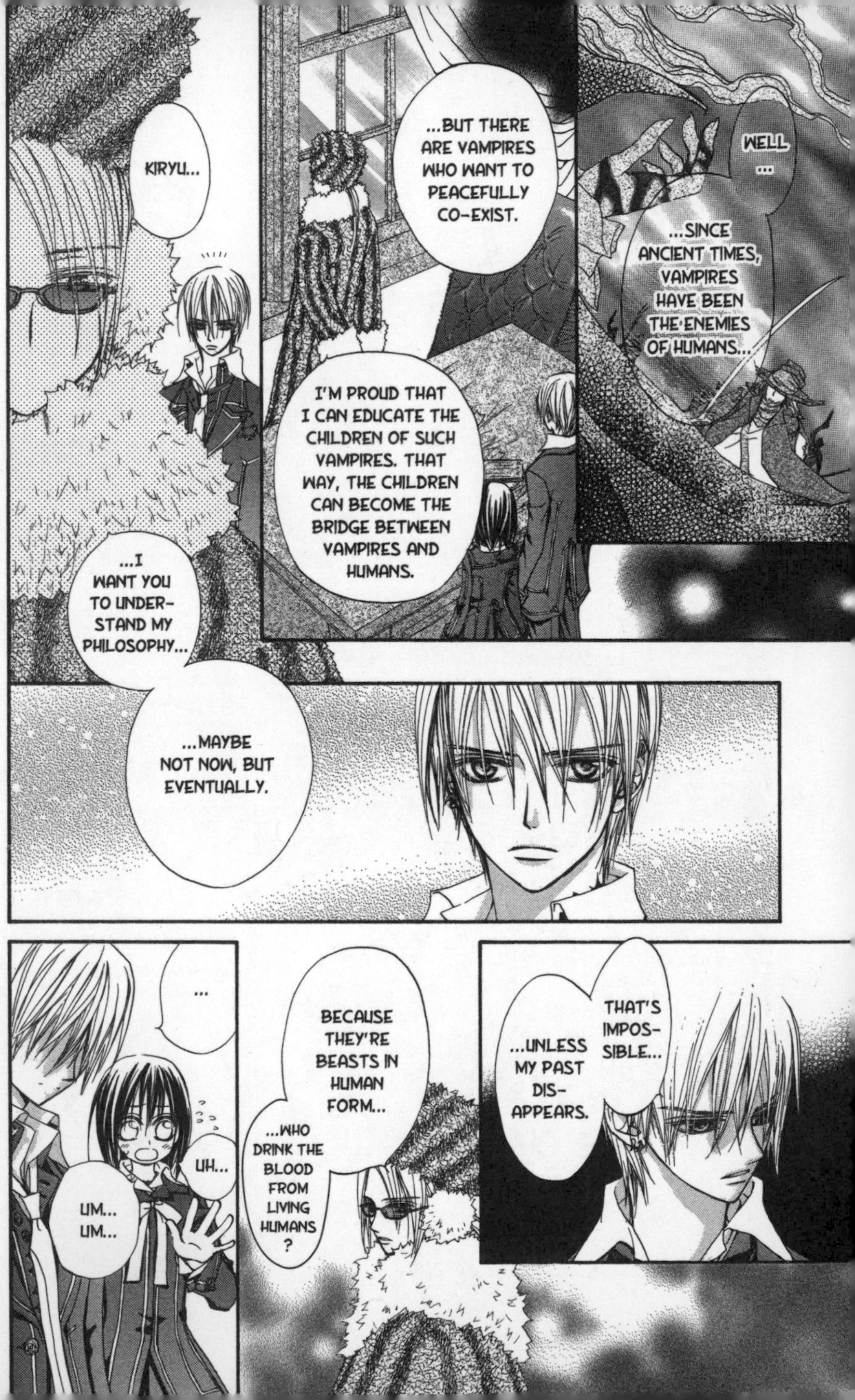
WELL ...
...SINCE ANCIENT TIMES, VAMPIRES HAVE BEEN THE ENEMIES OF HUMANS...
...BUT THERE ARE VAMPIRES WHO WANT TO PEACEFULLY CO-EXIST.
I'M PROUD THAT I CAN EDUCATE THE CHILDREN OF SUCH VAMPIRES. THAT WAY, THE CHILDREN CAN BECOME THE BRIDGE BETWEEN VAMPIRES AND HUMANS.
KIRYU...
...I WANT YOU TO UNDER-STAND MY PHILOSOPHY...
...MAYBE NOT NOW, BUT EVENTUALLY.
THAT'S IMPOS-SIBLE...
...UNLESS MY PAST DIS-APPEARS.
BECAUSE THEY'RE BEASTS IN HUMAN FORM...
...WHO DRINK THE BLOOD FROM LIVING HUMANS ?
...
UH...
UM... UM...

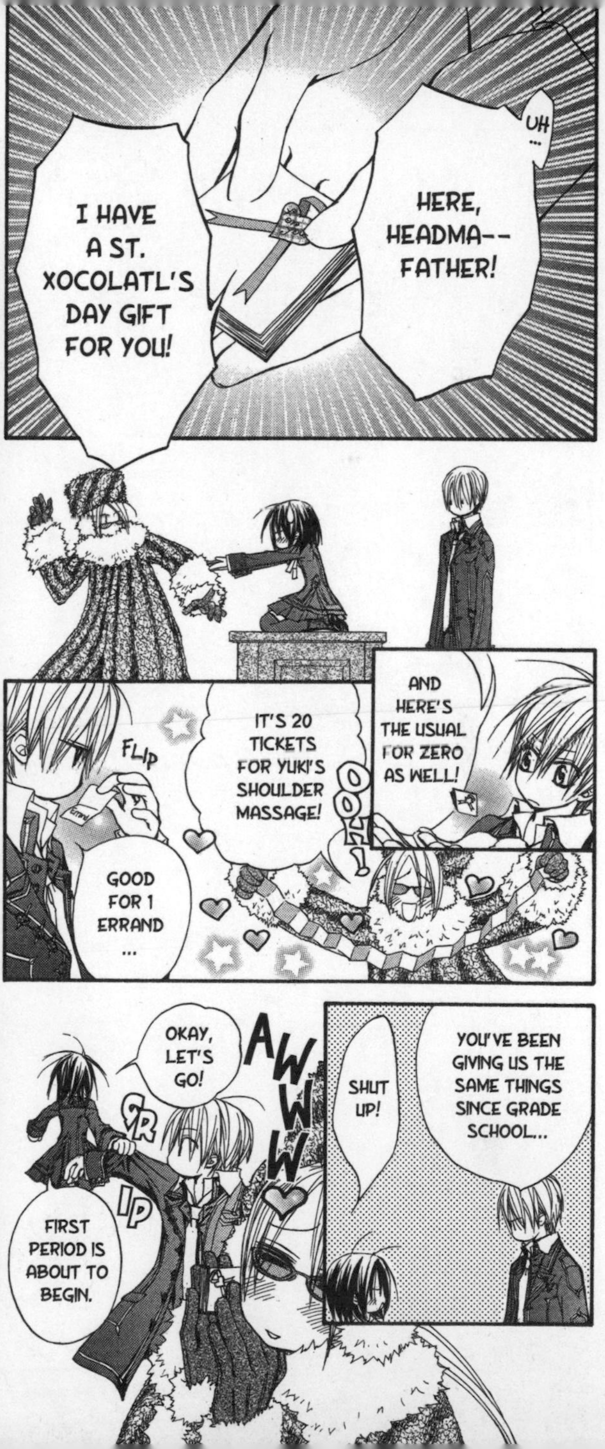
UH...
HERE, HEADMA-- FATHER!
I HAVE A ST. XOCOLATL'S DAY GIFT FOR YOU!
AND HERE'S THE USUAL FOR ZERO AS WELL!
OOH!
IT'S 20 TICKETS FOR YUKI'S SHOULDER MASSAGE!
FLIP
GOOD FOR 1 ERRAND ...
YOU'VE BEEN GIVING US THE SAME THINGS SINCE GRADE SCHOOL...
SHUT UP!
AWWW
OKAY, LET'S GO!
GR
IP
FIRST PERIOD IS ABOUT TO BEGIN.

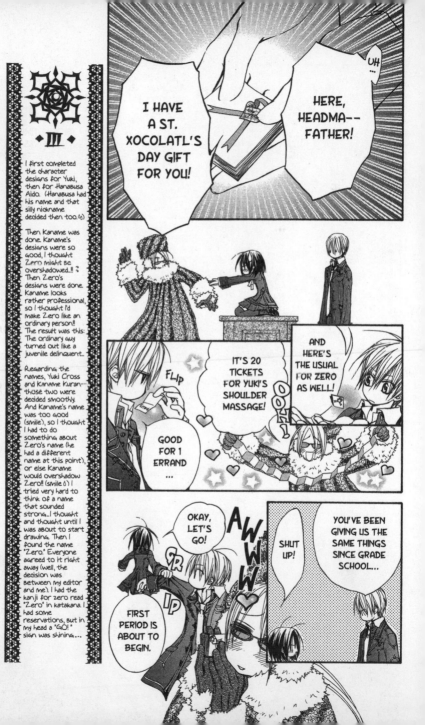

III

I first completed the character designs for Yuki, then for Hanabusa Aido. (Hanabusa had his name and that silly nickname decided then too.)

Then Kaname was done. Kaname's designs were so good, I thought Zero might be overshadowed..!! Then Zero's designs were done. Kaname looks rather professional, so I thought I'd make Zero like an ordinary person!! The result was this: The ordinary guy turned out like a juvenile delinquent...

Regarding the names, Yuki Cross and Kaname Kuran--those two were decided smoothly. And Kaname's name was too good (smile), so I thought I had to do something about Zero's name (he had a different name at this point), or else Kaname would overshadow Zero!! (smile) I tried very hard to think of a name that sounded strong... I thought and thought until I was about to start drawing. Then I found the name "Zero." Everyone agreed to it right away (well, the decision was between my editor and me). I had the kanji for zero read "Zero" in katakana. I had some reservations, but in my head a "GO!" sign was shining...

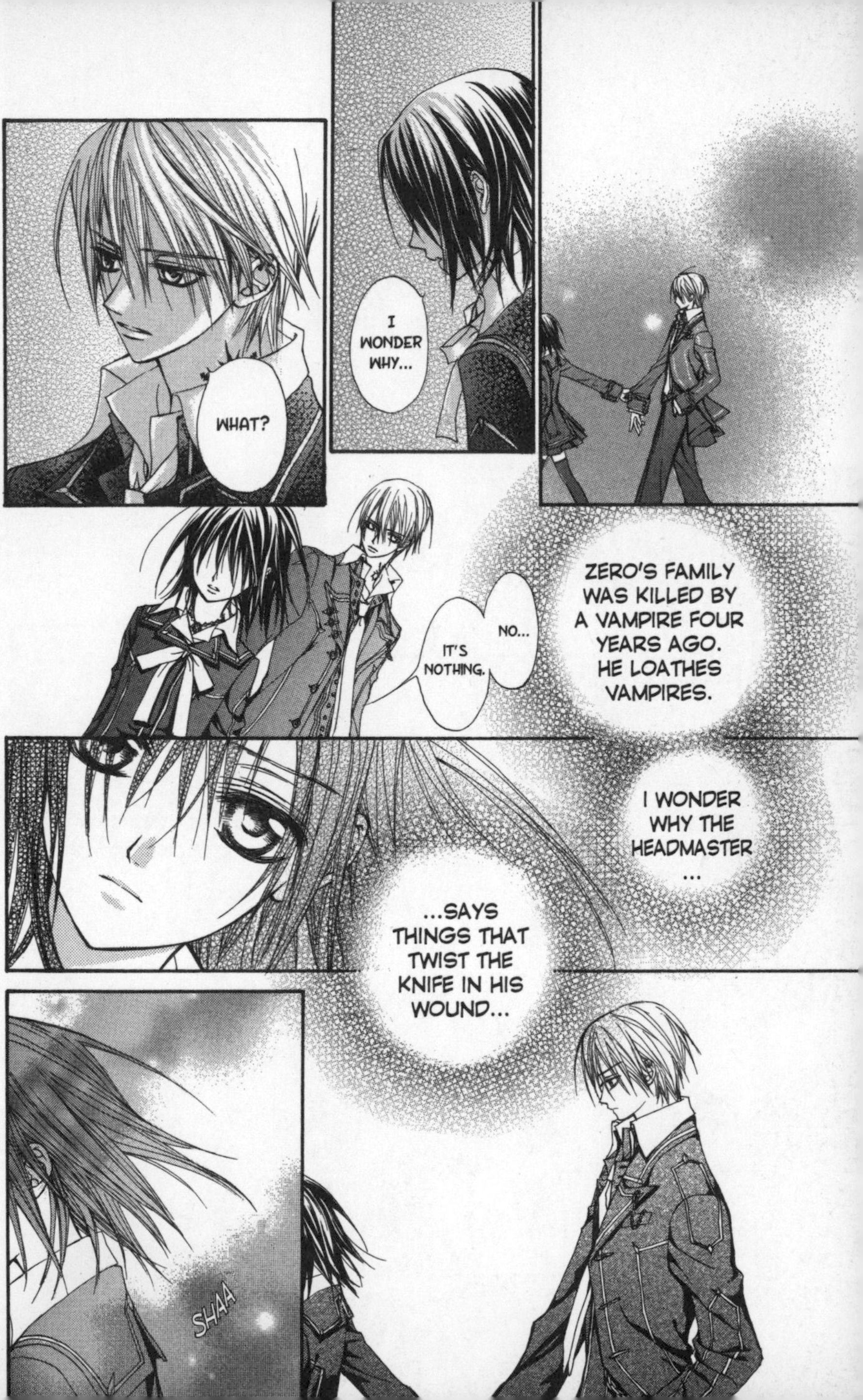
I WONDER WHY...
WHAT?
ZERO'S FAMILY WAS KILLED BY A VAMPIRE FOUR YEARS AGO. HE LOATHES VAMPIRES.
NO... IT'S NOTHING.
I WONDER WHY THE HEADMASTER ...
...SAYS THINGS THAT TWIST THE KNIFE IN HIS WOUND...
SHAA

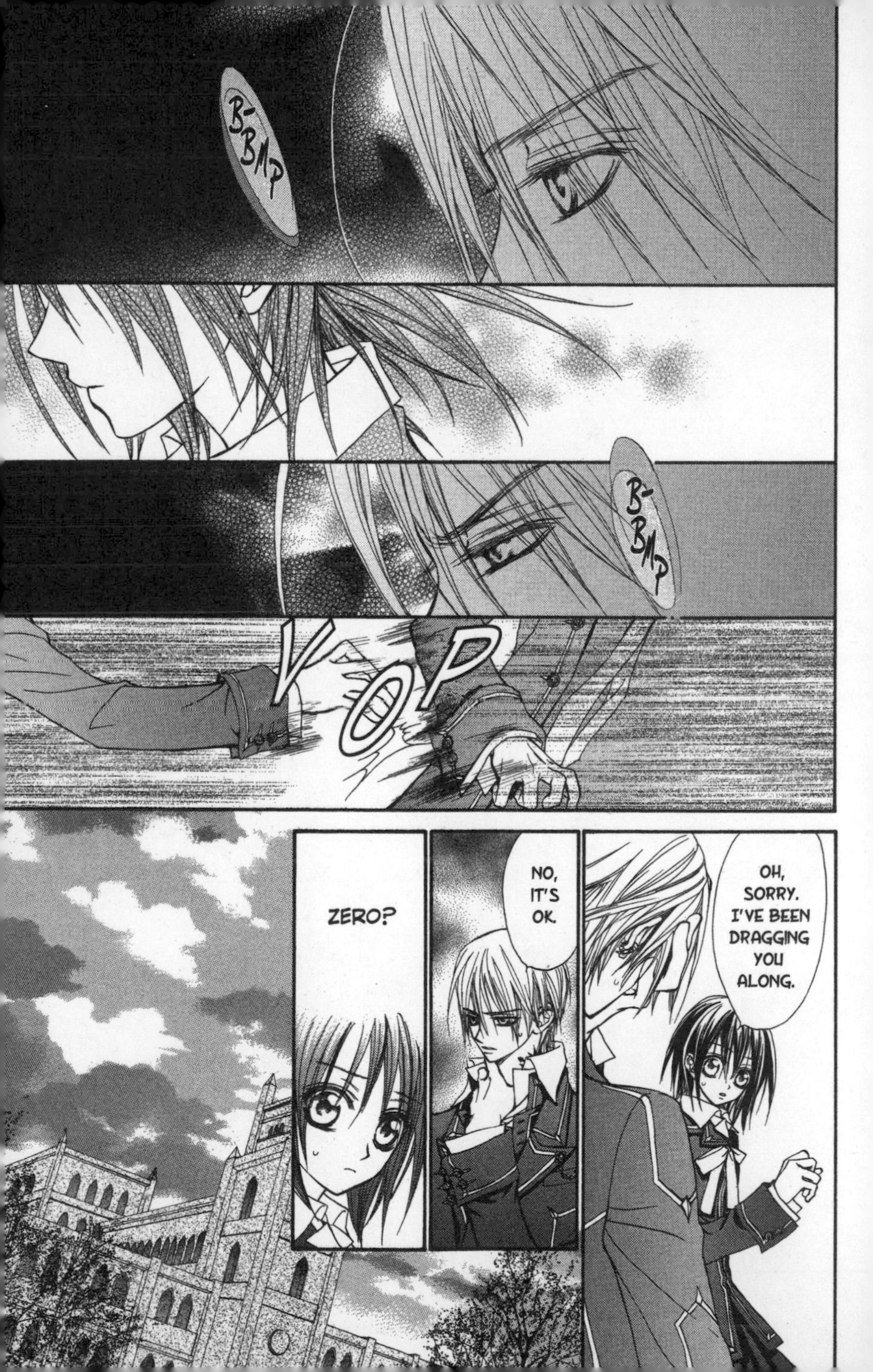
B-BMP
B-BMP
VOP
OH, SORRY. I'VE BEEN DRAGGING YOU ALONG.
NO, IT'S OK.
ZERO?

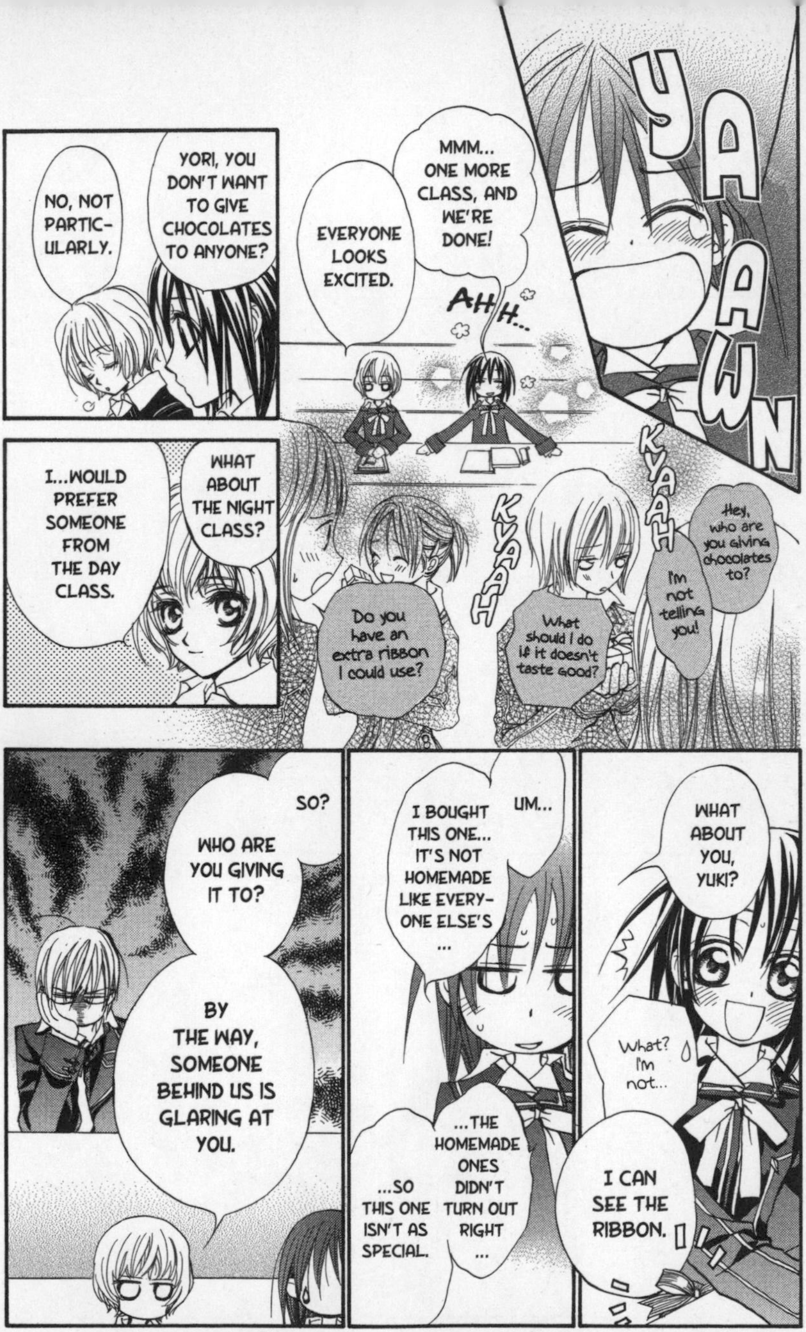
YAAAWN
MMM... ONE MORE CLASS, AND WE'RE DONE!
EVERYONE LOOKS EXCITED.
AHHH...
YORI, YOU DON'T WANT TO GIVE CHOCOLATES TO ANYONE?
NO, NOT PARTIC-ULARLY.
Hey, who are you giving chocolates to?
I'm not telling you!
KYAAH
What should I do if it doesn't taste good?
KYAAH
Do you have an extra ribbon I could use?
WHAT ABOUT THE NIGHT CLASS?
I...WOULD PREFER SOMEONE FROM THE DAY CLASS.
WHAT ABOUT YOU, YUKI?
What? I'm not...
I CAN SEE THE RIBBON.
UM...
I BOUGHT THIS ONE... IT'S NOT HOMEMADE LIKE EVERY-ONE ELSE'S ...
...THE HOMEMADE ONES DIDN'T TURN OUT RIGHT ...
...SO THIS ONE ISN'T AS SPECIAL.
SO?
WHO ARE YOU GIVING IT TO?
BY THE WAY, SOMEONE BEHIND US IS GLARING AT YOU.

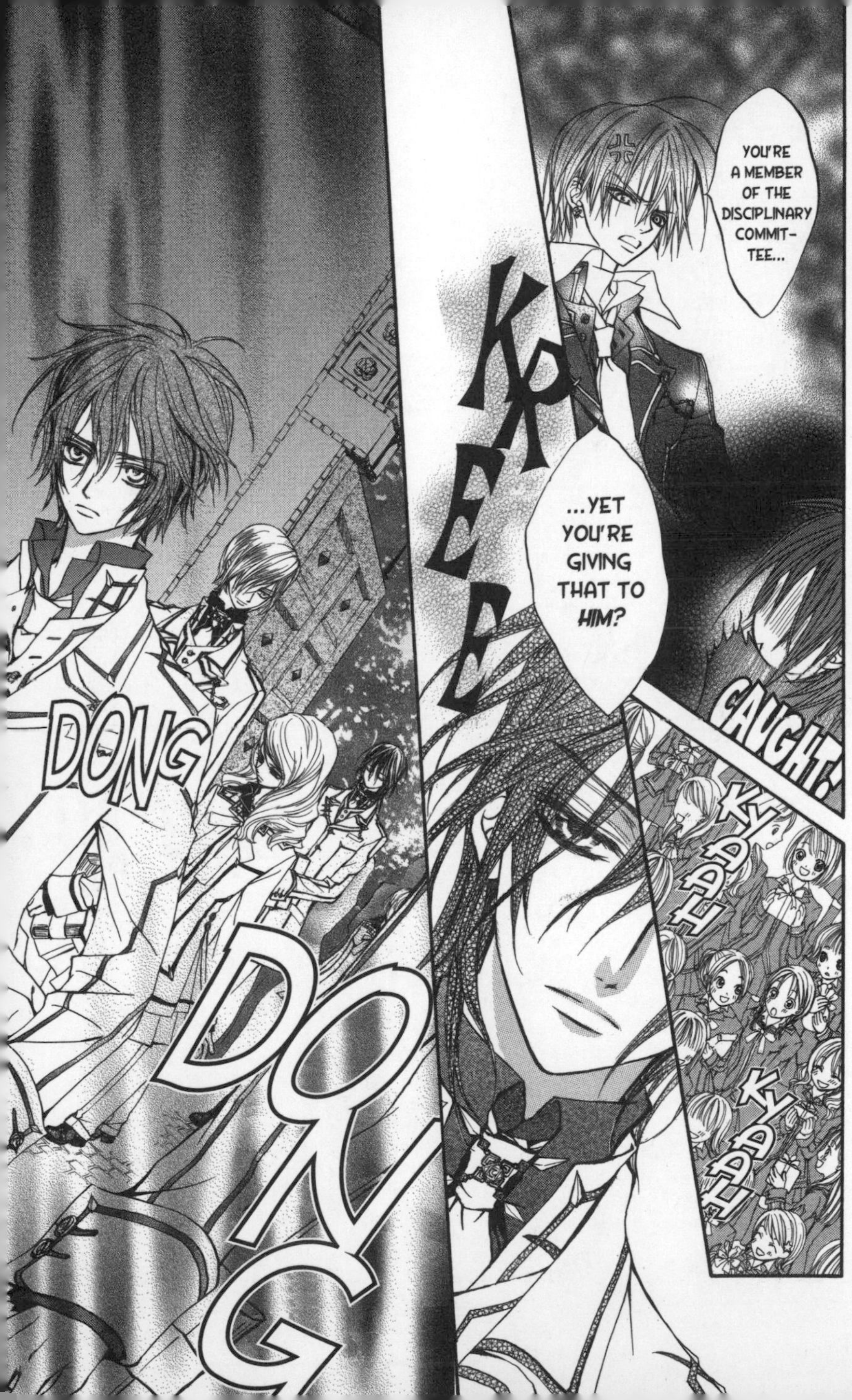
YOU'RE A MEMBER OF THE DISCIPLINARY COMMIT-TEE...
KREEE
...YET YOU'RE GIVING THAT TO *HIM*?
CAUGHT!
KYAAH
KYAAH
DONG
DONG

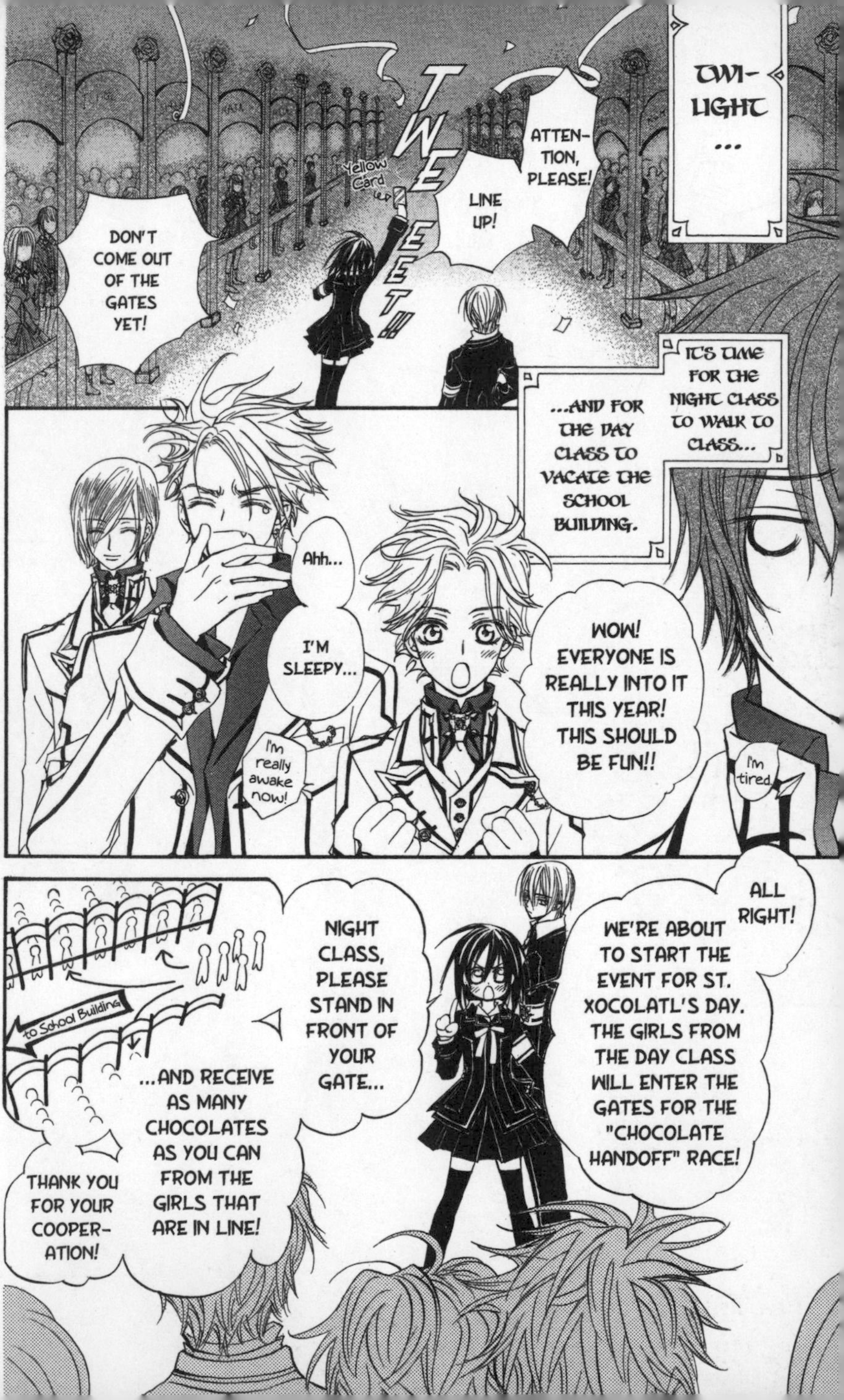
TWI-LIGHT...
ATTENTION, PLEASE!
LINE UP!
TWEEETH!!
Yellow Card up
DON'T COME OUT OF THE GATES YET!
IT'S TIME FOR THE NIGHT CLASS TO WALK TO CLASS...
...AND FOR THE DAY CLASS TO VACATE THE SCHOOL BUILDING.
I'm tired
WOW! EVERYONE IS REALLY INTO IT THIS YEAR! THIS SHOULD BE FUN!!
Ahh...
I'M SLEEPY...
I'm really awake now!
ALL RIGHT!
WE'RE ABOUT TO START THE EVENT FOR ST. XOCOLATL'S DAY. THE GIRLS FROM THE DAY CLASS WILL ENTER THE GATES FOR THE "CHOCOLATE HANDOFF" RACE!
NIGHT CLASS, PLEASE STAND IN FRONT OF YOUR GATE...
...AND RECEIVE AS MANY CHOCOLATES AS YOU CAN FROM THE GIRLS THAT ARE IN LINE!
to School Building
THANK YOU FOR YOUR COOPERATION!

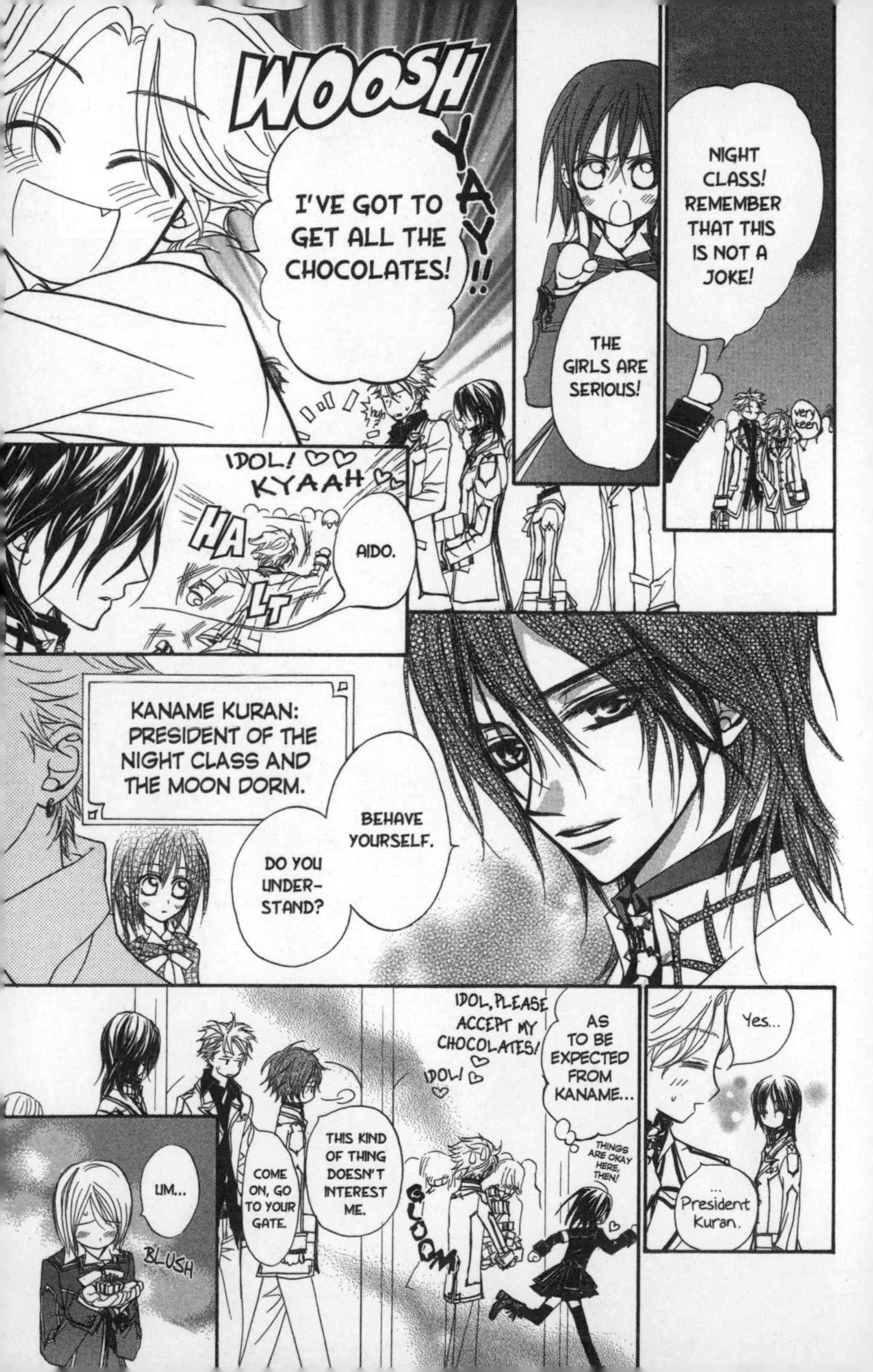
NIGHT CLASS! REMEMBER THAT THIS IS NOT A JOKE!
THE GIRLS ARE SERIOUS!
very keen
WOOSH
YAY!!
I'VE GOT TO GET ALL THE CHOCOLATES!
huh?
BEHAVE YOURSELF.
DO YOU UNDER-STAND?
IDOL! KYAAH
HALT
AIDO.
KANAME KURAN: PRESIDENT OF THE NIGHT CLASS AND THE MOON DORM.
Yes...
... President Kuran.
AS TO BE EXPECTED FROM KANAME...
IDOL, PLEASE ACCEPT MY CHOCOLATES!
IDOL!
THINGS ARE OKAY HERE, THEN!
GLOOM
THIS KIND OF THING DOESN'T INTEREST ME.
COME ON, GO TO YOUR GATE.
UM...
BLUSH

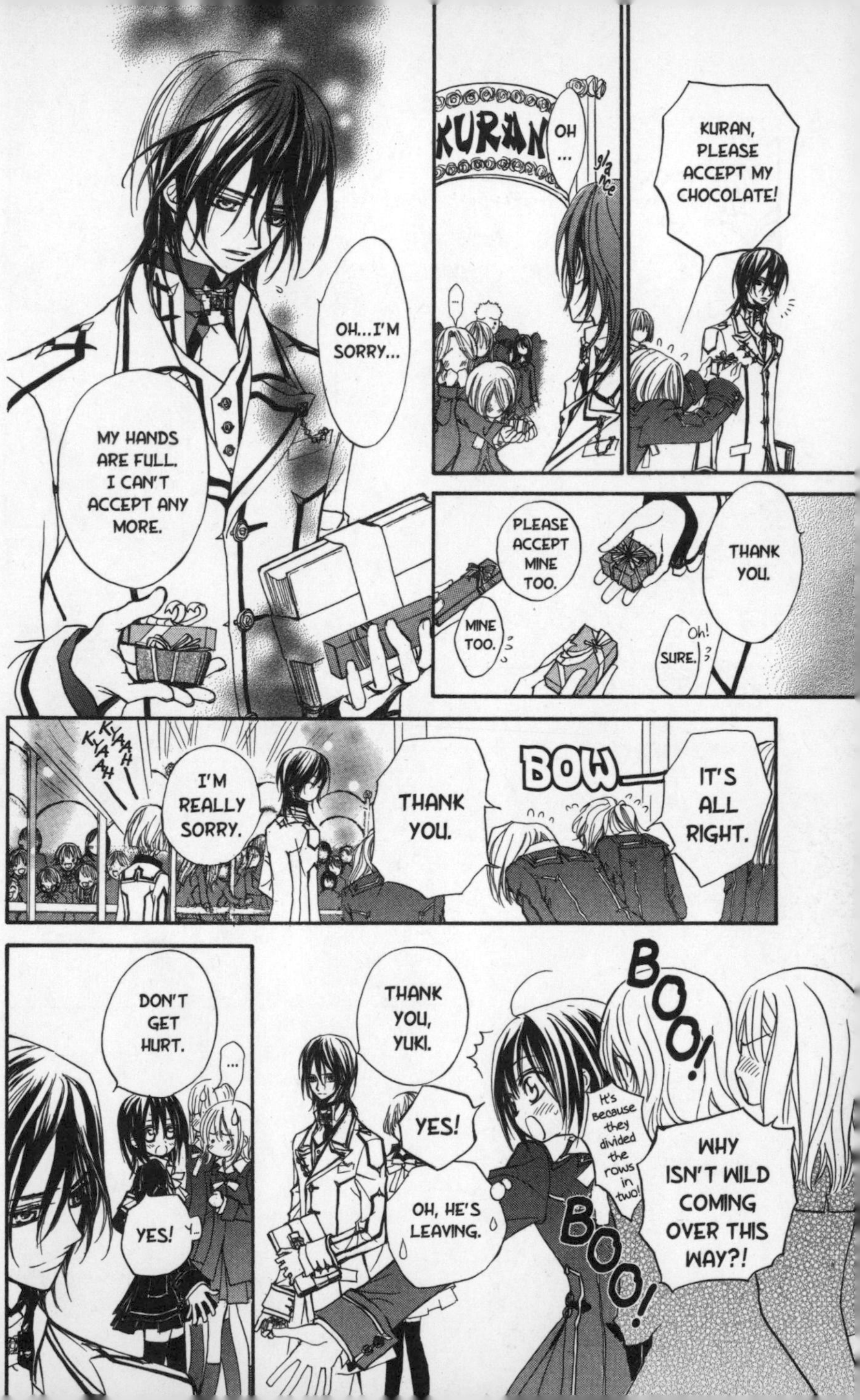
KURAN, PLEASE ACCEPT MY CHOCOLATE!
KURAN
OH ...
glance
...
THANK YOU.
Oh! SURE.
PLEASE ACCEPT MINE TOO.
MINE TOO.
OH...I'M SORRY...
MY HANDS ARE FULL. I CAN'T ACCEPT ANY MORE.
IT'S ALL RIGHT.
BOW
THANK YOU.
I'M REALLY SORRY.
KYAAH KYAAH
WHY ISN'T WILD COMING OVER THIS WAY?!
BOO!
BOO!
It's because they divided the rows in two!
OH, HE'S LEAVING.
THANK YOU, YUKI.
YES!
DON'T GET HURT.
...
YES!
Y...

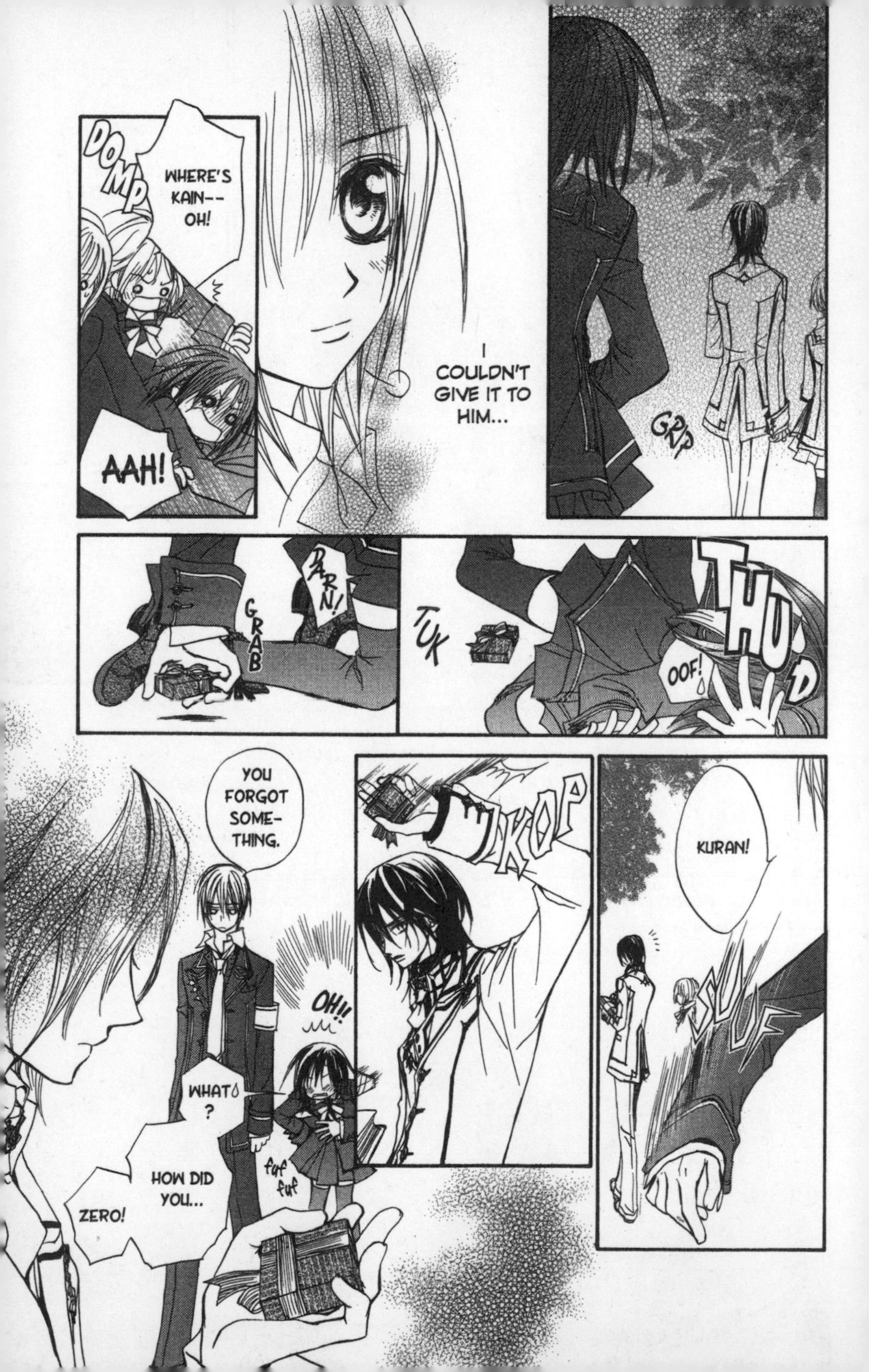
GRIP
I COULDN'T GIVE IT TO HIM...
DOMP
WHERE'S KAIN-- OH!
AAH!
THUD
OOF!
TUK
DARN!
GRAB
KURAN!
KOP
YOU FORGOT SOMETHING.
OH!!
WHAT?
fuf fuf
HOW DID YOU...
ZERO!

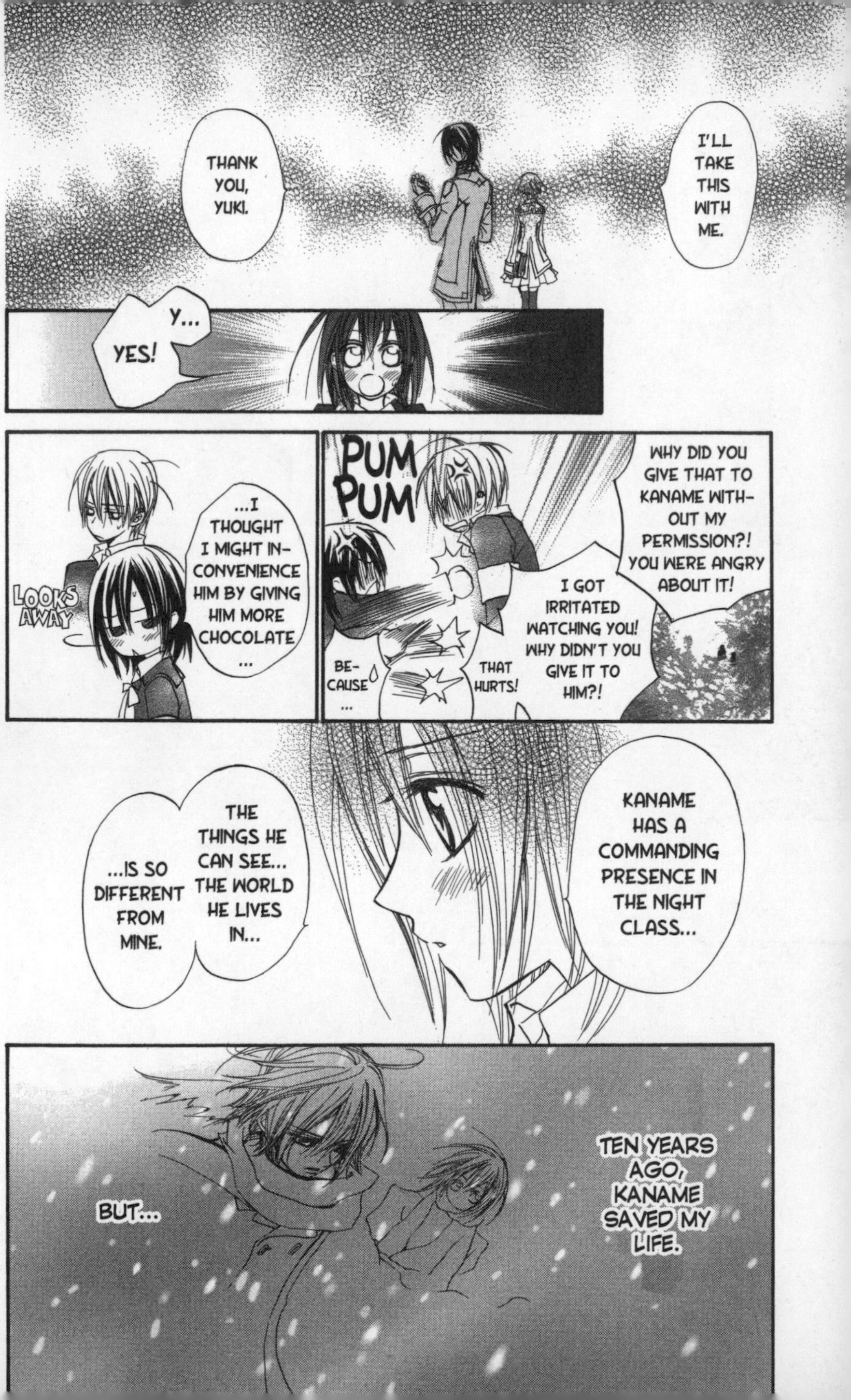
I'LL TAKE THIS WITH ME.
THANK YOU, YUKI.
Y... YES!
WHY DID YOU GIVE THAT TO KANAME WITH-OUT MY PERMISSION?! YOU WERE ANGRY ABOUT IT!
I GOT IRRITATED WATCHING YOU! WHY DIDN'T YOU GIVE IT TO HIM?!
PUM PUM
THAT HURTS!
BE-CAUSE ...
...I THOUGHT I MIGHT IN-CONVENIENCE HIM BY GIVING HIM MORE CHOCOLATE ...
LOOKS AWAY
KANAME HAS A COMMANDING PRESENCE IN THE NIGHT CLASS...
THE THINGS HE CAN SEE... THE WORLD HE LIVES IN...
...IS SO DIFFERENT FROM MINE.
TEN YEARS AGO, KANAME SAVED MY LIFE.
BUT...

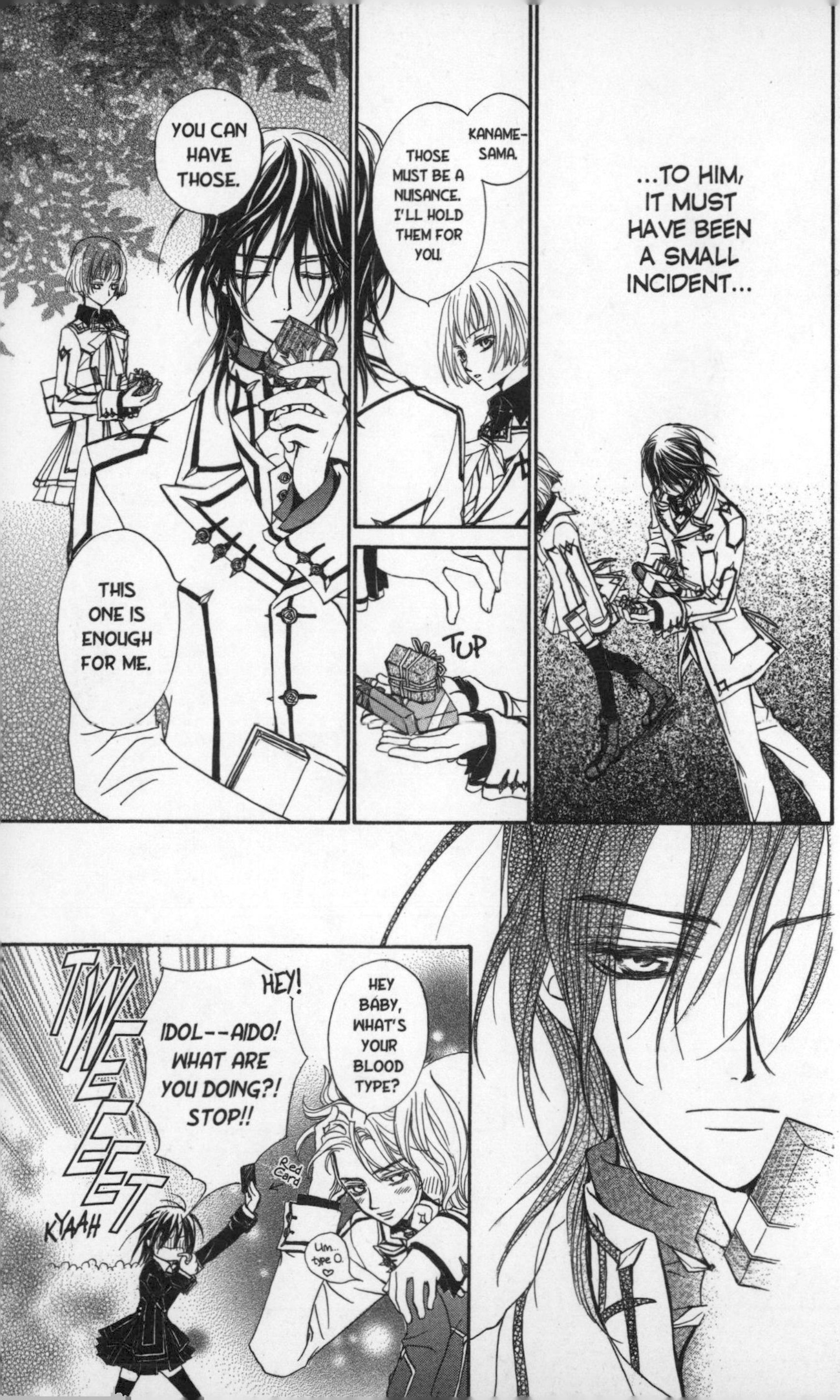
...TO HIM, IT MUST HAVE BEEN A SMALL INCIDENT...
KANAME-SAMA.
THOSE MUST BE A NUISANCE. I'LL HOLD THEM FOR YOU.
TUP
YOU CAN HAVE THOSE.
THIS ONE IS ENOUGH FOR ME.
HEY BABY, WHAT'S YOUR BLOOD TYPE?
HEY!
IDOL--AIDO! WHAT ARE YOU DOING?! STOP!!
Red Card
Um... type O. ♡
TWEEEET
KYAAH

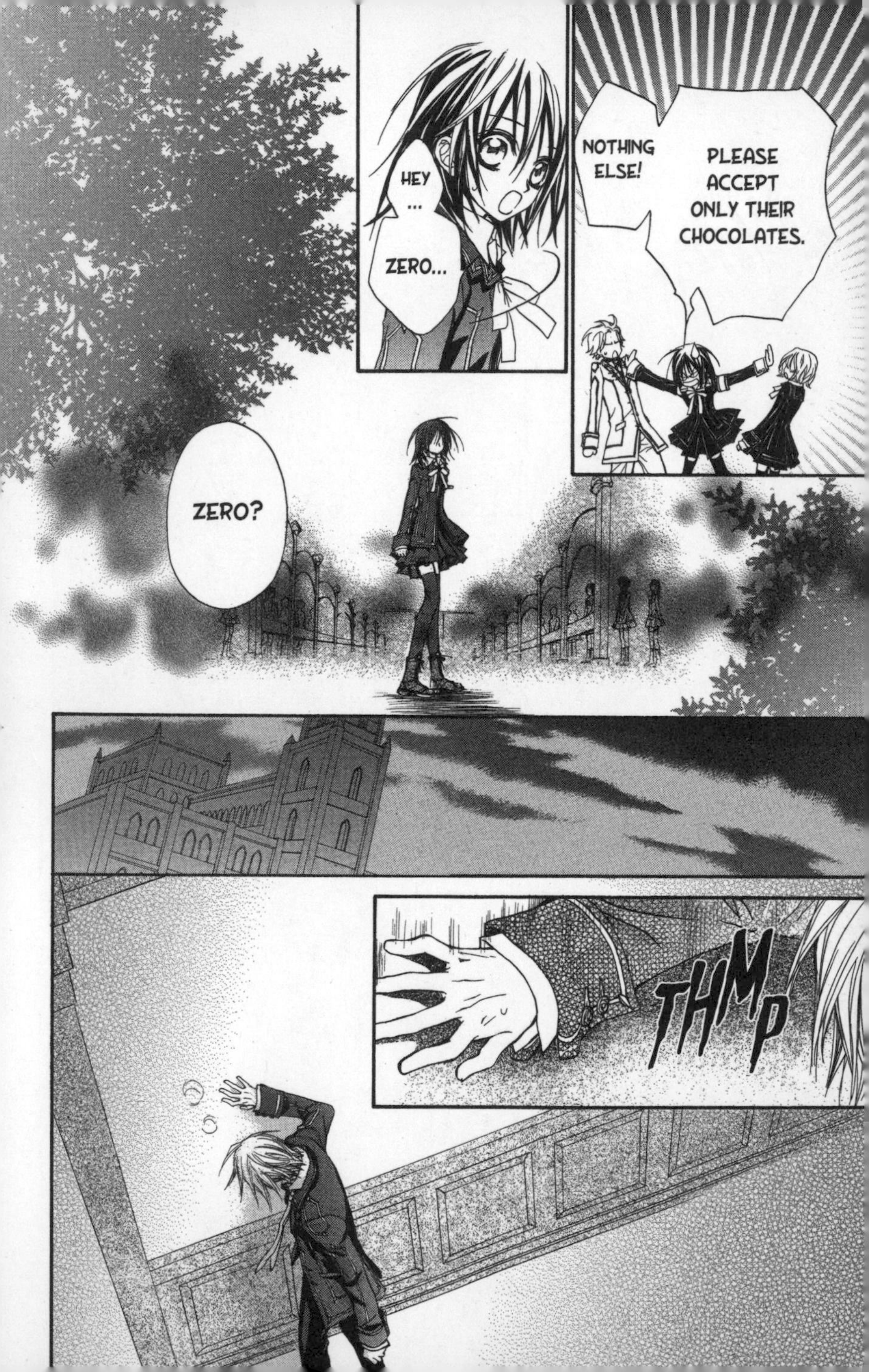
PLEASE ACCEPT ONLY THEIR CHOCOLATES.
NOTHING ELSE!
HEY ...
ZERO...
ZERO?
THMP

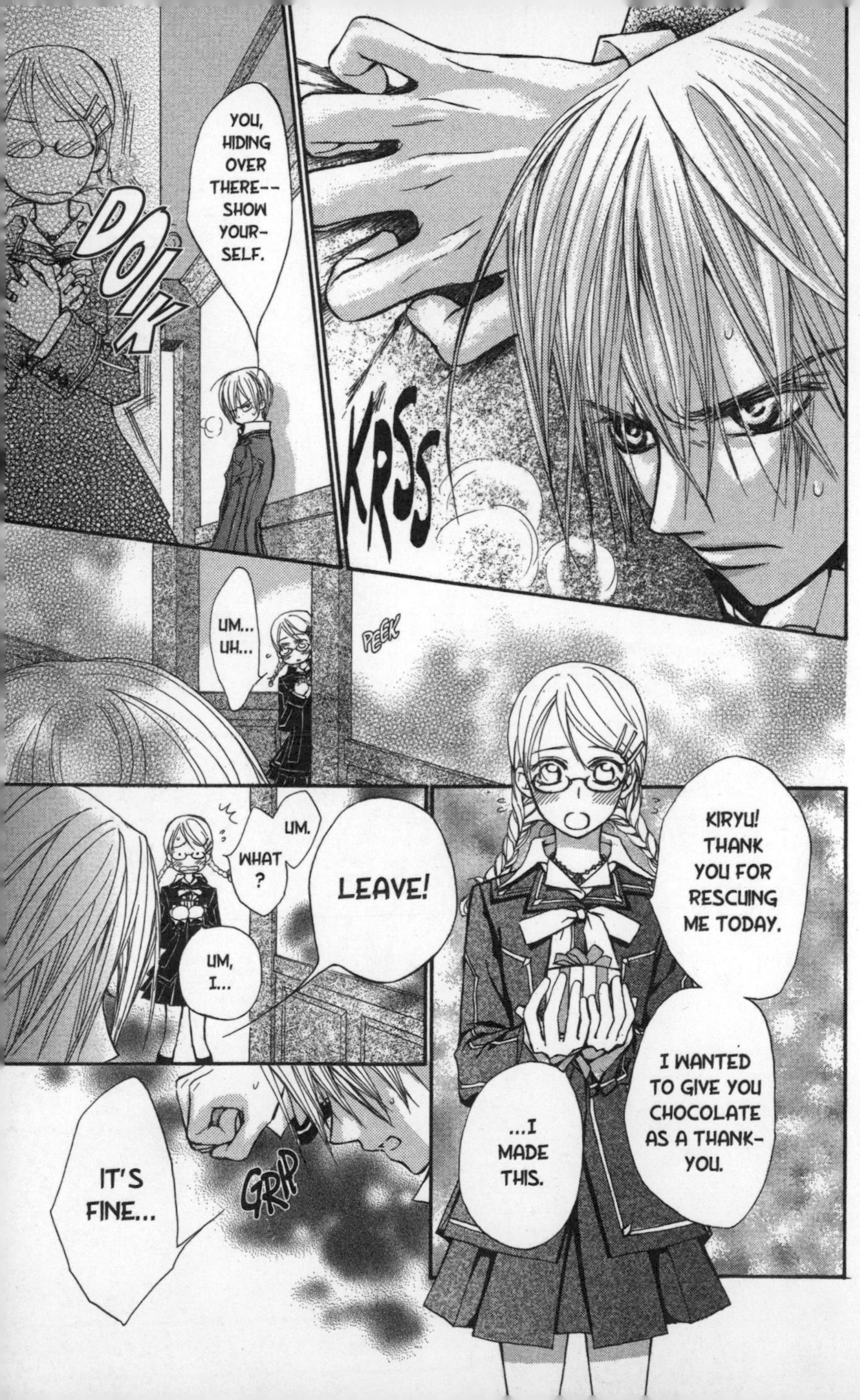
KRSS
YOU, HIDING OVER THERE-- SHOW YOURSELF.
DOIK
PEEK
KIRYU! THANK YOU FOR RESCUING ME TODAY.
I WANTED TO GIVE YOU CHOCOLATE AS A THANK-YOU.
...I MADE THIS.
UM... UH...
UM.
WHAT?
LEAVE!
UM, I...
IT'S FINE...
GRIP

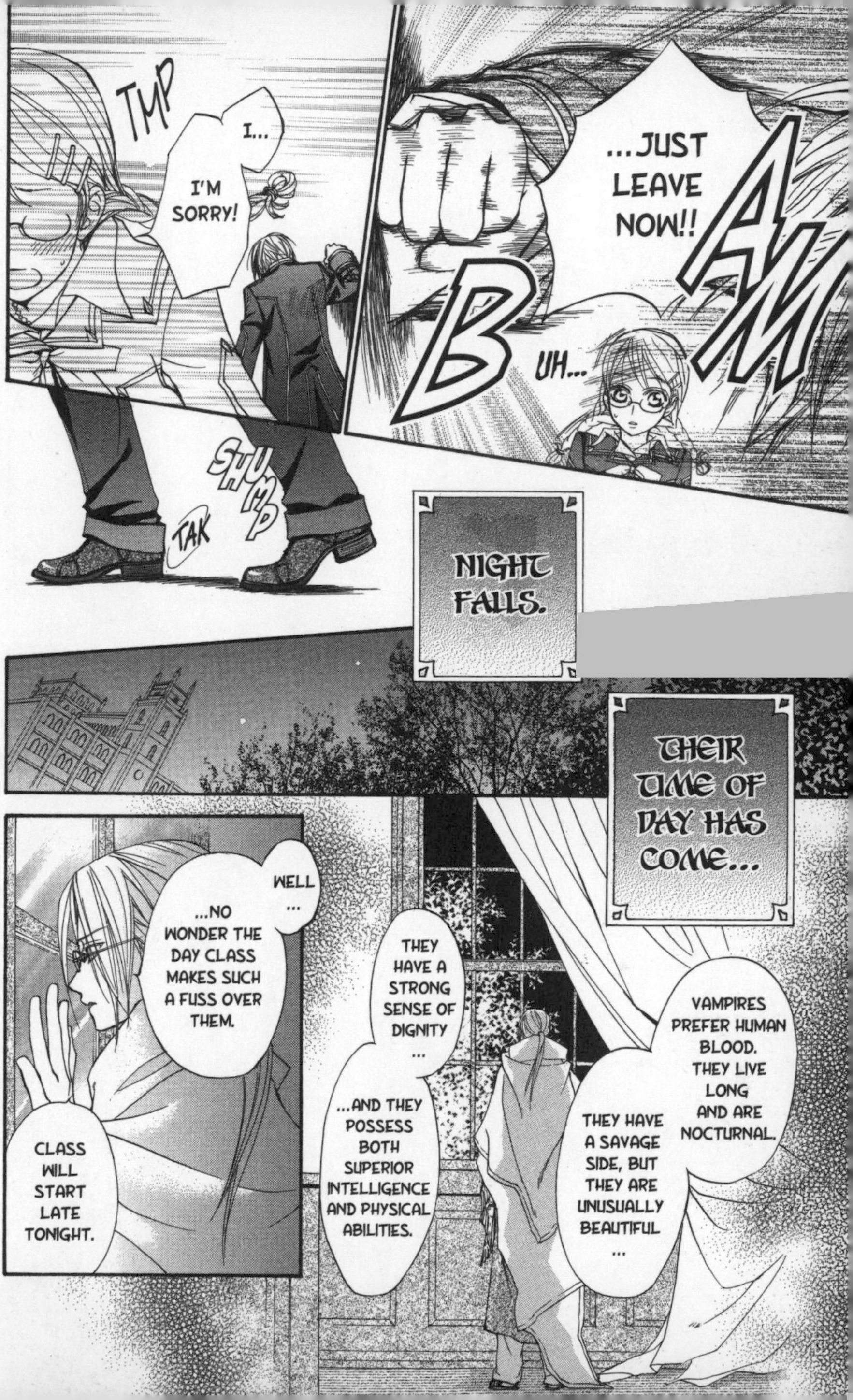
...JUST LEAVE NOW!!
BAM
UH...
TMP
I...
I'M SORRY!
SHUMP
TAK
NIGHT FALLS.
THEIR TIME OF DAY HAS COME...
VAMPIRES PREFER HUMAN BLOOD. THEY LIVE LONG AND ARE NOCTURNAL.
THEY HAVE A SAVAGE SIDE, BUT THEY ARE UNUSUALLY BEAUTIFUL...
THEY HAVE A STRONG SENSE OF DIGNITY...
...AND THEY POSSESS BOTH SUPERIOR INTELLIGENCE AND PHYSICAL ABILITIES.
WELL...
...NO WONDER THE DAY CLASS MAKES SUCH A FUSS OVER THEM.
CLASS WILL START LATE TONIGHT.

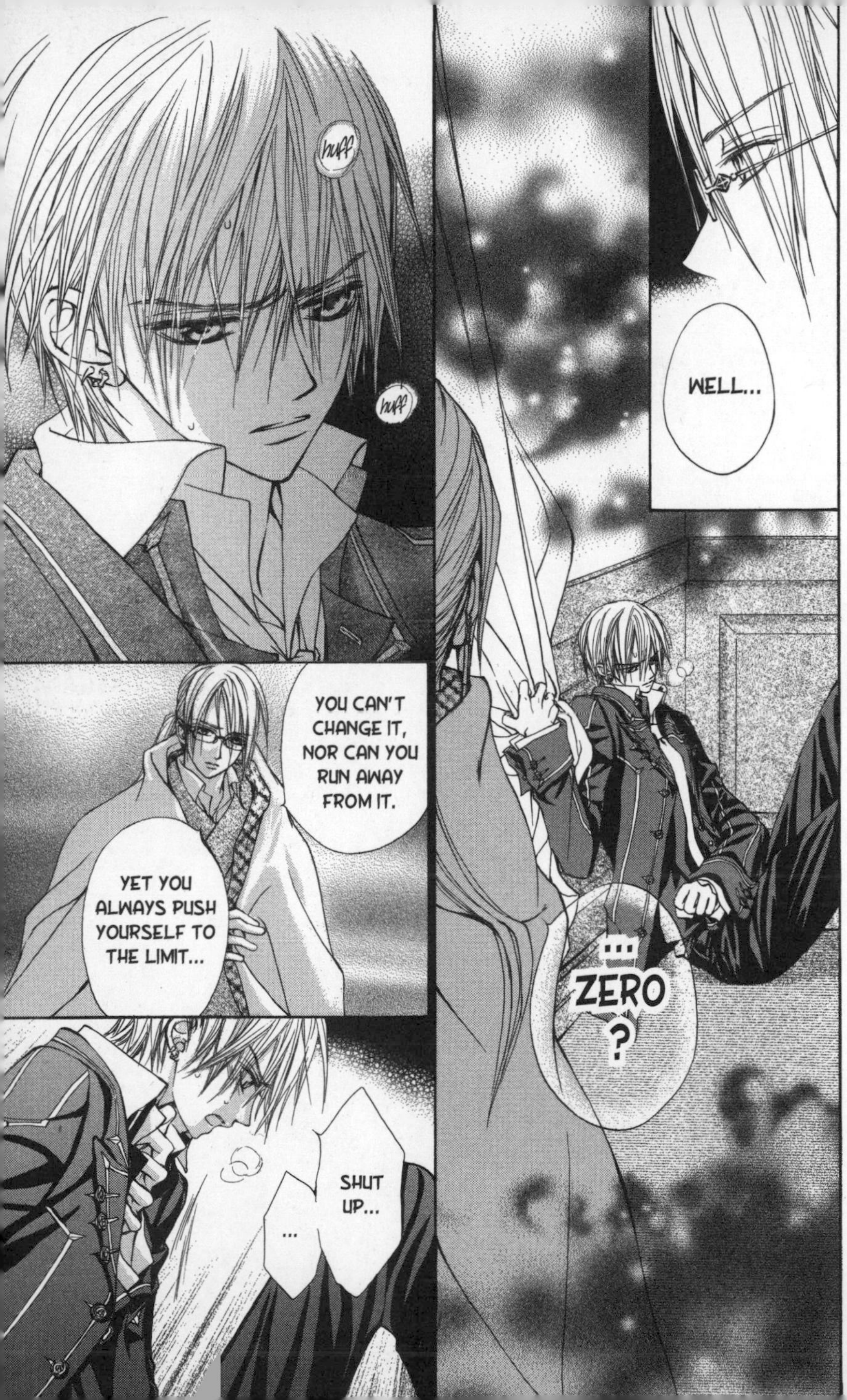
WELL...
...ZERO?
huff
huff
YOU CAN'T CHANGE IT, NOR CAN YOU RUN AWAY FROM IT.
YET YOU ALWAYS PUSH YOURSELF TO THE LIMIT...
SHUT UP...
...

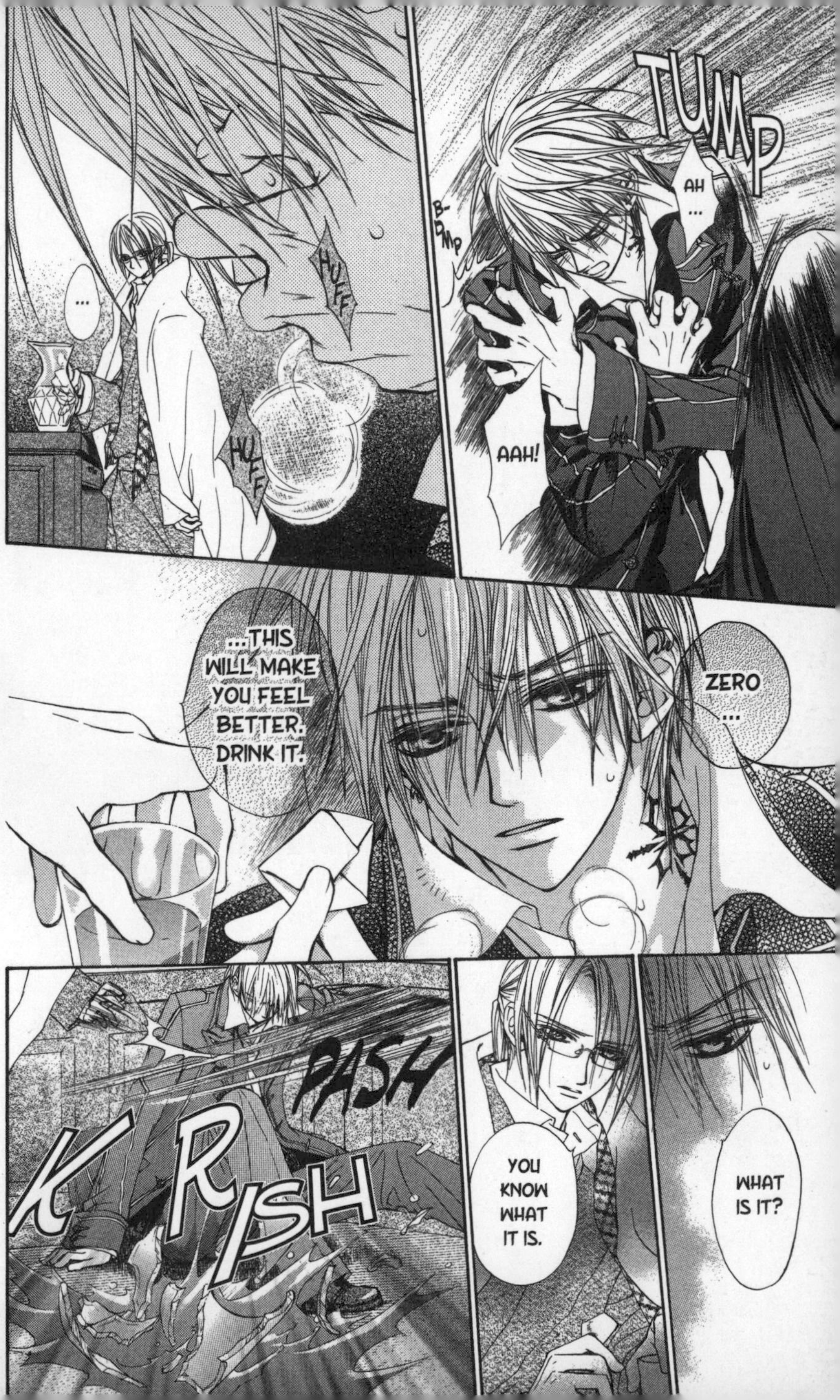
TUMP
AH ...
B-DMP
AAH!
HUFF
HUFF
...
ZERO ...
...THIS WILL MAKE YOU FEEL BETTER. DRINK IT.
WHAT IS IT?
YOU KNOW WHAT IT IS.
PASH
KRISH

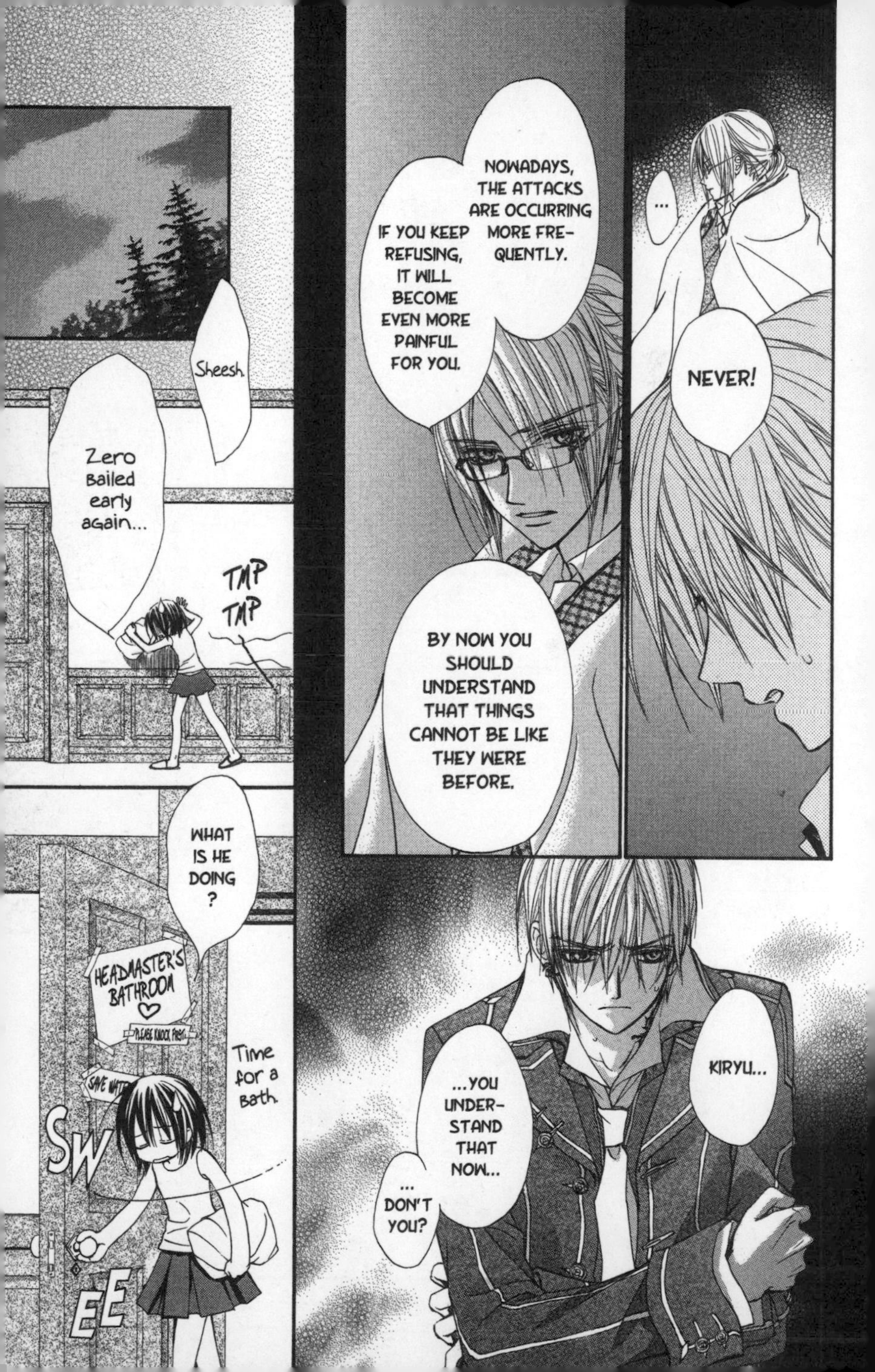
...
NEVER!
NOWADAYS, THE ATTACKS ARE OCCURRING MORE FRE-QUENTLY.
IF YOU KEEP REFUSING, IT WILL BECOME EVEN MORE PAINFUL FOR YOU.
BY NOW YOU SHOULD UNDERSTAND THAT THINGS CANNOT BE LIKE THEY WERE BEFORE.
KIRYU...
...YOU UNDER-STAND THAT NOW...
...DON'T YOU?
Sheesh.
Zero Bailed early again...
TMP TMP
WHAT IS HE DOING?
HEADMASTER'S BATHROOM ♡
PLEASE KNOCK FIRST
Time for a Bath.
SWEE

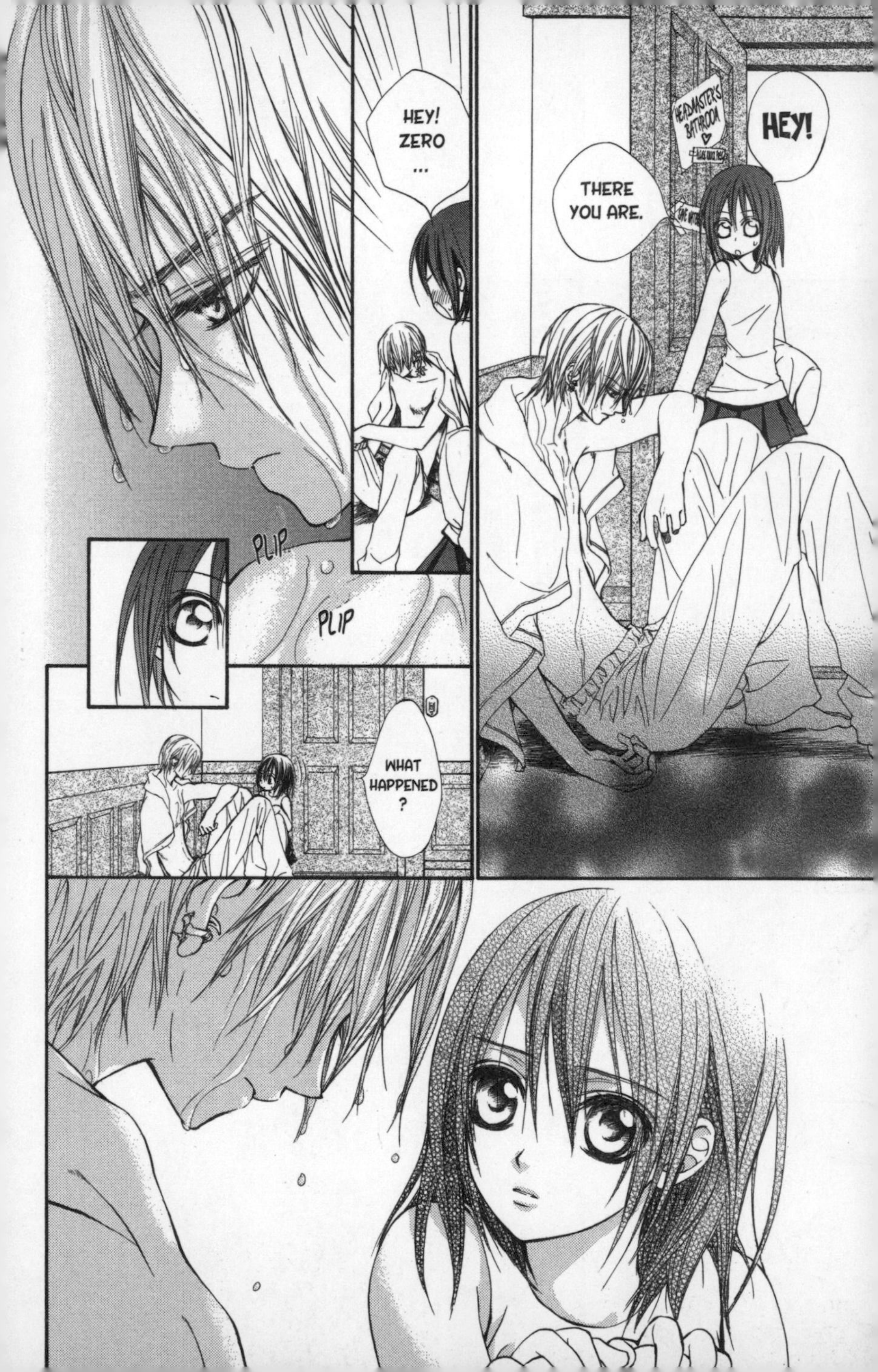
HEY!
THERE YOU ARE.
HEADMASTER'S BATHROOM
HEY! ZERO ...
PLIP
PLIP
WHAT HAPPENED ?

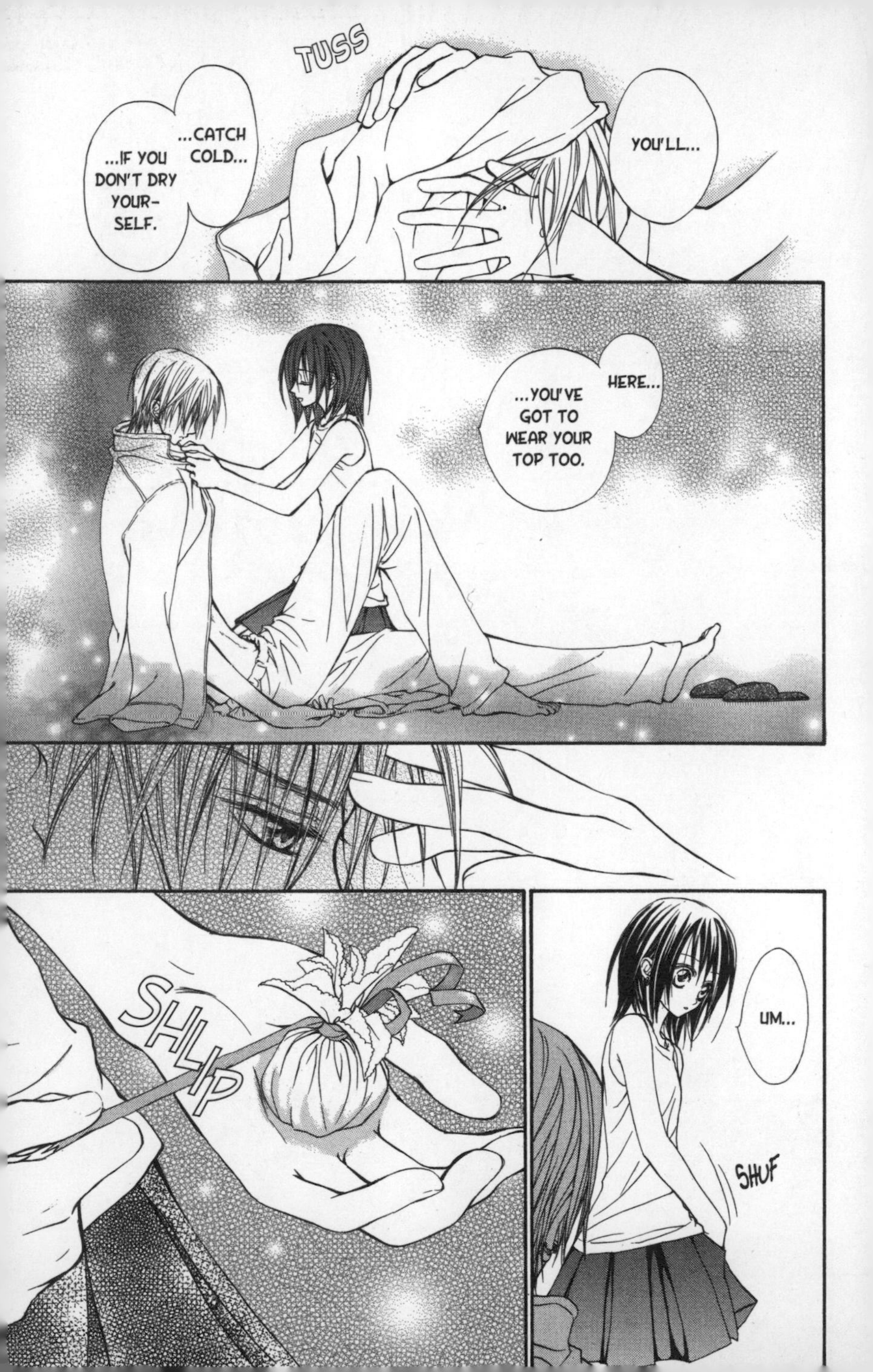
TUSS
YOU'LL...
...CATCH COLD...
...IF YOU DON'T DRY YOUR-SELF.
HERE...
...YOU'VE GOT TO WEAR YOUR TOP TOO.
UM...
SHUF
SHLIP

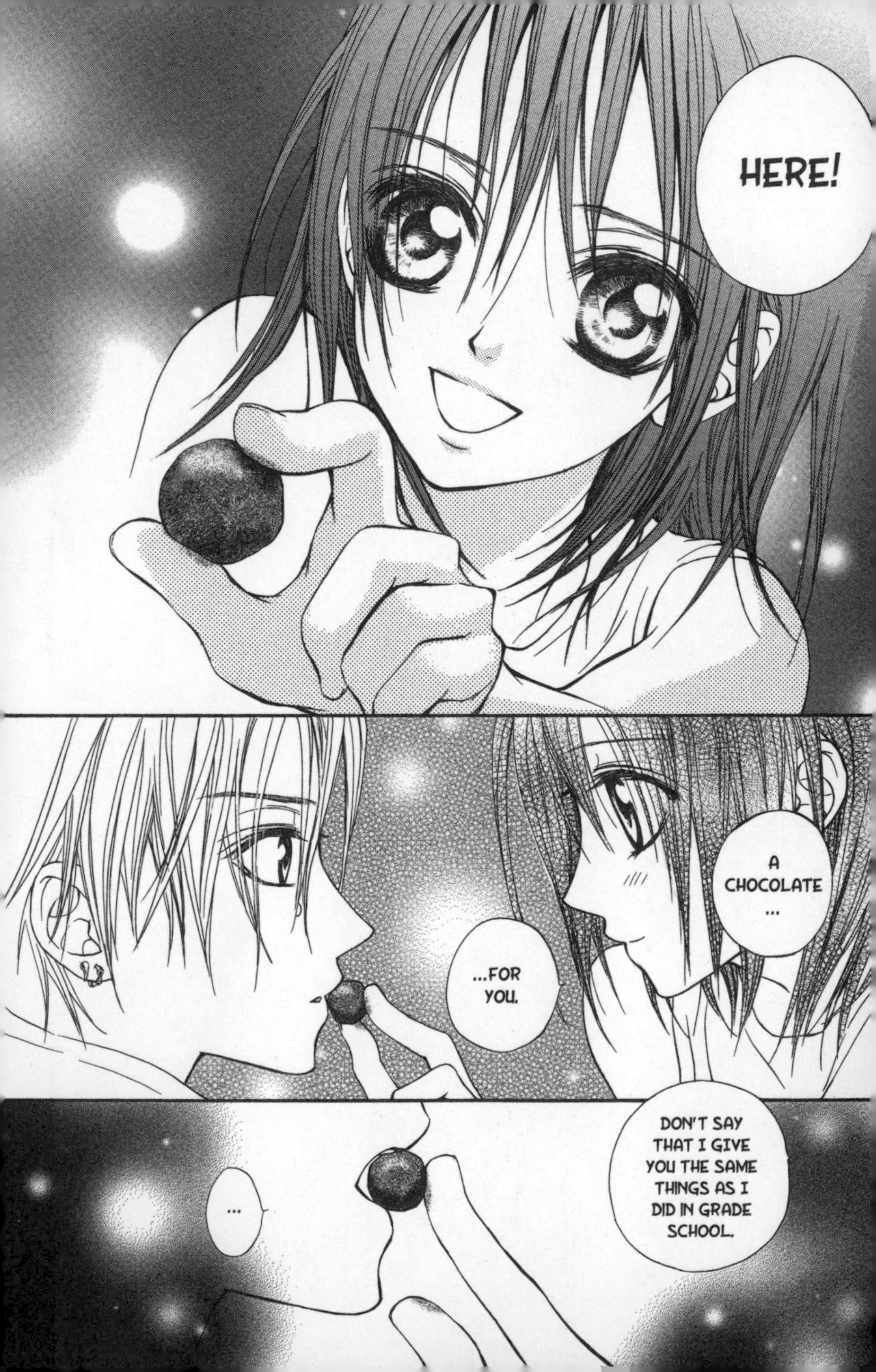
HERE!
A CHOCOLATE ...
...FOR YOU.
DON'T SAY THAT I GIVE YOU THE SAME THINGS AS I DID IN GRADE SCHOOL.
...

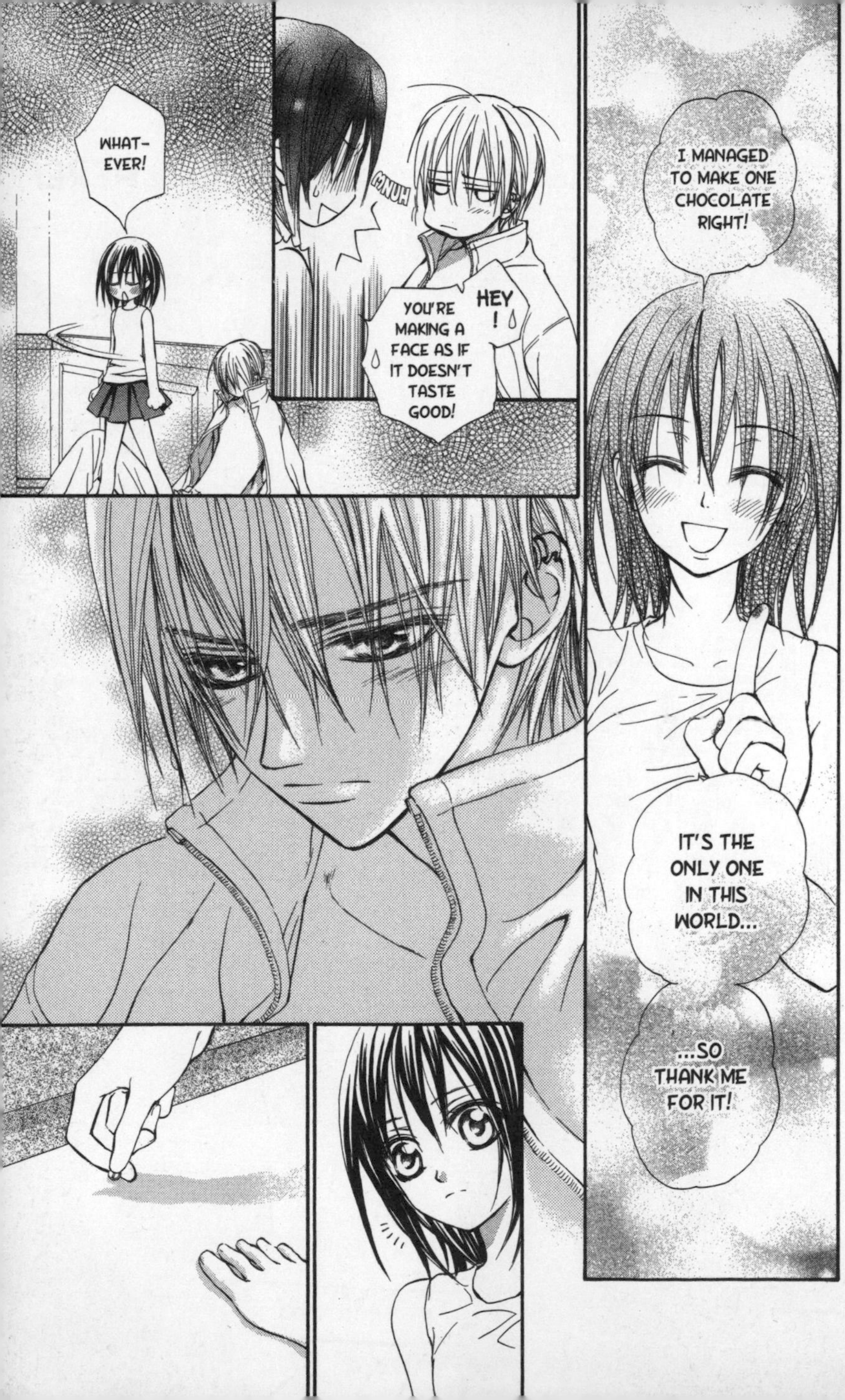
I MANAGED TO MAKE ONE CHOCOLATE RIGHT!
IT'S THE ONLY ONE IN THIS WORLD...
...SO THANK ME FOR IT!
HEY!
YOU'RE MAKING A FACE AS IF IT DOESN'T TASTE GOOD!
WHAT-EVER!

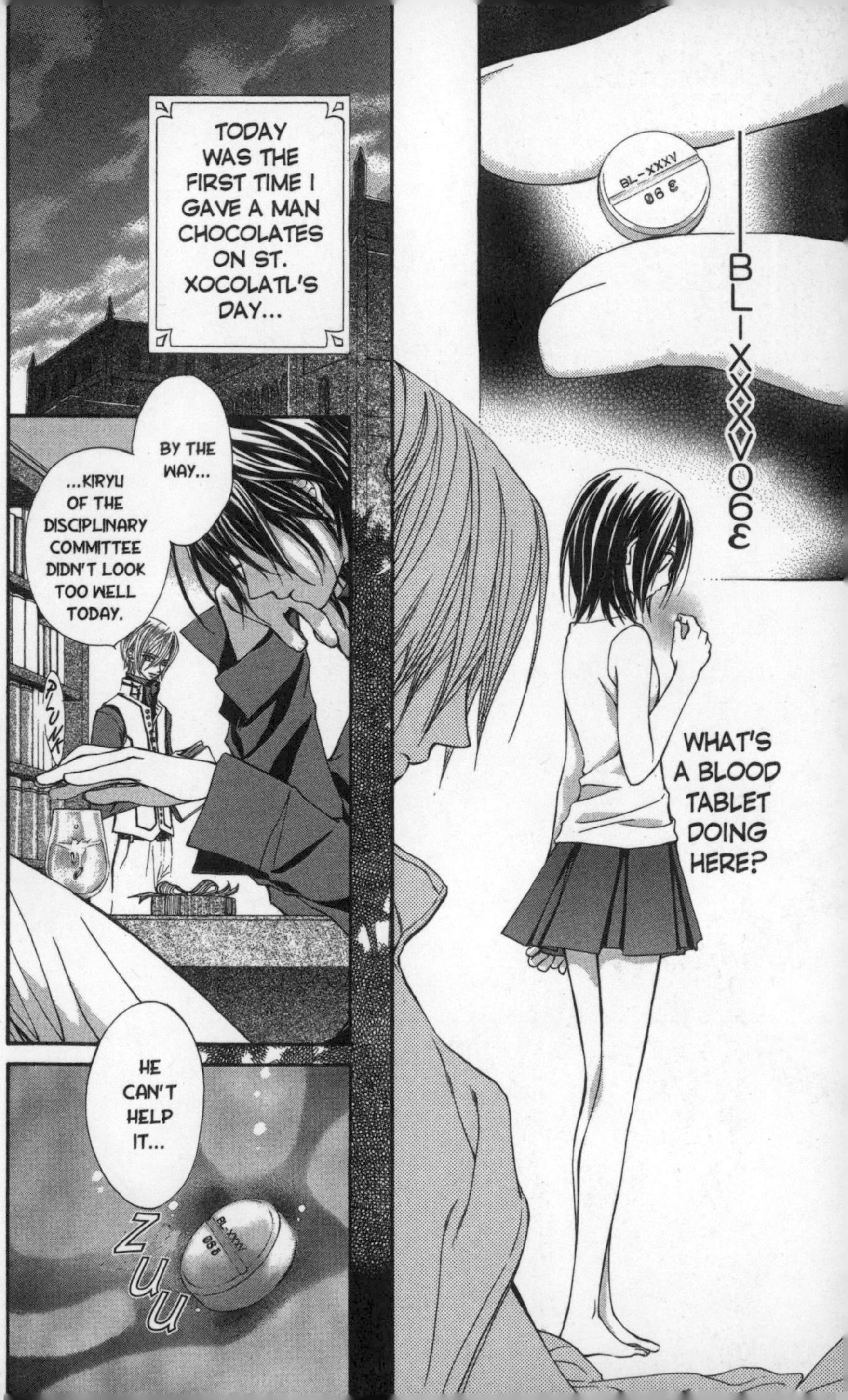
BL-XXXV
WHAT'S A BLOOD TABLET DOING HERE?
TODAY WAS THE FIRST TIME I GAVE A MAN CHOCOLATES ON ST. XOCOLATL'S DAY...
BY THE WAY...
...KIRYU OF THE DISCIPLINARY COMMITTEE DIDN'T LOOK TOO WELL TODAY.
PLUNK
HE CAN'T HELP IT...
BL-XXXV
ZUU

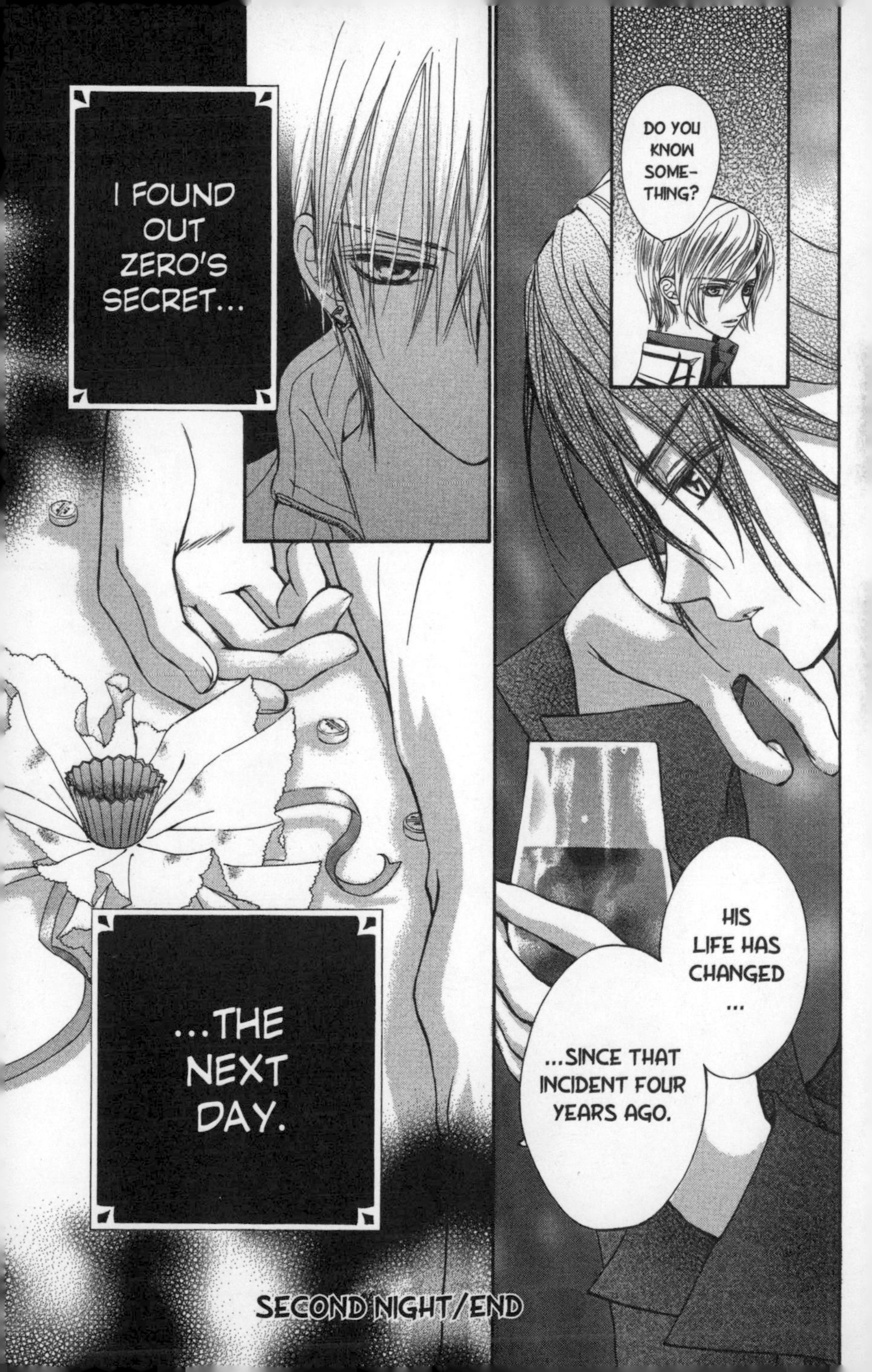
DO YOU KNOW SOME-THING?
HIS LIFE HAS CHANGED ...
...SINCE THAT INCIDENT FOUR YEARS AGO.
I FOUND OUT ZERO'S SECRET...
...THE NEXT DAY.
SECOND NIGHT/END

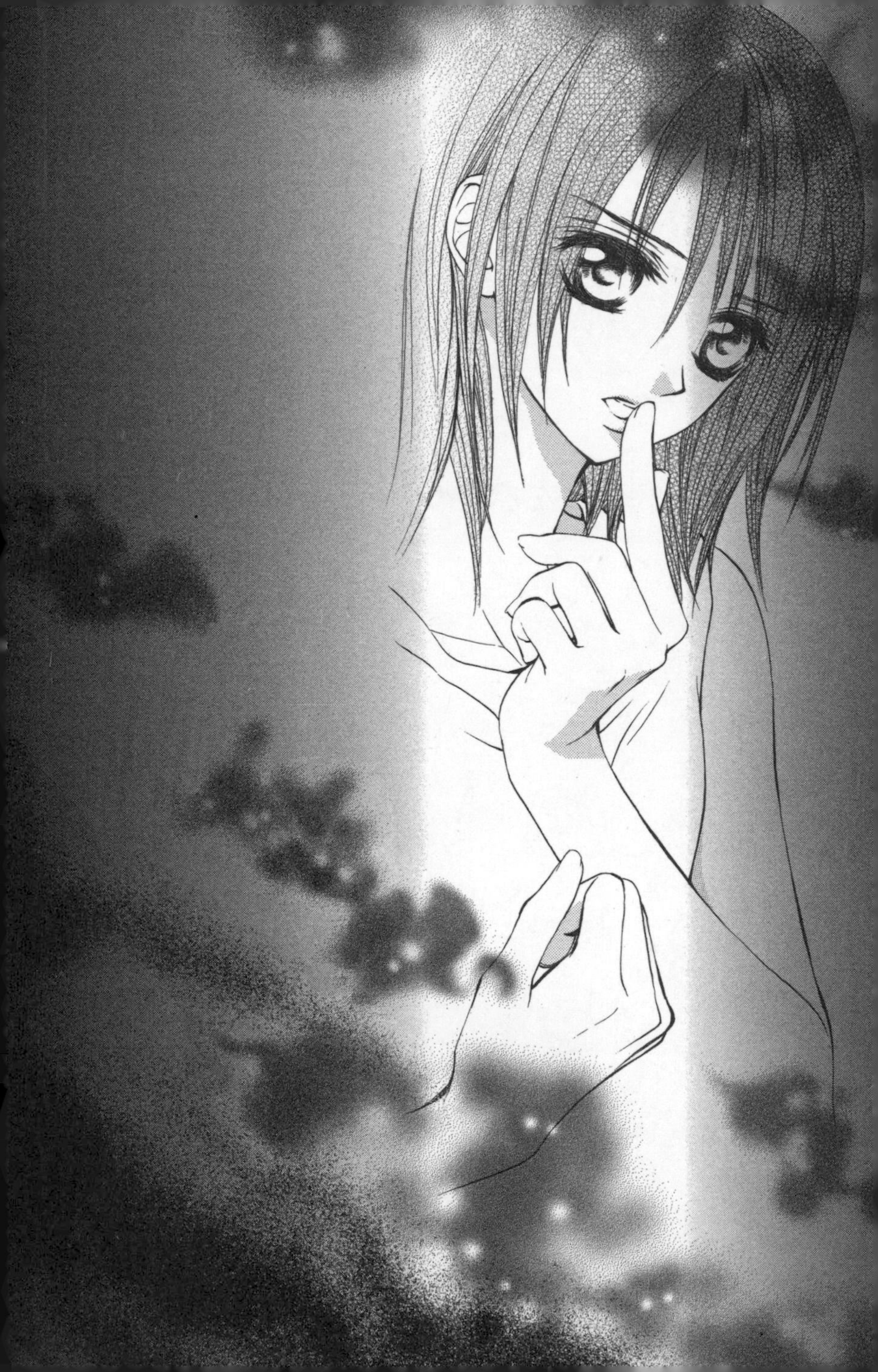

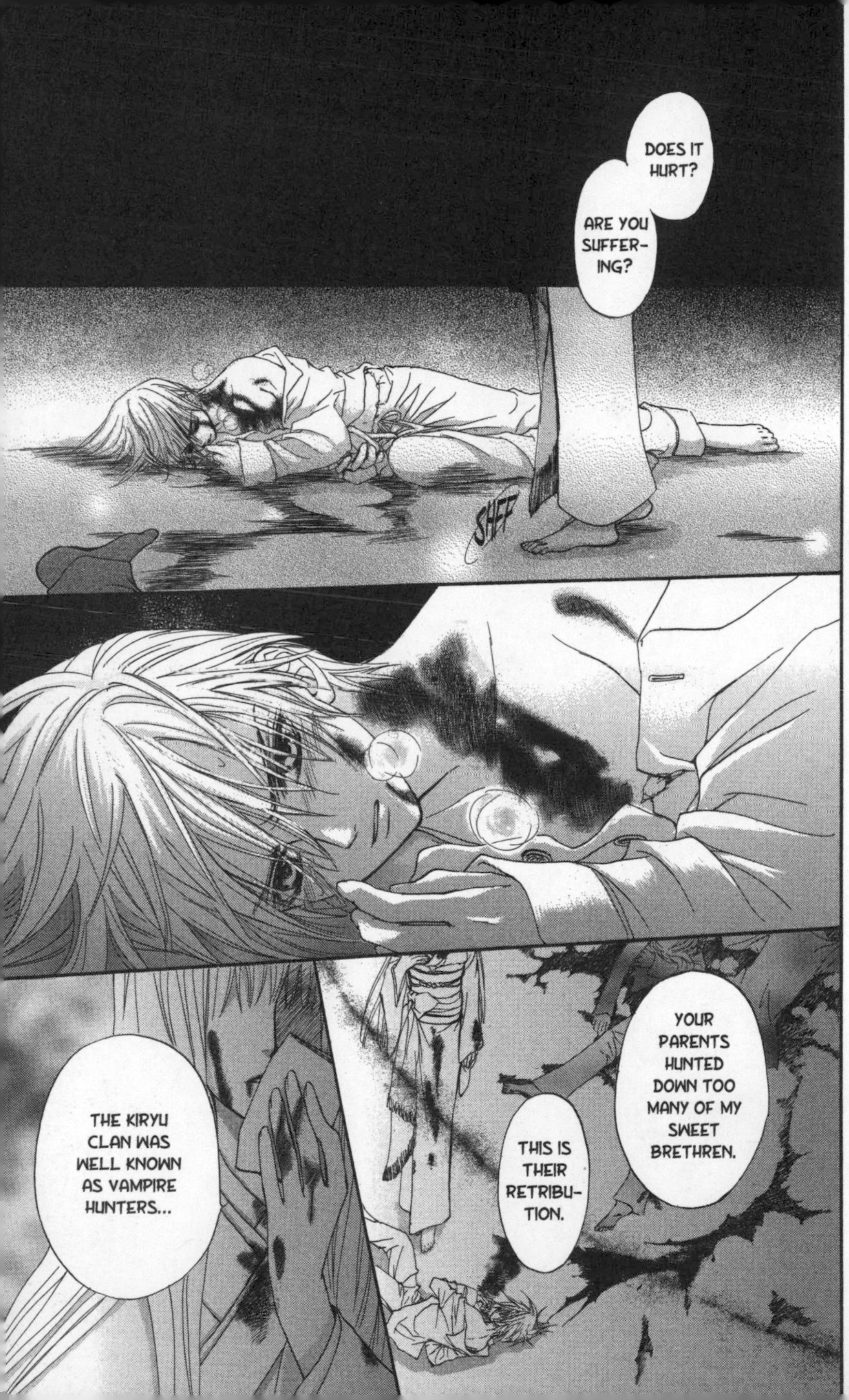
DOES IT HURT?
ARE YOU SUFFER-ING?
SHFF
YOUR PARENTS HUNTED DOWN TOO MANY OF MY SWEET BRETHREN.
THIS IS THEIR RETRIBU-TION.
THE KIRYU CLAN WAS WELL KNOWN AS VAMPIRE HUNTERS...

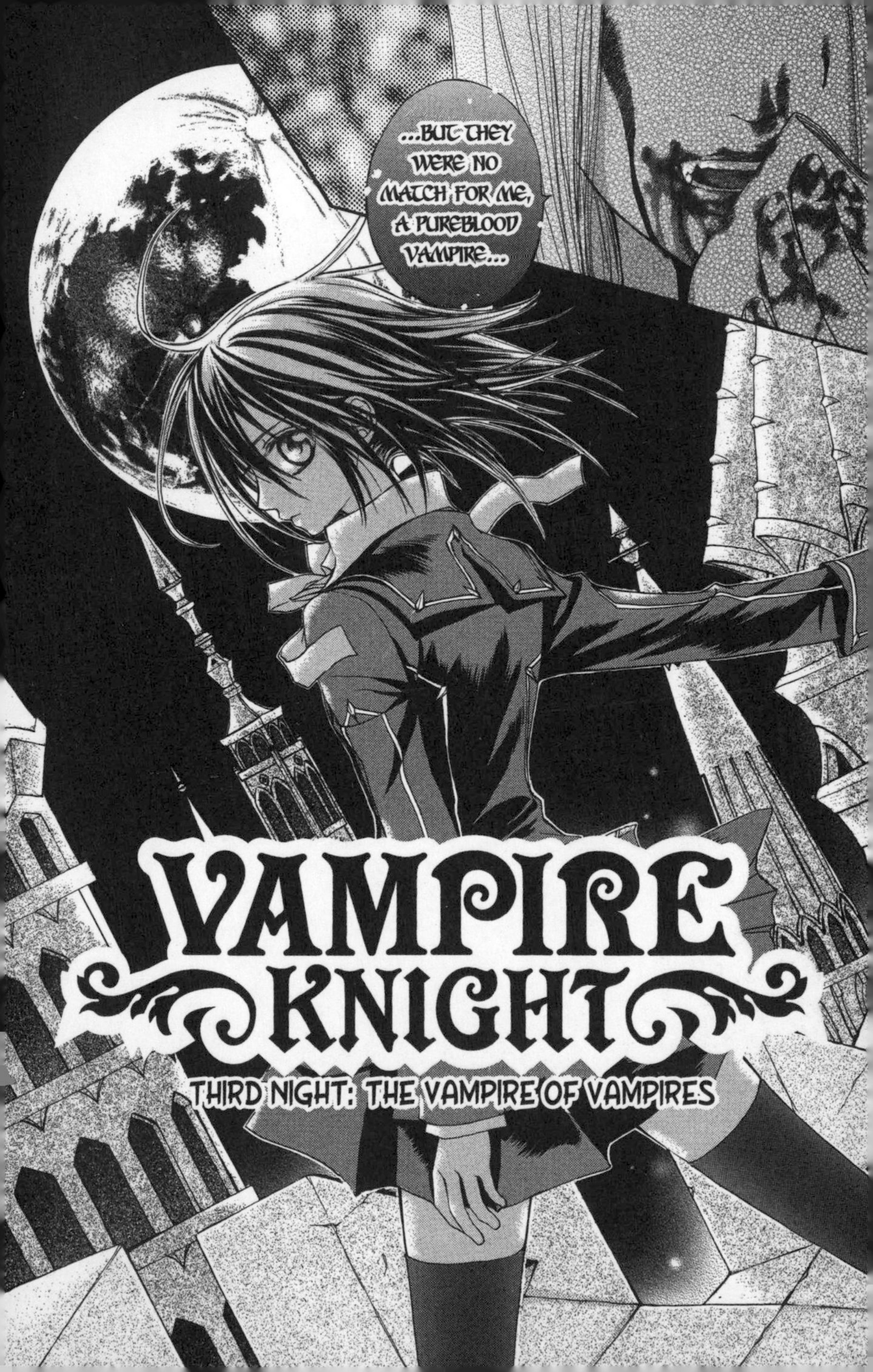
...BUT THEY WERE NO MATCH FOR ME, A PUREBLOOD VAMPIRE...
VAMPIRE KNIGHT
THIRD NIGHT: THE VAMPIRE OF VAMPIRES

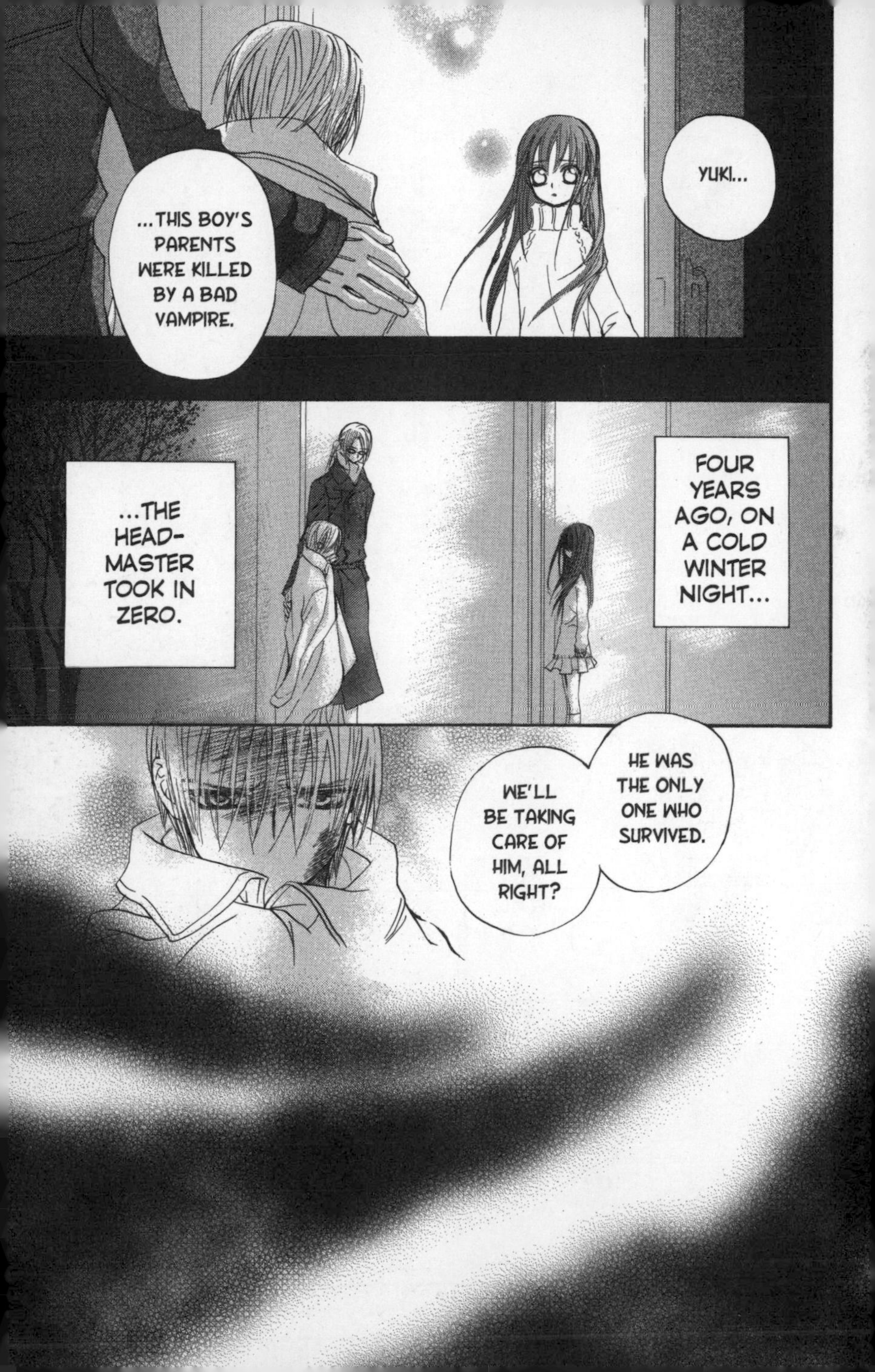
YUKI...
...THIS BOY'S PARENTS WERE KILLED BY A BAD VAMPIRE.
FOUR YEARS AGO, ON A COLD WINTER NIGHT...
...THE HEAD-MASTER TOOK IN ZERO.
HE WAS THE ONLY ONE WHO SURVIVED.
WE'LL BE TAKING CARE OF HIM, ALL RIGHT?

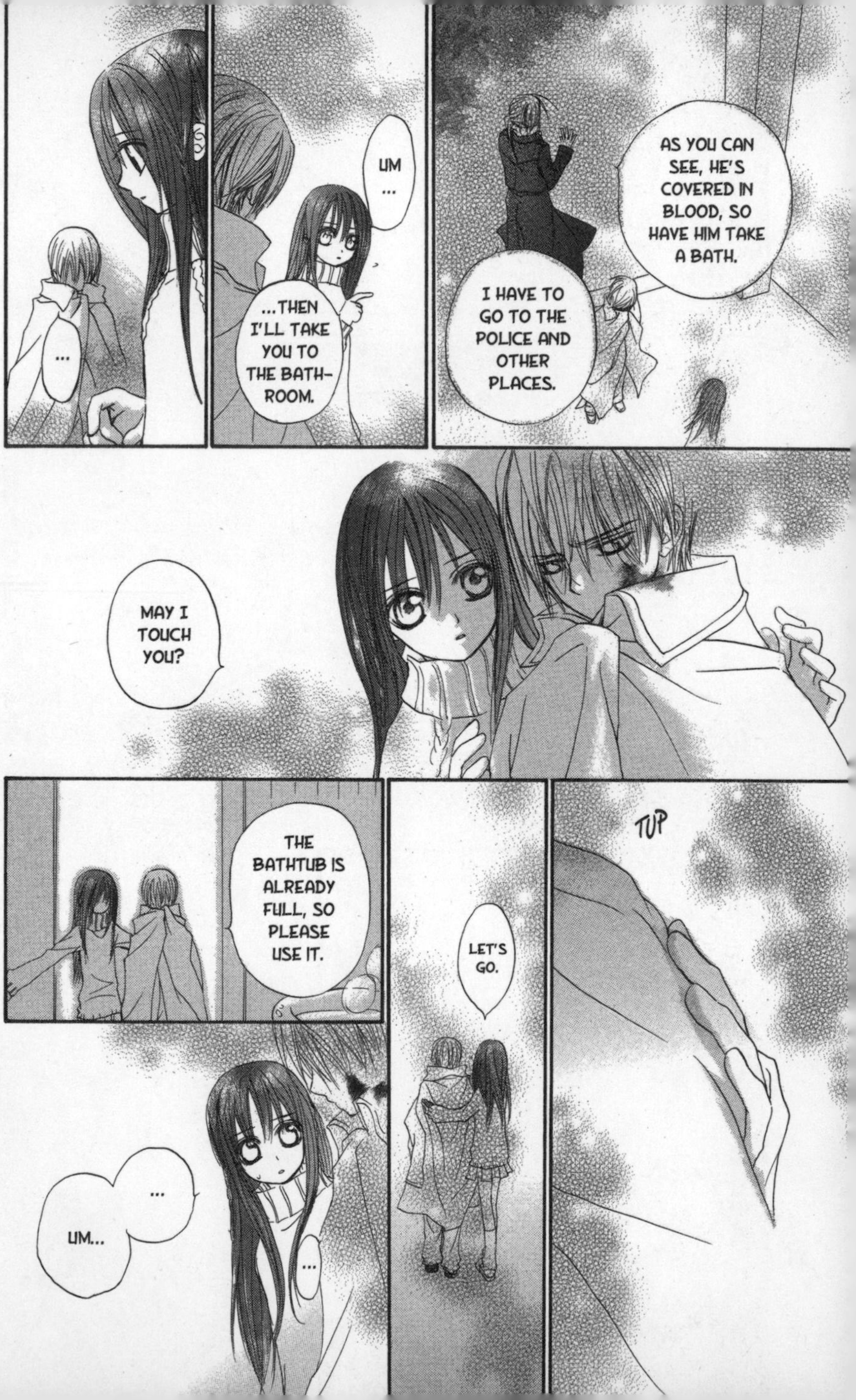
AS YOU CAN SEE, HE'S COVERED IN BLOOD, SO HAVE HIM TAKE A BATH.
I HAVE TO GO TO THE POLICE AND OTHER PLACES.
UM ...
...THEN I'LL TAKE YOU TO THE BATH-ROOM.
...
MAY I TOUCH YOU?
TUP
LET'S GO.
THE BATHTUB IS ALREADY FULL, SO PLEASE USE IT.
...
UM...
...

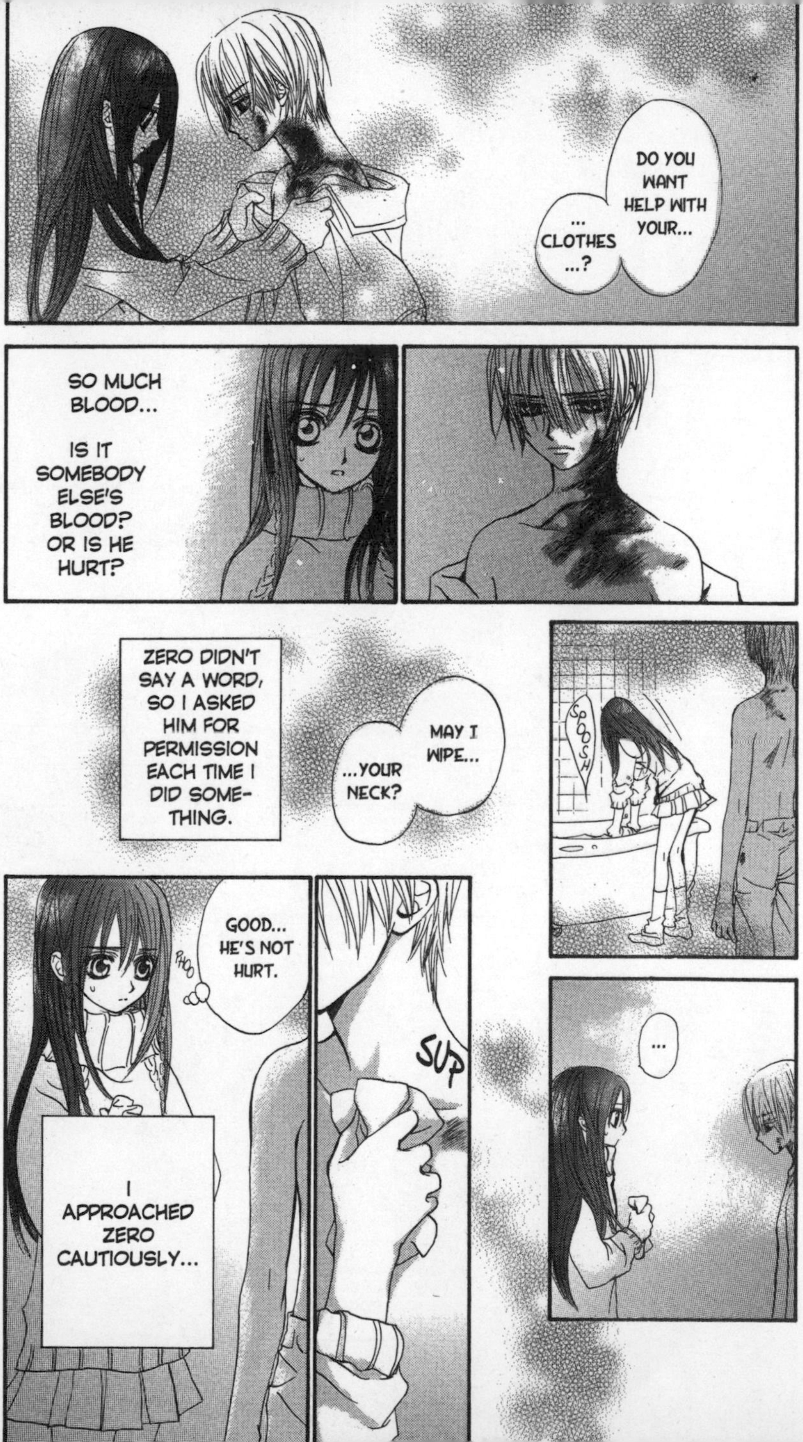
DO YOU WANT HELP WITH YOUR...
...CLOTHES ...?
SO MUCH BLOOD...
IS IT SOMEBODY ELSE'S BLOOD? OR IS HE HURT?
SPLOOSH
MAY I WIPE...
...YOUR NECK?
ZERO DIDN'T SAY A WORD, SO I ASKED HIM FOR PERMISSION EACH TIME I DID SOME-THING.
...
SUP
GOOD... HE'S NOT HURT.
PHOO
I APPROACHED ZERO CAUTIOUSLY...

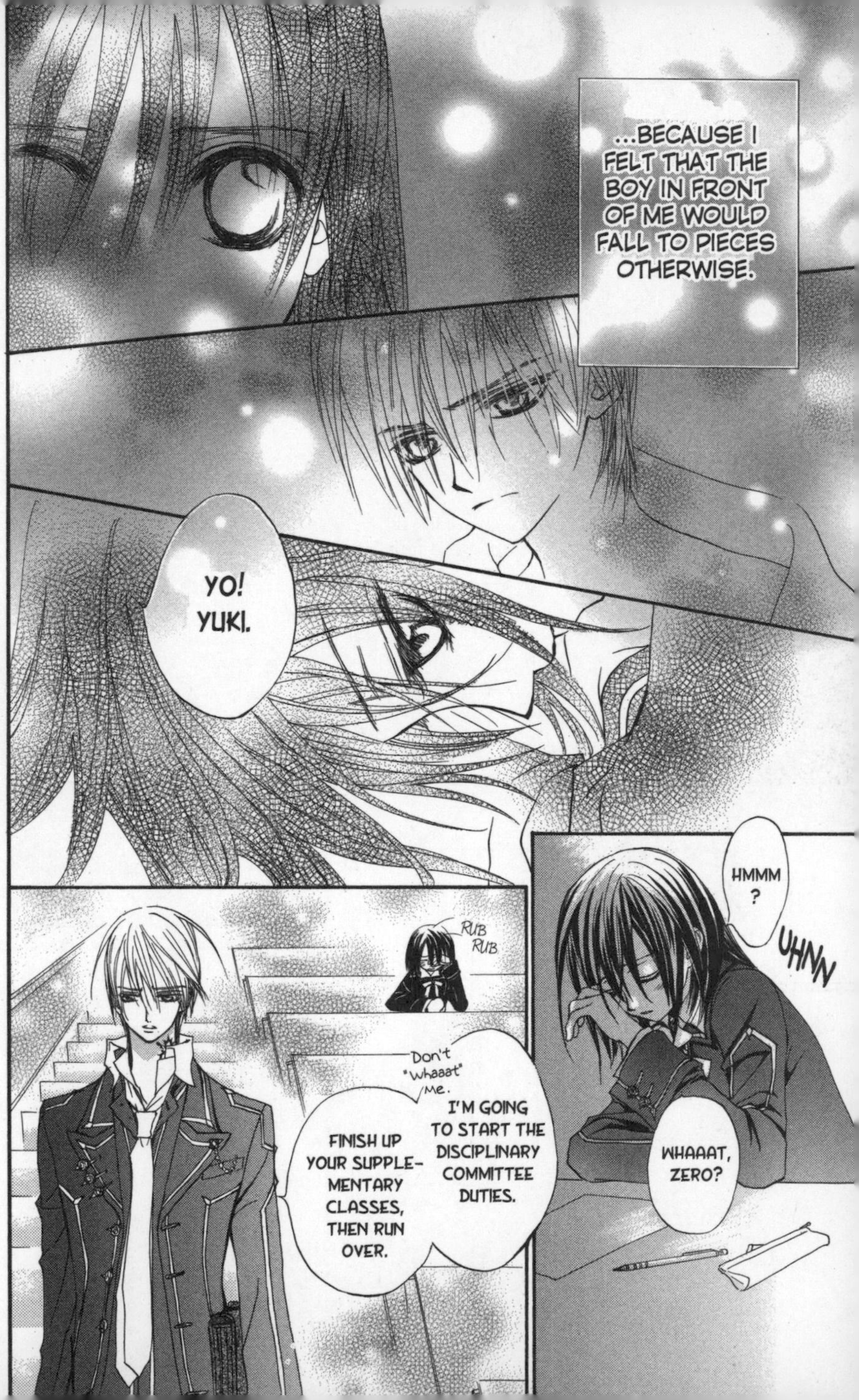
...BECAUSE I FELT THAT THE BOY IN FRONT OF ME WOULD FALL TO PIECES OTHERWISE.
YO! YUKI.
HMMM?
UHNN
WHAAAT, ZERO?
RUB RUB
Don't "whaaat" me.
I'M GOING TO START THE DISCIPLINARY COMMITTEE DUTIES.
FINISH UP YOUR SUPPLE-MENTARY CLASSES, THEN RUN OVER.

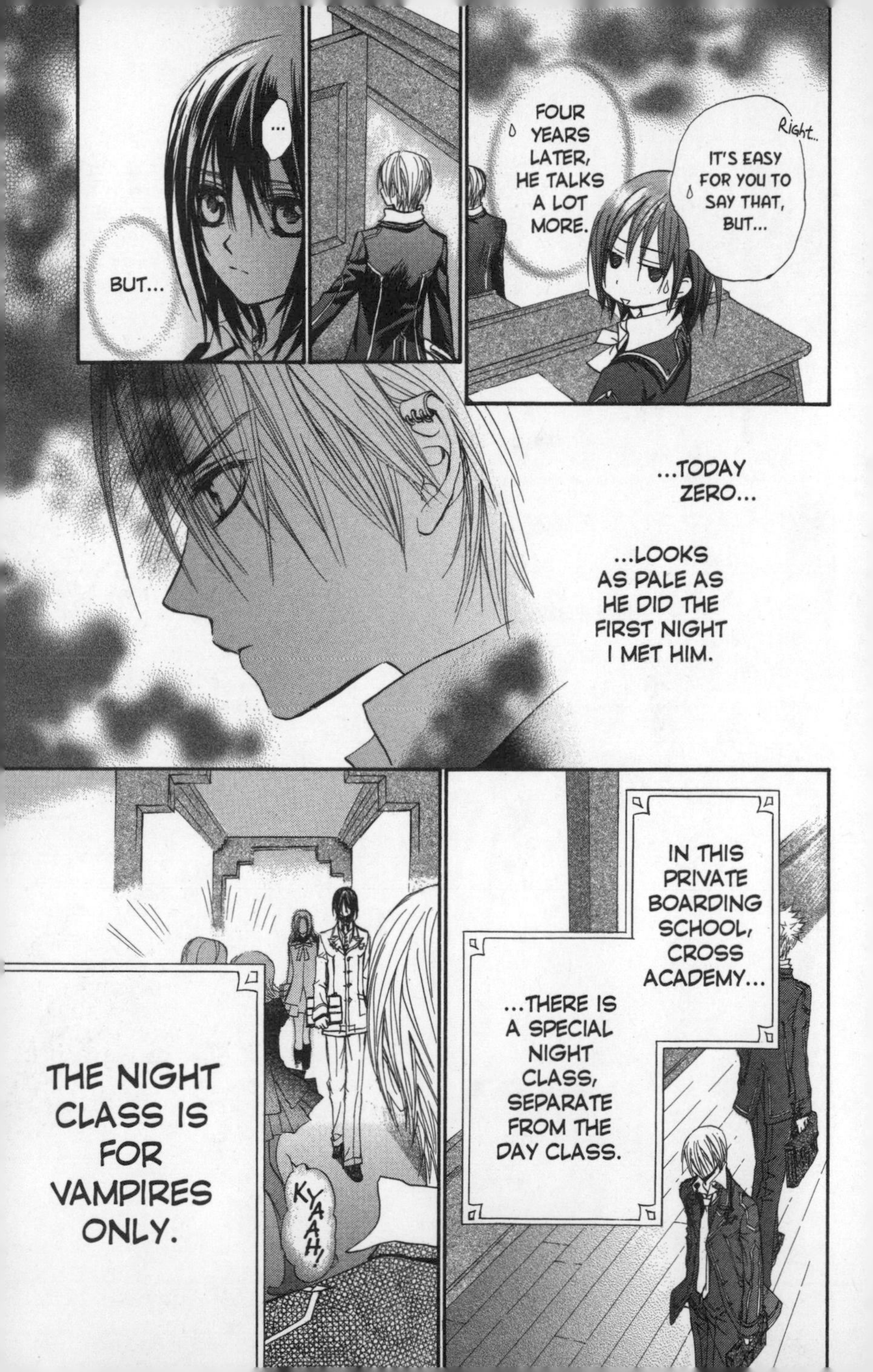
Right..
IT'S EASY FOR YOU TO SAY THAT, BUT...
FOUR YEARS LATER, HE TALKS A LOT MORE.
...
BUT...
...TODAY ZERO...
...LOOKS AS PALE AS HE DID THE FIRST NIGHT I MET HIM.
IN THIS PRIVATE BOARDING SCHOOL, CROSS ACADEMY...
...THERE IS A SPECIAL NIGHT CLASS, SEPARATE FROM THE DAY CLASS.
KYAAH!
THE NIGHT CLASS IS FOR VAMPIRES ONLY.

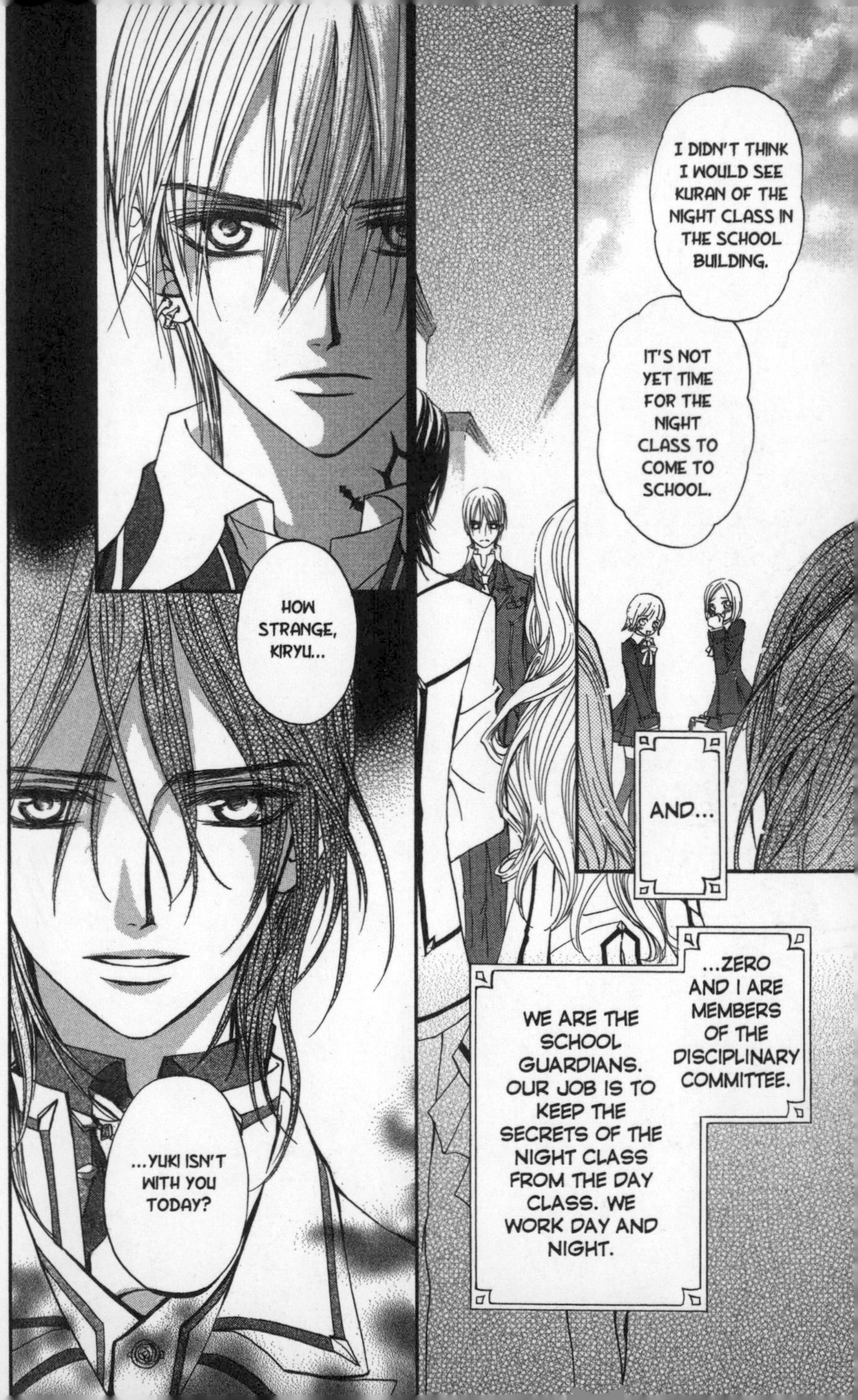
I DIDN'T THINK I WOULD SEE KURAN OF THE NIGHT CLASS IN THE SCHOOL BUILDING.
IT'S NOT YET TIME FOR THE NIGHT CLASS TO COME TO SCHOOL.
AND...
...ZERO AND I ARE MEMBERS OF THE DISCIPLINARY COMMITTEE.
WE ARE THE SCHOOL GUARDIANS. OUR JOB IS TO KEEP THE SECRETS OF THE NIGHT CLASS FROM THE DAY CLASS. WE WORK DAY AND NIGHT.
HOW STRANGE, KIRYU...
...YUKI ISN'T WITH YOU TODAY?

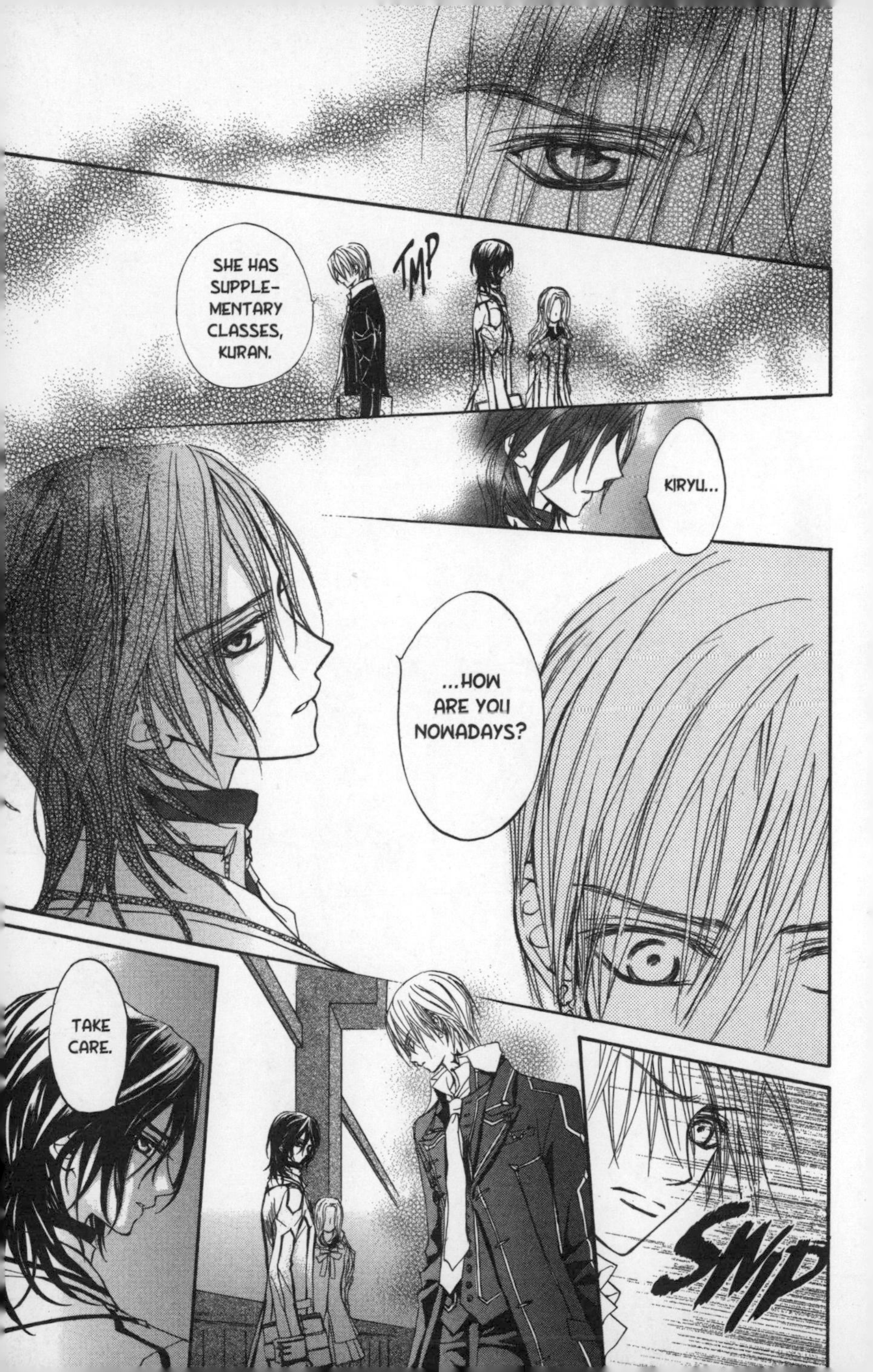
TMP
SHE HAS SUPPLE- MENTARY CLASSES, KURAN.
KIRYU...
...HOW ARE YOU NOWADAYS?
SNP
TAKE CARE.

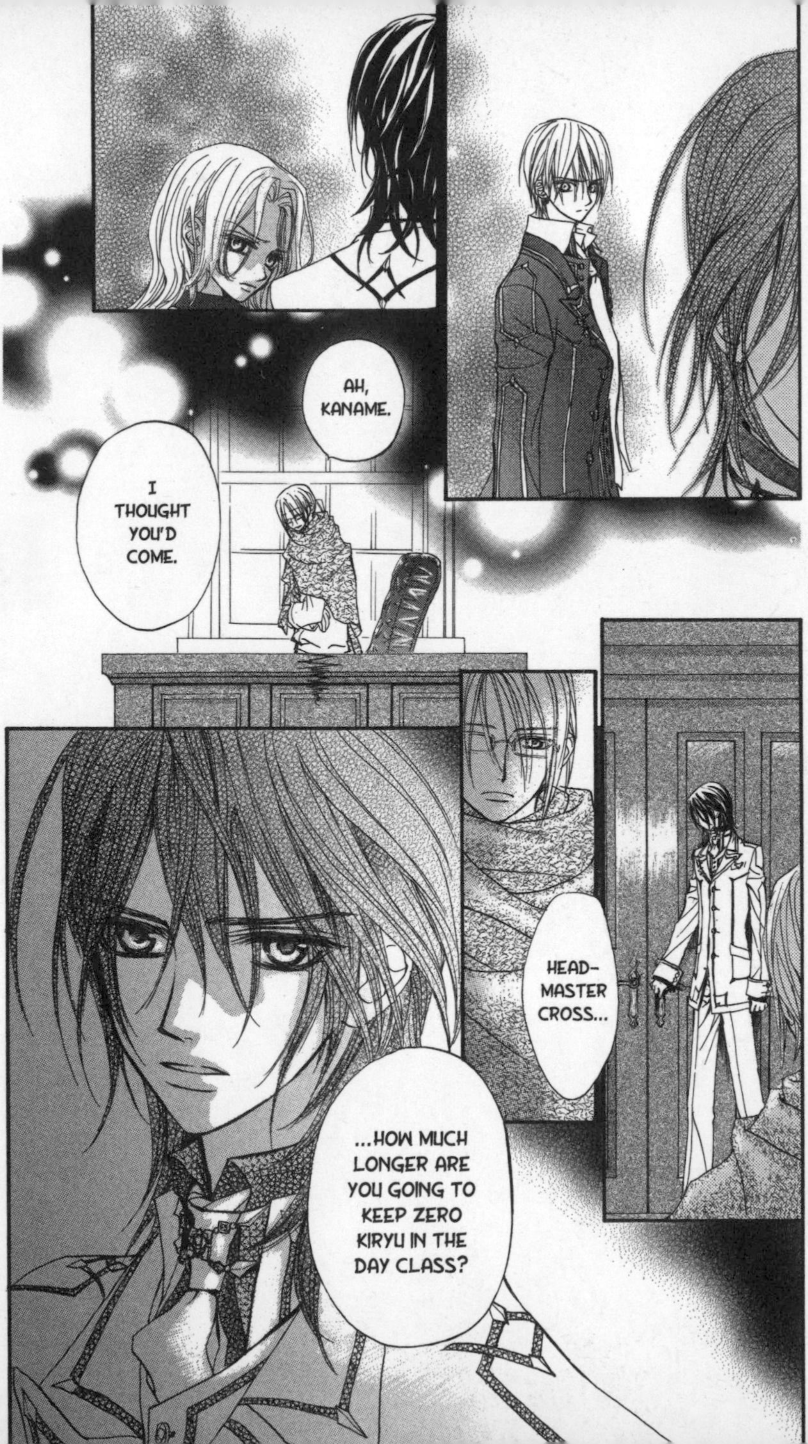
AH, KANAME.
I THOUGHT YOU'D COME.
HEAD-MASTER CROSS...
...HOW MUCH LONGER ARE YOU GOING TO KEEP ZERO KIRYU IN THE DAY CLASS?

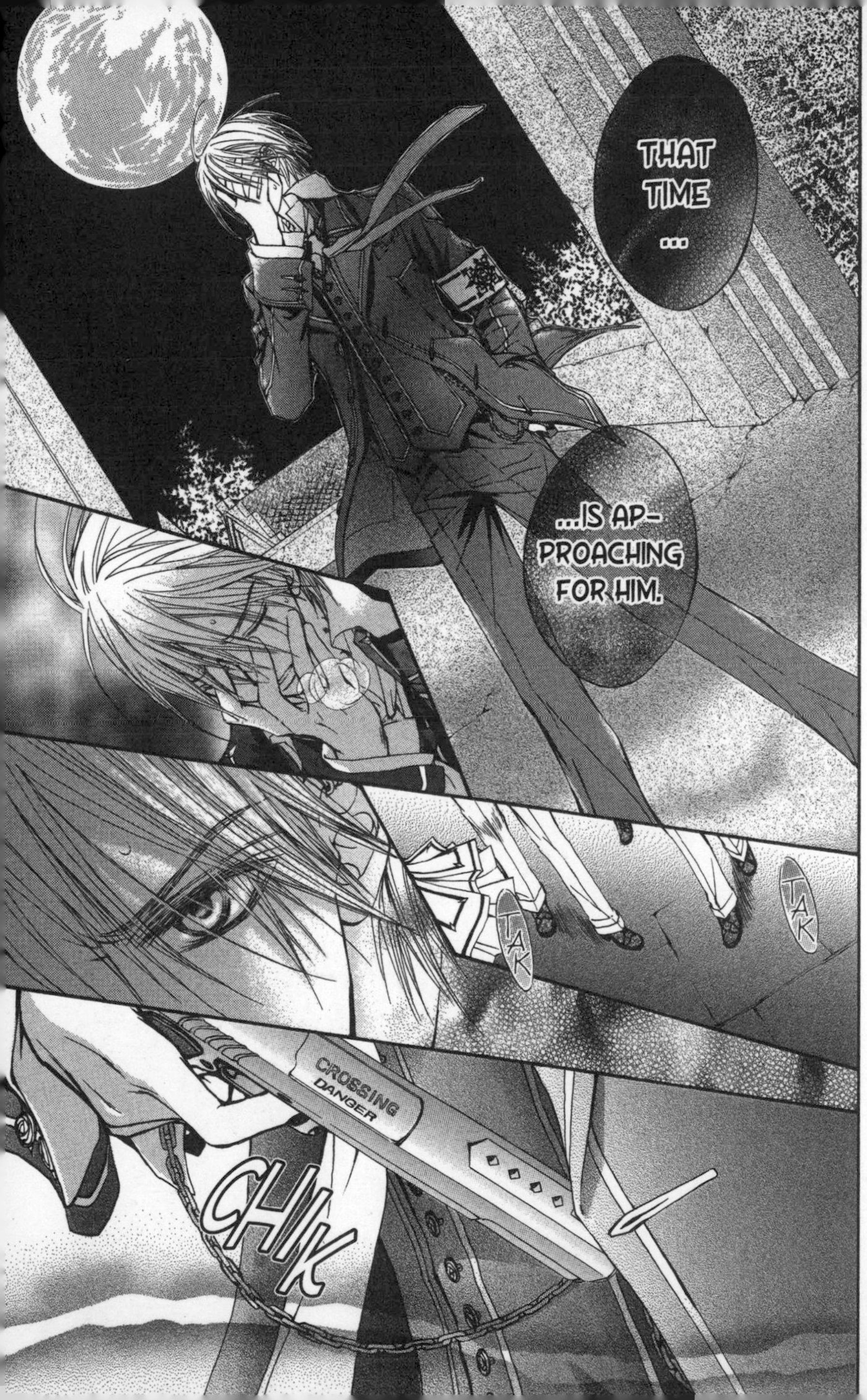
THAT TIME ...
...IS AP-PROACHING FOR HIM.
TAK
TAK
CROSSING DANGER
CHIK

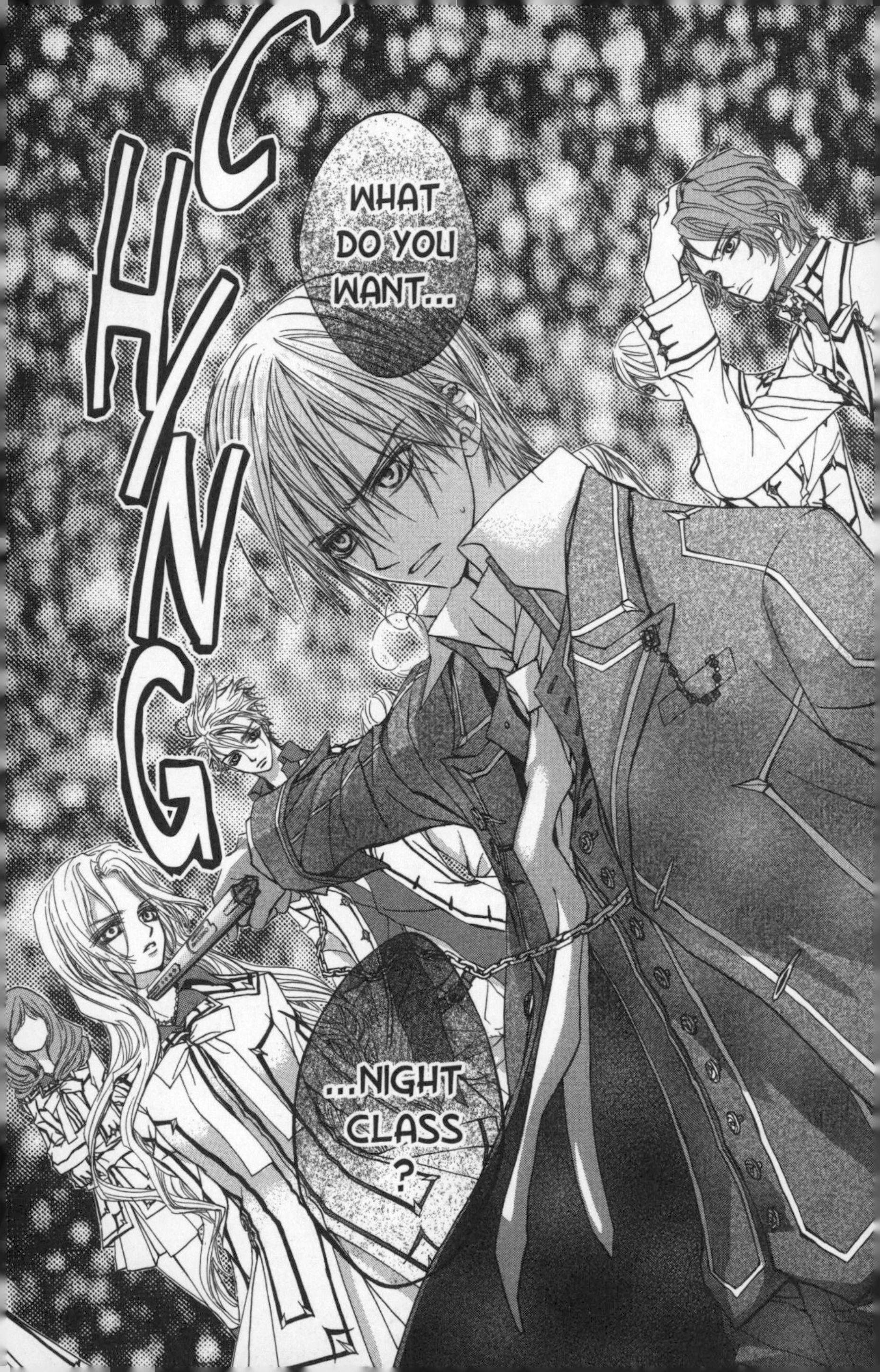
WHAT DO YOU WANT...
...NIGHT CLASS?
CHHNNG

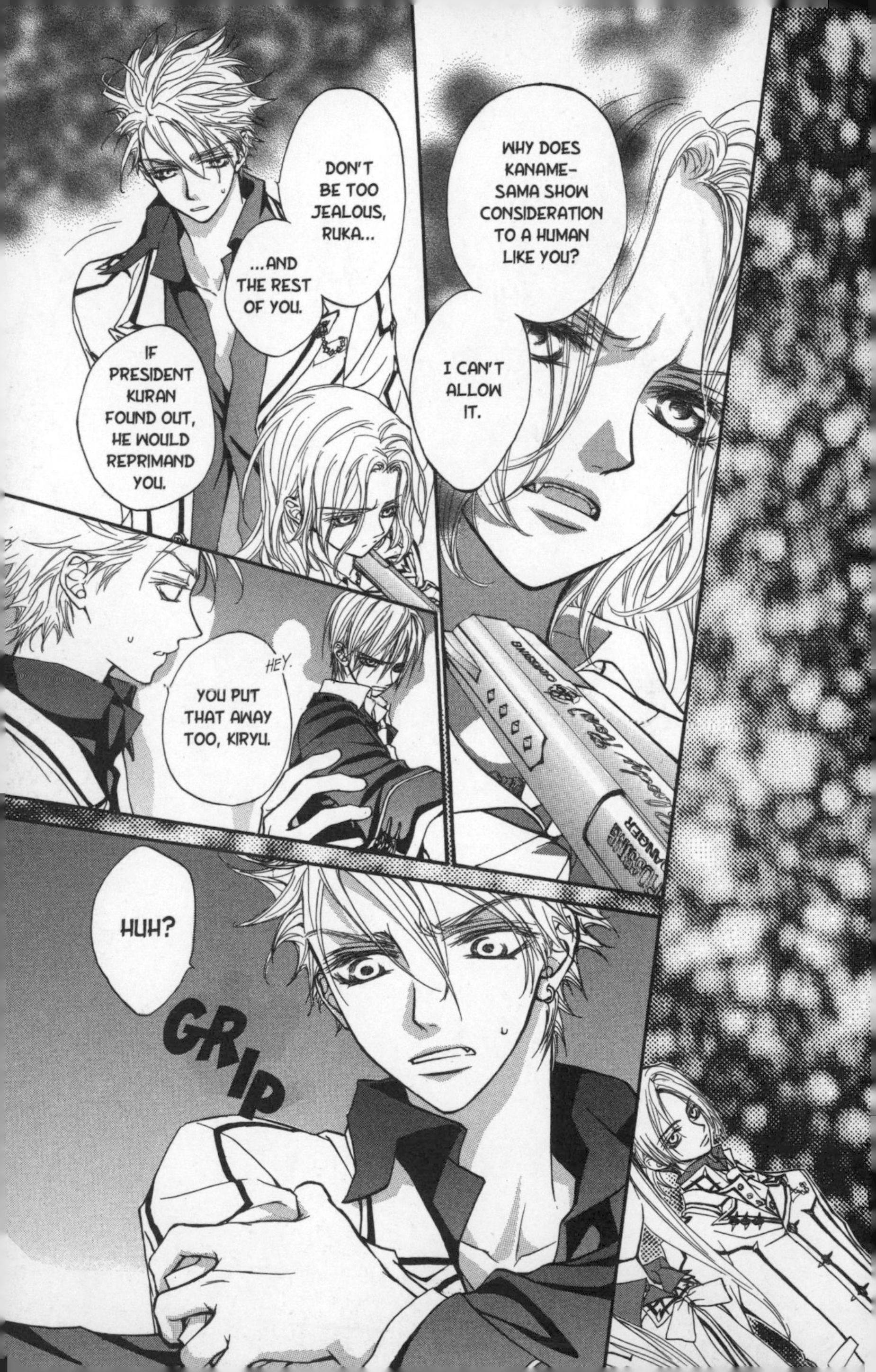
WHY DOES KANAME-SAMA SHOW CONSIDERATION TO A HUMAN LIKE YOU?
I CAN'T ALLOW IT.
DON'T BE TOO JEALOUS, RUKA...
...AND THE REST OF YOU.
IF PRESIDENT KURAN FOUND OUT, HE WOULD REPRIMAND YOU.
HEY.
YOU PUT THAT AWAY TOO, KIRYU.
HUH?
GRIP

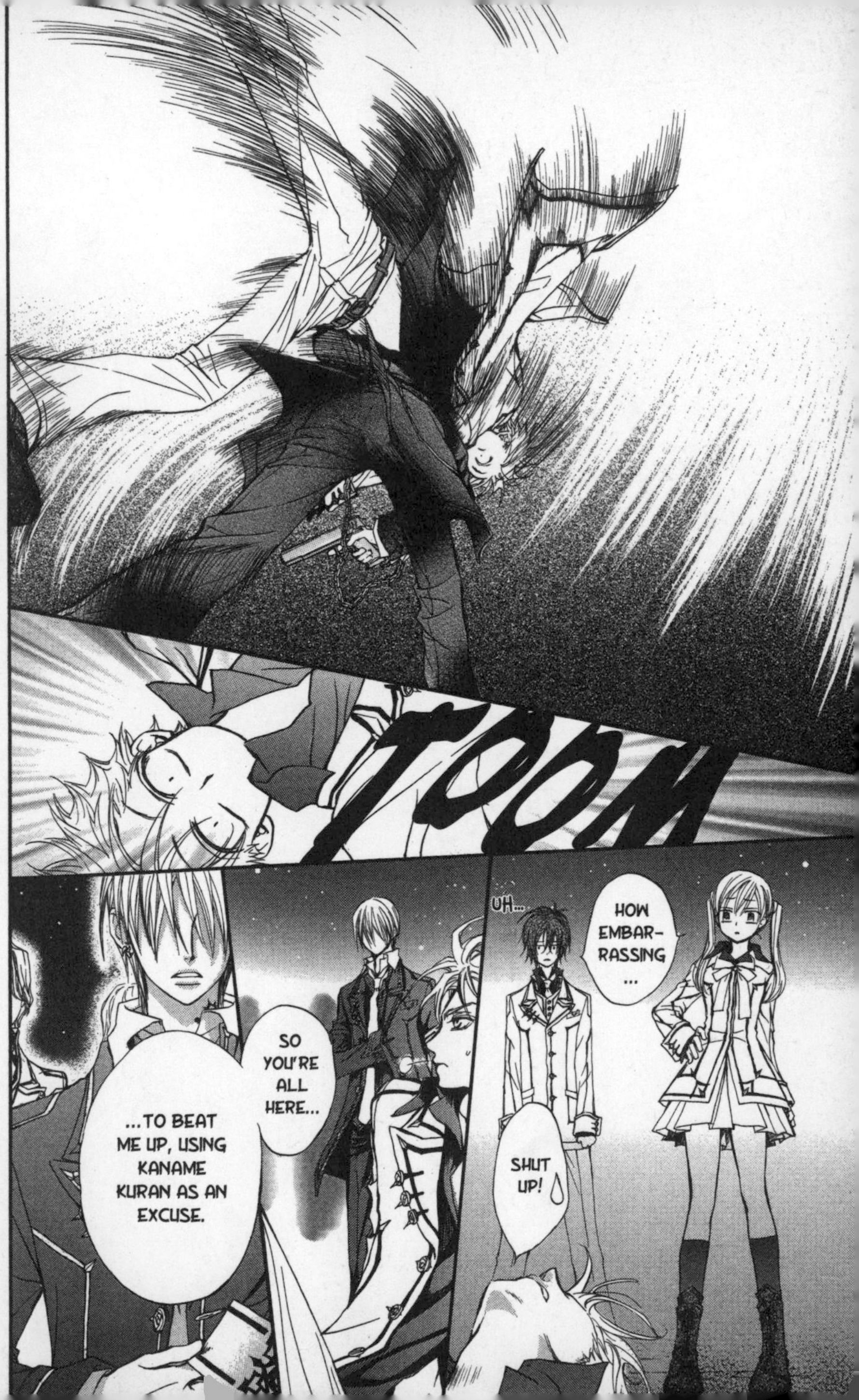
TOOM
HOW EMBAR-RASSING...
UH...
SHUT UP!
SO YOU'RE ALL HERE...
...TO BEAT ME UP, USING KANAME KURAN AS AN EXCUSE.

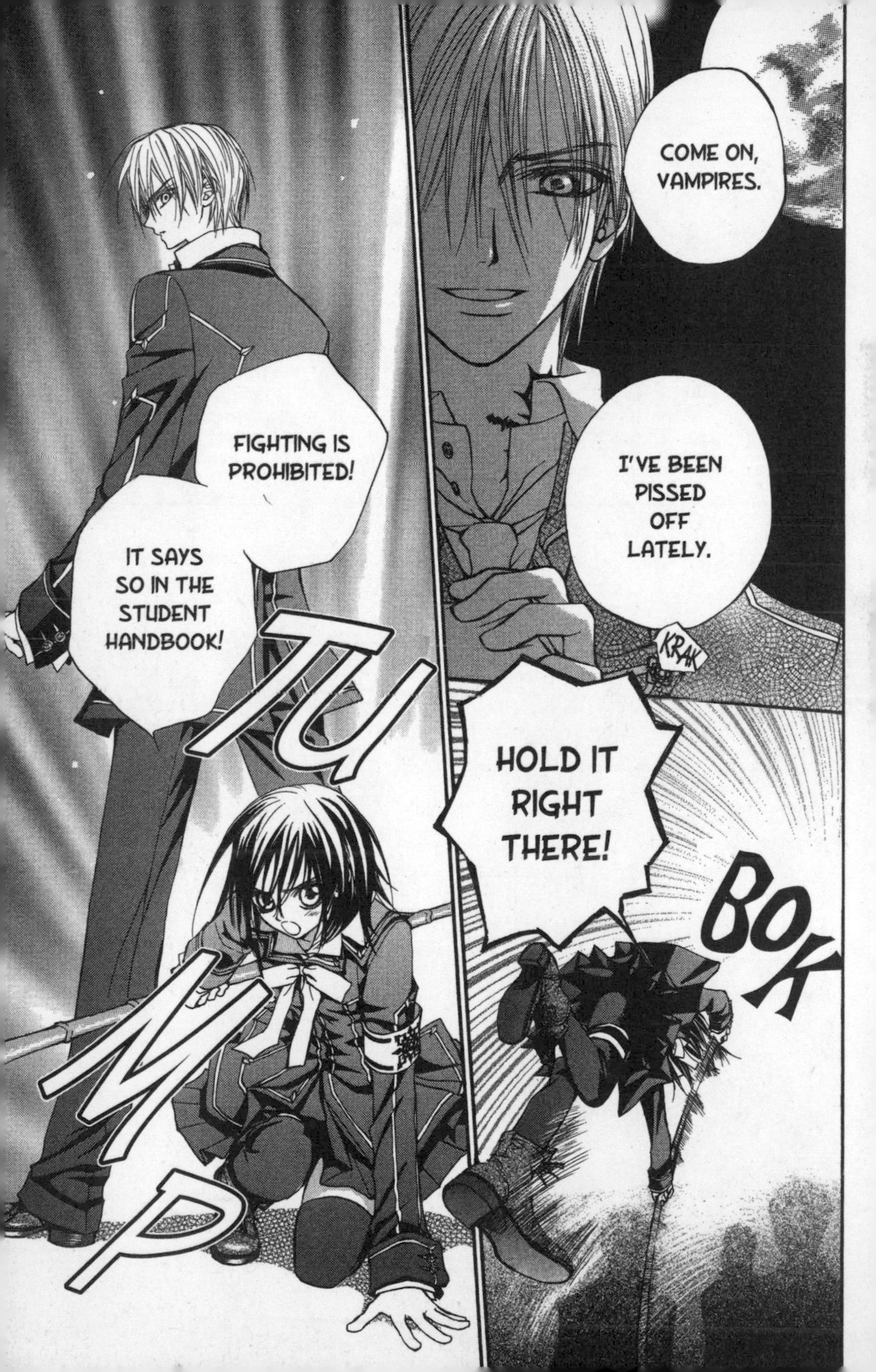
COME ON, VAMPIRES.
I'VE BEEN PISSED OFF LATELY.
KRAK
HOLD IT RIGHT THERE!
BOK
FIGHTING IS PROHIBITED!
IT SAYS SO IN THE STUDENT HANDBOOK!
JUMP

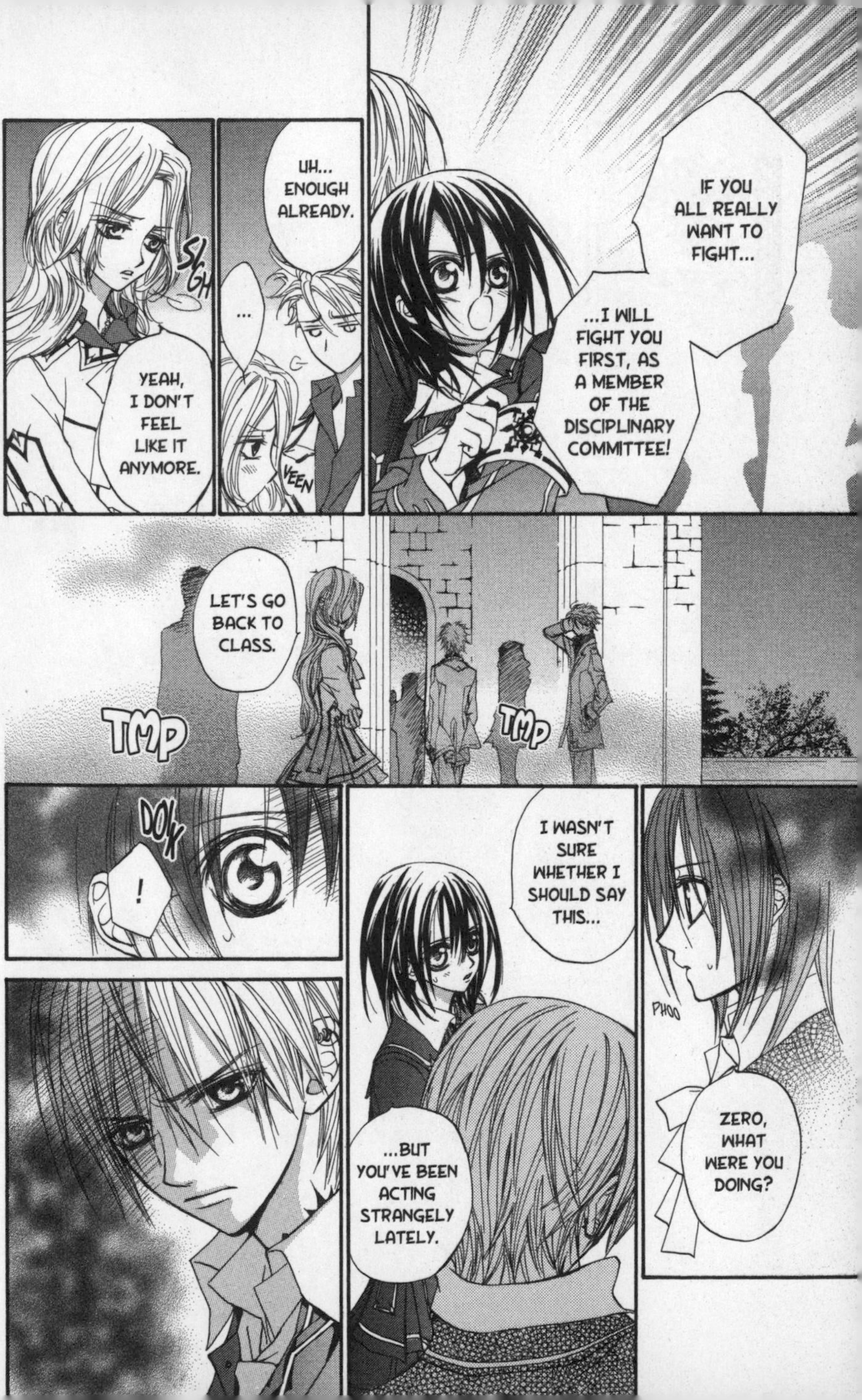
IF YOU ALL REALLY WANT TO FIGHT...
...I WILL FIGHT YOU FIRST, AS A MEMBER OF THE DISCIPLINARY COMMITTEE!
UH... ENOUGH ALREADY.
...
VEEN
SIGH
YEAH, I DON'T FEEL LIKE IT ANYMORE.
LET'S GO BACK TO CLASS.
TMP
TMP
PHOO
ZERO, WHAT WERE YOU DOING?
I WASN'T SURE WHETHER I SHOULD SAY THIS...
...BUT YOU'VE BEEN ACTING STRANGELY LATELY.
DOK
!

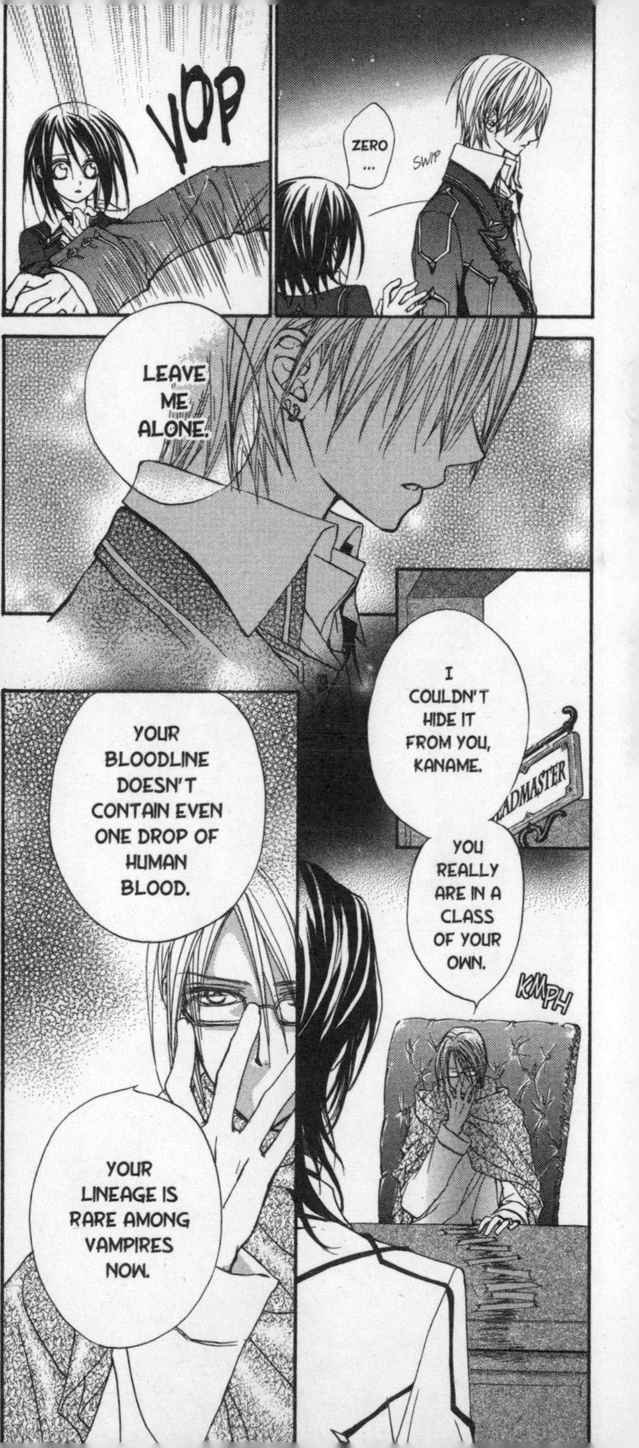
ZERO
...
SWIP
VOP
LEAVE ME ALONE.
I COULDN'T HIDE IT FROM YOU, KANAME.
HEADMASTER
YOU REALLY ARE IN A CLASS OF YOUR OWN.
KMPH
YOUR BLOODLINE DOESN'T CONTAIN EVEN ONE DROP OF HUMAN BLOOD.
YOUR LINEAGE IS RARE AMONG VAMPIRES NOW.

IV

And.
Regarding the characters' personalities, these were also fixed with Yuki first, then Kaname... With Zero, my editor and I worried and worried and made a big fuss, thinking, "If something isn't done, Kaname will overshadow Zero...!!!" (Kaname-sama, you're too scary. Please don't eat Zero any more than this...)

So Zero made me worry a lot, but because I tried very hard, he didn't turn out to be a weakling. It was good. Really.

Since Yuki is the heroine, I had her set from the beginning. But she still has many blanks to fill in, so I'm hoping (like an indulgent parent) that by filling in those blanks, she'll mature. Kaname...is filled as if there are no blanks left. Probably... (Probably?)

Vol. 1 is like a prologue of sorts, so the Night Class students, including Kaname, haven't really started to move yet (the Headmaster too...), but please look forward to it.

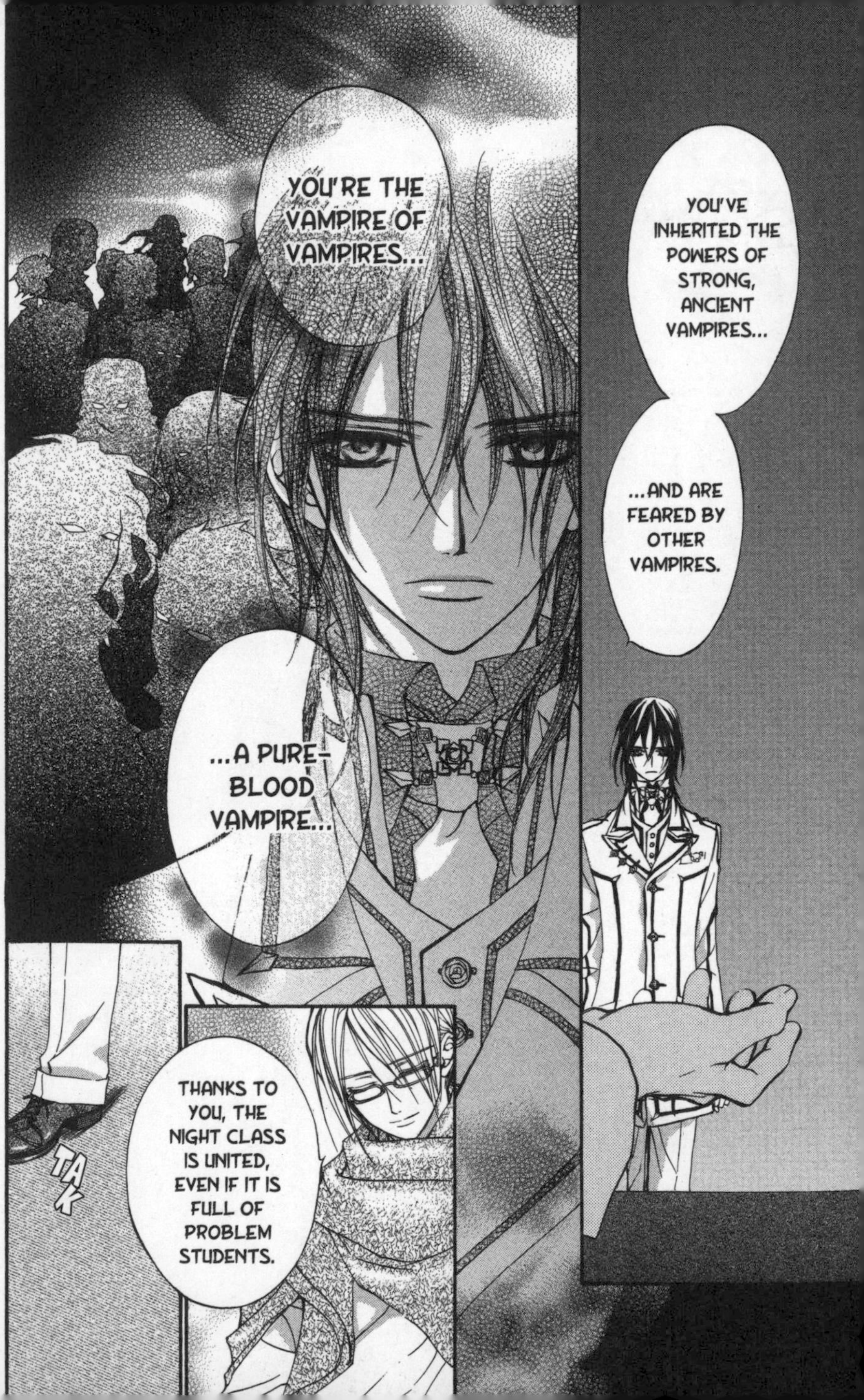
YOU'VE INHERITED THE POWERS OF STRONG, ANCIENT VAMPIRES...
...AND ARE FEARED BY OTHER VAMPIRES.
YOU'RE THE VAMPIRE OF VAMPIRES...
...A PURE-BLOOD VAMPIRE...
THANKS TO YOU, THE NIGHT CLASS IS UNITED, EVEN IF IT IS FULL OF PROBLEM STUDENTS.
TAK

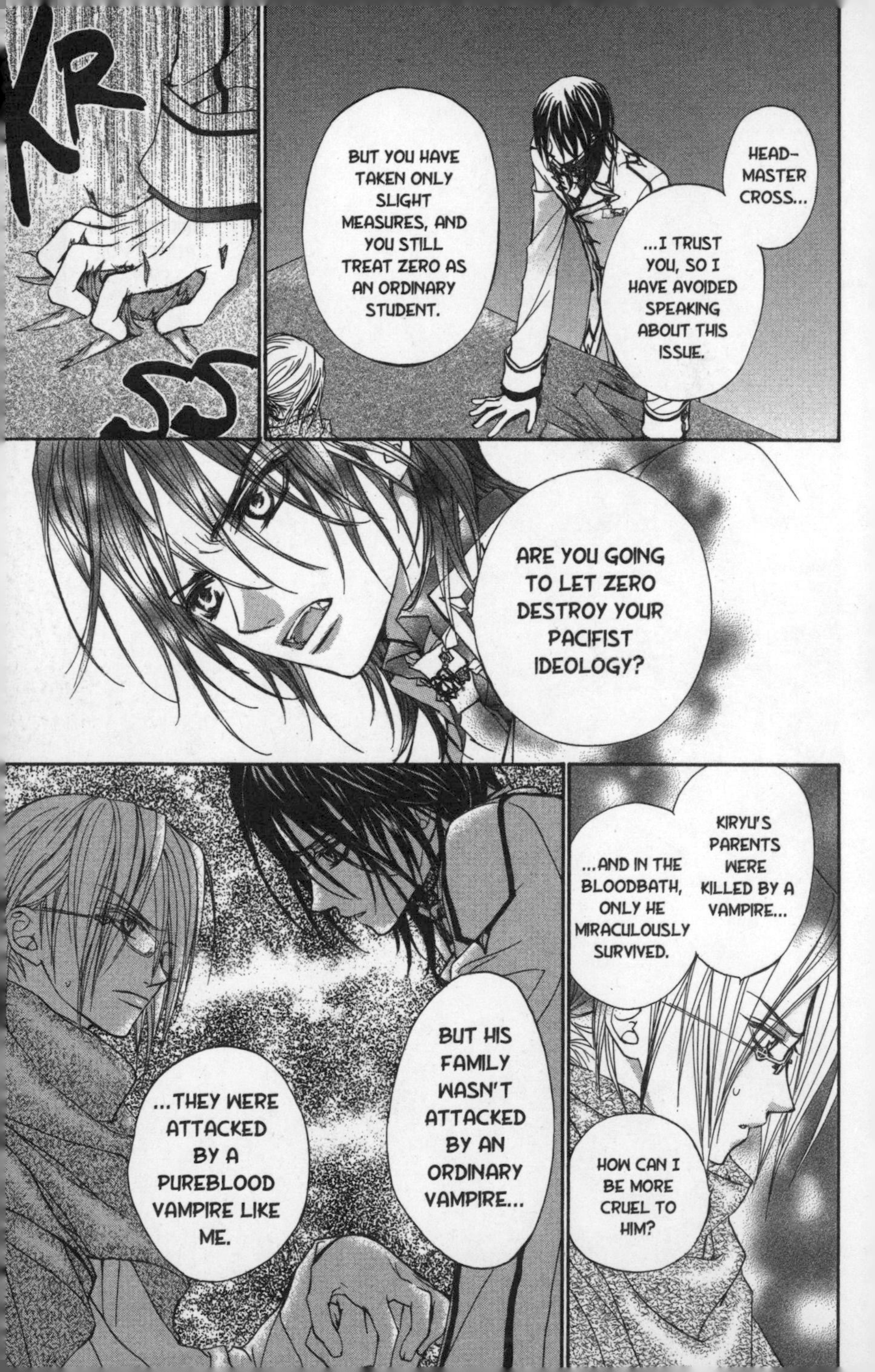
HEAD-MASTER CROSS...
...I TRUST YOU, SO I HAVE AVOIDED SPEAKING ABOUT THIS ISSUE.
BUT YOU HAVE TAKEN ONLY SLIGHT MEASURES, AND YOU STILL TREAT ZERO AS AN ORDINARY STUDENT.
KR
ARE YOU GOING TO LET ZERO DESTROY YOUR PACIFIST IDEOLOGY?
KIRYU'S PARENTS WERE KILLED BY A VAMPIRE...
...AND IN THE BLOODBATH, ONLY HE MIRACULOUSLY SURVIVED.
HOW CAN I BE MORE CRUEL TO HIM?
BUT HIS FAMILY WASN'T ATTACKED BY AN ORDINARY VAMPIRE...
...THEY WERE ATTACKED BY A PUREBLOOD VAMPIRE LIKE ME.

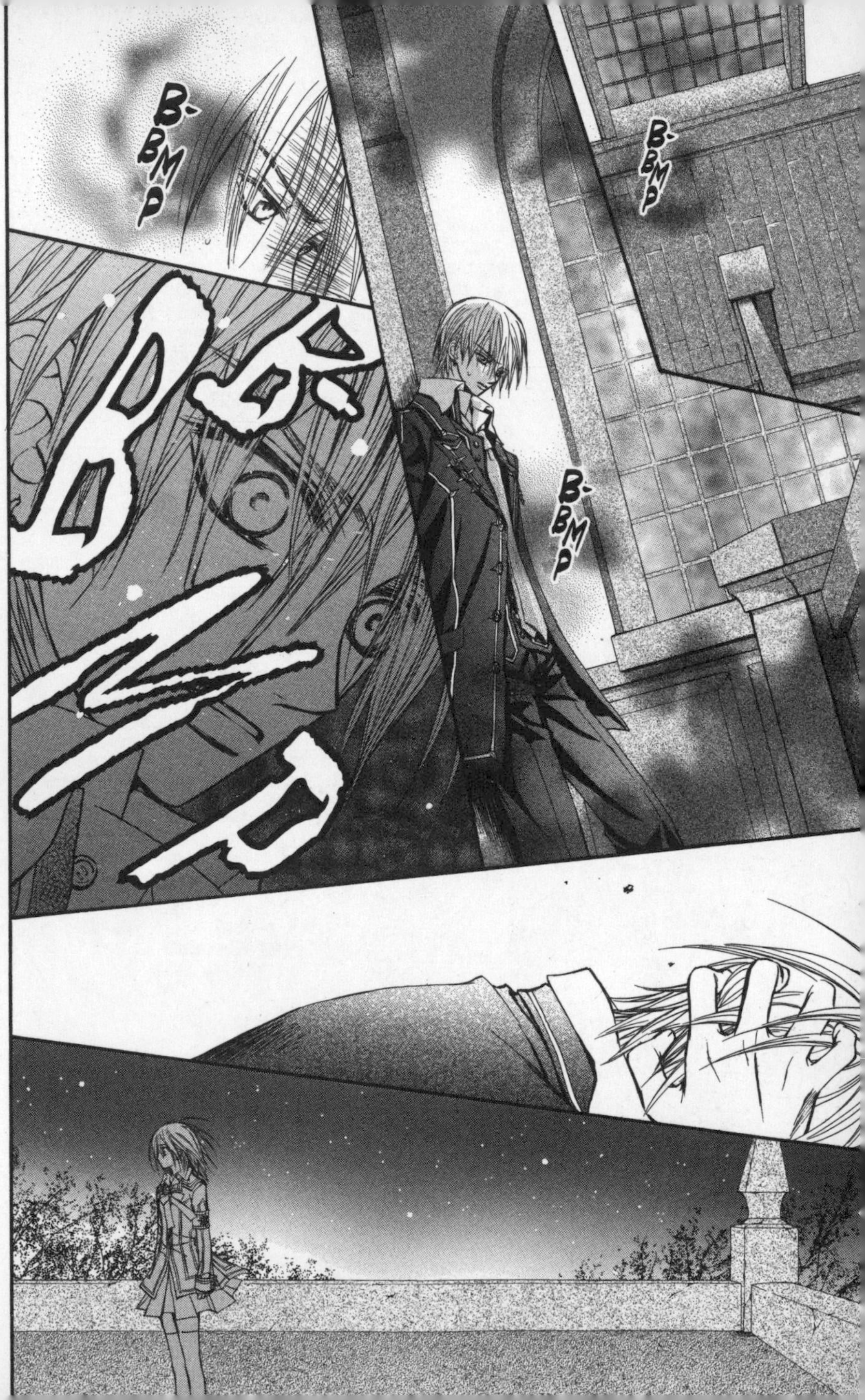
B-BMP
B-BMP
B-BMP
B-BMP

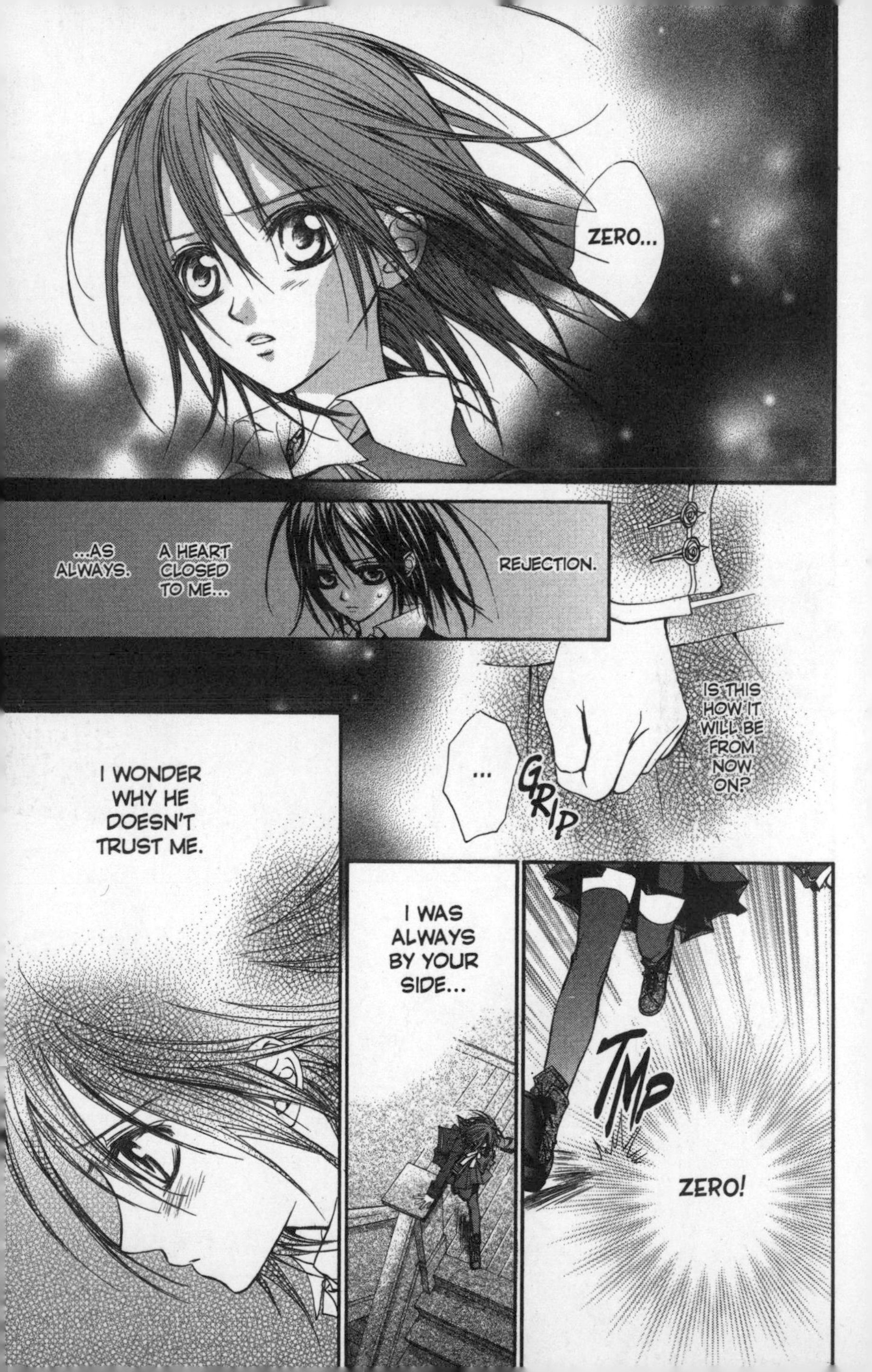
ZERO...
REJECTION.
A HEART CLOSED TO ME...
...AS ALWAYS.
IS THIS HOW IT WILL BE FROM NOW ON?
...
GRIP
TMP
ZERO!
I WAS ALWAYS BY YOUR SIDE...
I WONDER WHY HE DOESN'T TRUST ME.

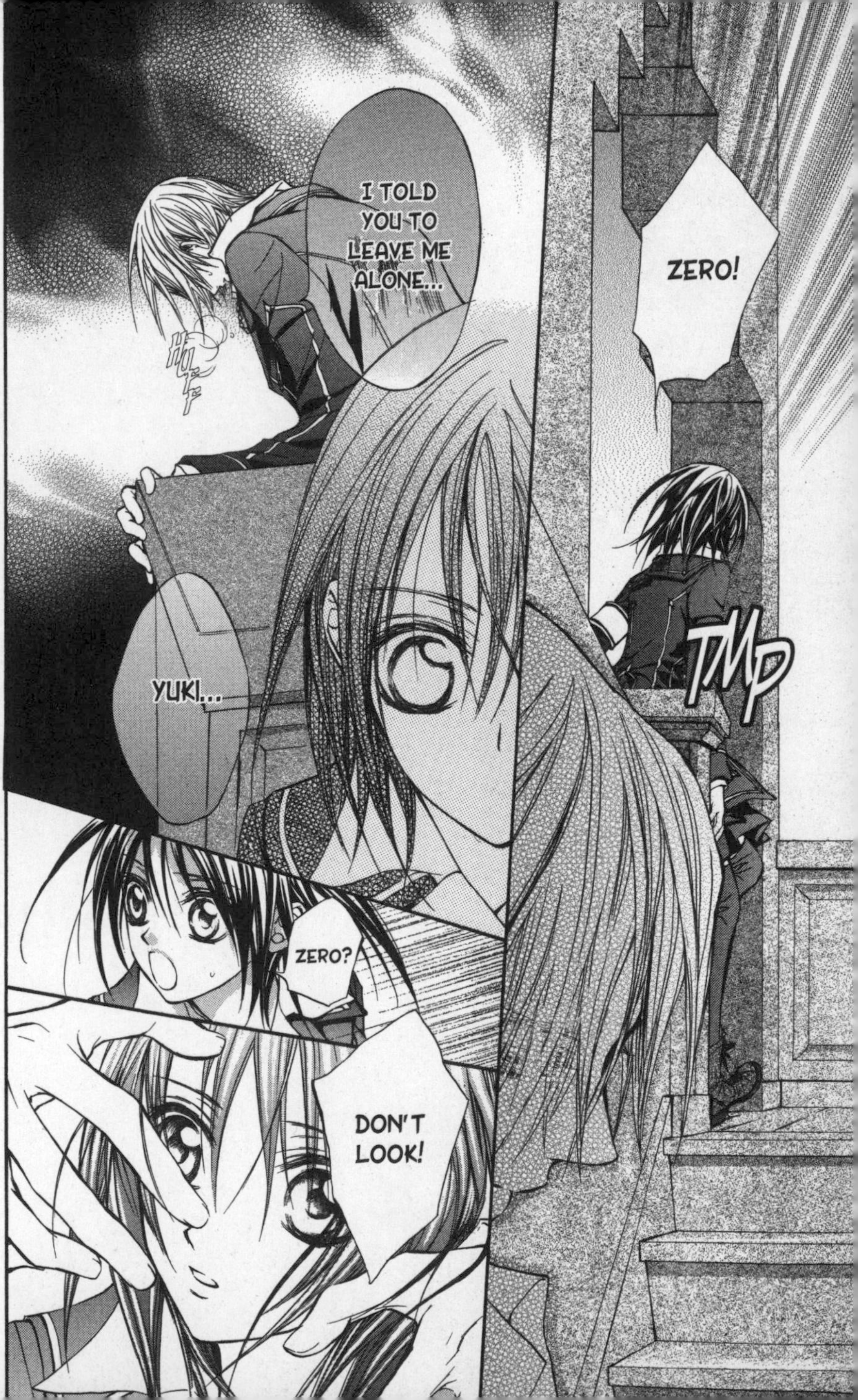
ZERO!
TMP
I TOLD YOU TO LEAVE ME ALONE...
HUFF
YUKI...
ZERO?
DON'T LOOK!

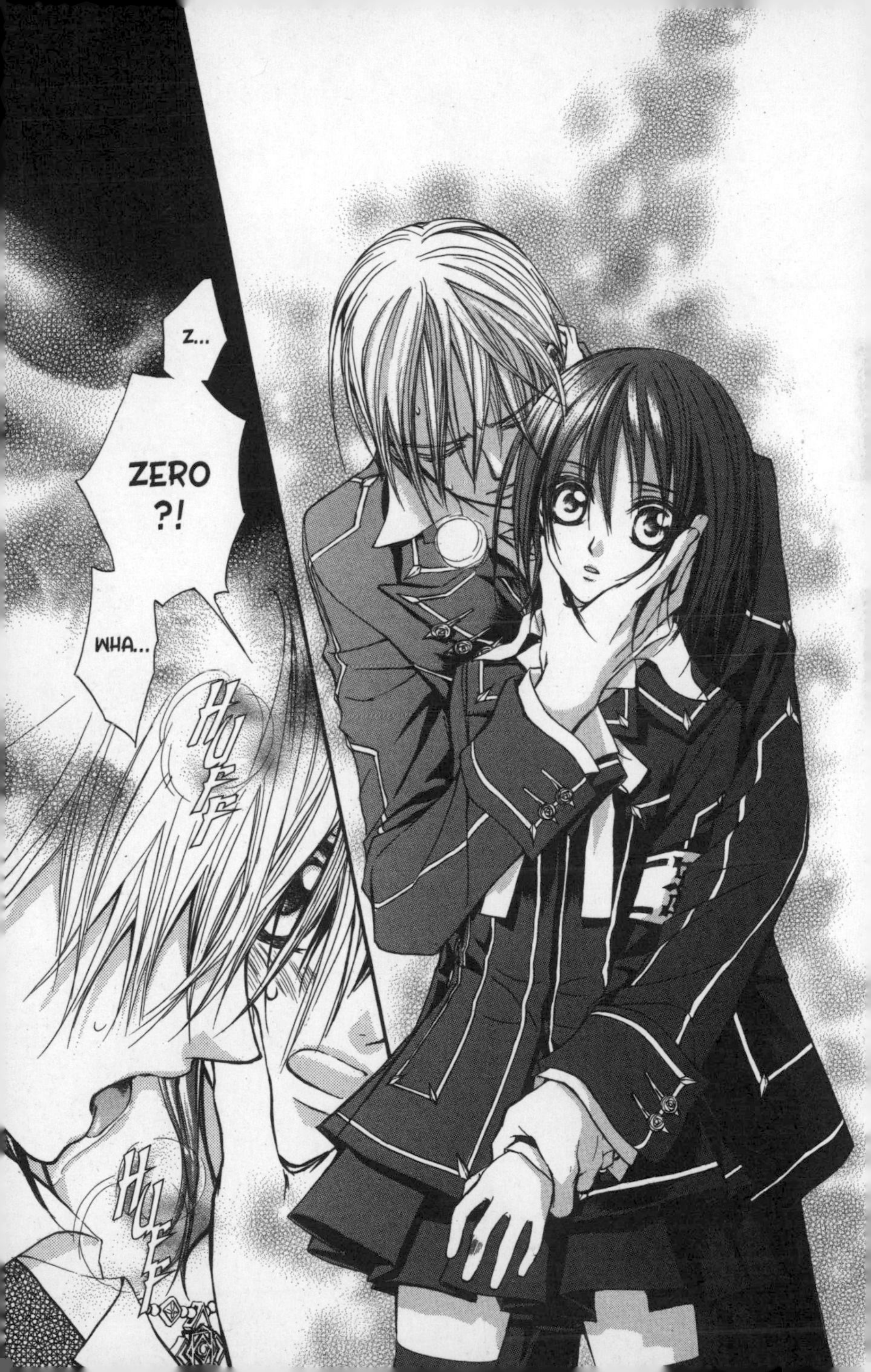
Z...
ZERO ?!
WHA...
HUFF
HUFF

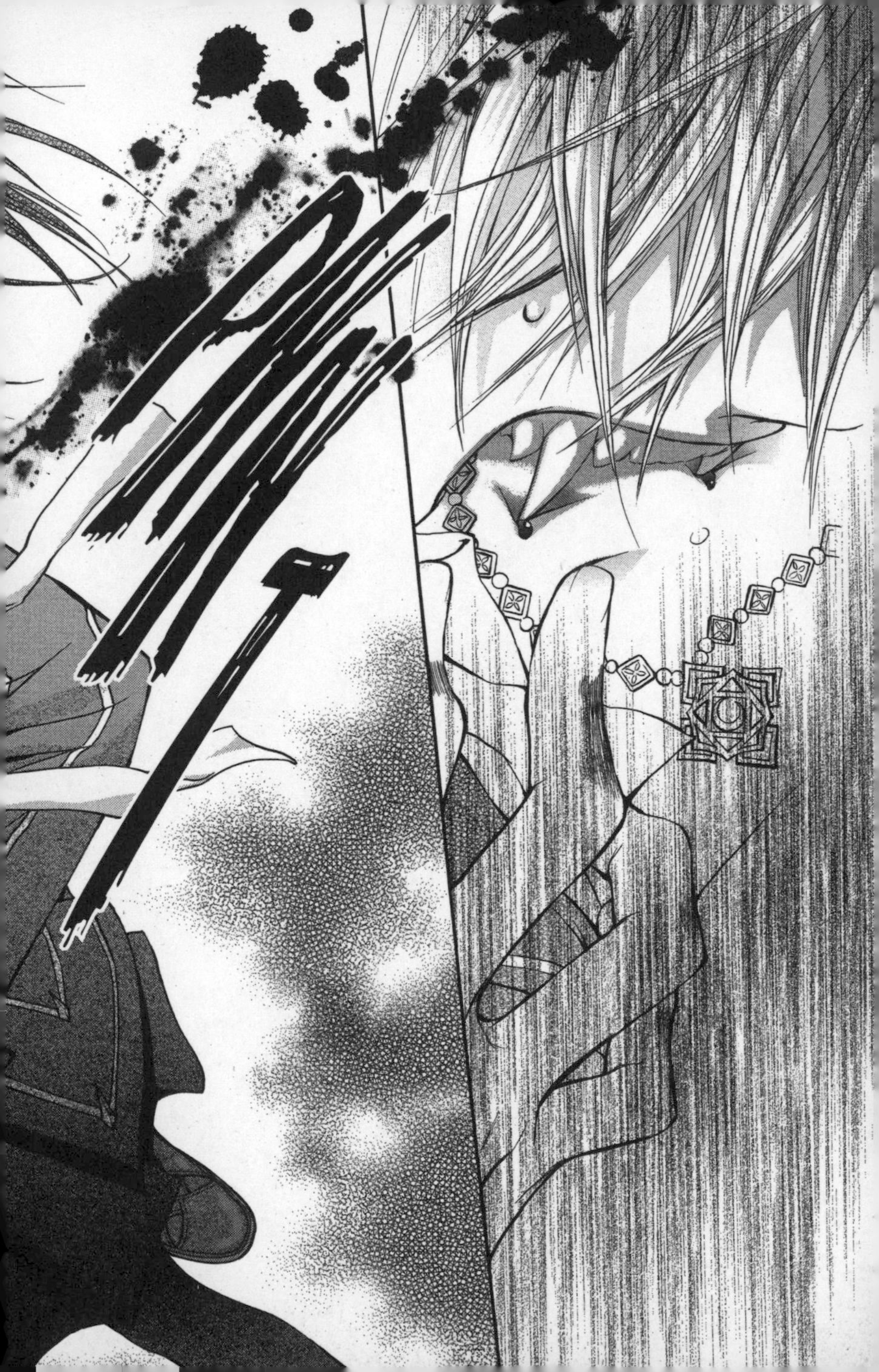

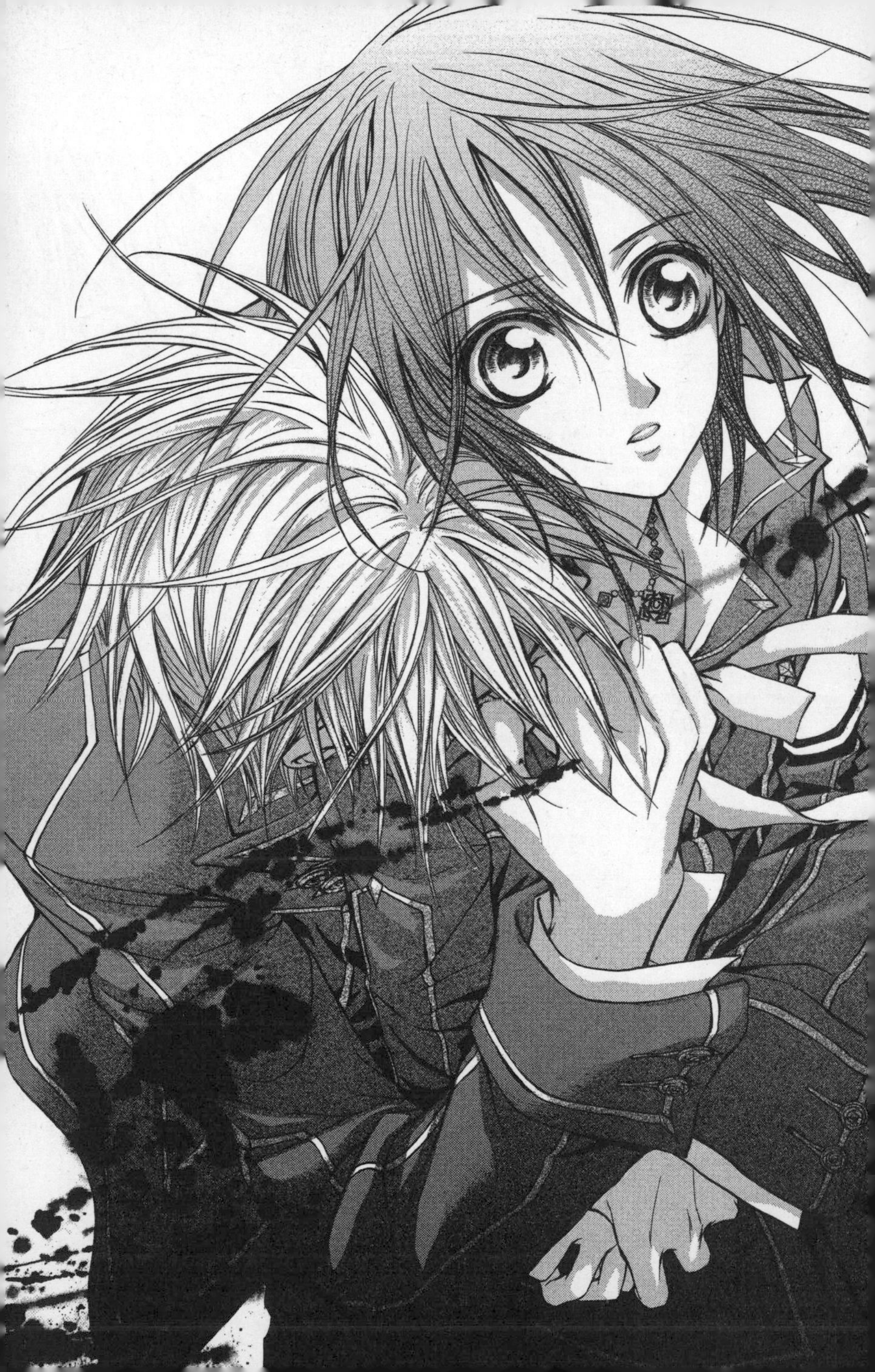

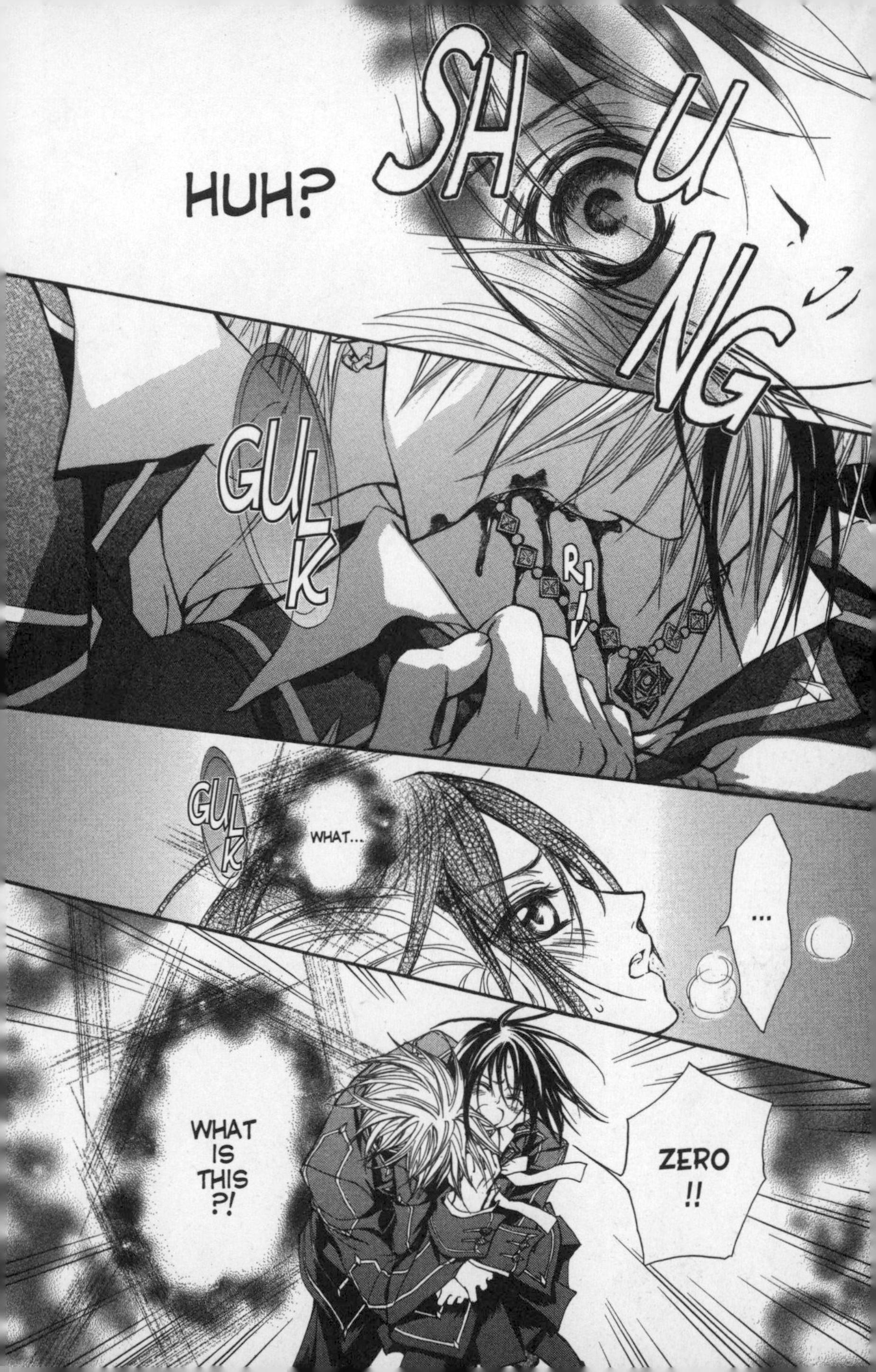
SHUNG
HUH?
GULK
RIP
GULK
...
WHAT...
ZERO!!
WHAT IS THIS?!

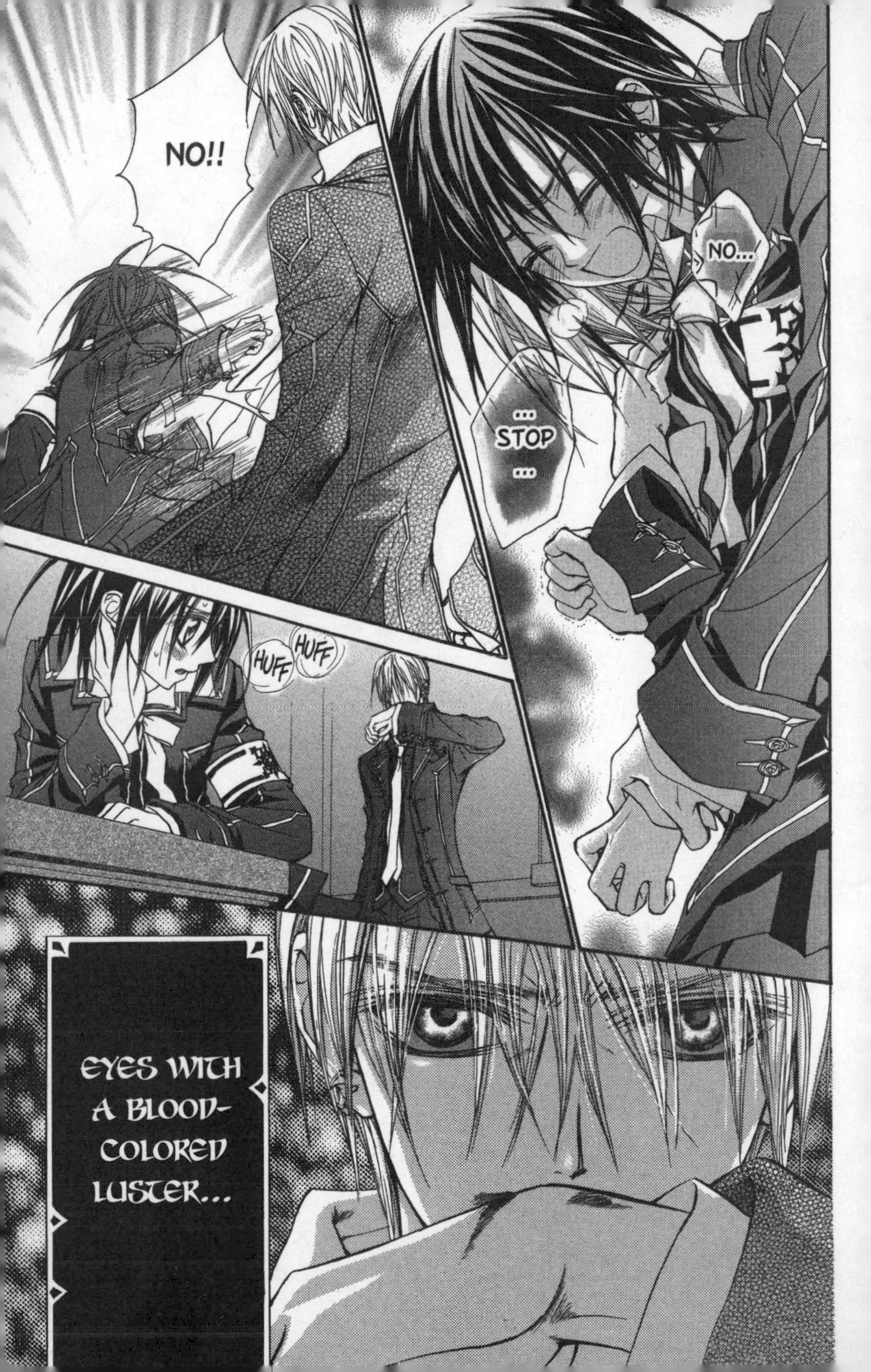
NO...
...
STOP
...
NO!!
HUFF
HUFF
EYES WITH A BLOOD-COLORED LUSTER...

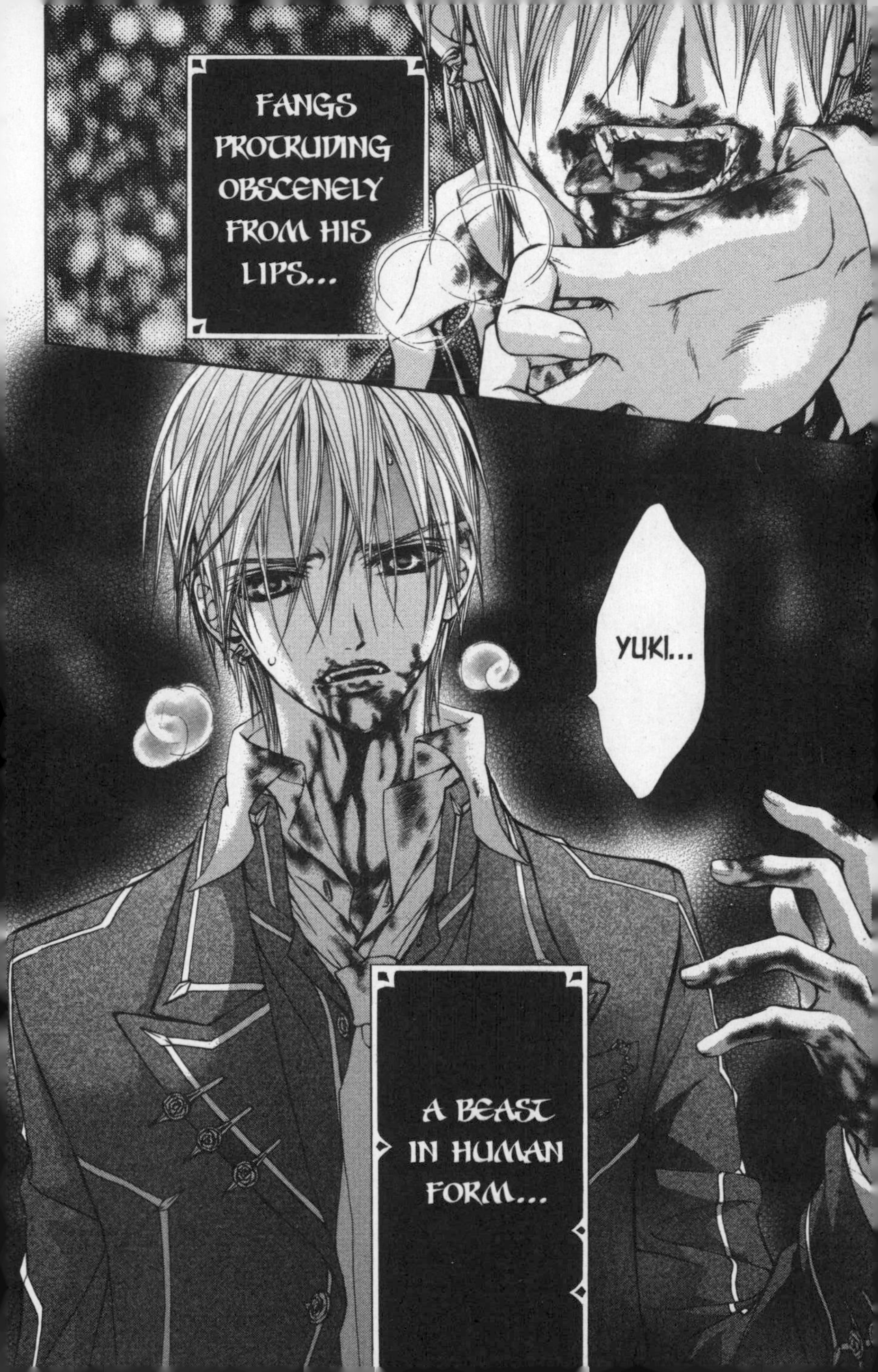
FANGS PROTRUDING OBSCENELY FROM HIS LIPS...
YUKI...
A BEAST IN HUMAN FORM...

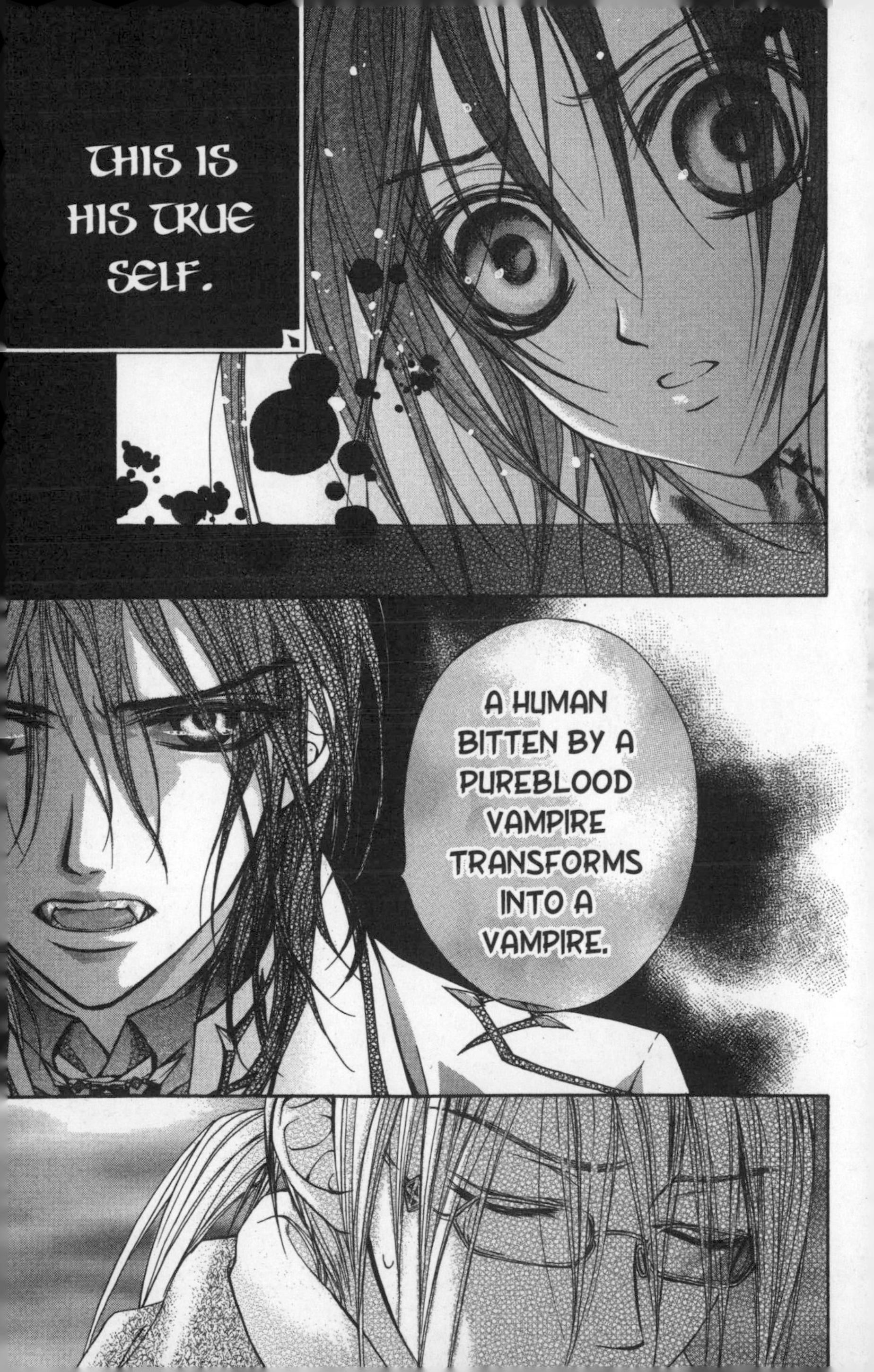
THIS IS HIS TRUE SELF.
A HUMAN BITTEN BY A PUREBLOOD VAMPIRE TRANSFORMS INTO A VAMPIRE.

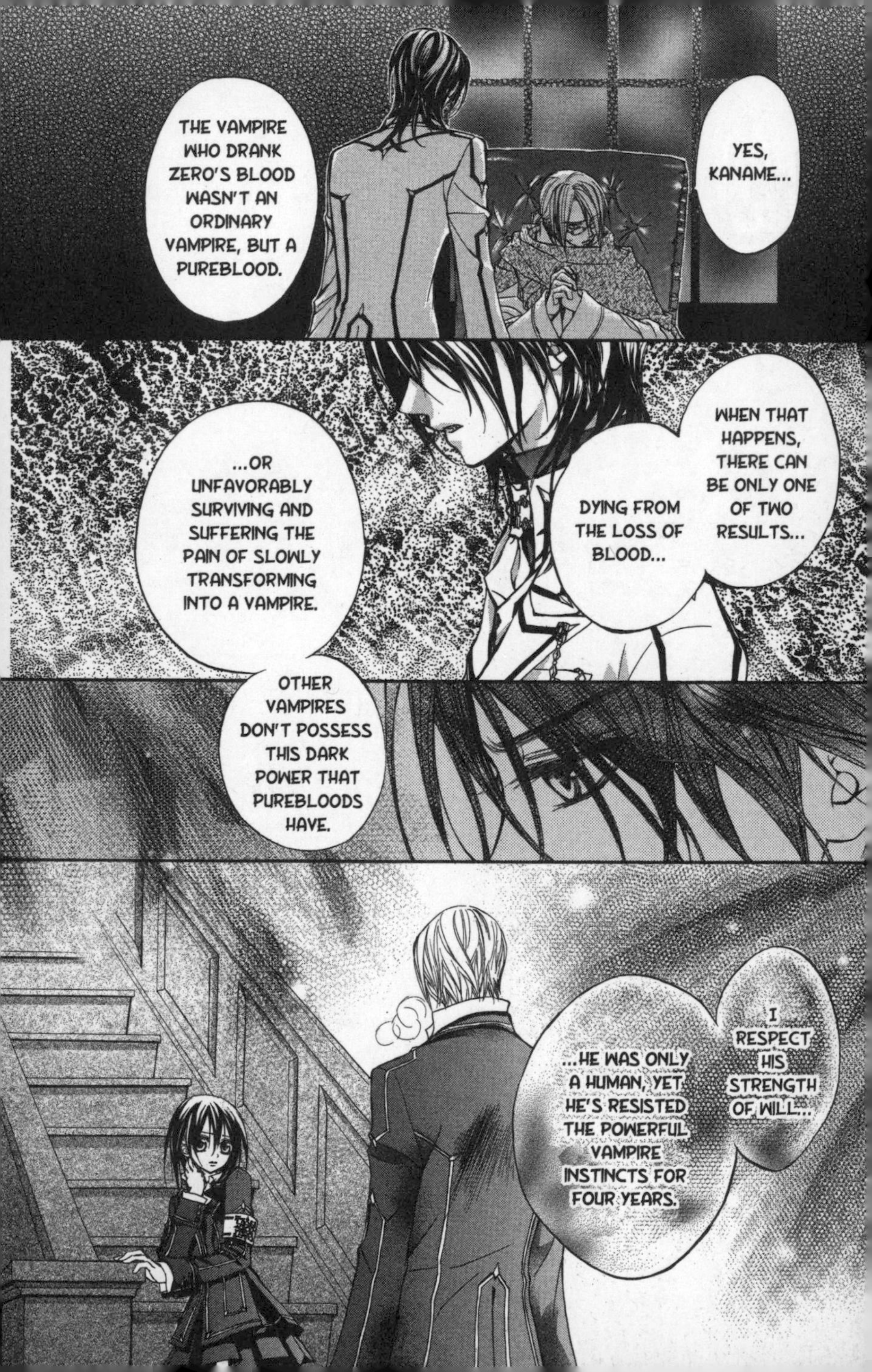
YES, KANAME...
THE VAMPIRE WHO DRANK ZERO'S BLOOD WASN'T AN ORDINARY VAMPIRE, BUT A PUREBLOOD.
WHEN THAT HAPPENS, THERE CAN BE ONLY ONE OF TWO RESULTS...
DYING FROM THE LOSS OF BLOOD...
...OR UNFAVORABLY SURVIVING AND SUFFERING THE PAIN OF SLOWLY TRANSFORMING INTO A VAMPIRE.
OTHER VAMPIRES DON'T POSSESS THIS DARK POWER THAT PUREBLOODS HAVE.
I RESPECT HIS STRENGTH OF WILL...
...HE WAS ONLY A HUMAN, YET HE'S RESISTED THE POWERFUL VAMPIRE INSTINCTS FOR FOUR YEARS.

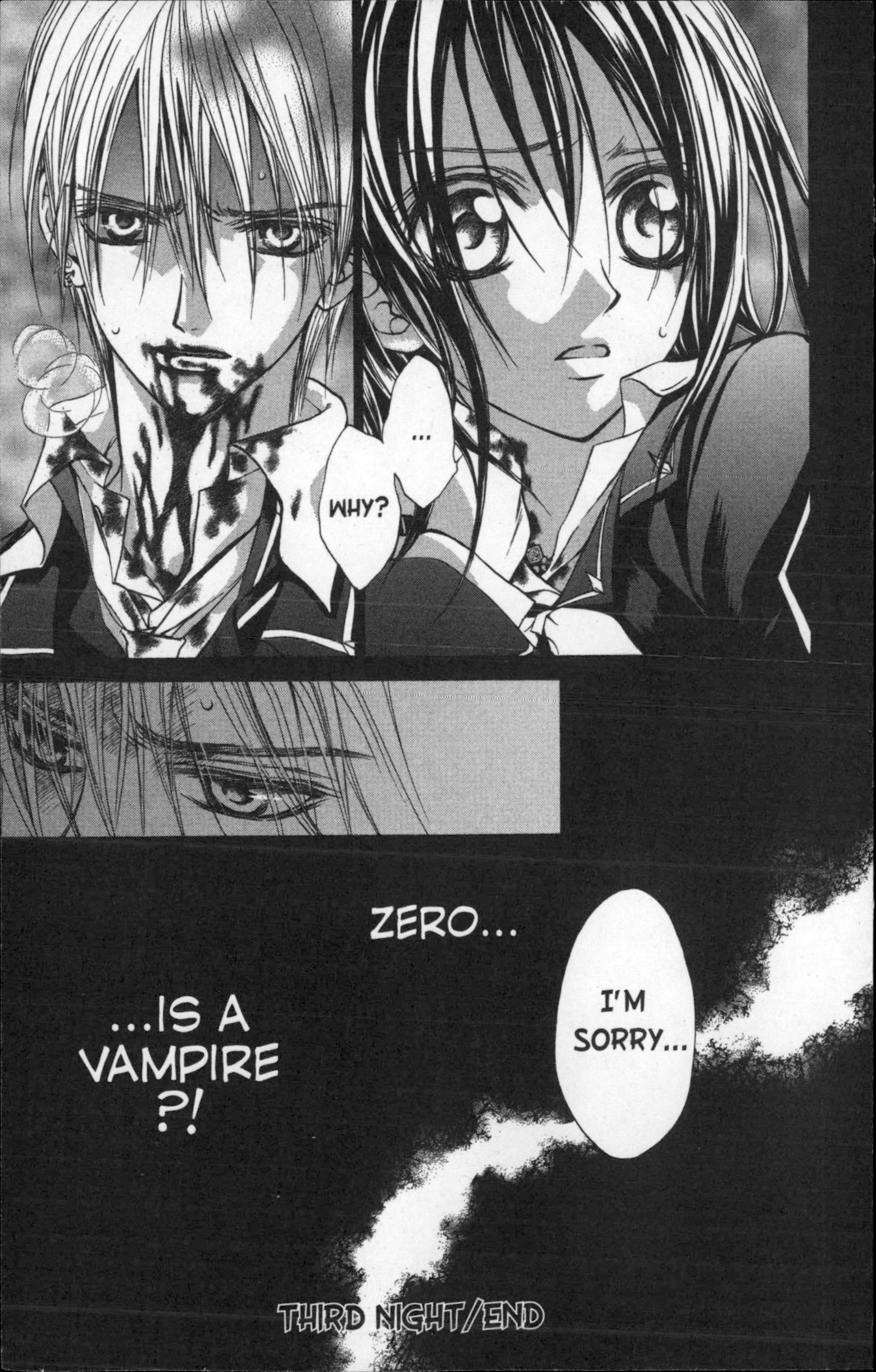
...
WHY?
I'M SORRY...
ZERO...
...IS A VAMPIRE ?!
THIRD NIGHT/END

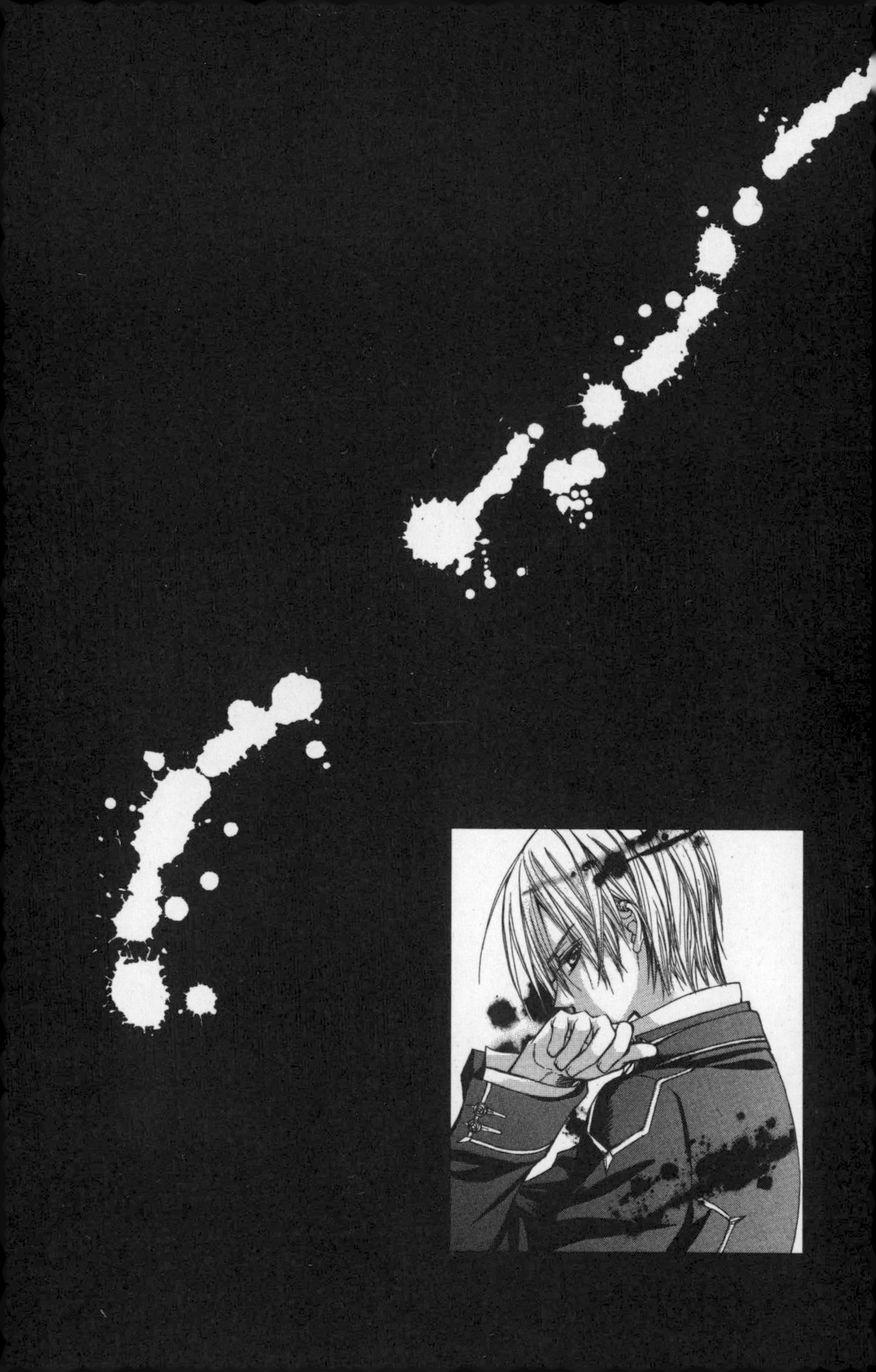

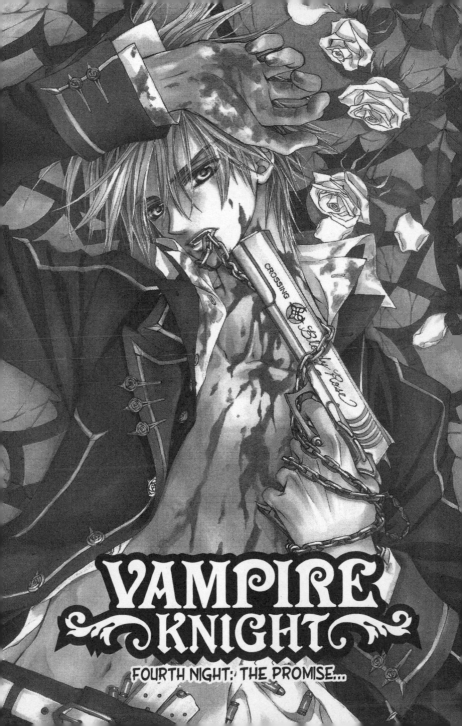

# VAMPIRE KNIGHT

### FOURTH NIGHT: THE PROMISE...

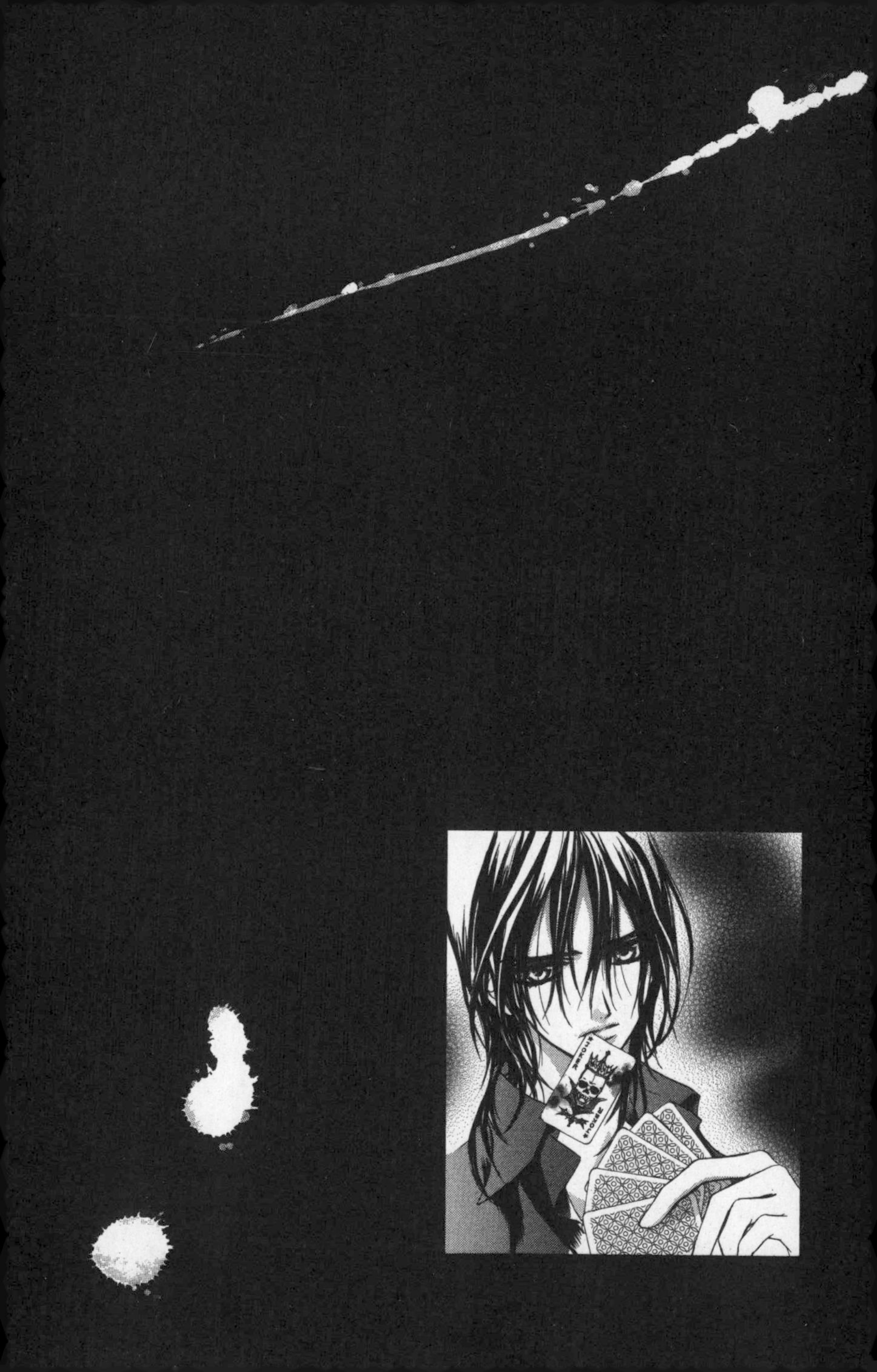

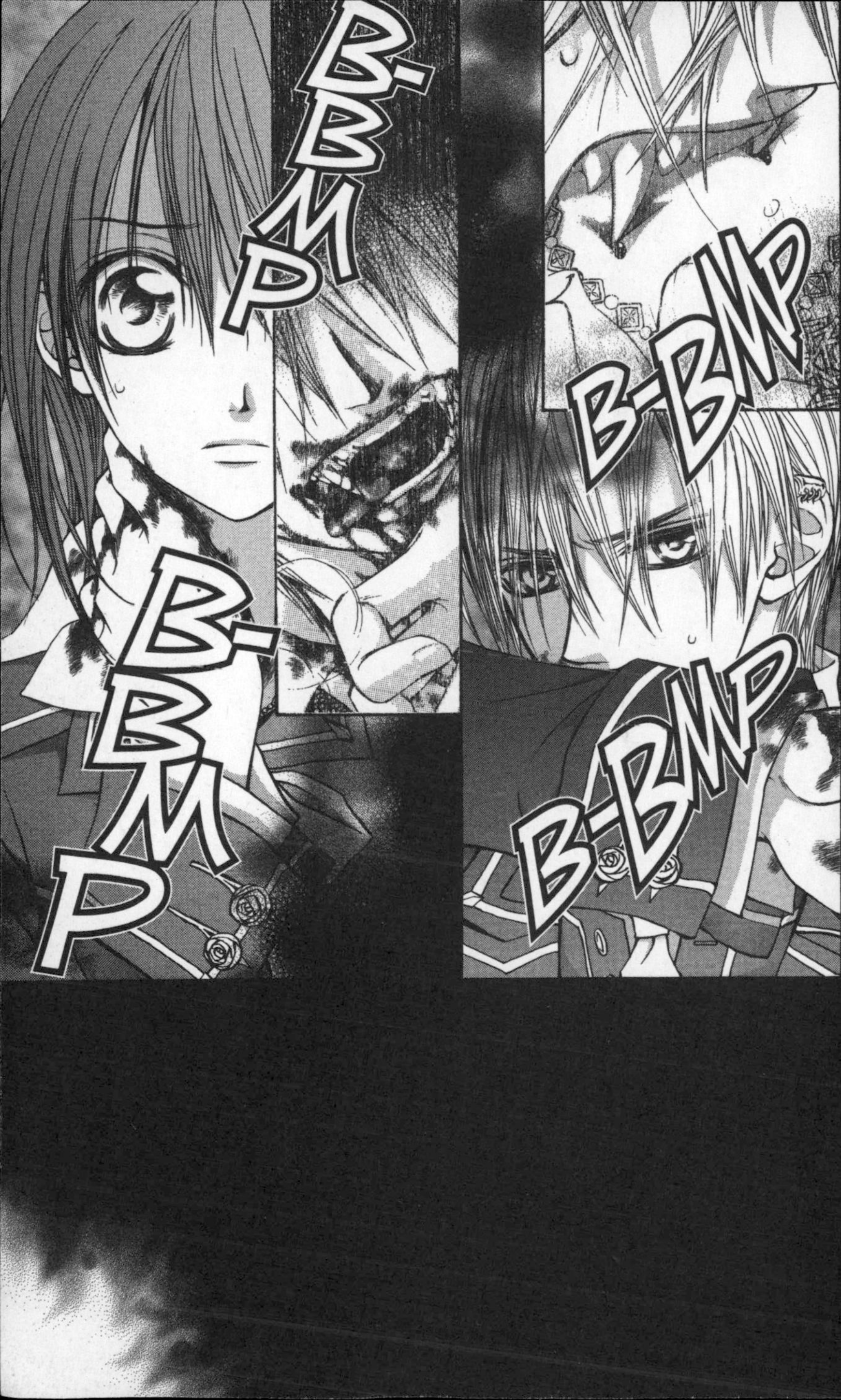

B-BMP
B-BMP
B-BMP
B-BMP

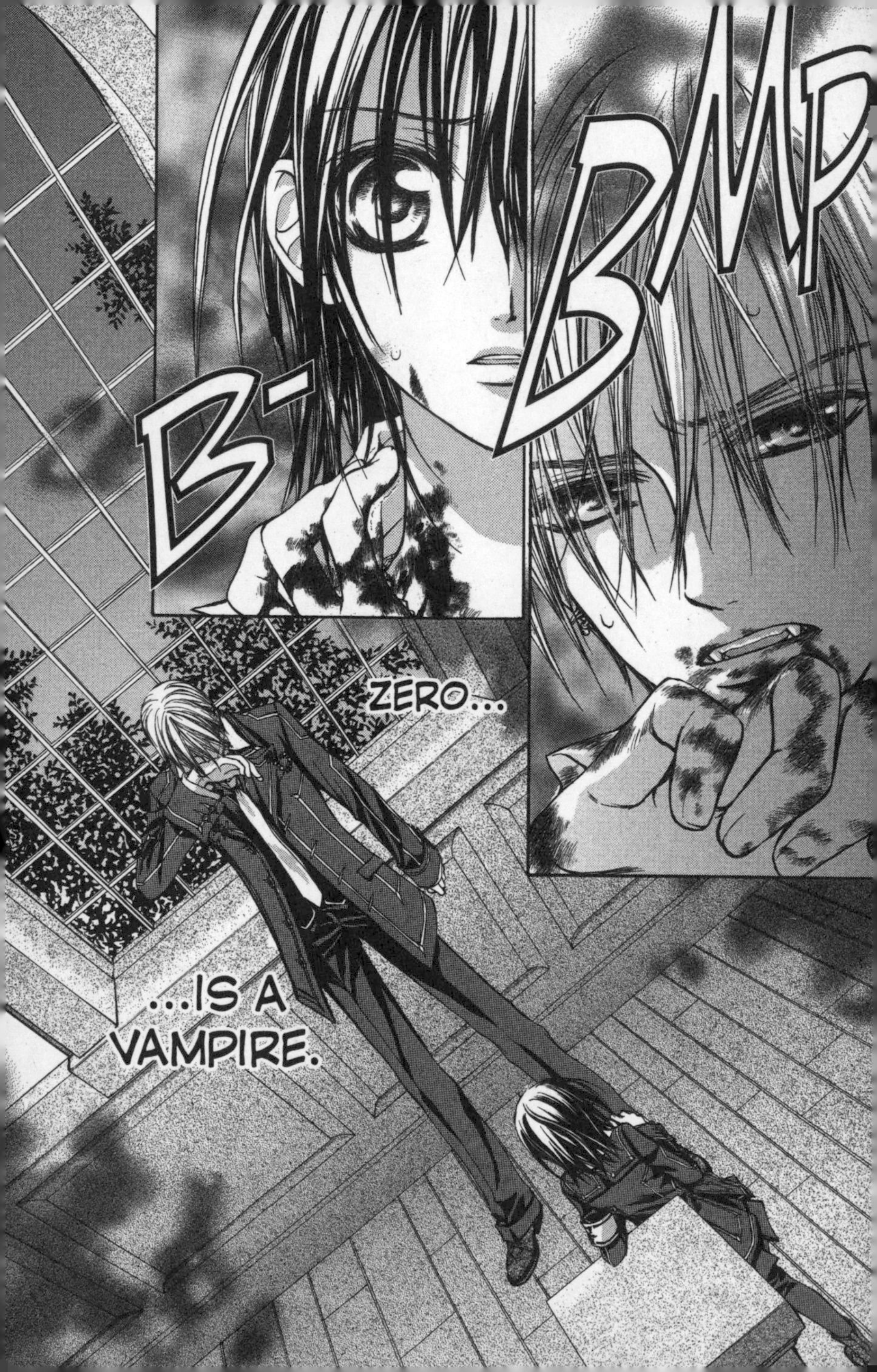
B-BMP
ZERO...
...IS A VAMPIRE.

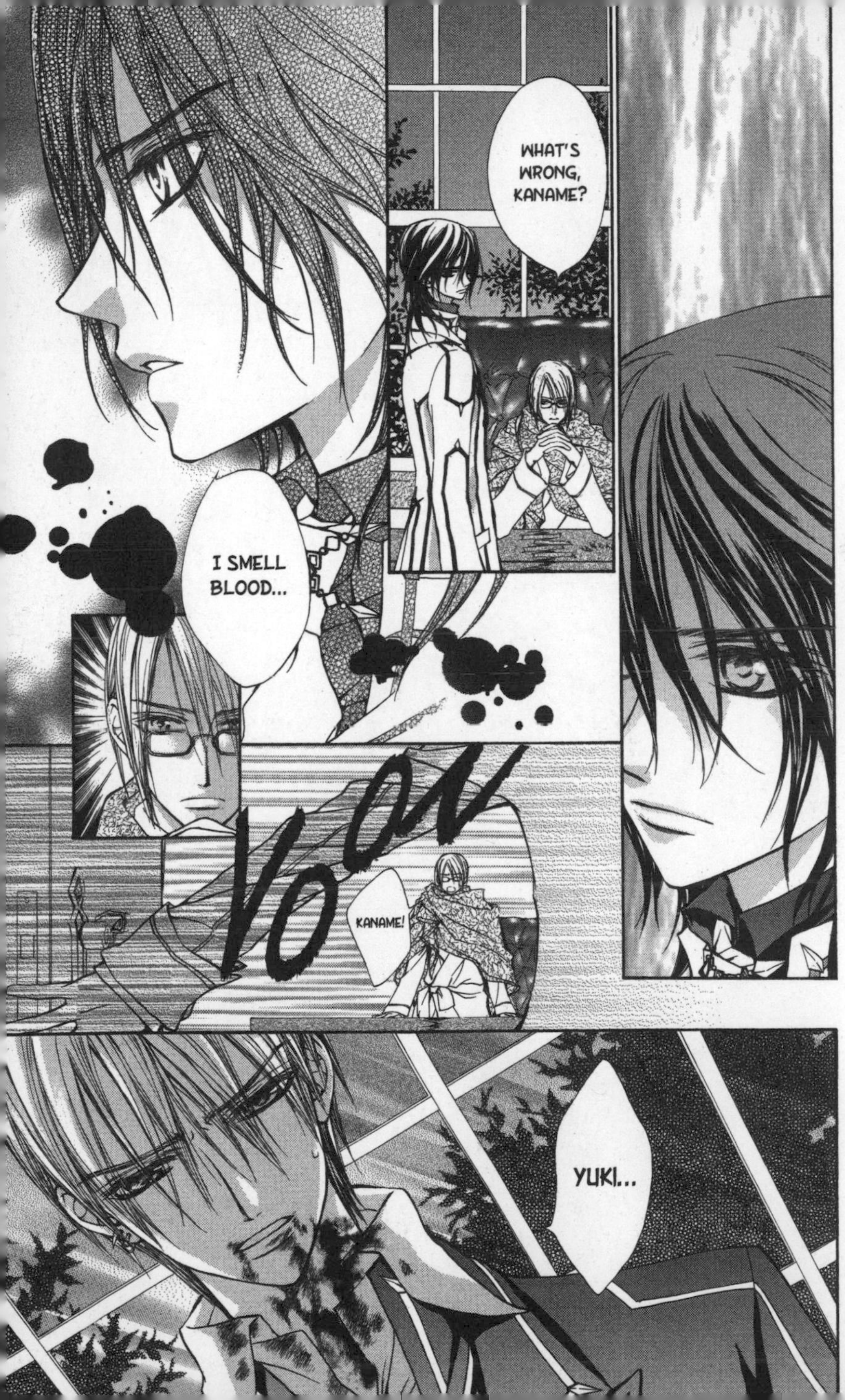
WHAT'S WRONG, KANAME?
I SMELL BLOOD...
VOOM
KANAME!
YUKI...

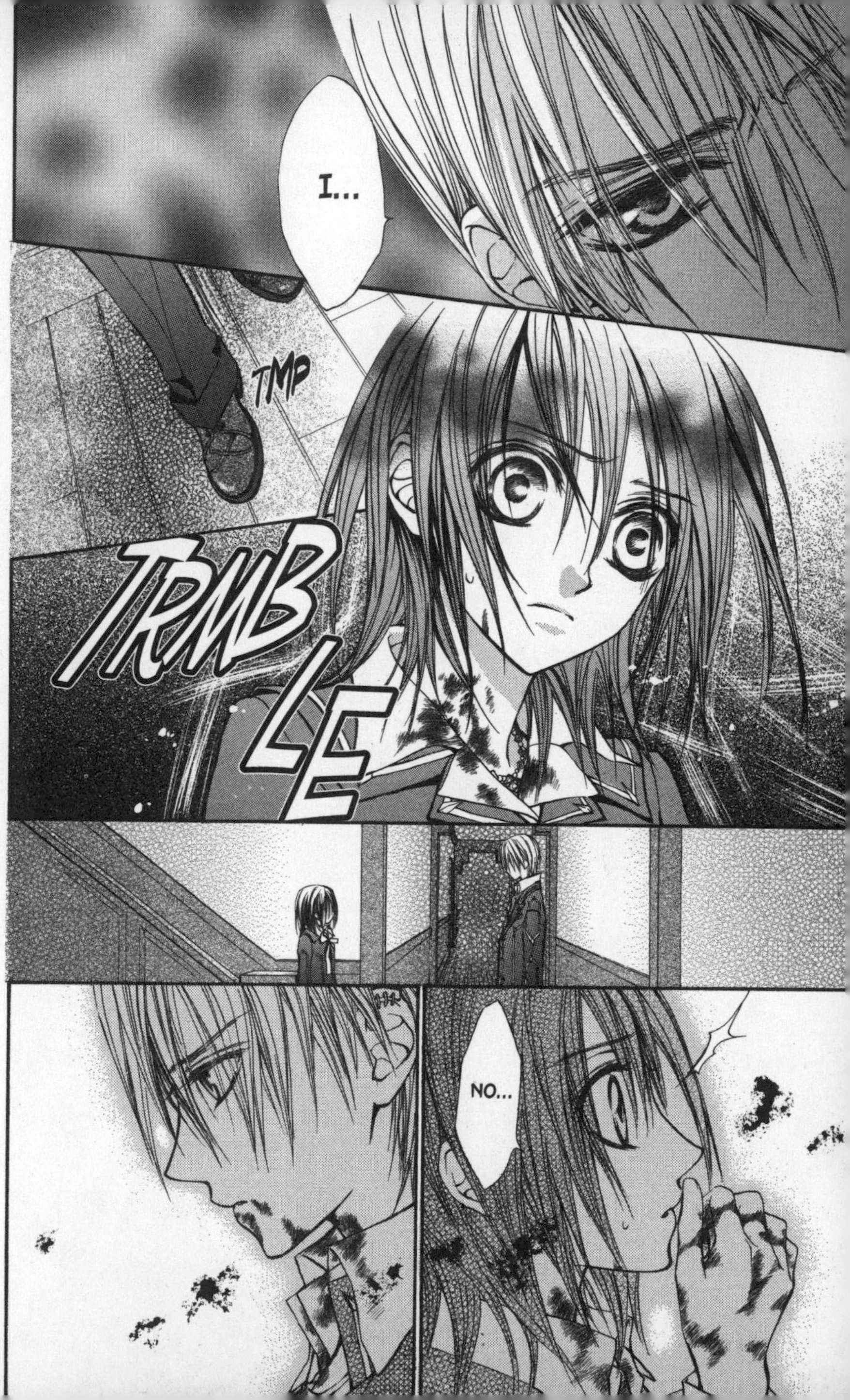
I...
TMP
TRMBLE
NO...

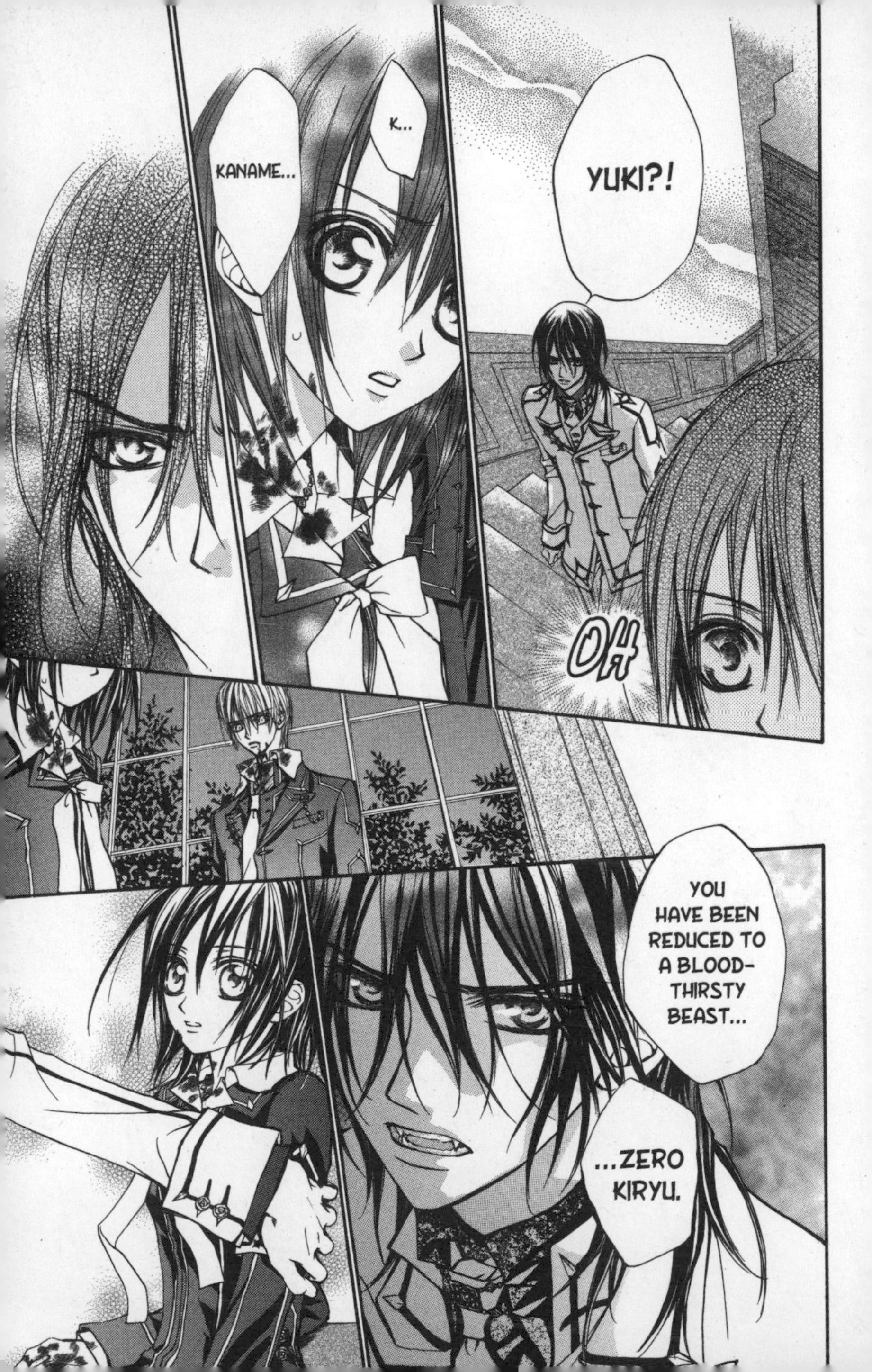
YUKI?!
OH
K...
KANAME...
YOU HAVE BEEN REDUCED TO A BLOOD-THIRSTY BEAST...
...ZERO KIRYU.

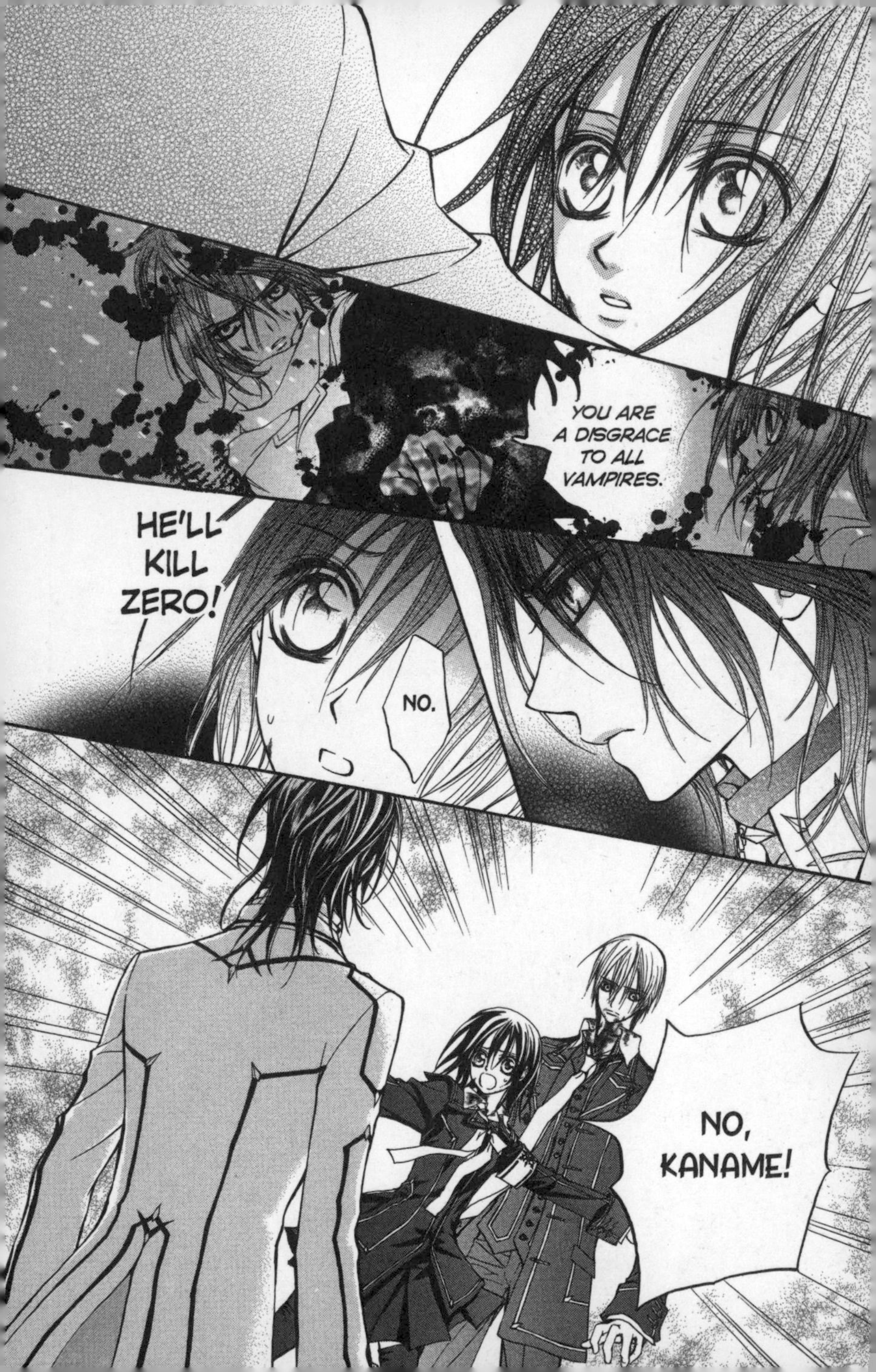
YOU ARE A DISGRACE TO ALL VAMPIRES.
HE'LL KILL ZERO!
NO.
NO, KANAME!

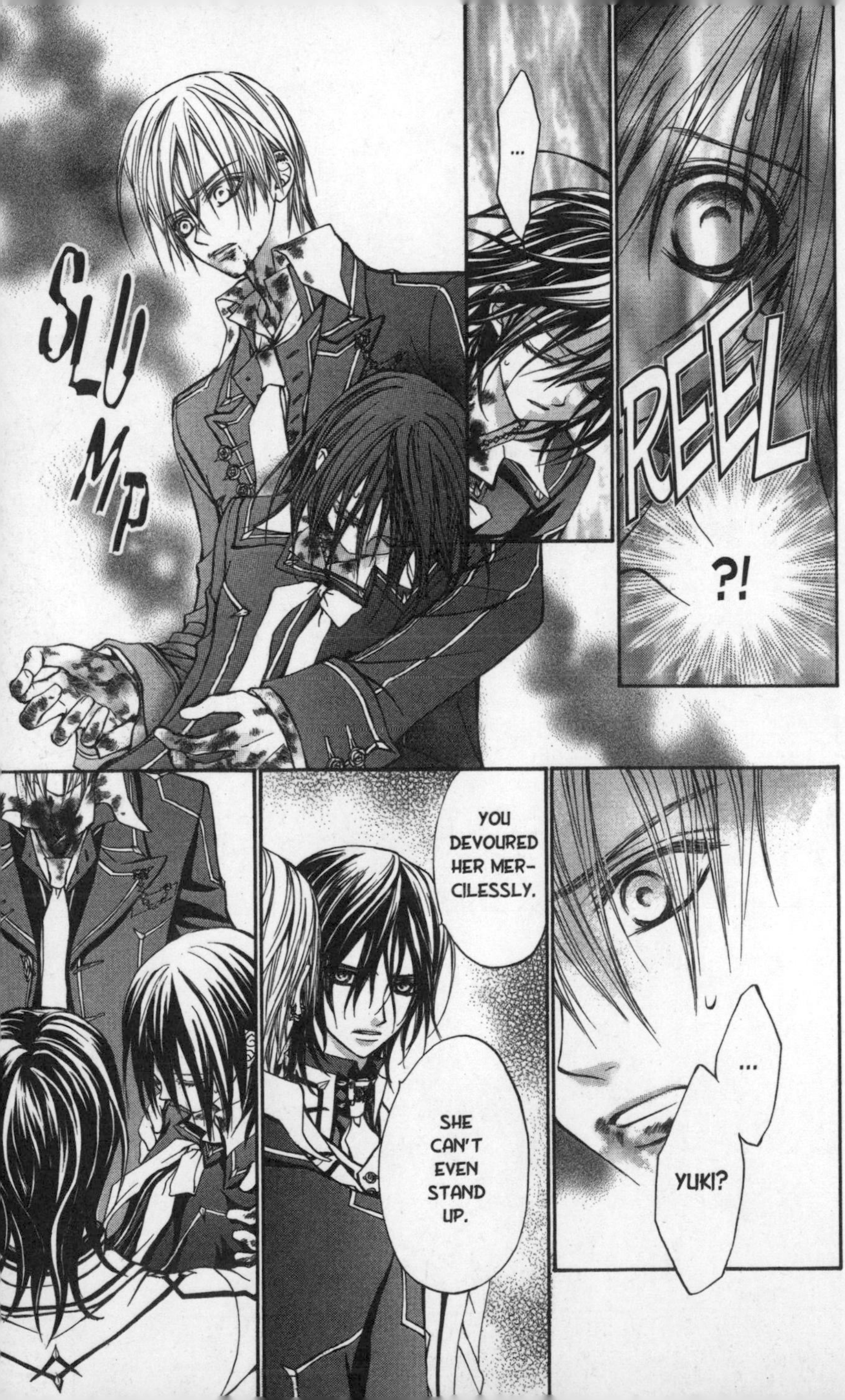
REEL
?!
...
SLUMP
...
YUKI?
YOU DEVOURED HER MERCILESSLY.
SHE CAN'T EVEN STAND UP.

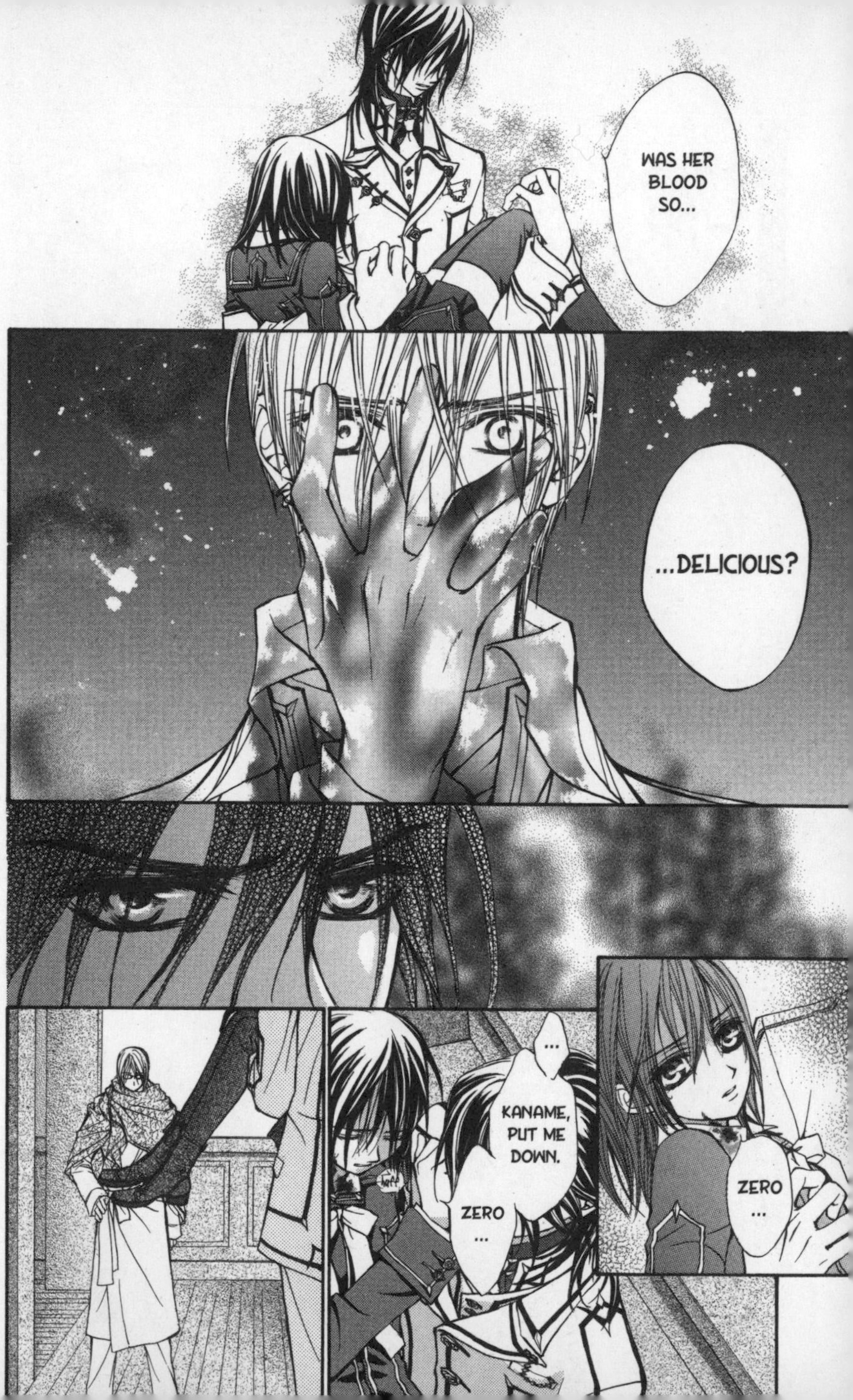
WAS HER BLOOD SO...
...DELICIOUS?
ZERO ...
...
KANAME, PUT ME DOWN.
huff
ZERO ...

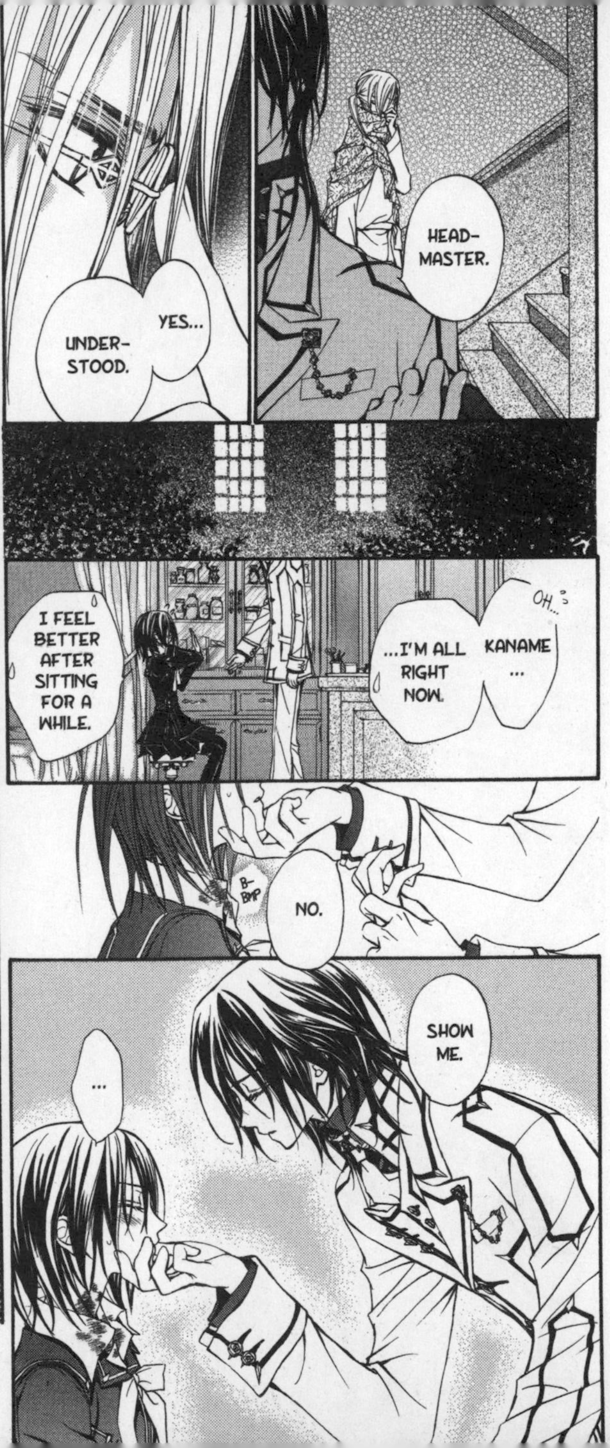
HEAD-MASTER.
YES...
UNDER-STOOD.
OH...
KANAME ...
...I'M ALL RIGHT NOW.
I FEEL BETTER AFTER SITTING FOR A WHILE.
NO.
B-BMP
SHOW ME.
...

**V**

I included the *LaLa* cover illustration for the January 2005 issue and the two-page spread in this volume. There's an image of Yuki, Zero, and Kaname, but because I wanted to unify the color scheme, I made them wear Day Class uniforms in one image, and then Night Class uniforms in the spread. Because Zero wore a white uniform once, and because Zero turned out that way, some readers thought, "Will he go to the Night Class?!" Hee hee. If that happened, Zero would be in real trouble... I feel like I want to draw extra manga for "if x happened." You must check out the extra pages in volume 2 and on, maybe?!

I've drawn extra stuff in this volume too, so please check it out.

About the colors of the uniform... At first I was going to make the Day Class uniforms white, and the Night Class uniforms black. This is because I was simply thinking vampires=black. Then I thought, "Aren't uniforms usually black?" "Shouldn't elites wear white?" So it changed. It's good it wasn't the opposite, because I believe the current colors suit the characters.

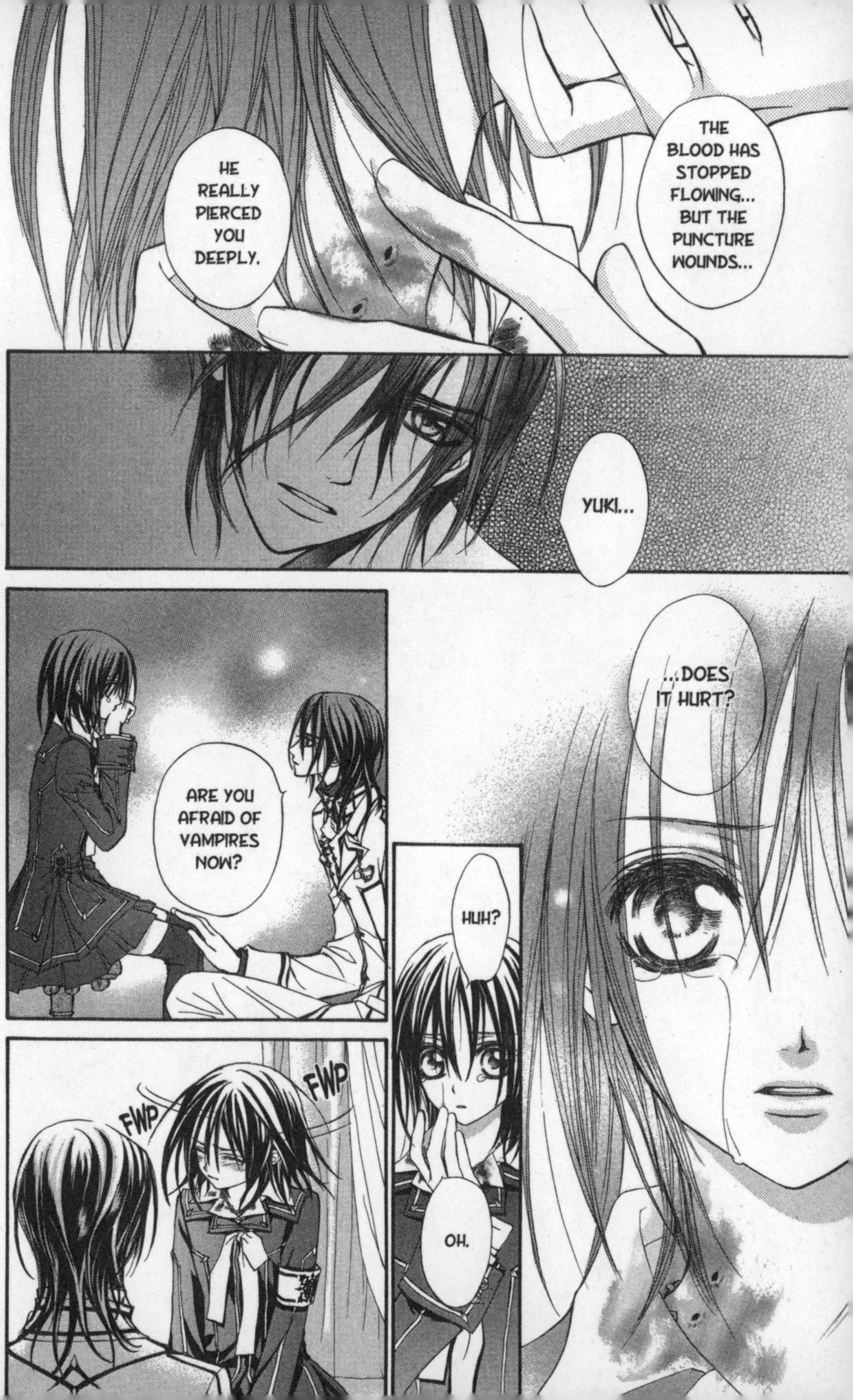
THE BLOOD HAS STOPPED FLOWING... BUT THE PUNCTURE WOUNDS...
HE REALLY PIERCED YOU DEEPLY.
YUKI...
...DOES IT HURT?
ARE YOU AFRAID OF VAMPIRES NOW?
HUH?
OH.
FWP
FWP

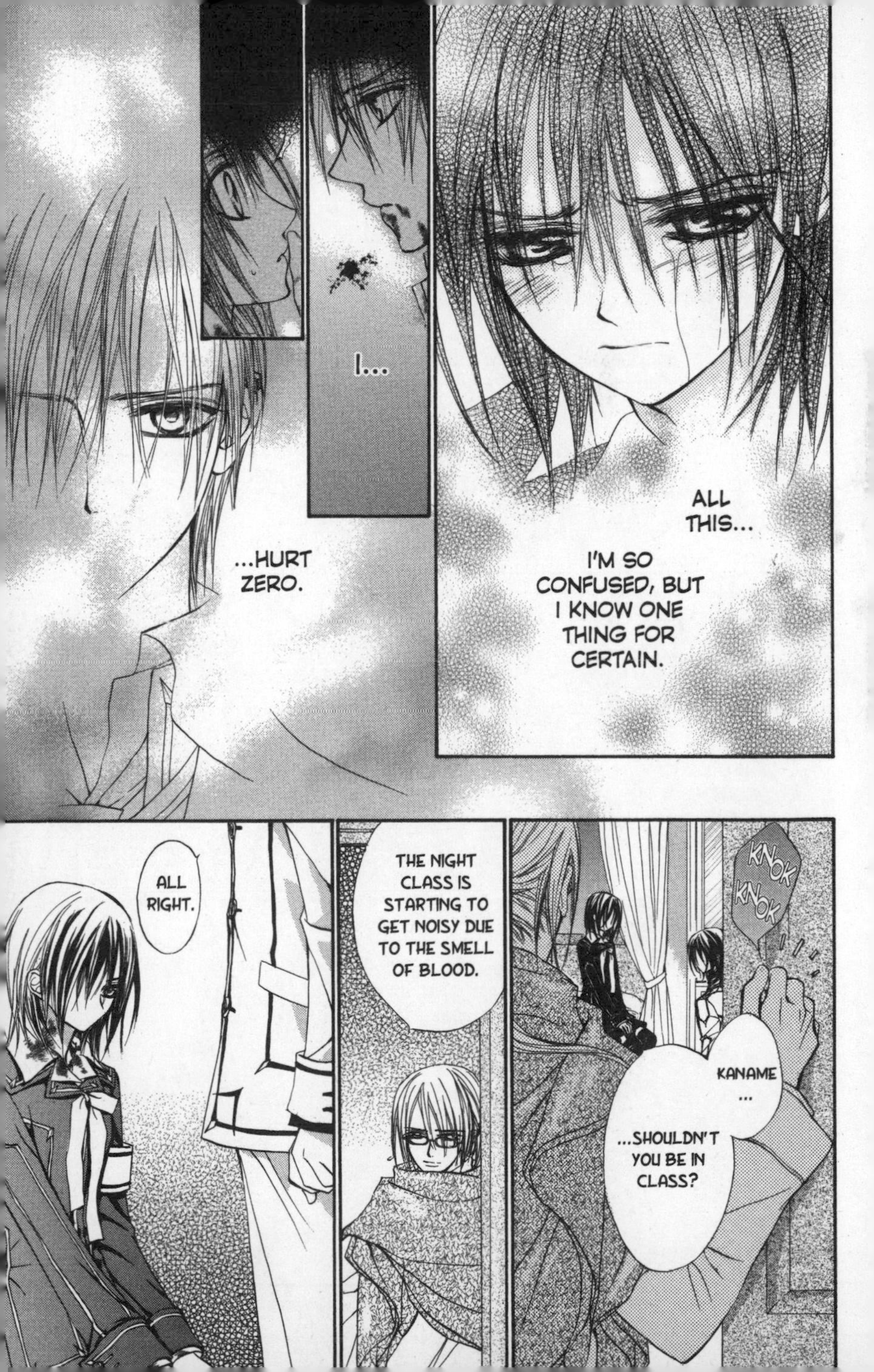
ALL THIS...
I'M SO CONFUSED, BUT I KNOW ONE THING FOR CERTAIN.
I...
...HURT ZERO.
KNOK KNOK
KANAME ...
...SHOULDN'T YOU BE IN CLASS?
THE NIGHT CLASS IS STARTING TO GET NOISY DUE TO THE SMELL OF BLOOD.
ALL RIGHT.

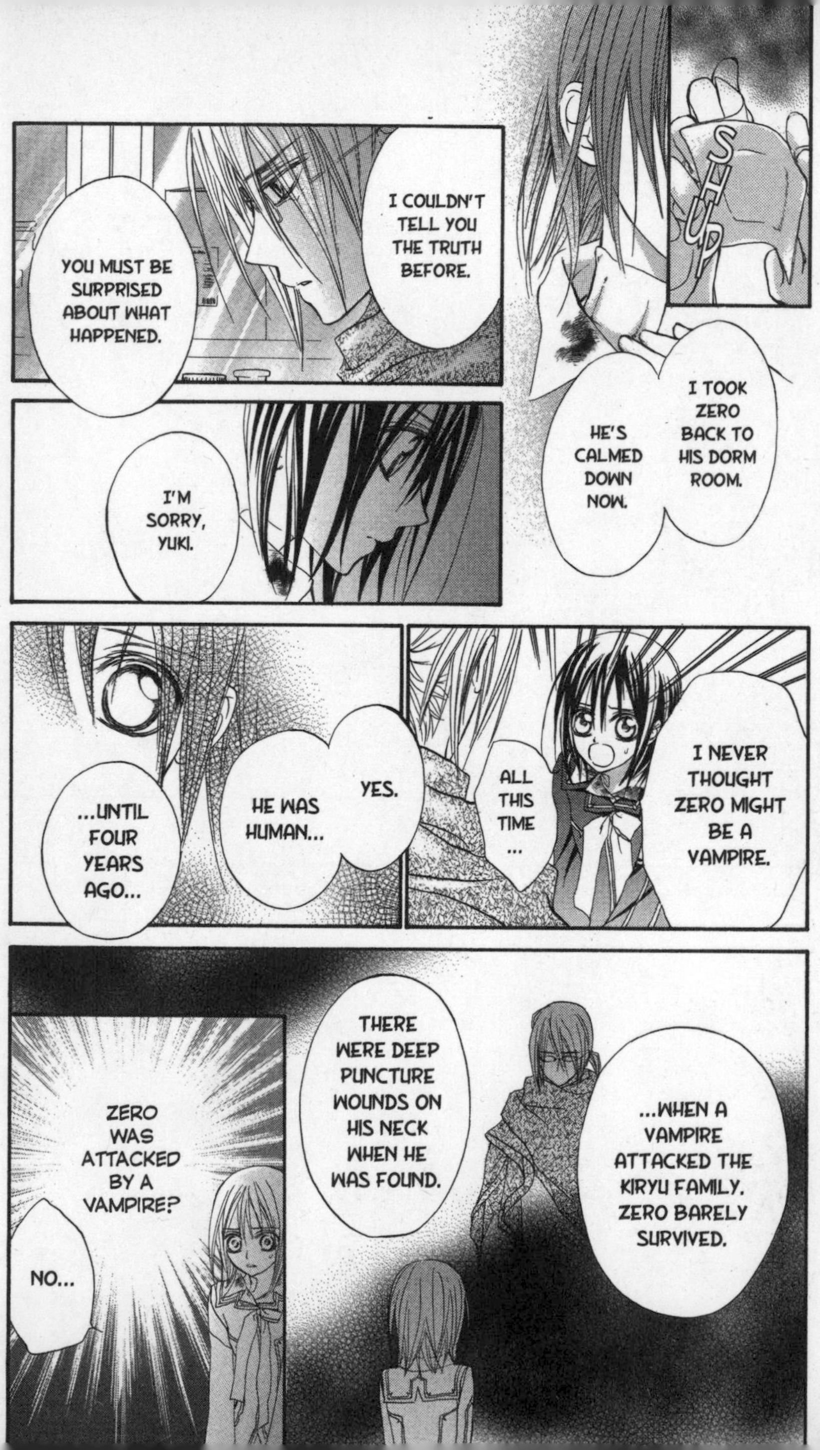
SHUP
I TOOK ZERO BACK TO HIS DORM ROOM.
HE'S CALMED DOWN NOW.
I COULDN'T TELL YOU THE TRUTH BEFORE.
YOU MUST BE SURPRISED ABOUT WHAT HAPPENED.
I'M SORRY, YUKI.
I NEVER THOUGHT ZERO MIGHT BE A VAMPIRE.
ALL THIS TIME...
YES.
HE WAS HUMAN...
...UNTIL FOUR YEARS AGO...
...WHEN A VAMPIRE ATTACKED THE KIRYU FAMILY. ZERO BARELY SURVIVED.
THERE WERE DEEP PUNCTURE WOUNDS ON HIS NECK WHEN HE WAS FOUND.
ZERO WAS ATTACKED BY A VAMPIRE?
NO...

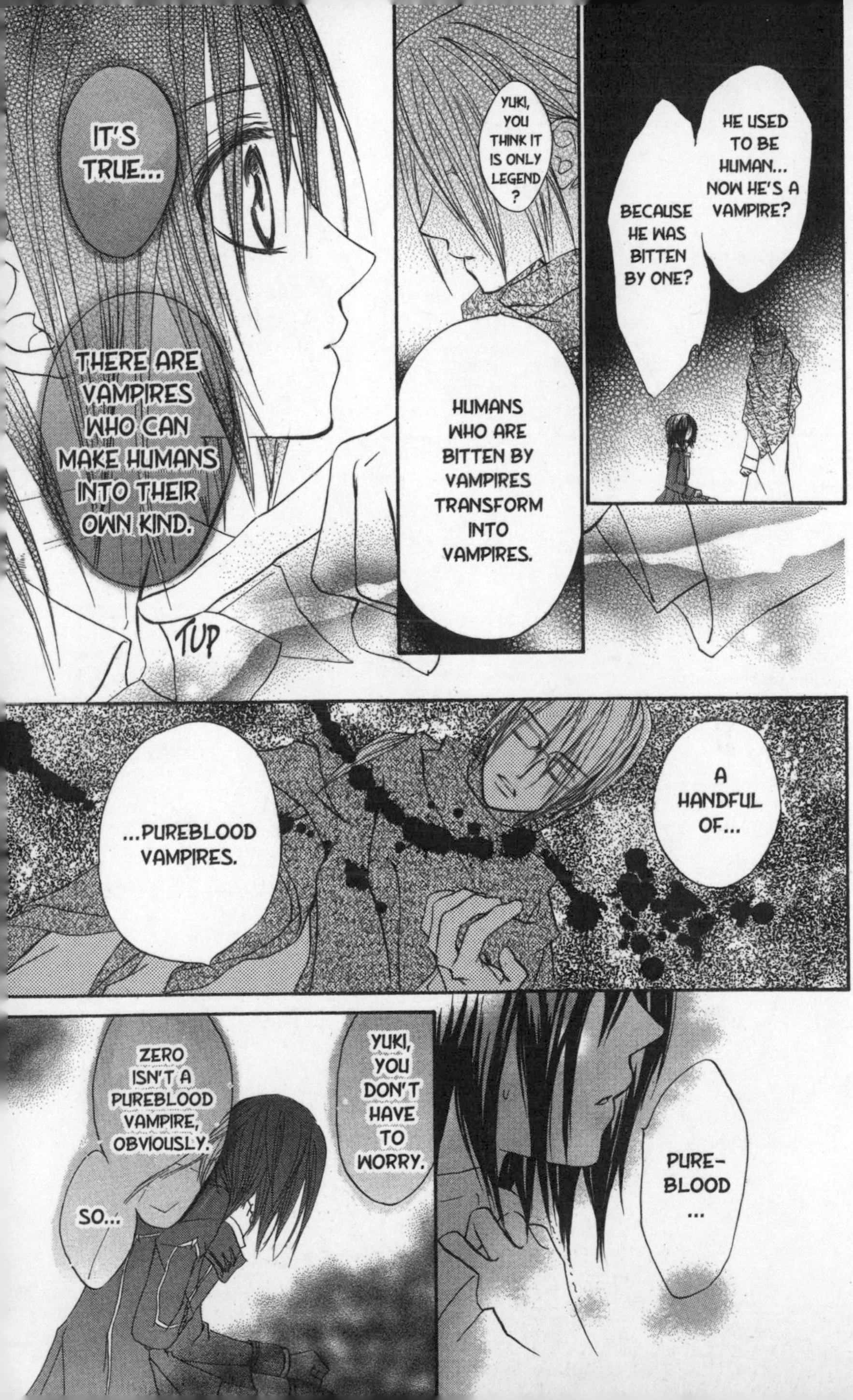
HE USED TO BE HUMAN... NOW HE'S A VAMPIRE?
BECAUSE HE WAS BITTEN BY ONE?
YUKI, YOU THINK IT IS ONLY LEGEND?
HUMANS WHO ARE BITTEN BY VAMPIRES TRANSFORM INTO VAMPIRES.
IT'S TRUE...
THERE ARE VAMPIRES WHO CAN MAKE HUMANS INTO THEIR OWN KIND.
TUP
A HANDFUL OF...
...PUREBLOOD VAMPIRES.
PURE-BLOOD...
YUKI, YOU DON'T HAVE TO WORRY.
ZERO ISN'T A PUREBLOOD VAMPIRE, OBVIOUSLY.
SO...

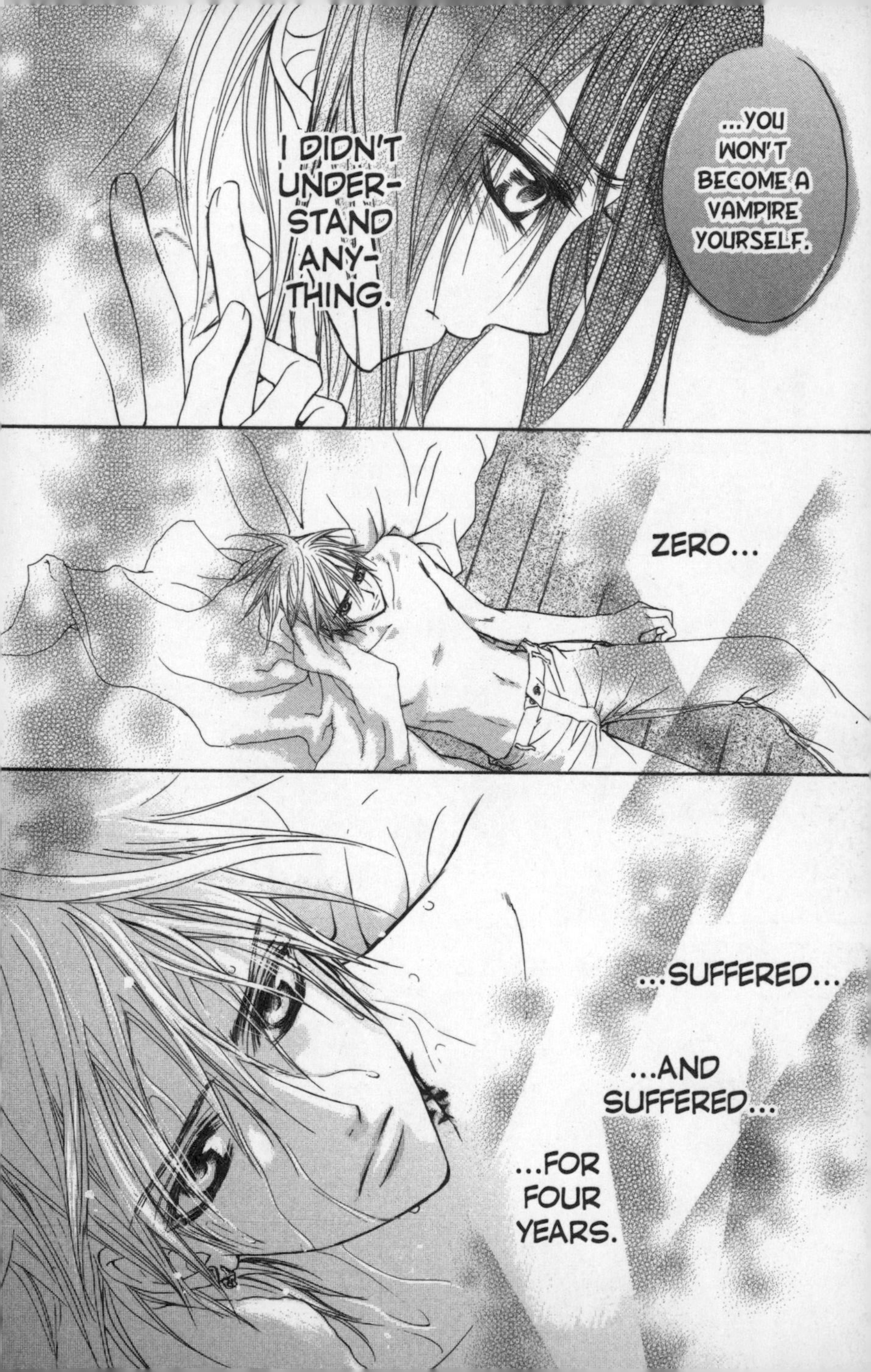
...YOU WON'T BECOME A VAMPIRE YOURSELF.
I DIDN'T UNDER-STAND ANY-THING.
ZERO...
...SUFFERED...
...AND SUFFERED...
...FOR FOUR YEARS.

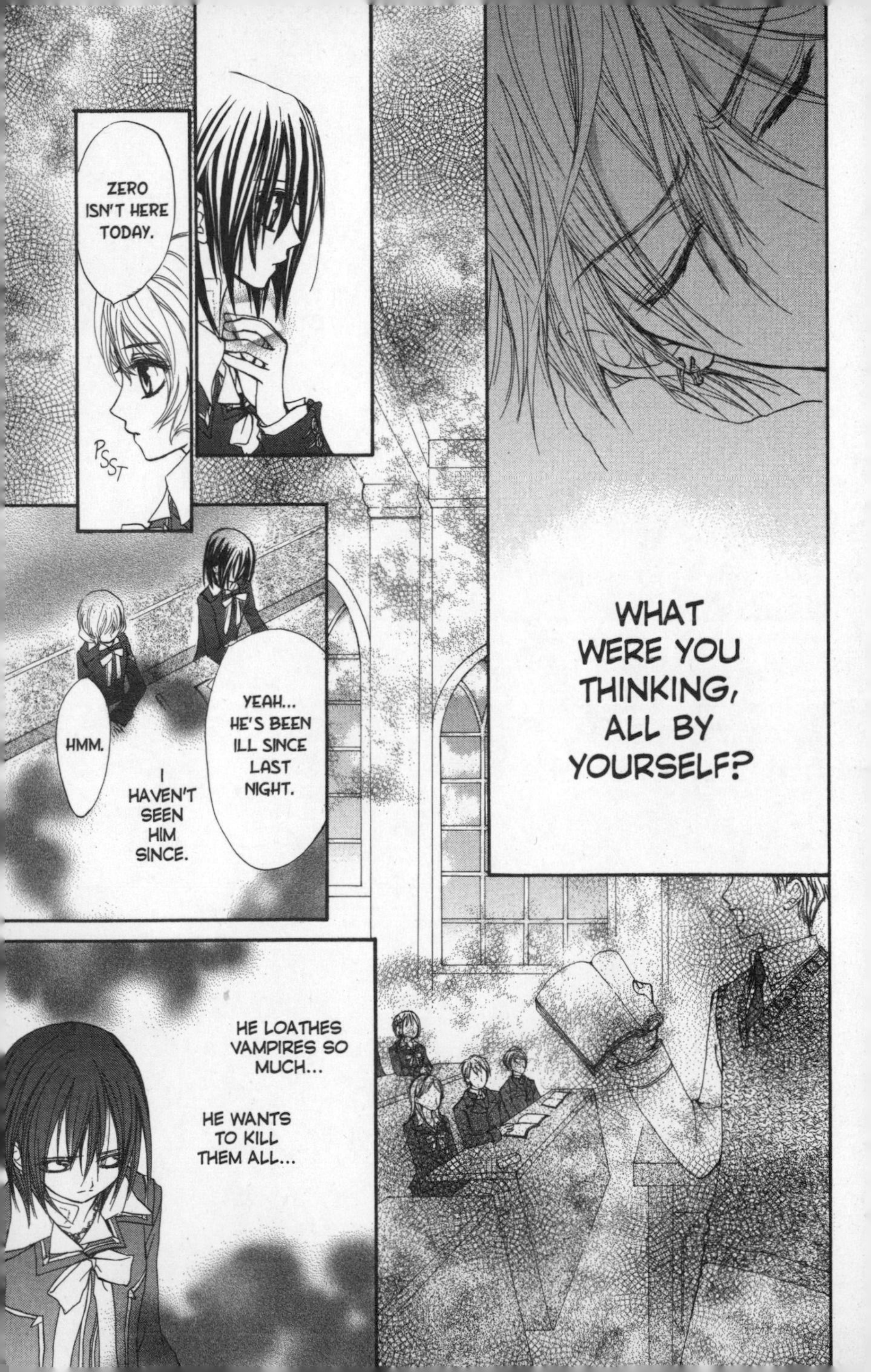
WHAT WERE YOU THINKING, ALL BY YOURSELF?
ZERO ISN'T HERE TODAY.
PSST
YEAH... HE'S BEEN ILL SINCE LAST NIGHT.
I HAVEN'T SEEN HIM SINCE.
HMM.
HE LOATHES VAMPIRES SO MUCH...
HE WANTS TO KILL THEM ALL...

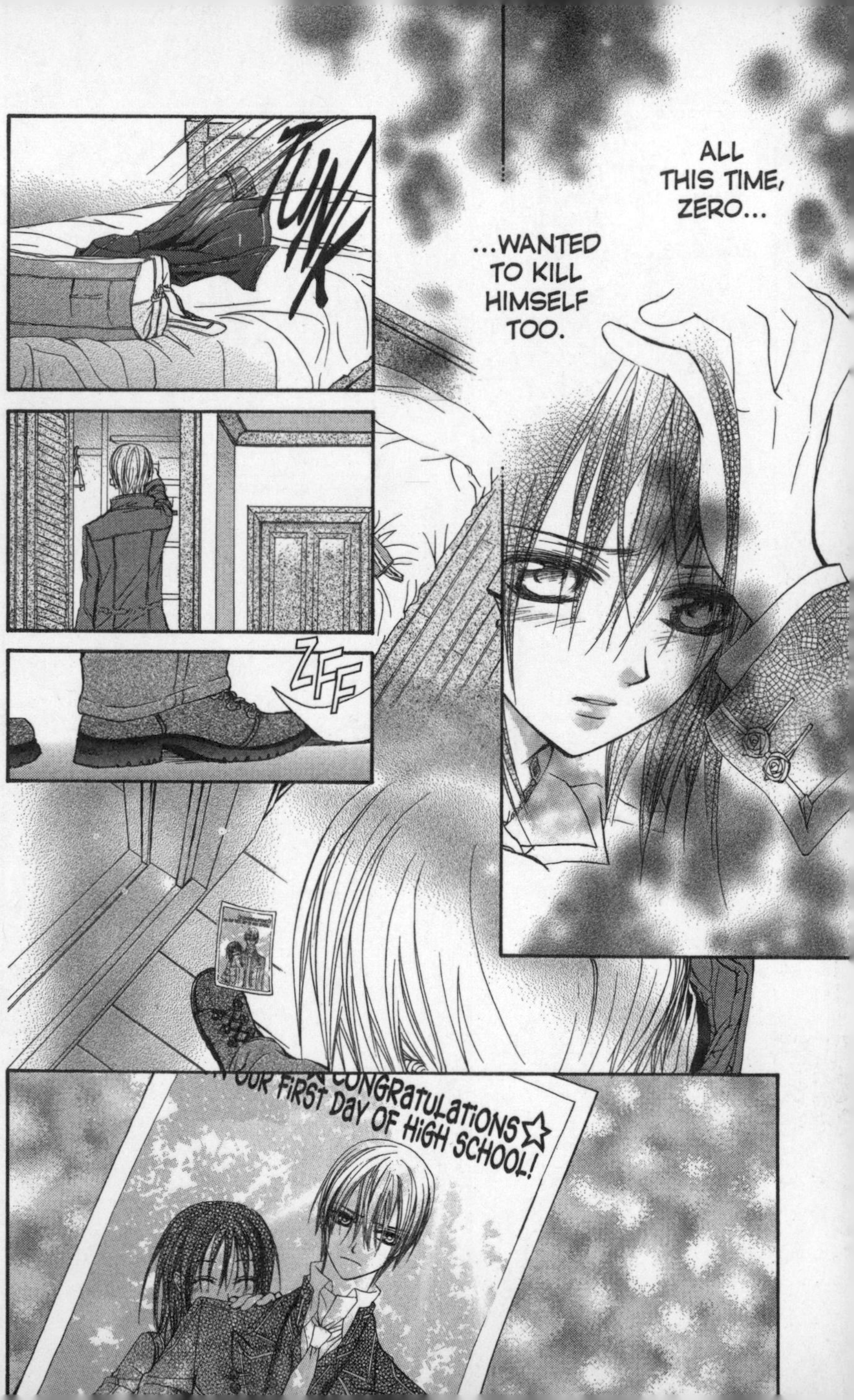
ALL THIS TIME, ZERO...
...WANTED TO KILL HIMSELF TOO.
TUNK
ZFF
CONGRATULATIONS☆
OUR FIRST DAY OF HIGH SCHOOL!

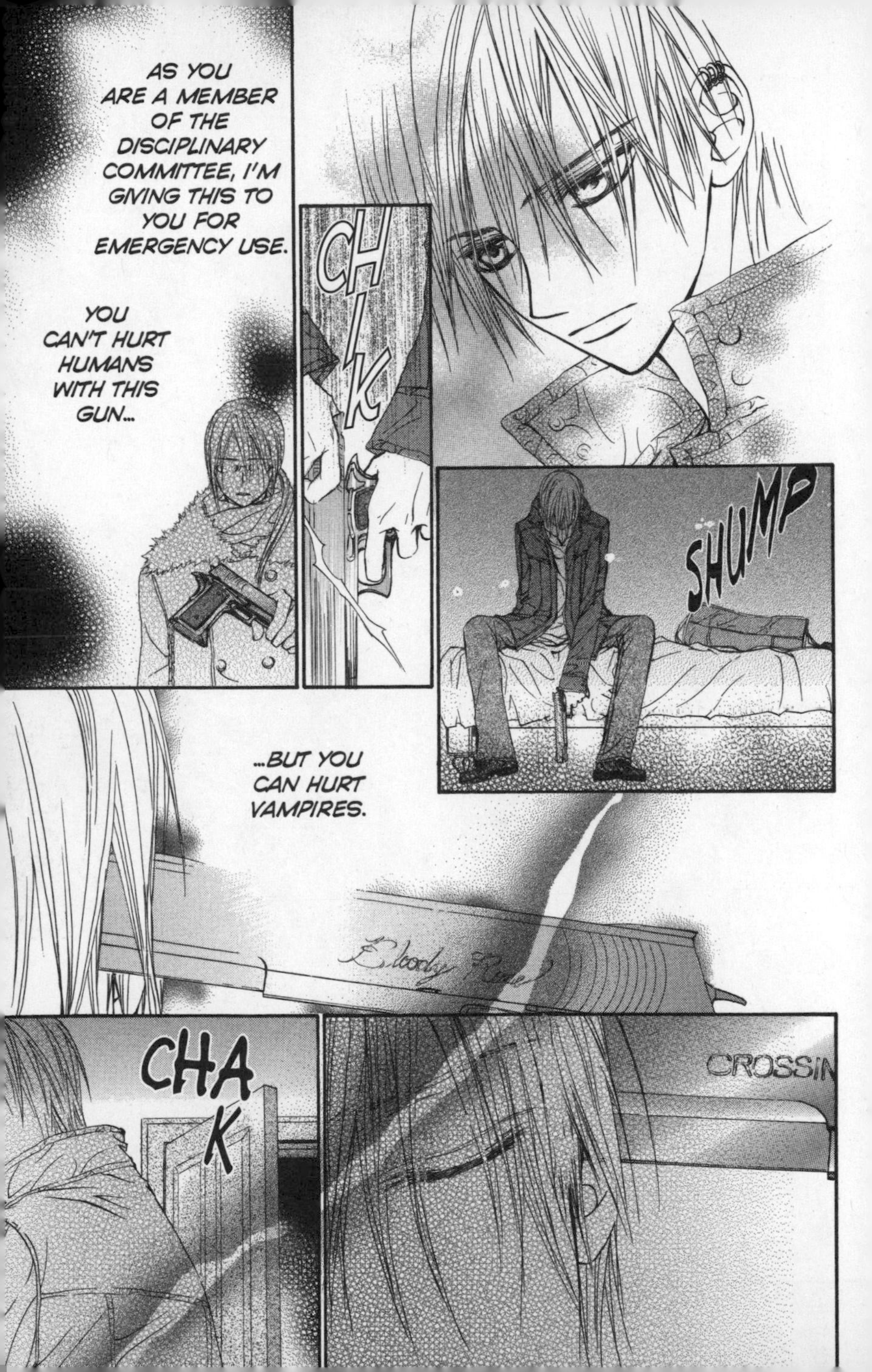
CHIK
AS YOU ARE A MEMBER OF THE DISCIPLINARY COMMITTEE, I'M GIVING THIS TO YOU FOR EMERGENCY USE.
YOU CAN'T HURT HUMANS WITH THIS GUN...
SHUMP
...BUT YOU CAN HURT VAMPIRES.
CROSSIN
CHA K

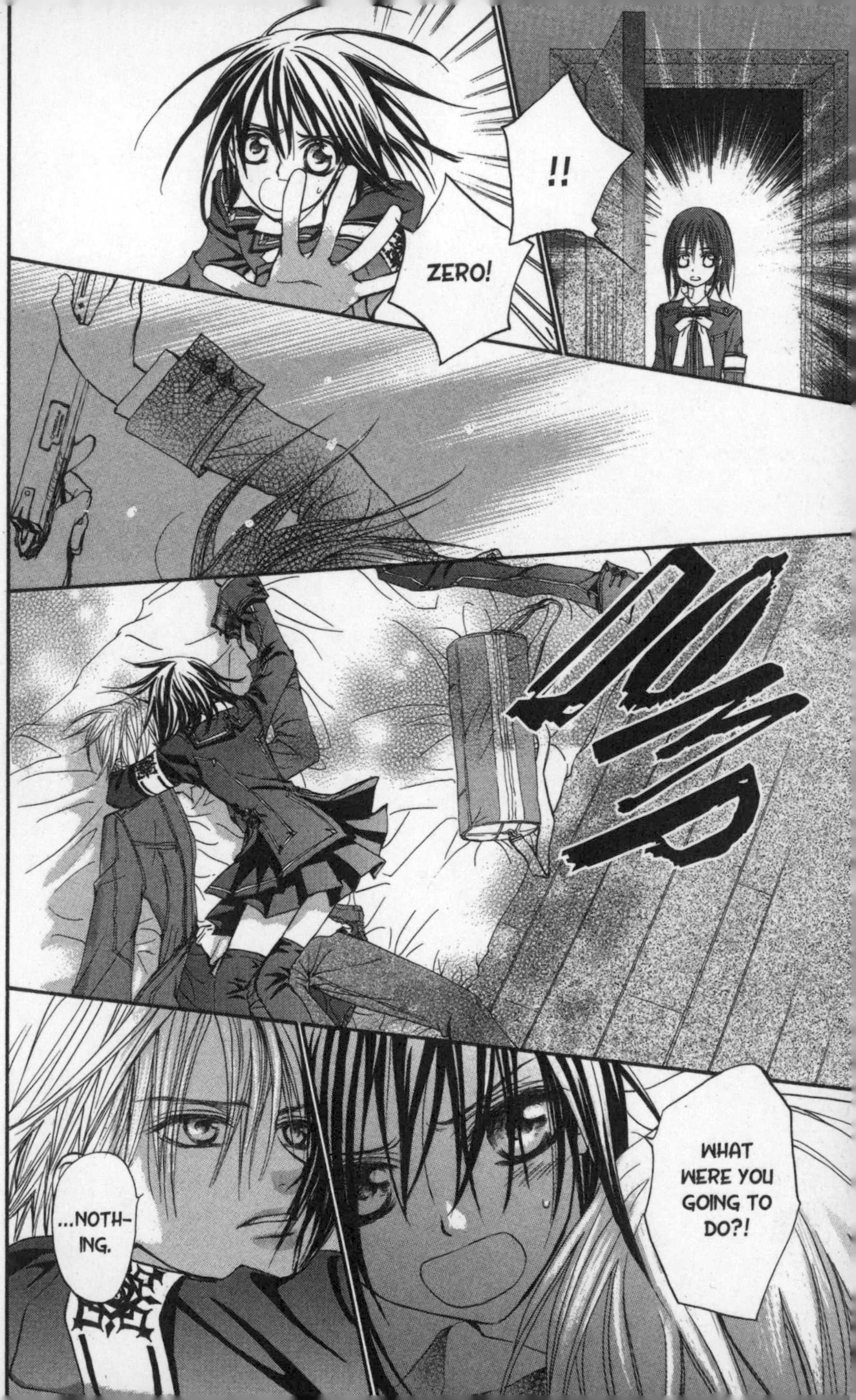
!!
ZERO!
WHAT WERE YOU GOING TO DO?!
...NOTH-ING.

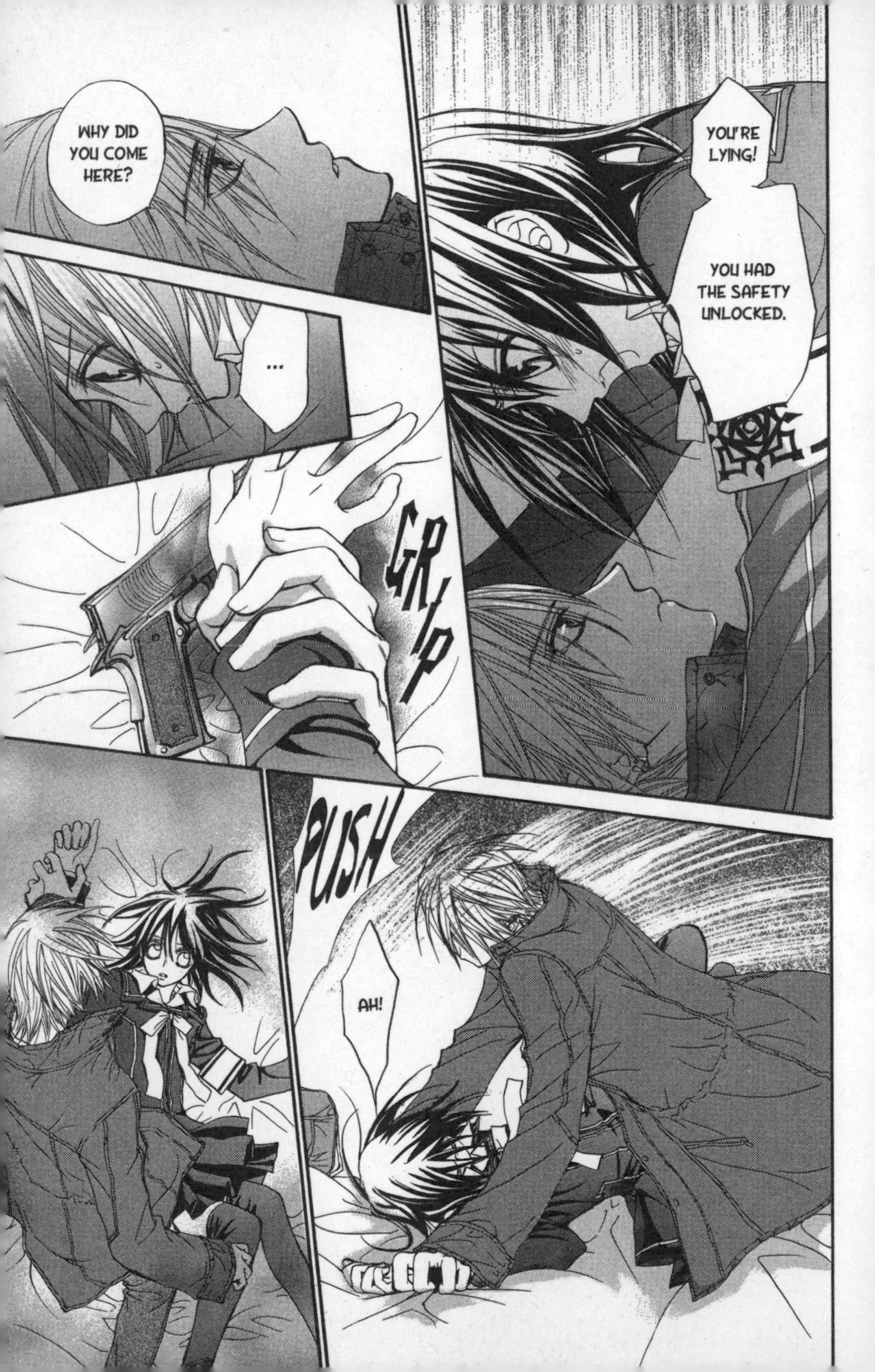
YOU'RE LYING!
YOU HAD THE SAFETY UNLOCKED.
WHY DID YOU COME HERE?
...
GRIP
PUSH
AH!

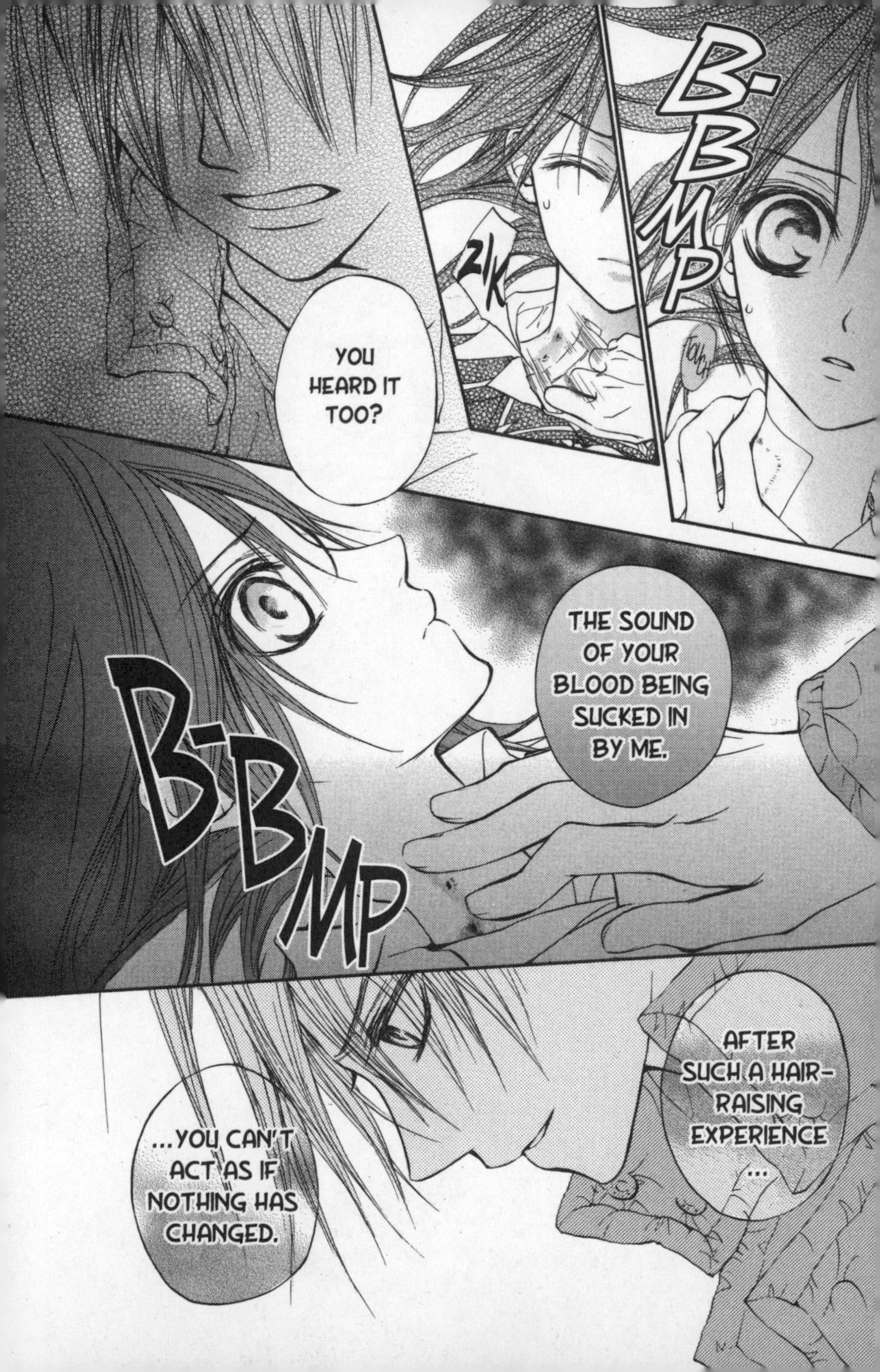
B-BMP
YOU HEARD IT TOO?
THE SOUND OF YOUR BLOOD BEING SUCKED IN BY ME.
B-BMP
AFTER SUCH A HAIR-RAISING EXPERIENCE ...
...YOU CAN'T ACT AS IF NOTHING HAS CHANGED.

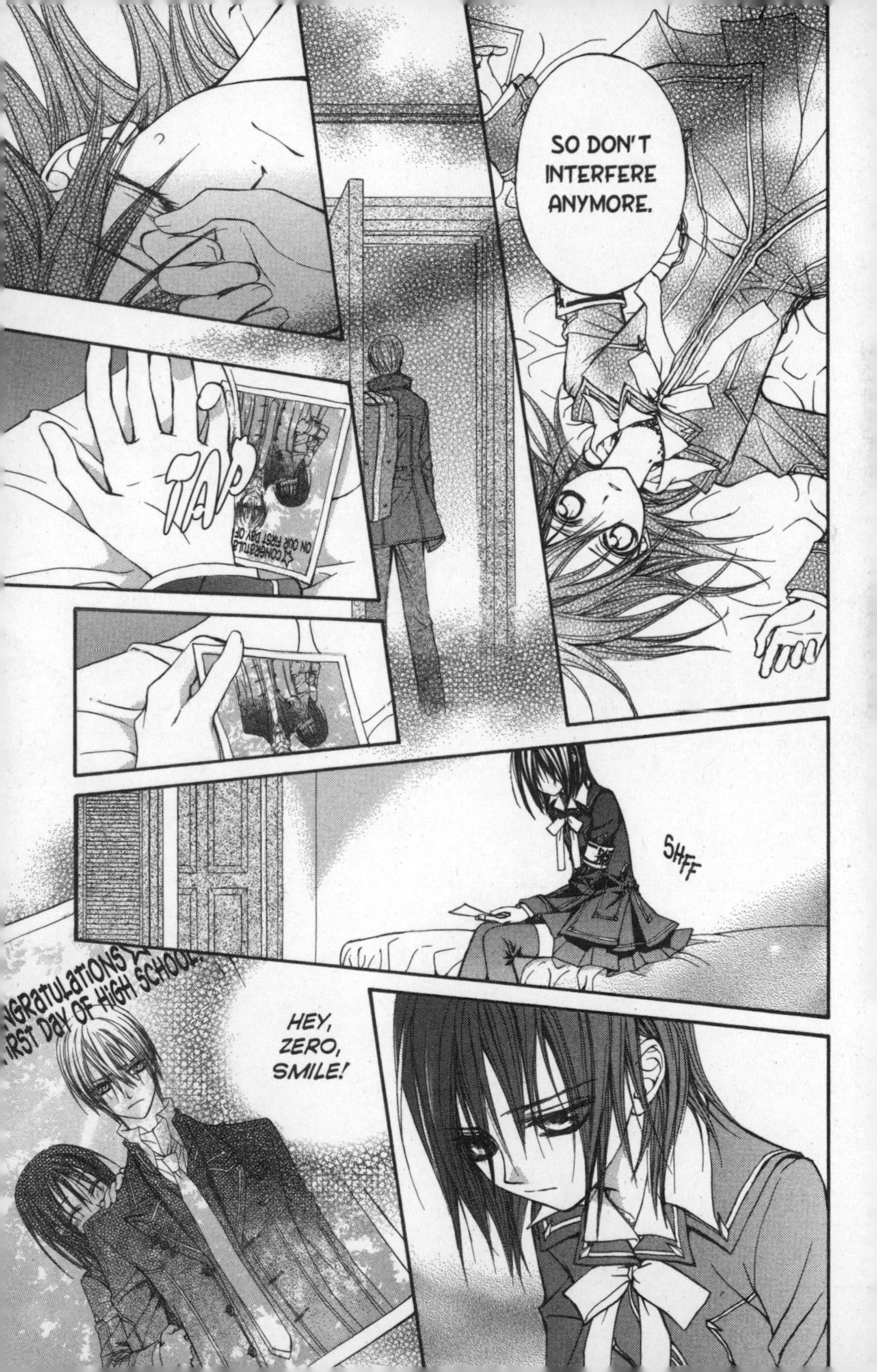
SO DON'T INTERFERE ANYMORE.
TAP
SHFF
HEY, ZERO, SMILE!
NGRATULATIONS ☆
RST DAY OF HIGH SCHOOL!

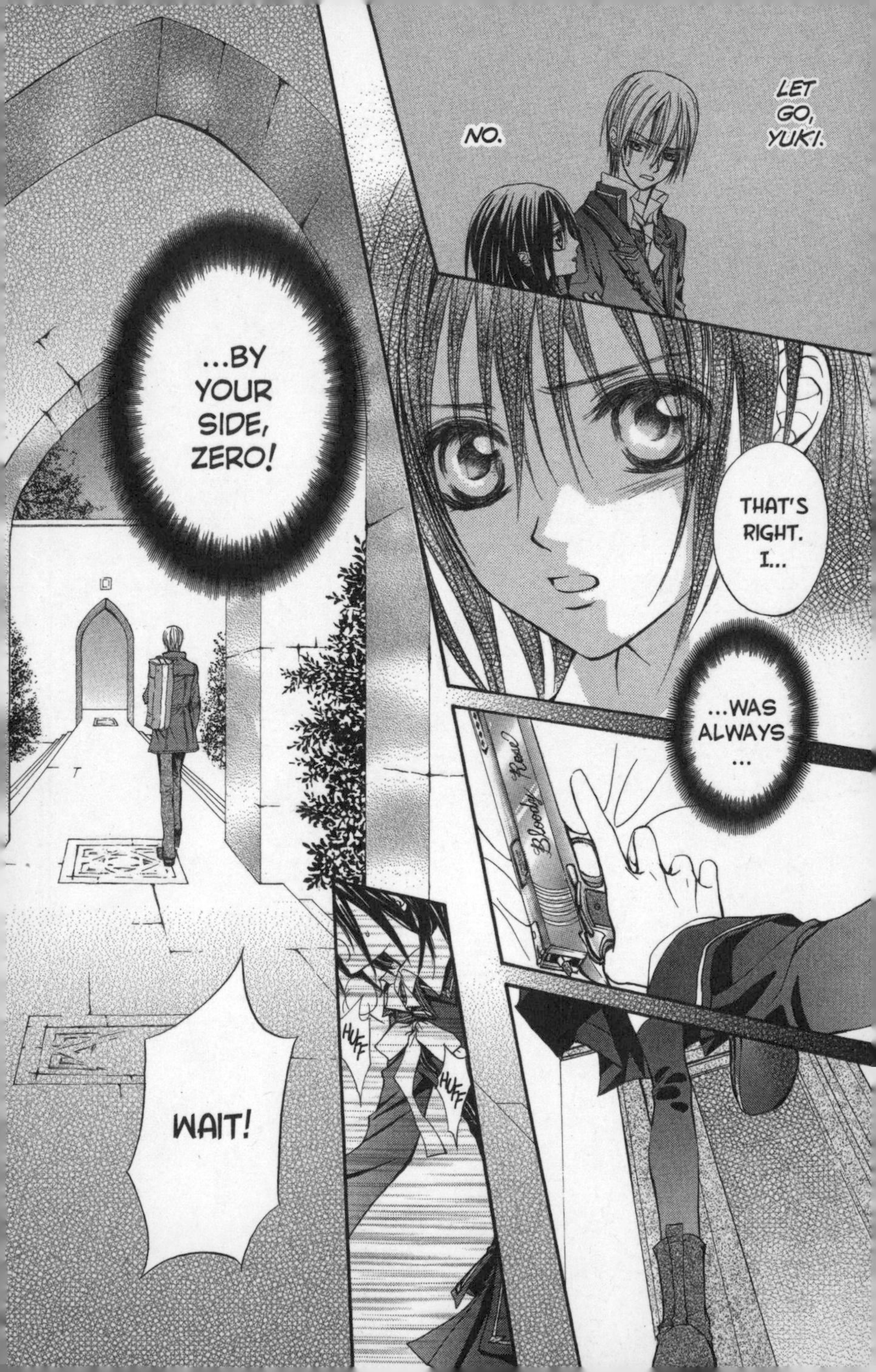
LET GO, YUKI.
NO.
THAT'S RIGHT. I...
...WAS ALWAYS ...
Bloody Rose
...BY YOUR SIDE, ZERO!
HUFF
HUFF
WAIT!

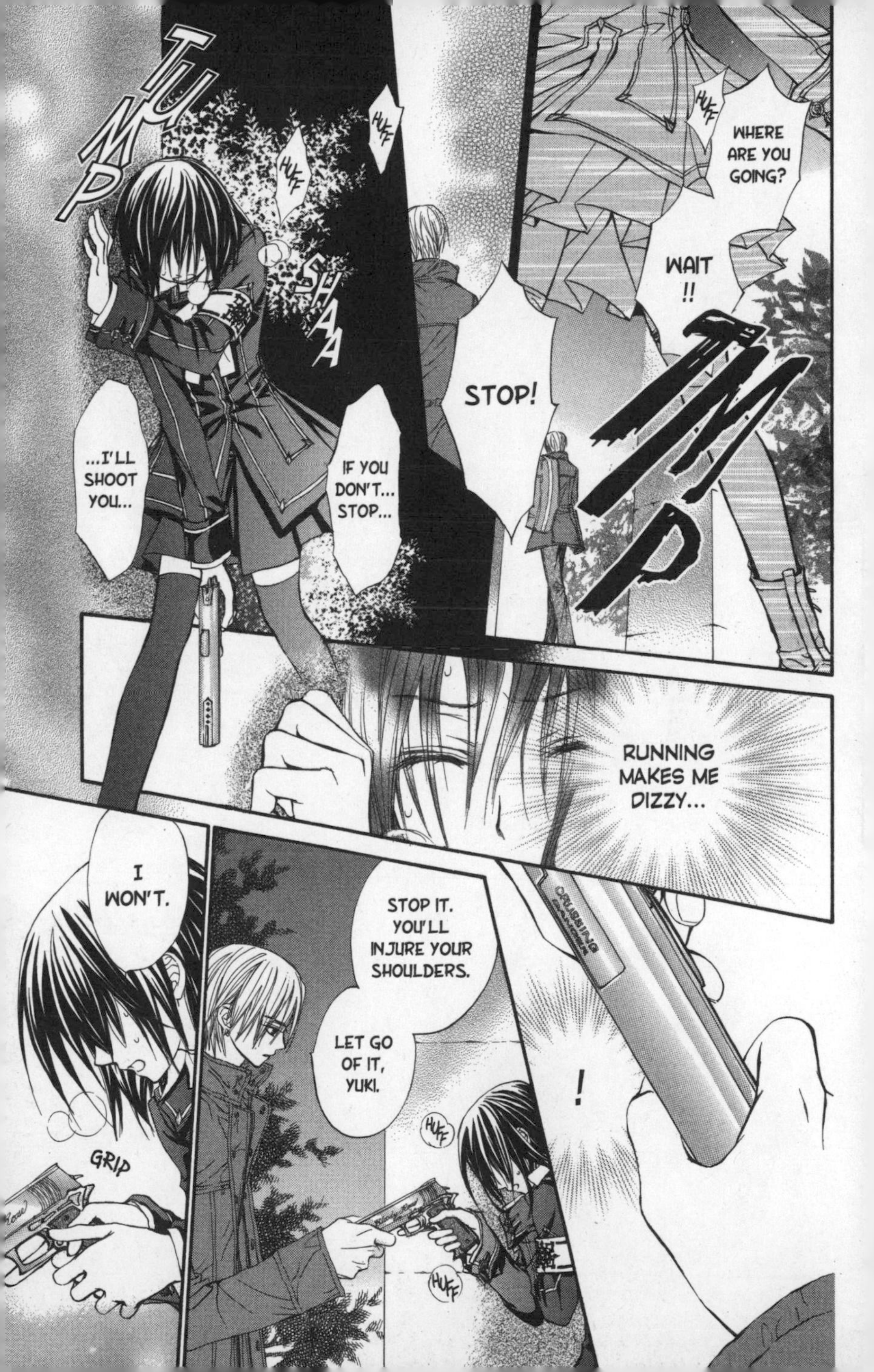
HUFF
WHERE ARE YOU GOING?
WAIT !!
TMP
STOP!
HUFF
HUFF
TUMP
SHAA
IF YOU DON'T... STOP...
...I'LL SHOOT YOU...
RUNNING MAKES ME DIZZY...
!
STOP IT. YOU'LL INJURE YOUR SHOULDERS.
LET GO OF IT, YUKI.
HUFF
HUFF
I WON'T.
GRIP

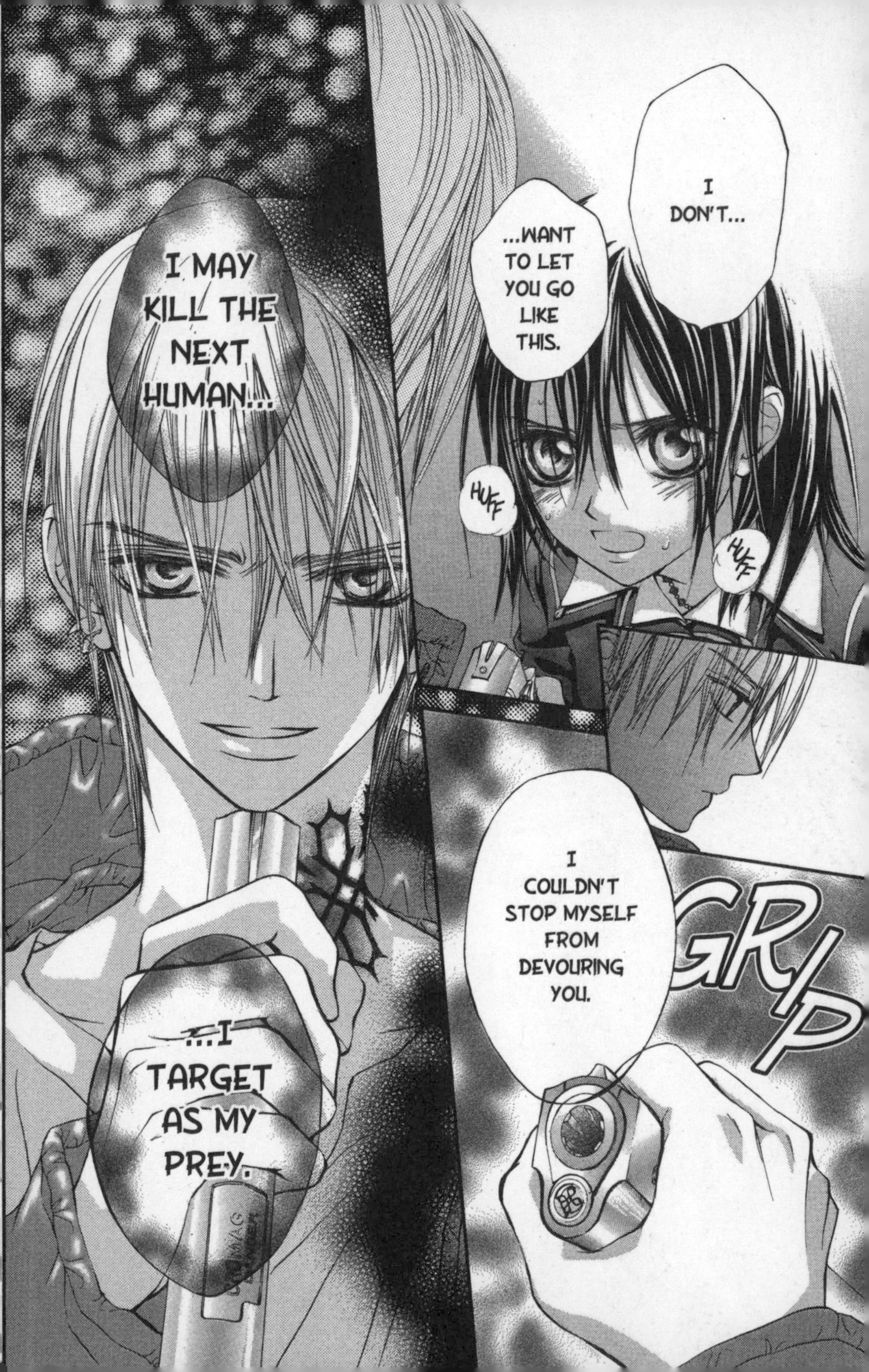
I DON'T...
...WANT TO LET YOU GO LIKE THIS.
HUFF
HUFF
I COULDN'T STOP MYSELF FROM DEVOURING YOU.
GRIP
I MAY KILL THE NEXT HUMAN...
...I TARGET AS MY PREY.

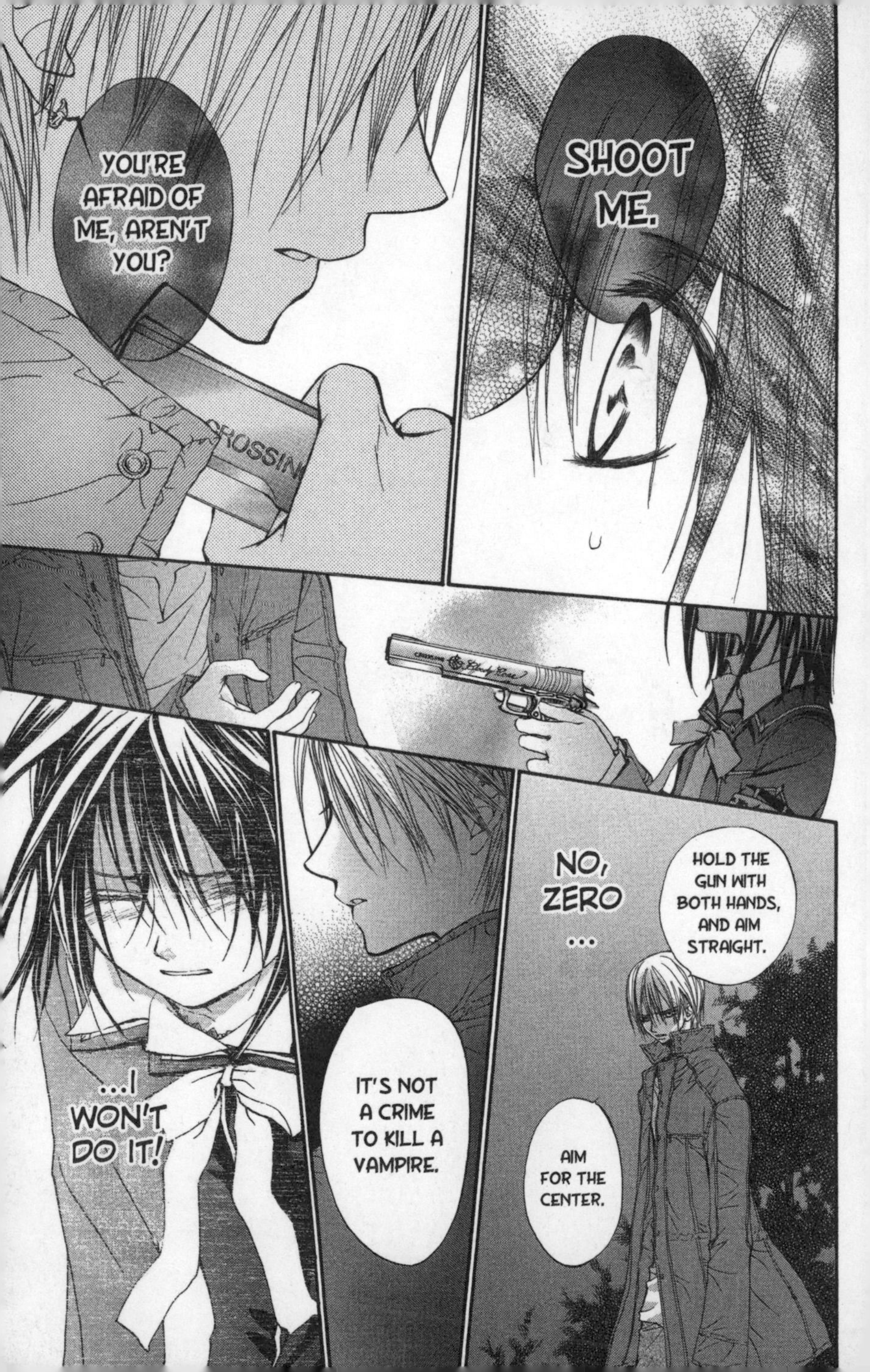
SHOOT ME.
YOU'RE AFRAID OF ME, AREN'T YOU?
HOLD THE GUN WITH BOTH HANDS, AND AIM STRAIGHT.
NO, ZERO...
AIM FOR THE CENTER.
IT'S NOT A CRIME TO KILL A VAMPIRE.
...I WON'T DO IT!

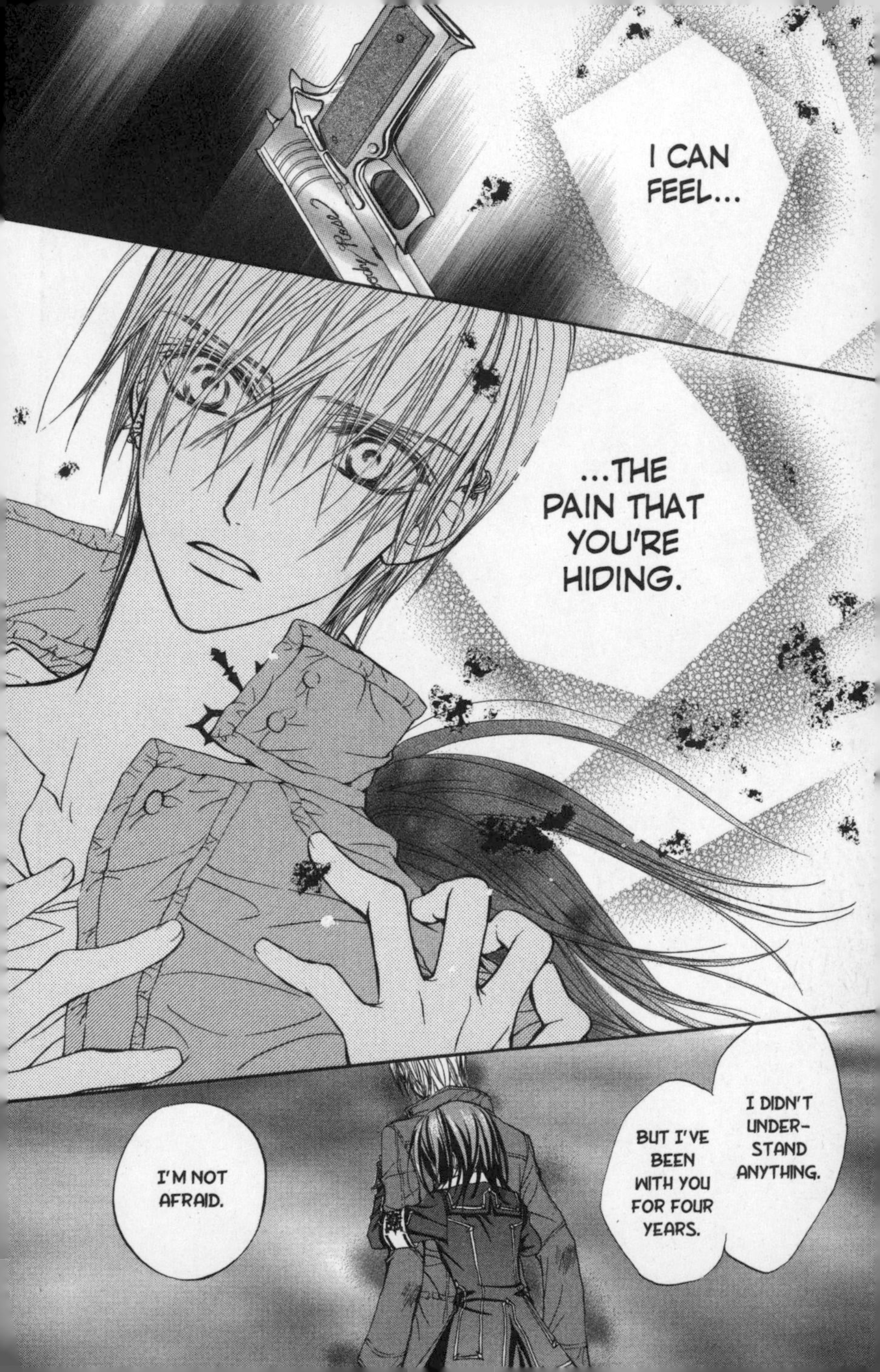
I CAN FEEL...
...THE PAIN THAT YOU'RE HIDING.
I DIDN'T UNDER-STAND ANYTHING.
BUT I'VE BEEN WITH YOU FOR FOUR YEARS.
I'M NOT AFRAID.

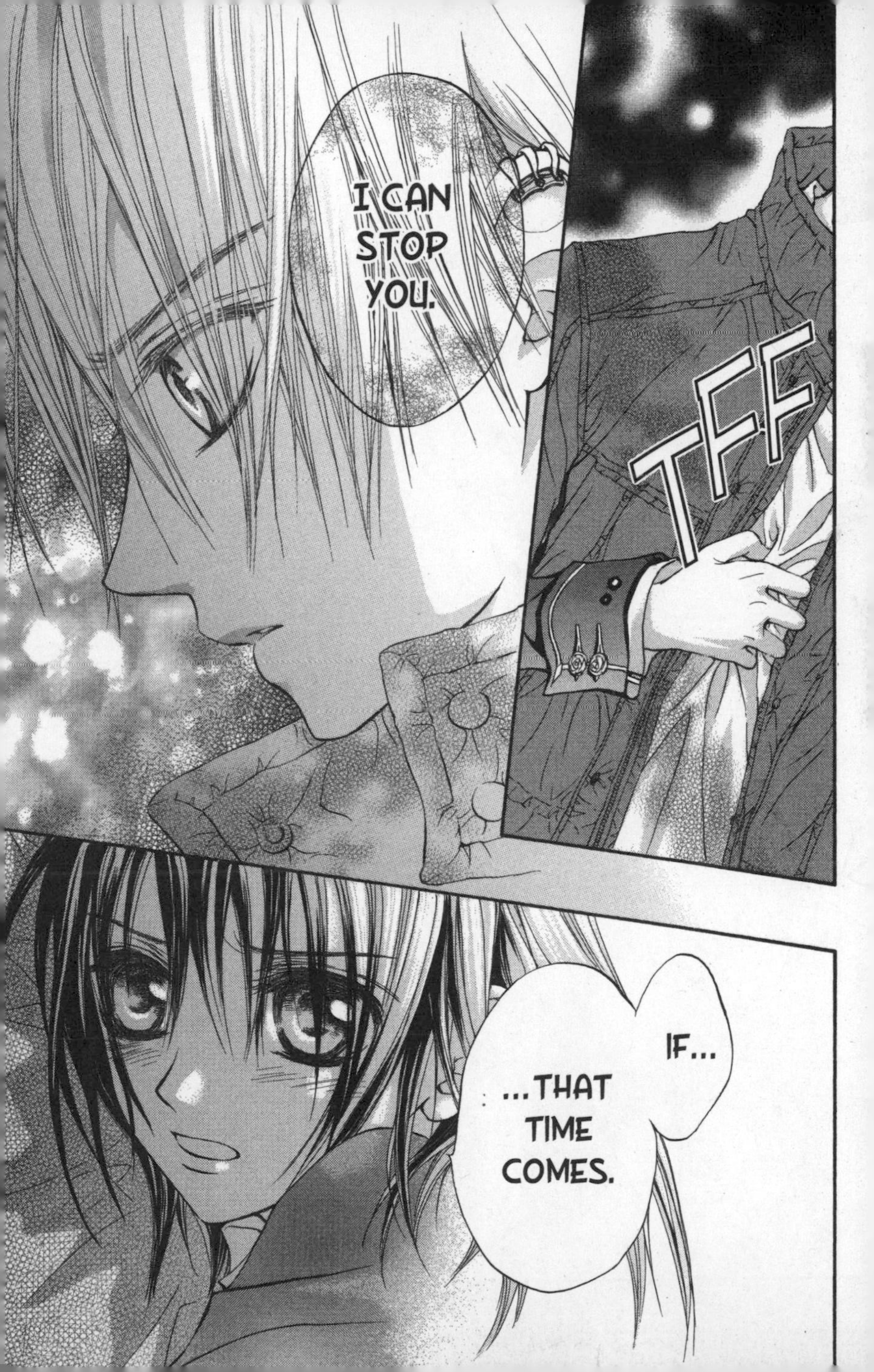
TFF
I CAN STOP YOU.
IF...
...THAT TIME COMES.

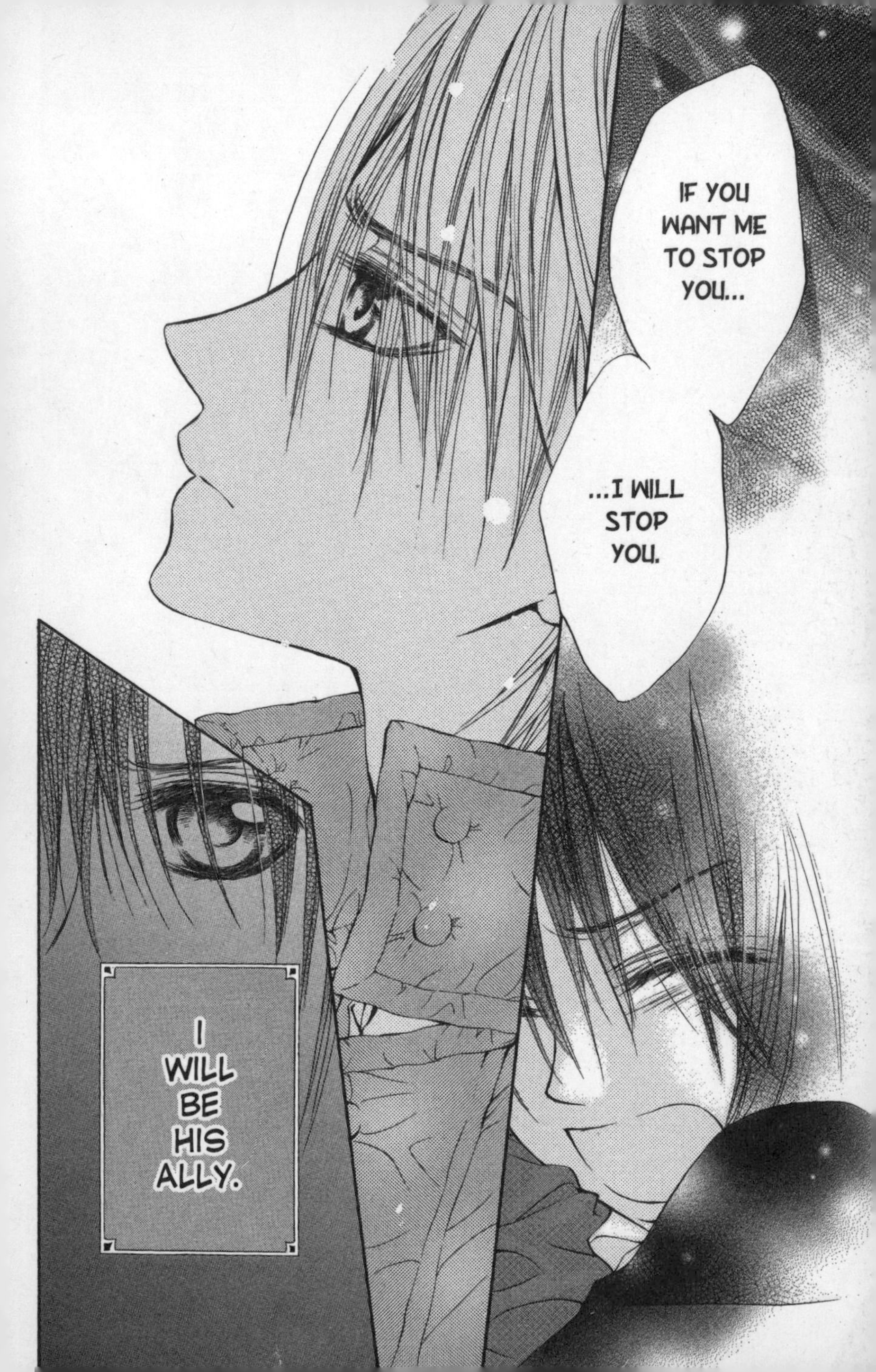
IF YOU WANT ME TO STOP YOU...
...I WILL STOP YOU.
I WILL BE HIS ALLY.

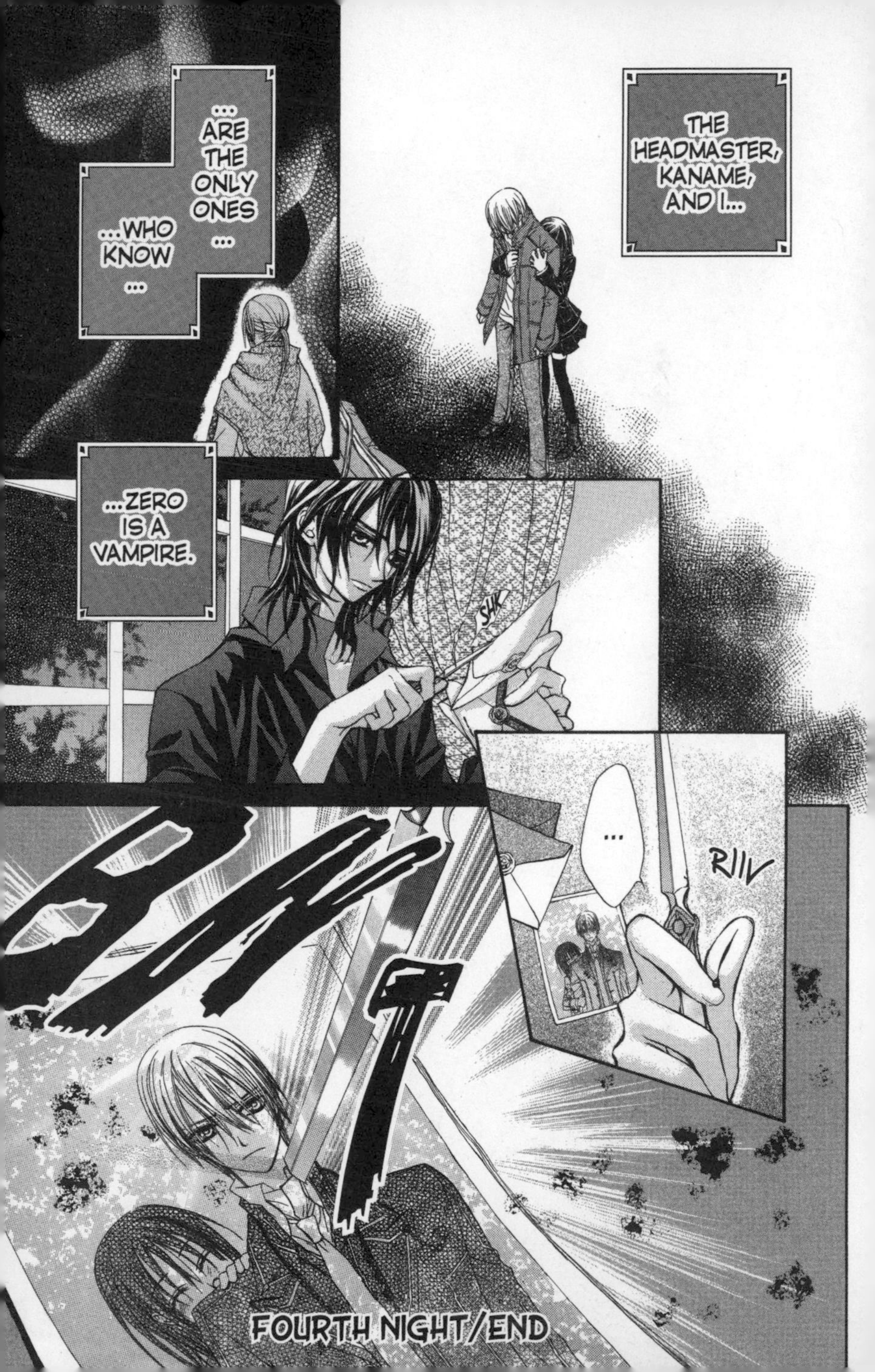
THE HEADMASTER, KANAME, AND I...
...ARE THE ONLY ONES...
...WHO KNOW...
...ZERO IS A VAMPIRE.
SHK
...
RIIV
FOURTH NIGHT/END

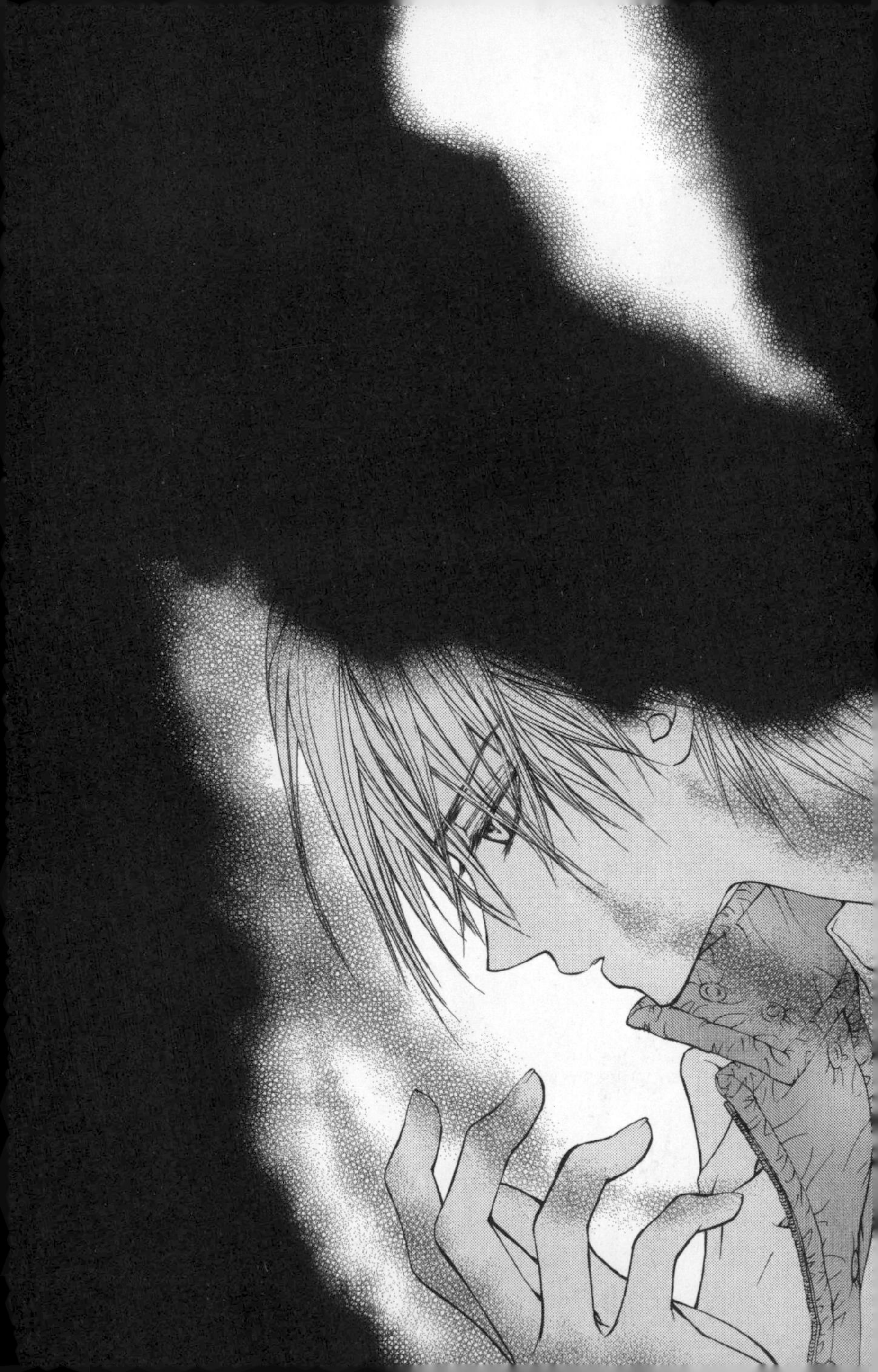

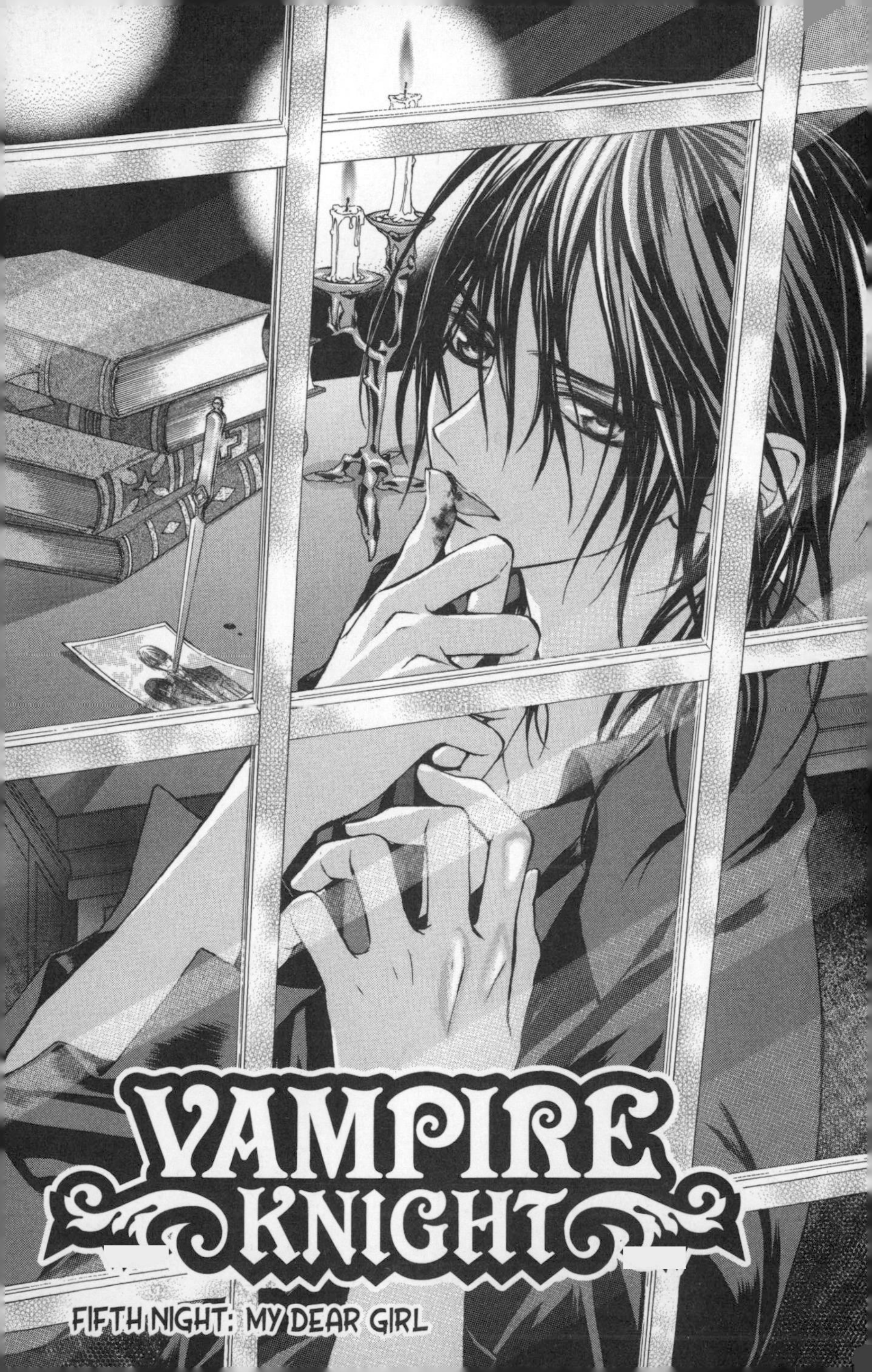
VAMPIRE KNIGHT
FIFTH NIGHT: MY DEAR GIRL

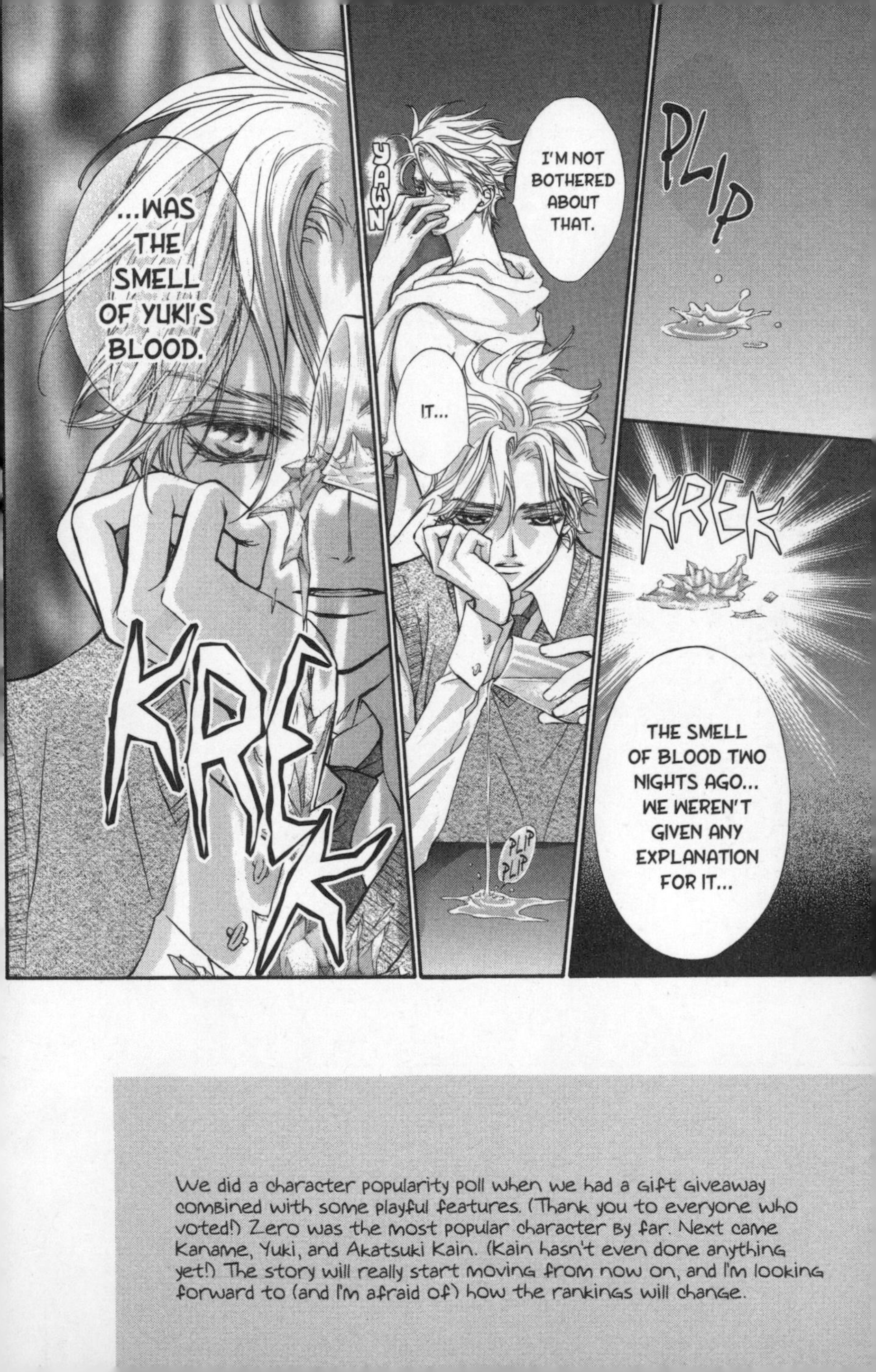
PLIP
KREK
THE SMELL OF BLOOD TWO NIGHTS AGO... WE WEREN'T GIVEN ANY EXPLANATION FOR IT...
I'M NOT BOTHERED ABOUT THAT.
YAWN
IT...
PLIP PLIP
...WAS THE SMELL OF YUKI'S BLOOD.
KREK

We did a character popularity poll when we had a gift giveaway combined with some playful features. (Thank you to everyone who voted!) Zero was the most popular character by far. Next came Kaname, Yuki, and Akatsuki Kain. (Kain hasn't even done anything yet!) The story will really start moving from now on, and I'm looking forward to (and I'm afraid of) how the rankings will change.

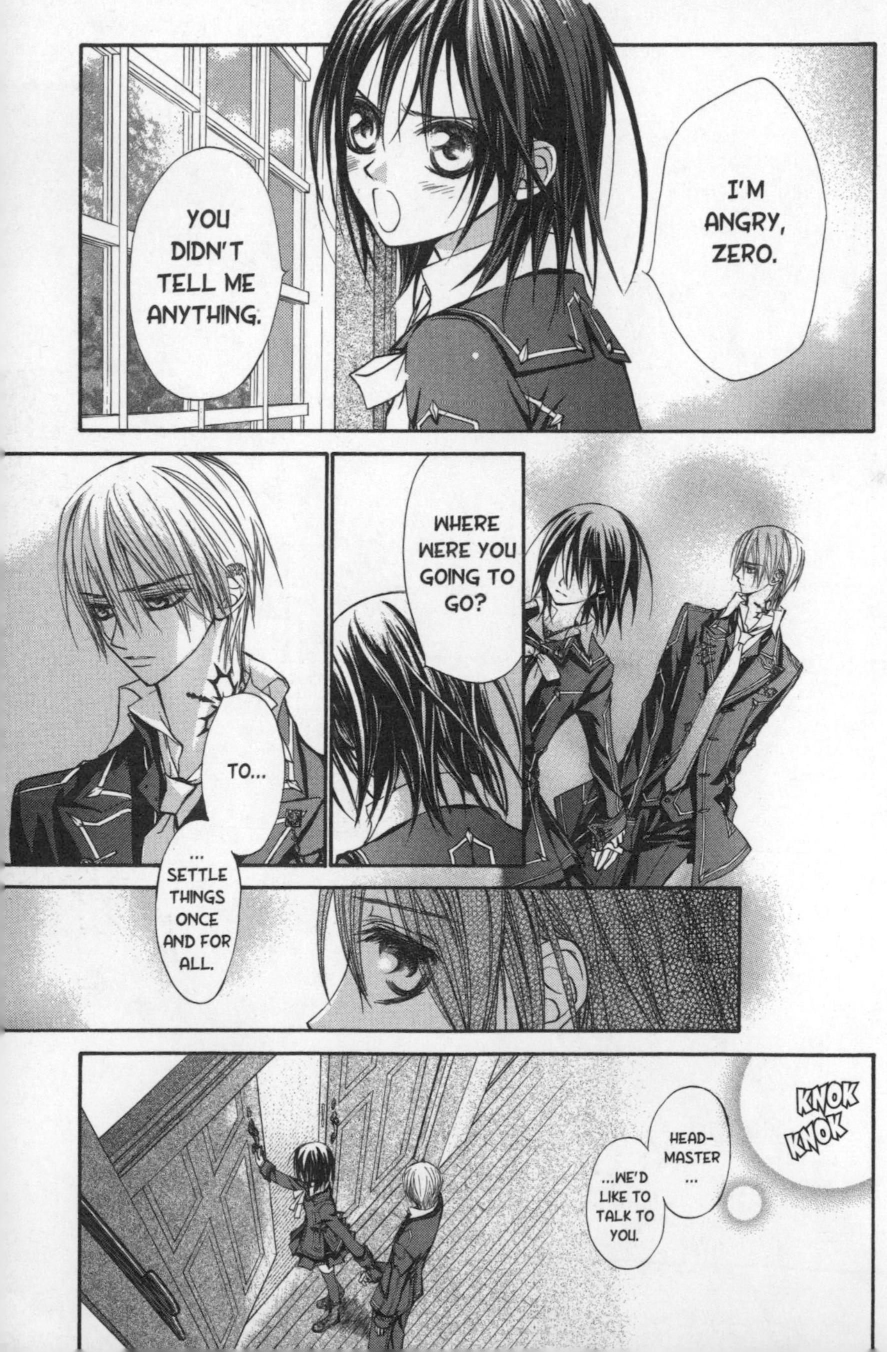
I'M ANGRY, ZERO.
YOU DIDN'T TELL ME ANYTHING.
WHERE WERE YOU GOING TO GO?
TO...
... SETTLE THINGS ONCE AND FOR ALL.
KNOK KNOK
HEAD-MASTER ...
...WE'D LIKE TO TALK TO YOU.

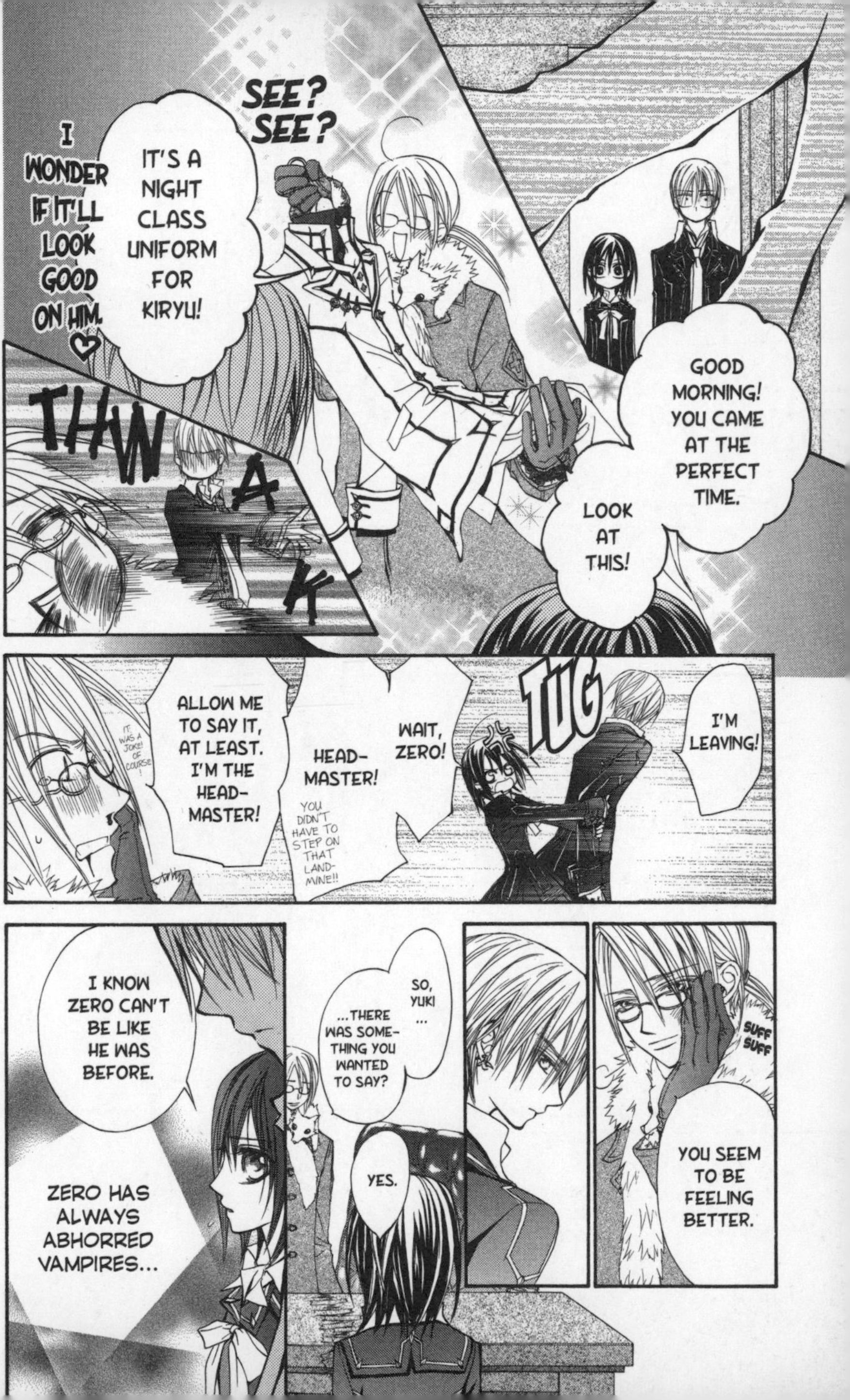
GOOD MORNING! YOU CAME AT THE PERFECT TIME.
LOOK AT THIS!
SEE? SEE?
IT'S A NIGHT CLASS UNIFORM FOR KIRYU!
I WONDER IF IT'LL LOOK GOOD ON HIM.
THWAK
I'M LEAVING!
TUG
WAIT, ZERO!
HEAD-MASTER!
YOU DIDN'T HAVE TO STEP ON THAT LAND-MINE!!
ALLOW ME TO SAY IT, AT LEAST. I'M THE HEAD-MASTER!
IT WAS A JOKE!! OF COURSE!
SUFF SUFF
YOU SEEM TO BE FEELING BETTER.
SO, YUKI...
...THERE WAS SOME-THING YOU WANTED TO SAY?
YES.
I KNOW ZERO CAN'T BE LIKE HE WAS BEFORE.
ZERO HAS ALWAYS ABHORRED VAMPIRES...

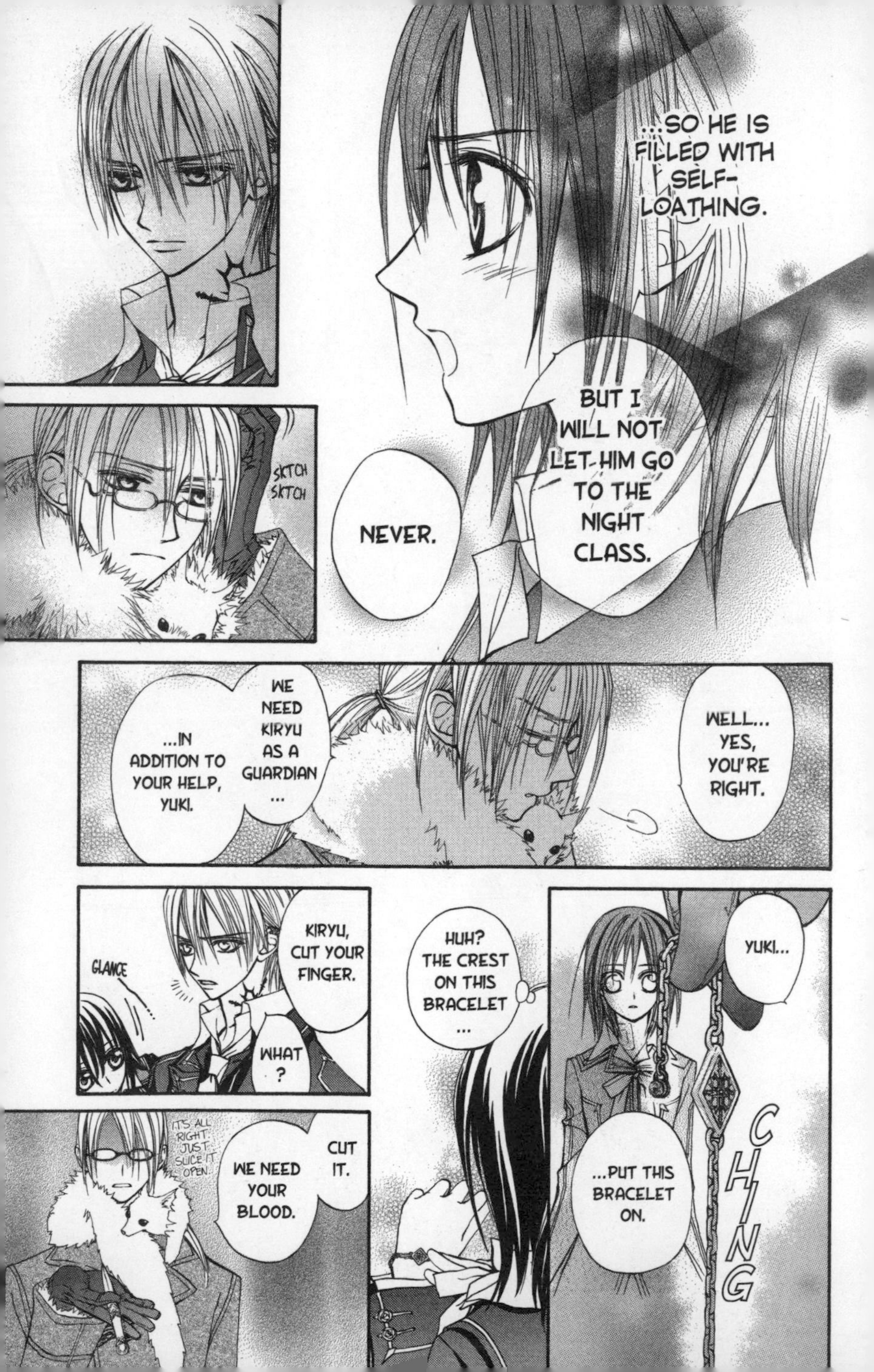
...SO HE IS FILLED WITH SELF-LOATHING.
BUT I WILL NOT LET HIM GO TO THE NIGHT CLASS.
NEVER.
SKTCH SKTCH
WELL... YES, YOU'RE RIGHT.
WE NEED KIRYU AS A GUARDIAN...
...IN ADDITION TO YOUR HELP, YUKI.
YUKI...
HUH? THE CREST ON THIS BRACELET...
...PUT THIS BRACELET ON.
CHING
KIRYU, CUT YOUR FINGER.
GLANCE
WHAT?
CUT IT.
WE NEED YOUR BLOOD.
IT'S ALL RIGHT. JUST SLICE IT OPEN.

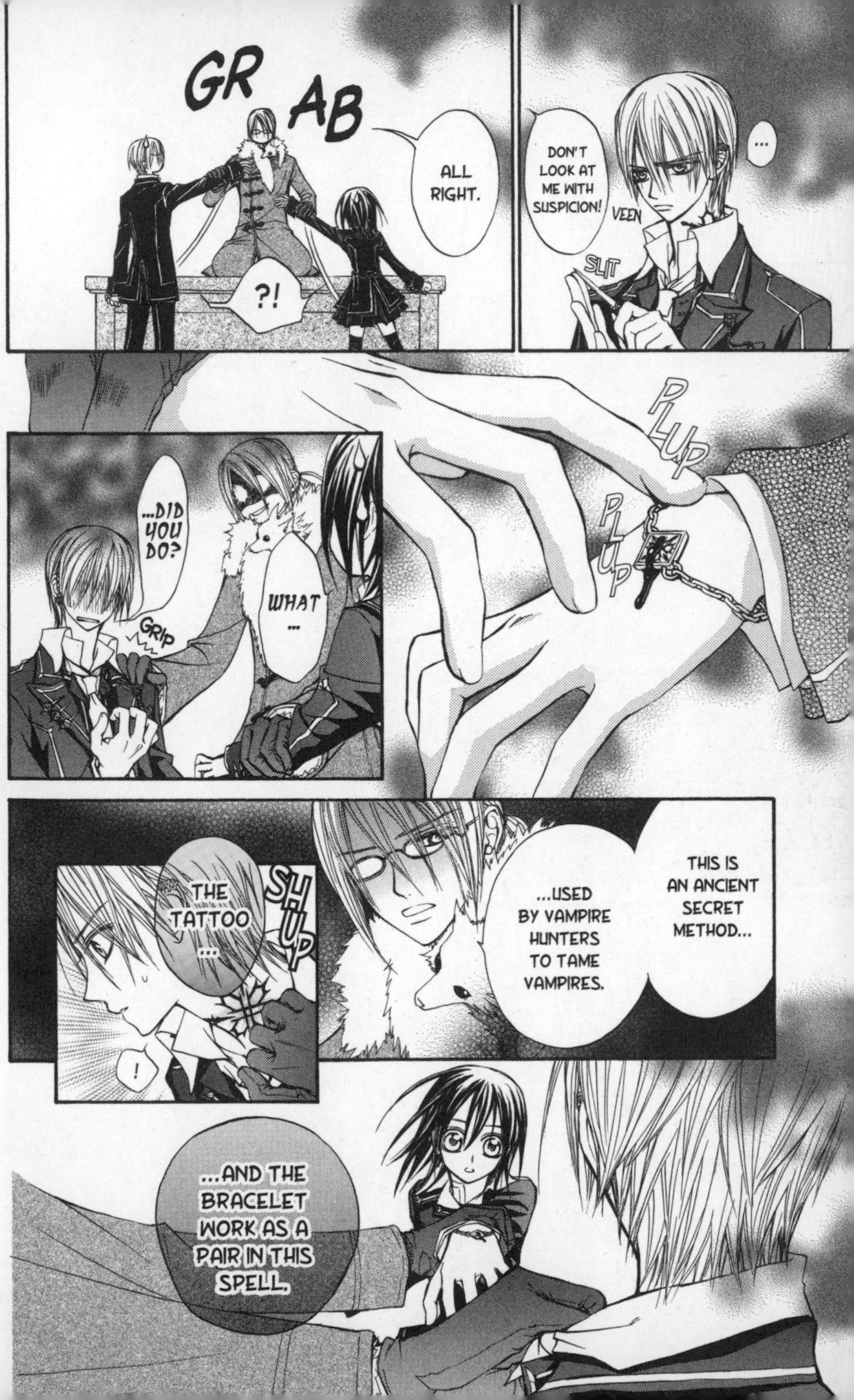
...
DON'T LOOK AT ME WITH SUSPICION!
VEEN
SLIT
GR AB
ALL RIGHT.
?!
PLUP
PLUP
PLUP
WHAT ...
...DID YOU DO?
GRIP
THIS IS AN ANCIENT SECRET METHOD...
...USED BY VAMPIRE HUNTERS TO TAME VAMPIRES.
SHUP
THE TATTOO ...
!
...AND THE BRACELET WORK AS A PAIR IN THIS SPELL.

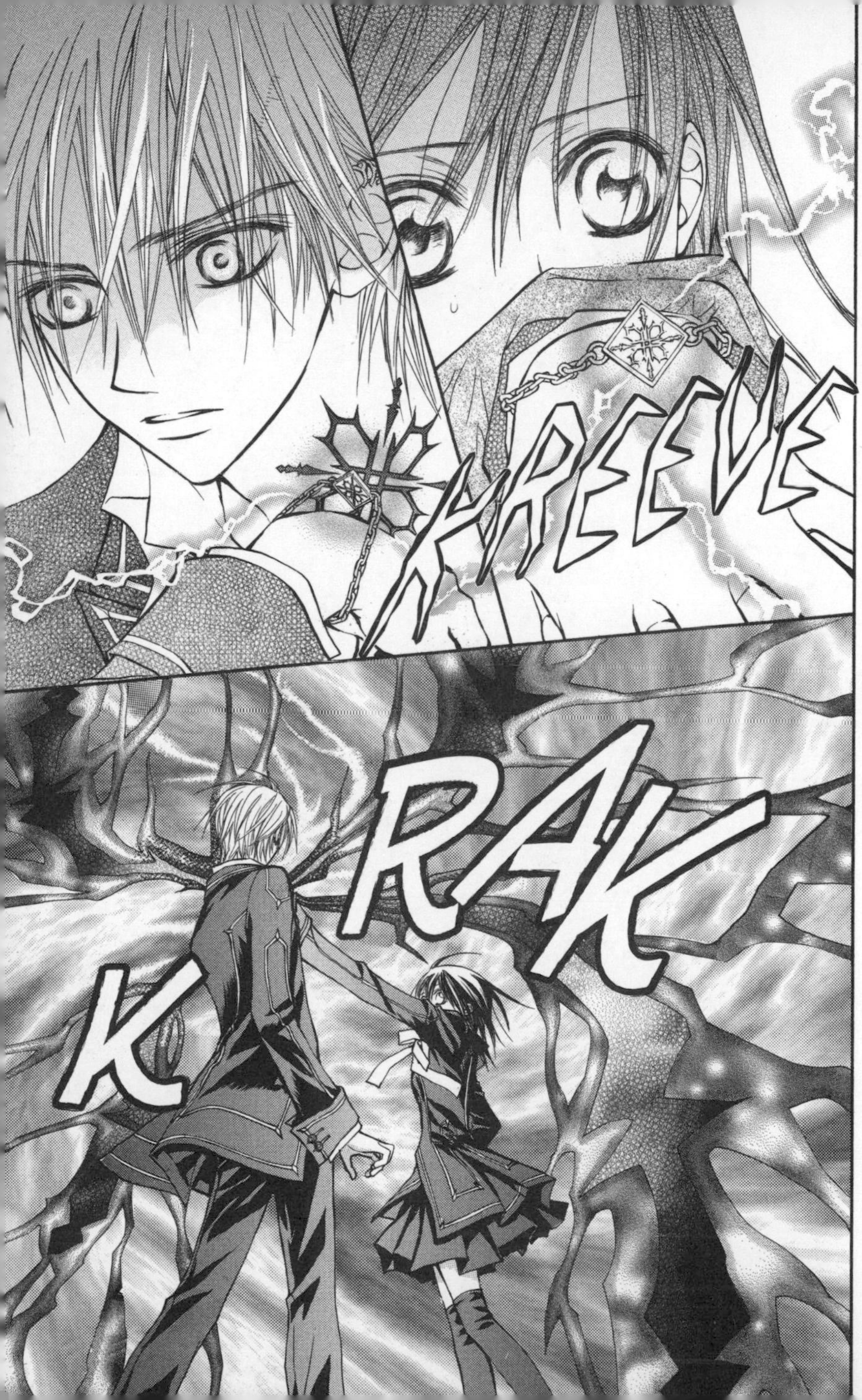
KREEVE
KRAK

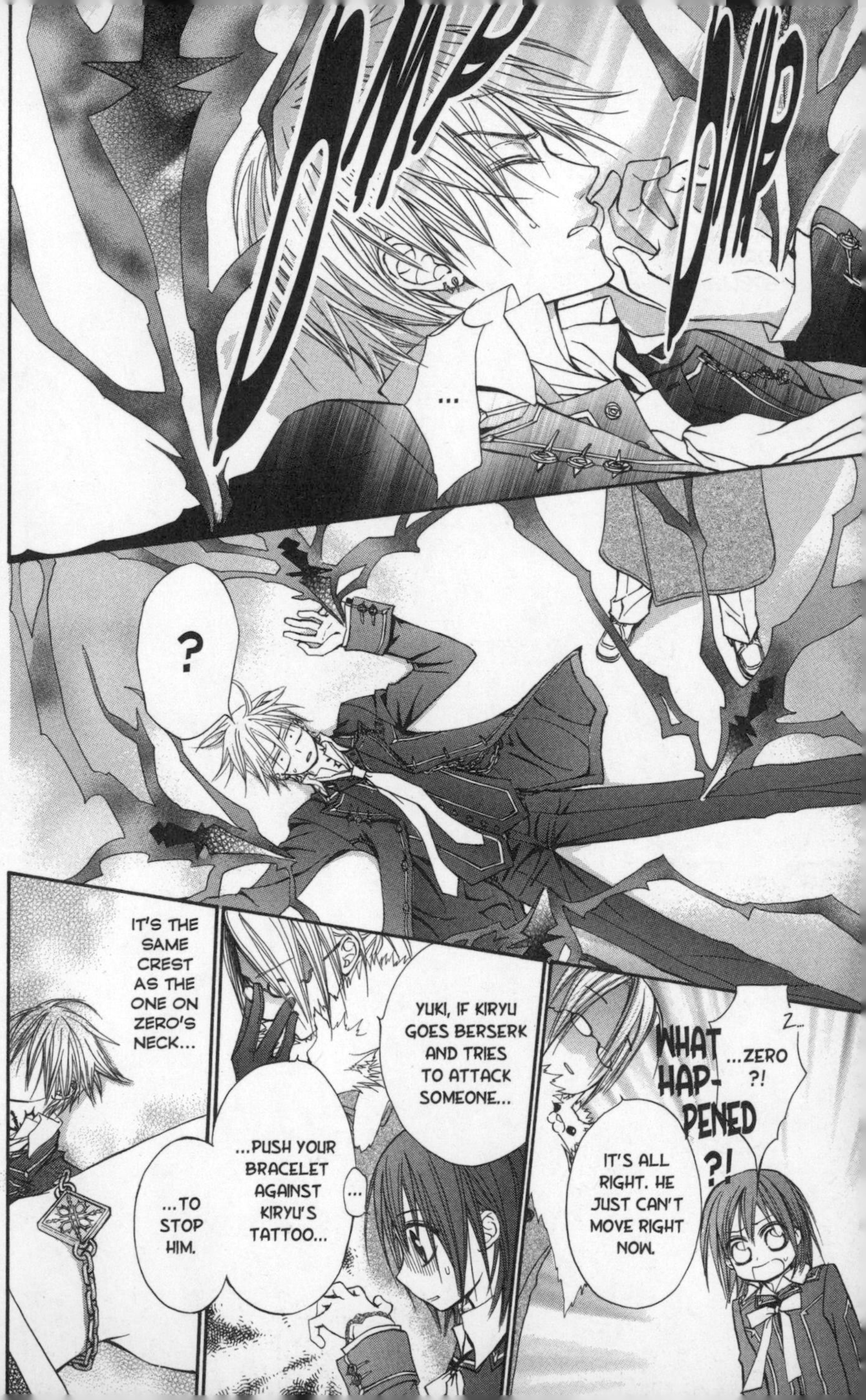
...
?
Z...
...ZERO ?!
WHAT HAP-PENED ?!
IT'S ALL RIGHT. HE JUST CAN'T MOVE RIGHT NOW.
YUKI, IF KIRYU GOES BERSERK AND TRIES TO ATTACK SOMEONE...
...PUSH YOUR BRACELET AGAINST KIRYU'S TATTOO...
...
...TO STOP HIM.
IT'S THE SAME CREST AS THE ONE ON ZERO'S NECK...

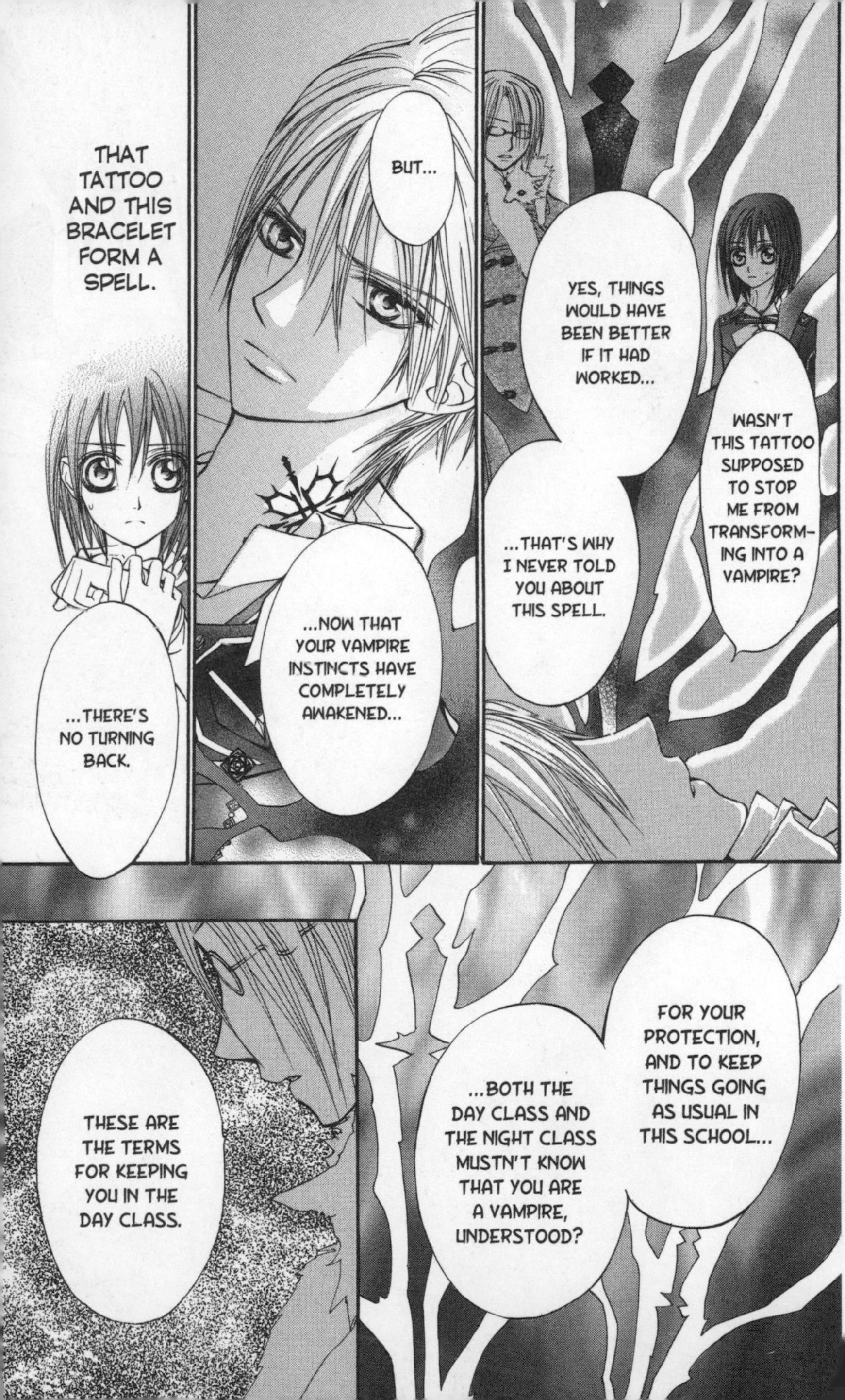
WASN'T THIS TATTOO SUPPOSED TO STOP ME FROM TRANSFORMING INTO A VAMPIRE?
YES, THINGS WOULD HAVE BEEN BETTER IF IT HAD WORKED...
...THAT'S WHY I NEVER TOLD YOU ABOUT THIS SPELL.
BUT...
...NOW THAT YOUR VAMPIRE INSTINCTS HAVE COMPLETELY AWAKENED...
THAT TATTOO AND THIS BRACELET FORM A SPELL.
...THERE'S NO TURNING BACK.
FOR YOUR PROTECTION, AND TO KEEP THINGS GOING AS USUAL IN THIS SCHOOL...
...BOTH THE DAY CLASS AND THE NIGHT CLASS MUSTN'T KNOW THAT YOU ARE A VAMPIRE, UNDERSTOOD?
THESE ARE THE TERMS FOR KEEPING YOU IN THE DAY CLASS.

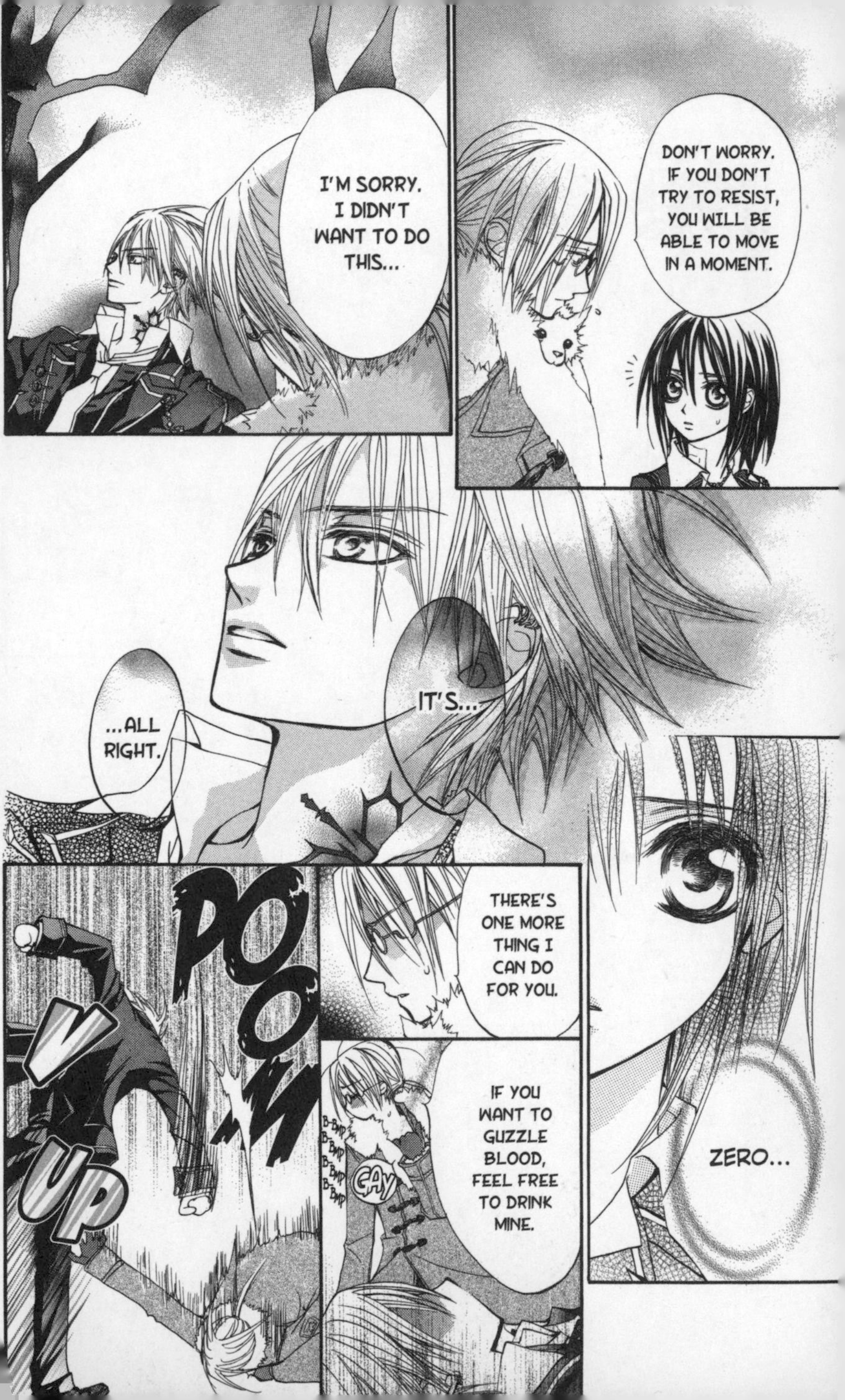
DON'T WORRY. IF YOU DON'T TRY TO RESIST, YOU WILL BE ABLE TO MOVE IN A MOMENT.
I'M SORRY. I DIDN'T WANT TO DO THIS...
IT'S...
...ALL RIGHT.
ZERO...
THERE'S ONE MORE THING I CAN DO FOR YOU.
IF YOU WANT TO GUZZLE BLOOD, FEEL FREE TO DRINK MINE.
B-BMP B-BMP B-BMP B-BMP
GAY
POOM
VUP

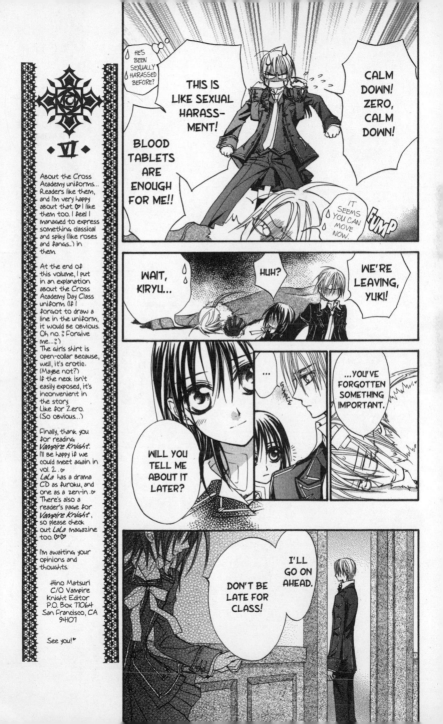

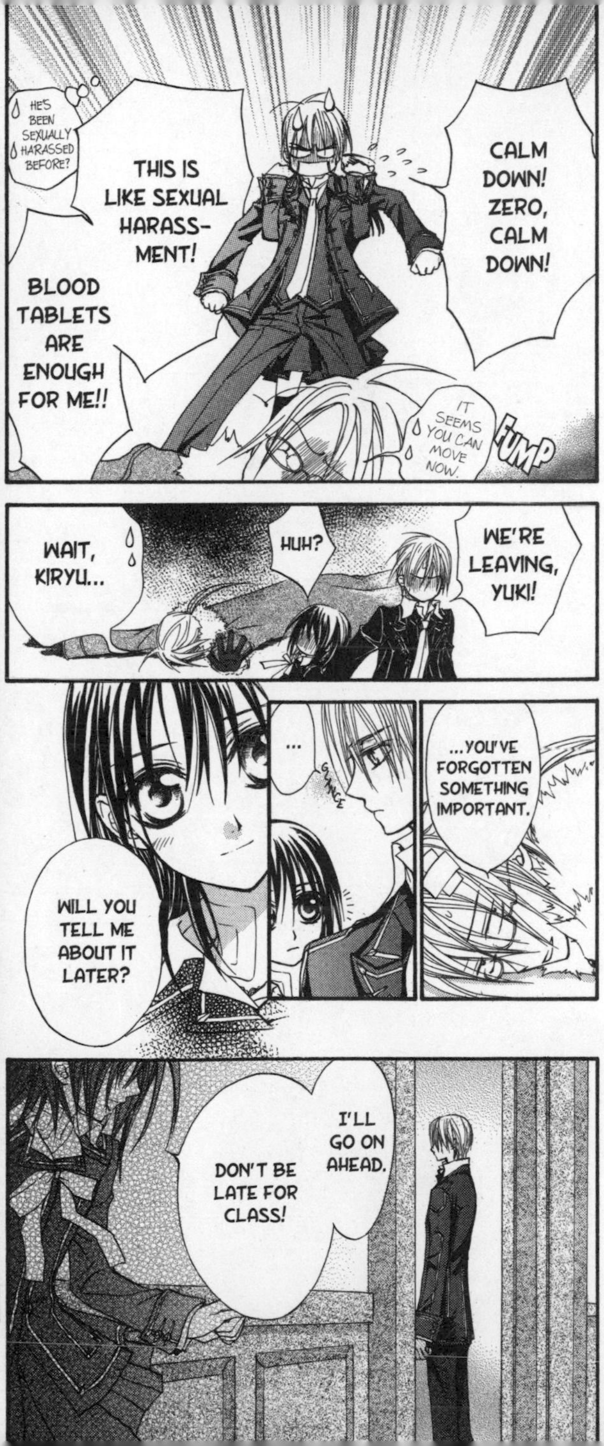
CALM DOWN! ZERO, CALM DOWN!
THIS IS LIKE SEXUAL HARASS-MENT!
HE'S BEEN SEXUALLY HARASSED BEFORE?
BLOOD TABLETS ARE ENOUGH FOR ME!!
IT SEEMS YOU CAN MOVE NOW.
FUMP
WE'RE LEAVING, YUKI!
HUH?
WAIT, KIRYU...
...YOU'VE FORGOTTEN SOMETHING IMPORTANT.
...
GLANCE
WILL YOU TELL ME ABOUT IT LATER?
I'LL GO ON AHEAD.
DON'T BE LATE FOR CLASS!

• VI •

About the Cross Academy uniforms... Readers like them, and I'm very happy about that. ♡ I like them too. I feel I managed to express something classical and spiky (like roses and fangs...) in them.

At the end of this volume, I put in an explanation about the Cross Academy Day Class uniform. (If I forgot to draw a line in the uniform, it would be obvious. Oh no. Forgive me...)
The girls shirt is open-collar because, well, it's erotic. (Maybe not?)
If the neck isn't easily exposed, it's inconvenient in the story.
Like for Zero.
(So obvious...)

Finally, thank you for reading *Vampire Knight*. I'll be happy if we could meet again in vol. 2. ♡
*LaLa* has a drama CD as furoku, and one as a zen-in. ♡
There's also a reader's page for *Vampire Knight*, so please check out *LaLa* magazine too. ♡♡

I'm awaiting your opinions and thoughts.

Hino Matsuri
C/O Vampire
Knight Editor
P.O. Box 77064
San Francisco, CA
94107

See you! ♥

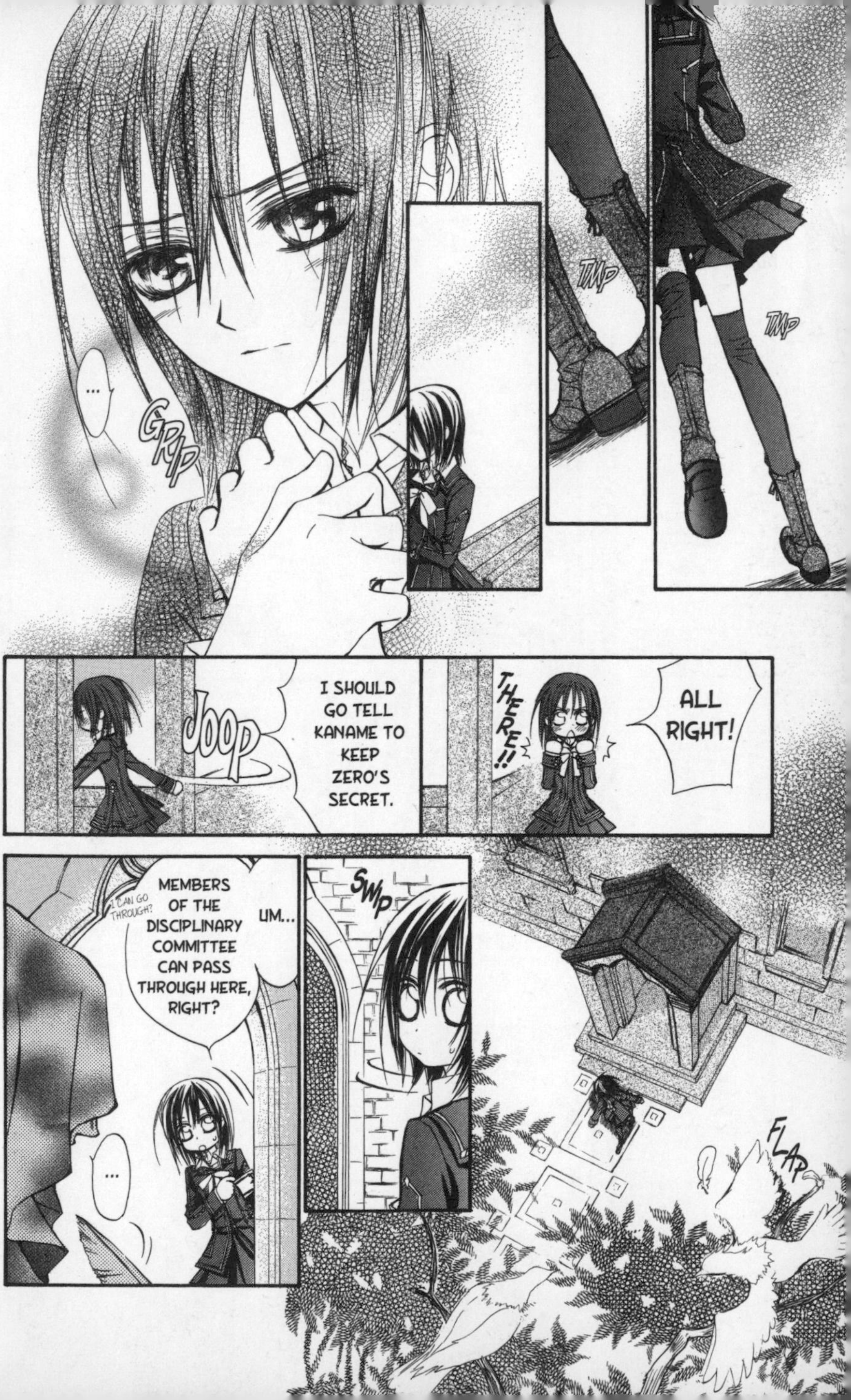
TMP
TMP
...
GRIP
ALL RIGHT!
THERE!!
I SHOULD GO TELL KANAME TO KEEP ZERO'S SECRET.
JOOP
FLAP
SWIP
UM...
MEMBERS OF THE DISCIPLINARY COMMITTEE CAN PASS THROUGH HERE, RIGHT?
I CAN GO THROUGH?
...

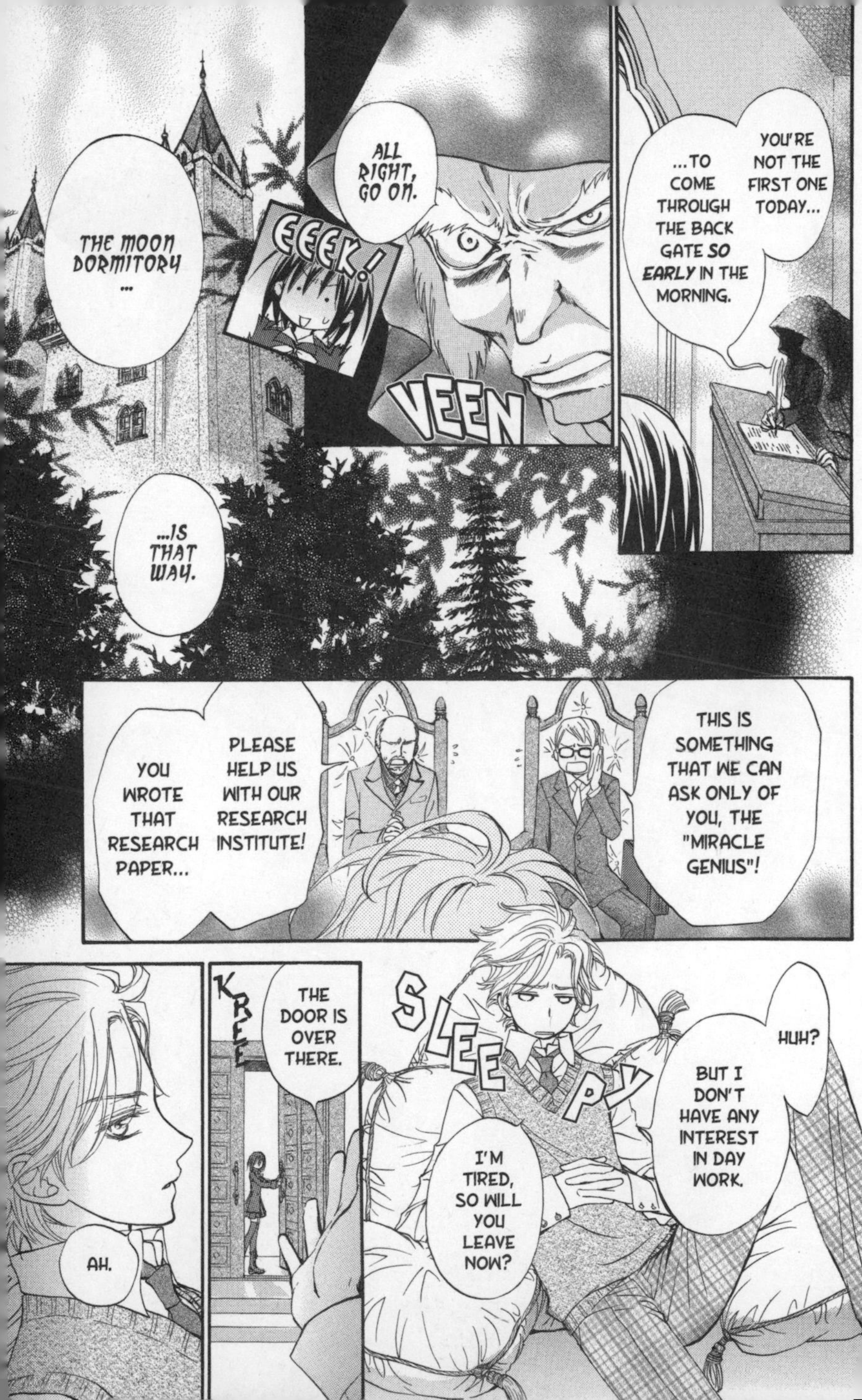
YOU'RE NOT THE FIRST ONE TODAY...
...TO COME THROUGH THE BACK GATE SO *EARLY* IN THE MORNING.
ALL RIGHT, GO ON.
VEEN
EEEK!
THE MOON DORMITORY ...
...IS THAT WAY.
THIS IS SOMETHING THAT WE CAN ASK ONLY OF YOU, THE "MIRACLE GENIUS"!
PLEASE HELP US WITH OUR RESEARCH INSTITUTE!
YOU WROTE THAT RESEARCH PAPER...
HUH?
BUT I DON'T HAVE ANY INTEREST IN DAY WORK.
SLEEPY
I'M TIRED, SO WILL YOU LEAVE NOW?
KREE
THE DOOR IS OVER THERE.
AH.

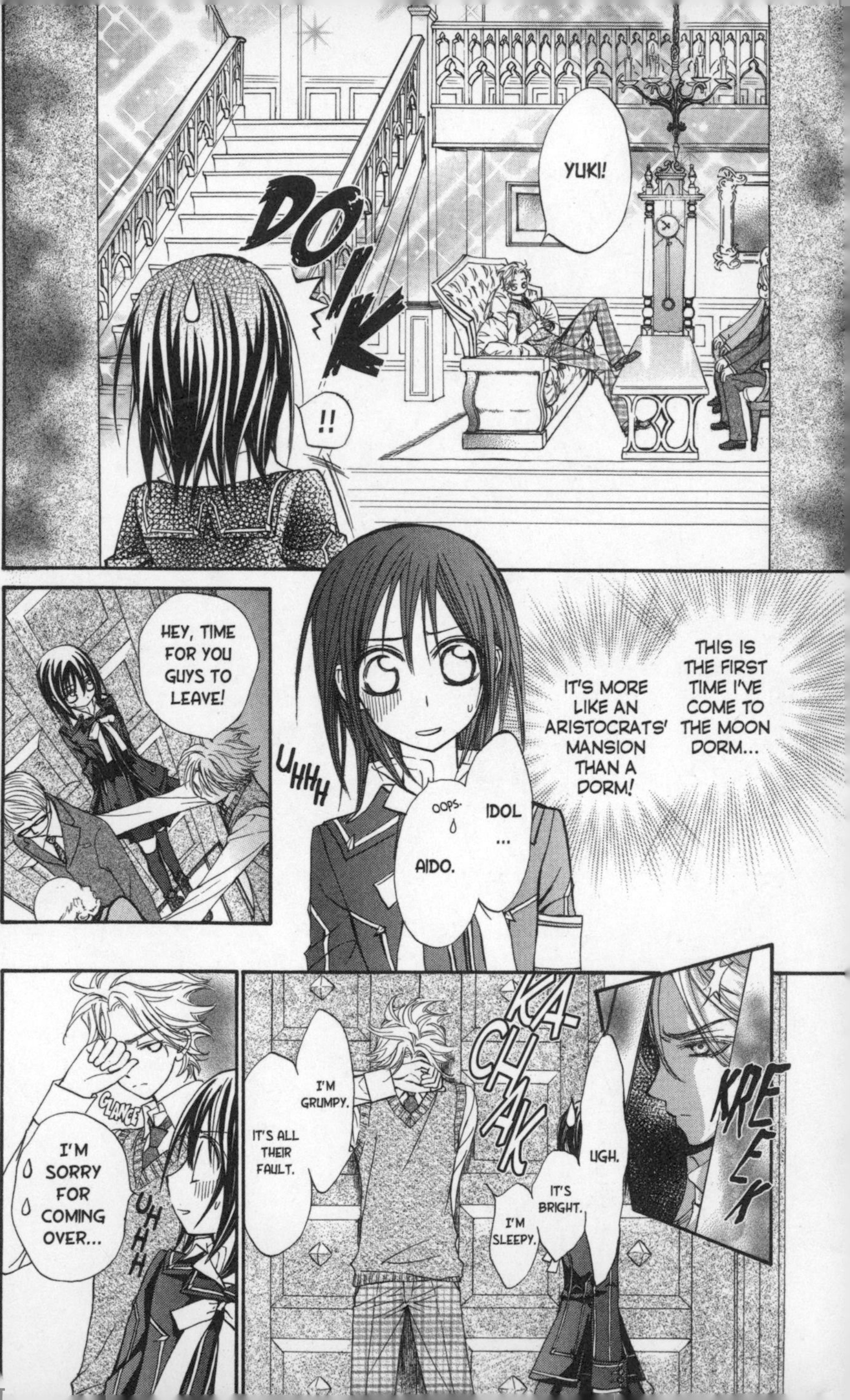
YUKI!
DOINK
!!
THIS IS THE FIRST TIME I'VE COME TO THE MOON DORM...
IT'S MORE LIKE AN ARISTOCRATS' MANSION THAN A DORM!
IDOL ...
OOPS.
AIDO.
UHHH
HEY, TIME FOR YOU GUYS TO LEAVE!
KREEK
KA-CHAK
UGH.
IT'S BRIGHT.
I'M SLEEPY.
I'M GRUMPY.
IT'S ALL THEIR FAULT.
GLANCE
I'M SORRY FOR COMING OVER...
UHHH

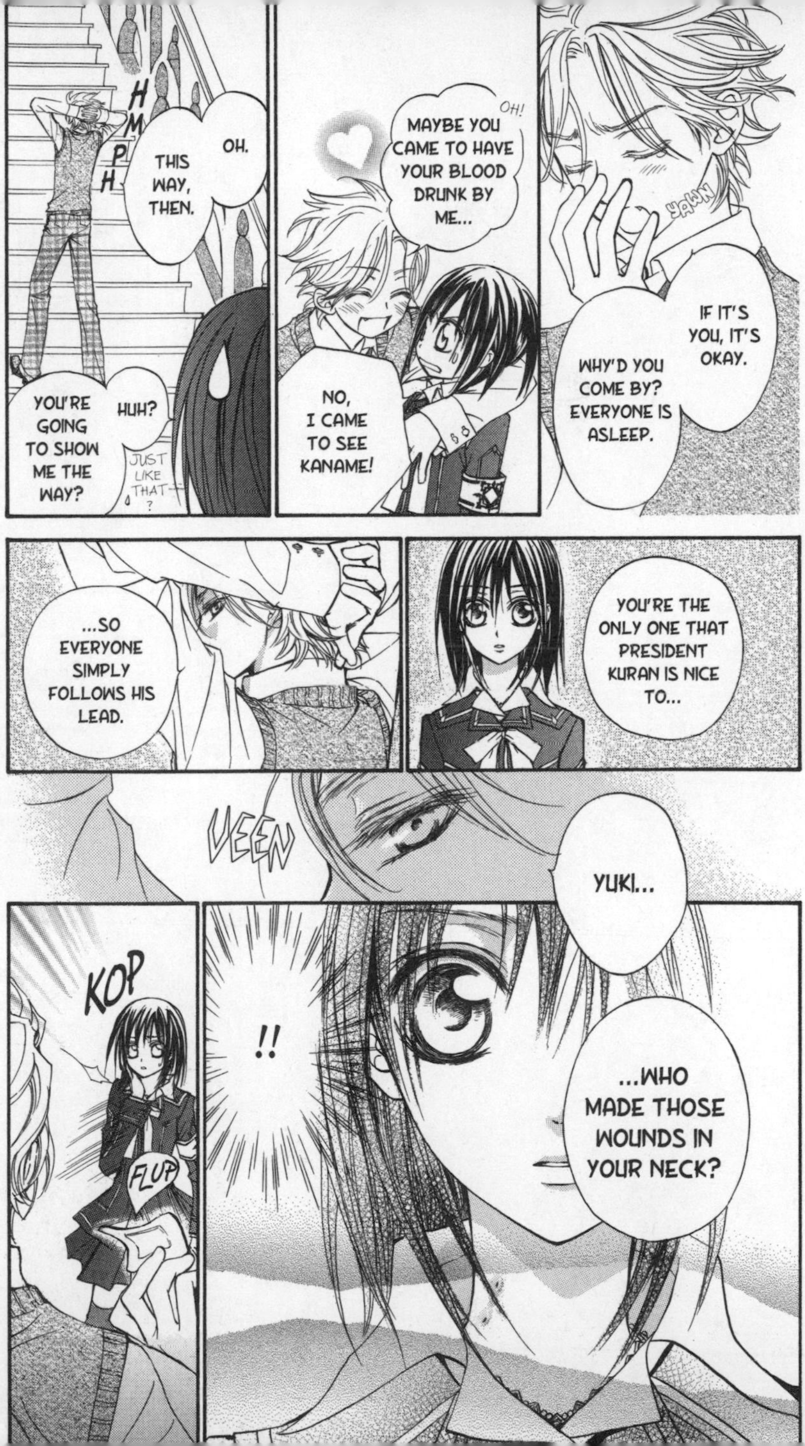
YAWN
IF IT'S YOU, IT'S OKAY.
WHY'D YOU COME BY? EVERYONE IS ASLEEP.
OH!
MAYBE YOU CAME TO HAVE YOUR BLOOD DRUNK BY ME...
NO, I CAME TO SEE KANAME!
OH.
THIS WAY, THEN.
HMPH
HUH?
YOU'RE GOING TO SHOW ME THE WAY?
JUST LIKE THAT?
YOU'RE THE ONLY ONE THAT PRESIDENT KURAN IS NICE TO...
...SO EVERYONE SIMPLY FOLLOWS HIS LEAD.
YUKI...
VEEN
...WHO MADE THOSE WOUNDS IN YOUR NECK?
!!
KOP
FLUP

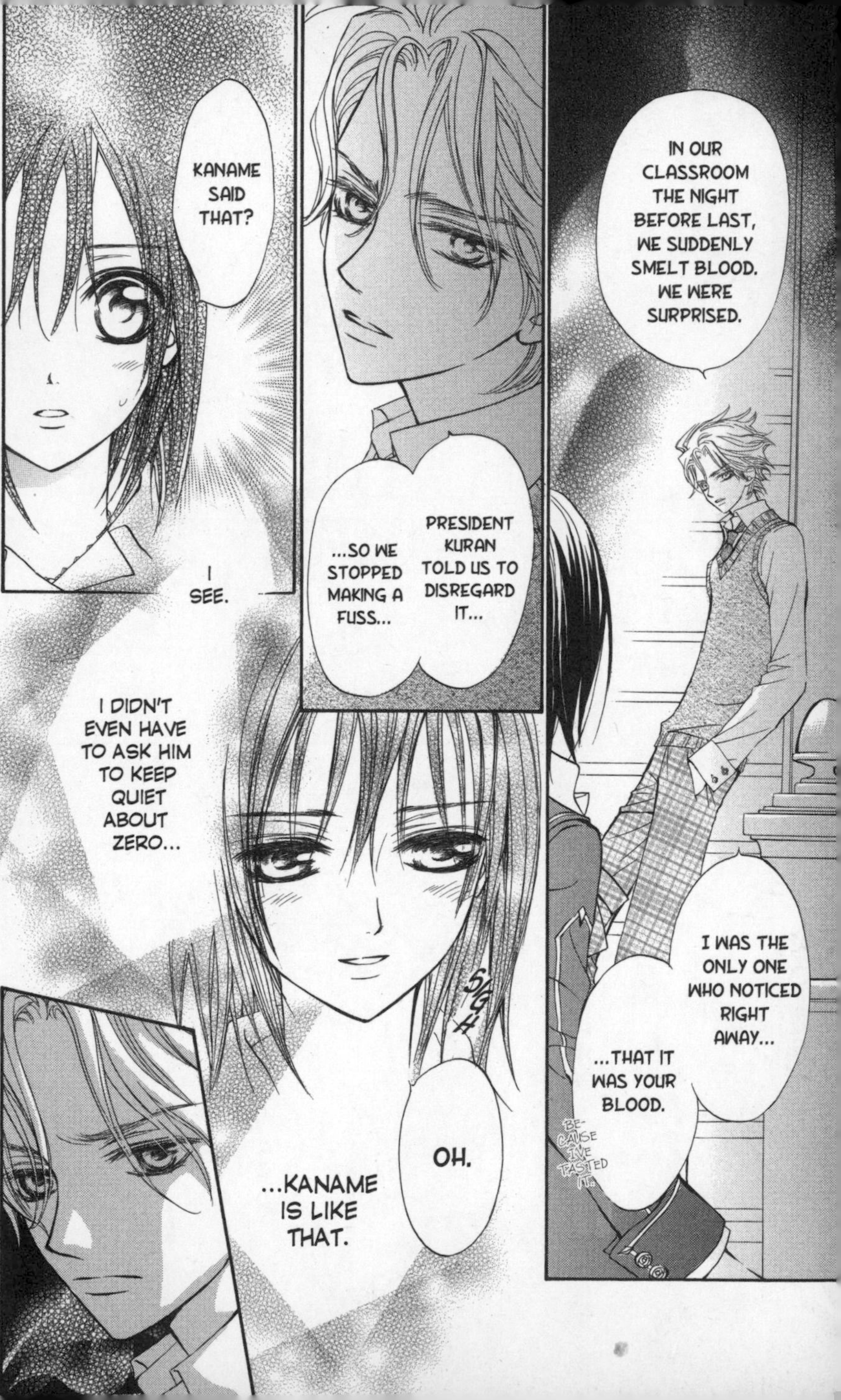
IN OUR CLASSROOM THE NIGHT BEFORE LAST, WE SUDDENLY SMELT BLOOD. WE WERE SURPRISED.
I WAS THE ONLY ONE WHO NOTICED RIGHT AWAY...
...THAT IT WAS YOUR BLOOD.
BE-CAUSE I'VE TASTED IT.
PRESIDENT KURAN TOLD US TO DISREGARD IT...
...SO WE STOPPED MAKING A FUSS...
KANAME SAID THAT?
I SEE.
I DIDN'T EVEN HAVE TO ASK HIM TO KEEP QUIET ABOUT ZERO...
SIGH
OH.
...KANAME IS LIKE THAT.

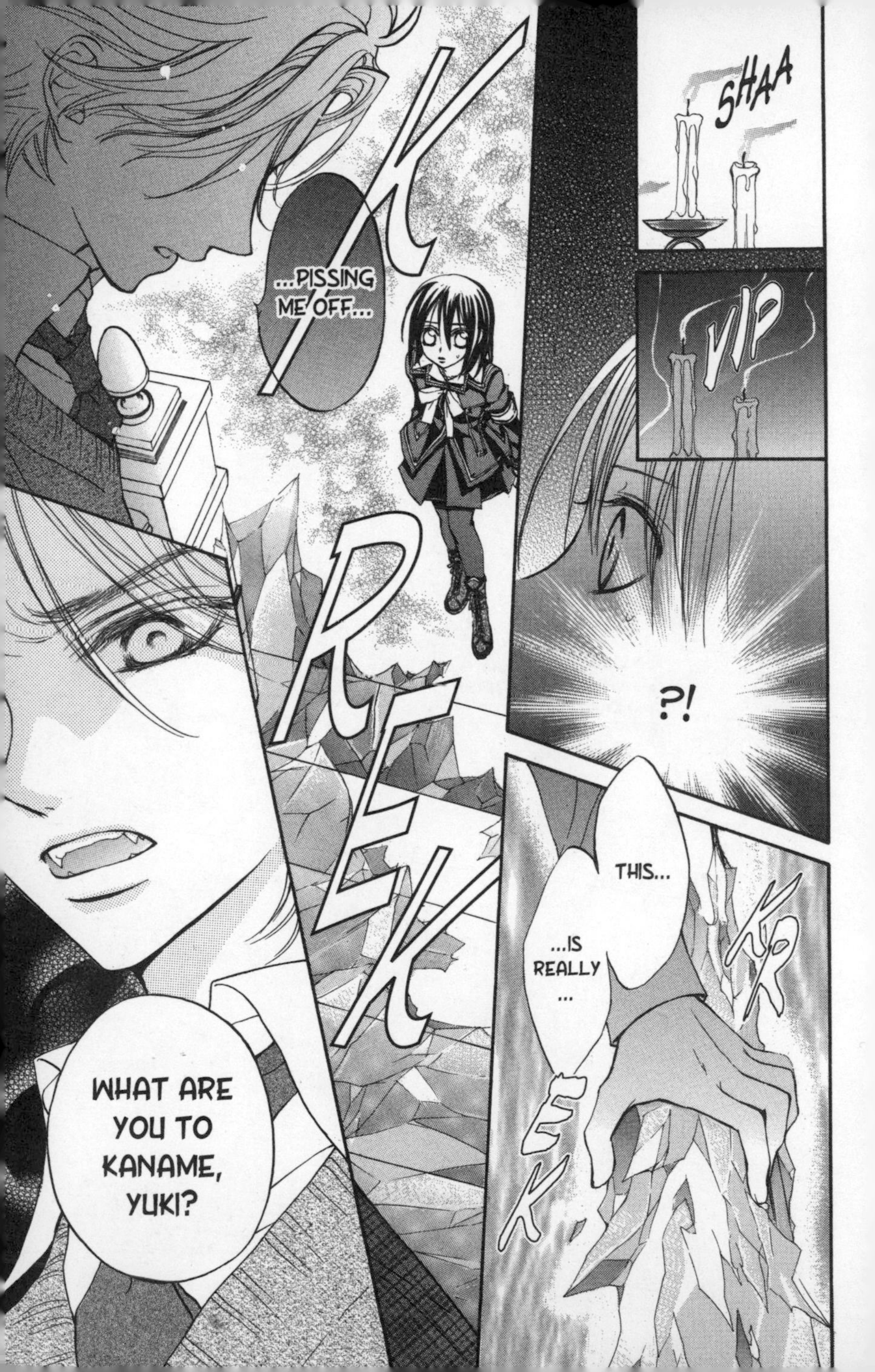
SHAA
VIP
...PISSING ME OFF...
KREK
?!
THIS...
...IS REALLY ...
KR
EEK
WHAT ARE YOU TO KANAME, YUKI?

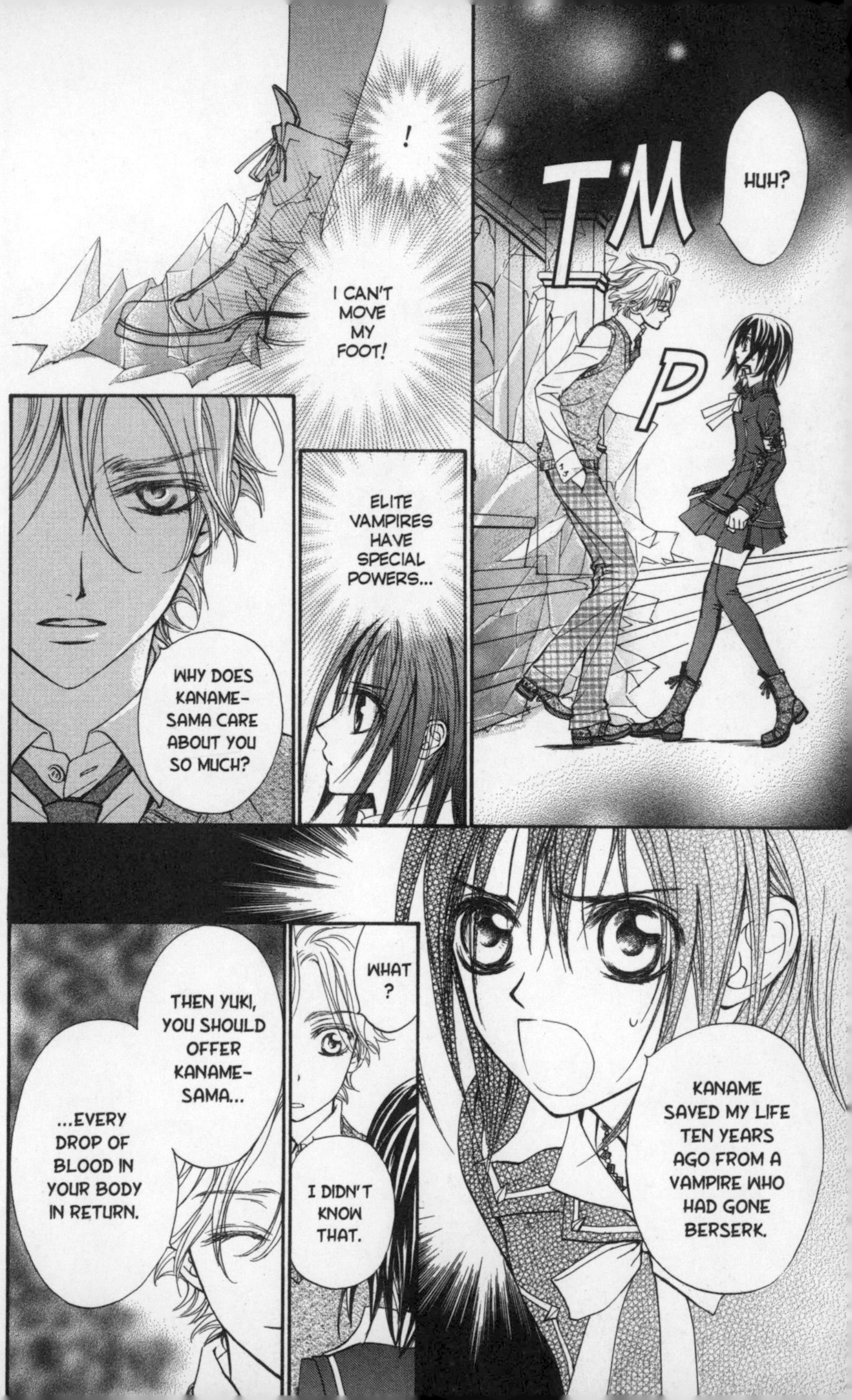
TMP
HUH?
!
I CAN'T MOVE MY FOOT!
ELITE VAMPIRES HAVE SPECIAL POWERS...
WHY DOES KANAME-SAMA CARE ABOUT YOU SO MUCH?
KANAME SAVED MY LIFE TEN YEARS AGO FROM A VAMPIRE WHO HAD GONE BERSERK.
WHAT?
I DIDN'T KNOW THAT.
THEN YUKI, YOU SHOULD OFFER KANAME-SAMA...
...EVERY DROP OF BLOOD IN YOUR BODY IN RETURN.

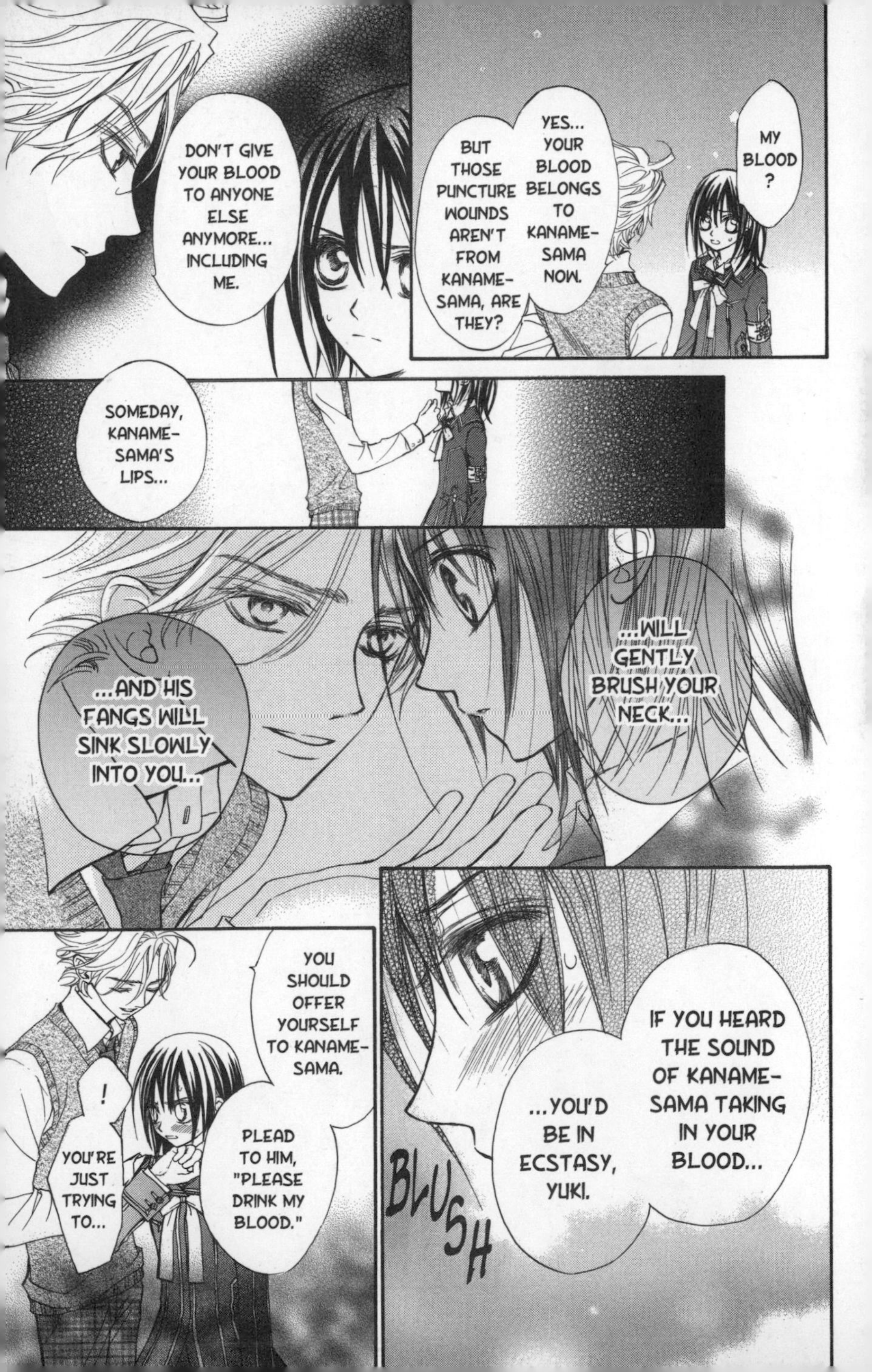
MY BLOOD ?
YES... YOUR BLOOD BELONGS TO KANAME-SAMA NOW.
BUT THOSE PUNCTURE WOUNDS AREN'T FROM KANAME-SAMA, ARE THEY?
DON'T GIVE YOUR BLOOD TO ANYONE ELSE ANYMORE... INCLUDING ME.
SOMEDAY, KANAME-SAMA'S LIPS...
...WILL GENTLY BRUSH YOUR NECK...
...AND HIS FANGS WILL SINK SLOWLY INTO YOU...
IF YOU HEARD THE SOUND OF KANAME-SAMA TAKING IN YOUR BLOOD...
...YOU'D BE IN ECSTASY, YUKI.
BLUSH
YOU SHOULD OFFER YOURSELF TO KANAME-SAMA.
PLEAD TO HIM, "PLEASE DRINK MY BLOOD."
!
YOU'RE JUST TRYING TO...

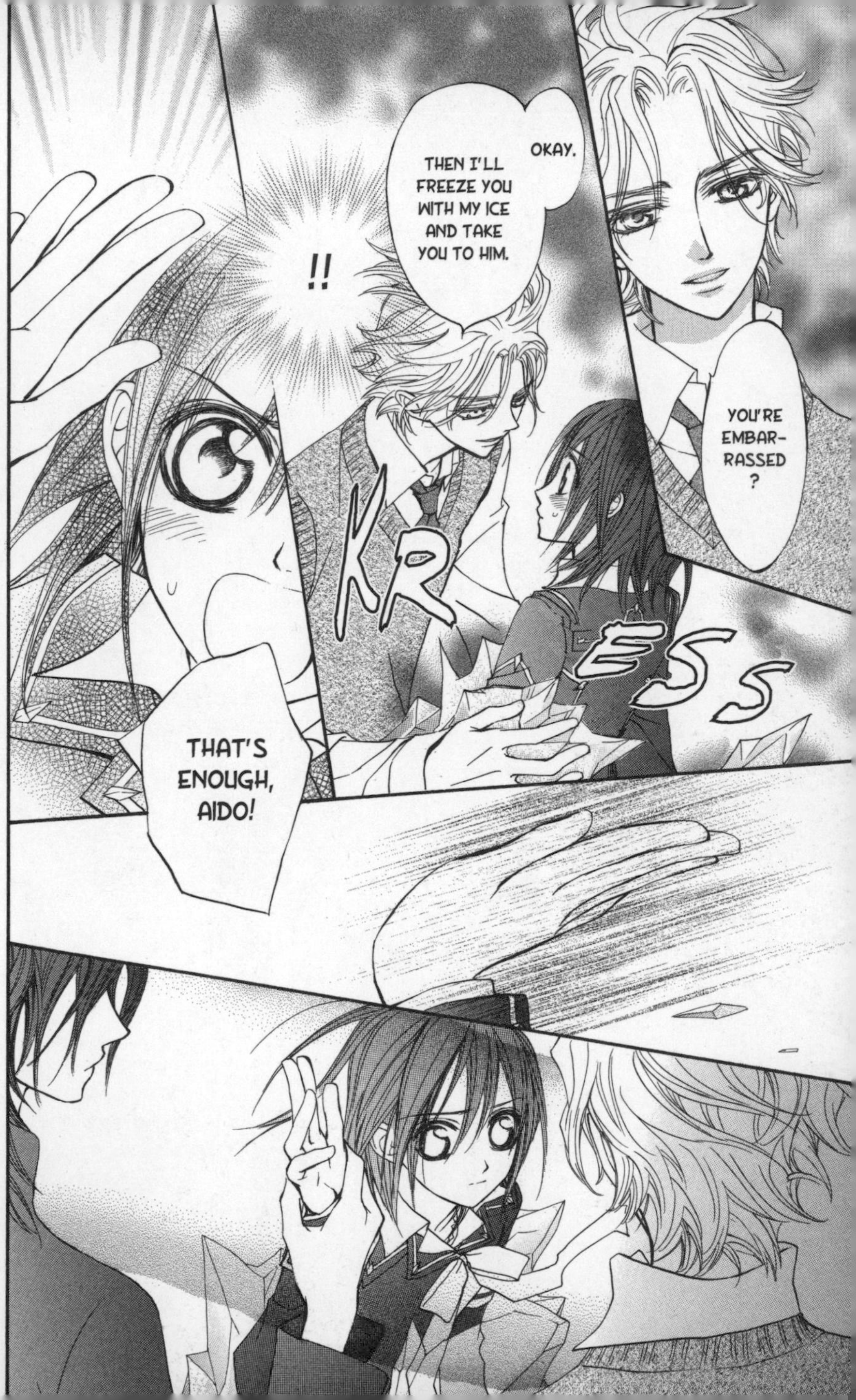
YOU'RE EMBARRASSED?
OKAY.
THEN I'LL FREEZE YOU WITH MY ICE AND TAKE YOU TO HIM.
!!
KRESS
THAT'S ENOUGH, AIDO!

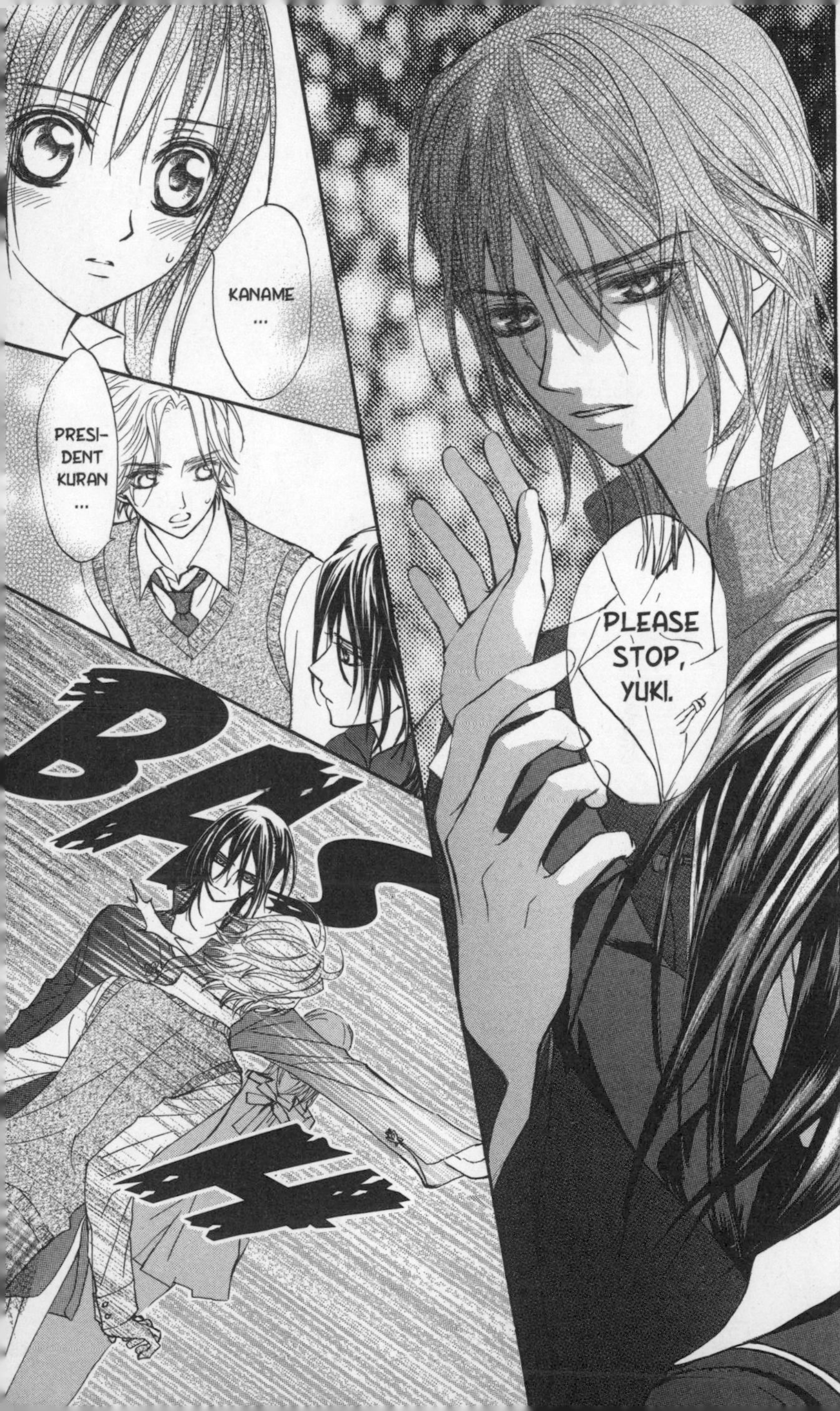
PLEASE STOP, YUKI.
KANAME ...
PRESI-DENT KURAN ...
BASH

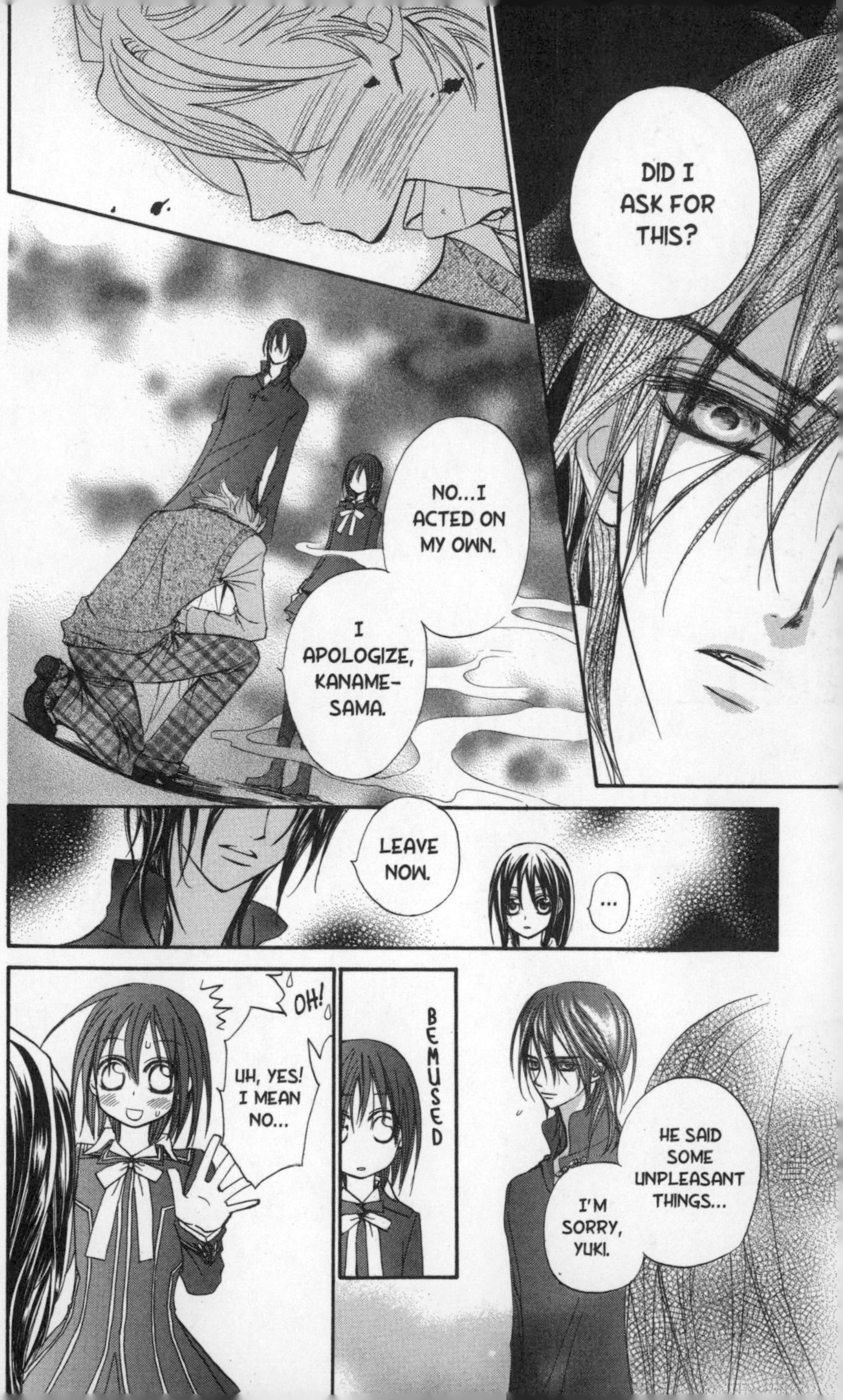
DID I ASK FOR THIS?
NO...I ACTED ON MY OWN.
I APOLOGIZE, KANAME-SAMA.
LEAVE NOW.
...
HE SAID SOME UNPLEASANT THINGS...
I'M SORRY, YUKI.
BEMUSED
OH!
UH, YES! I MEAN NO...

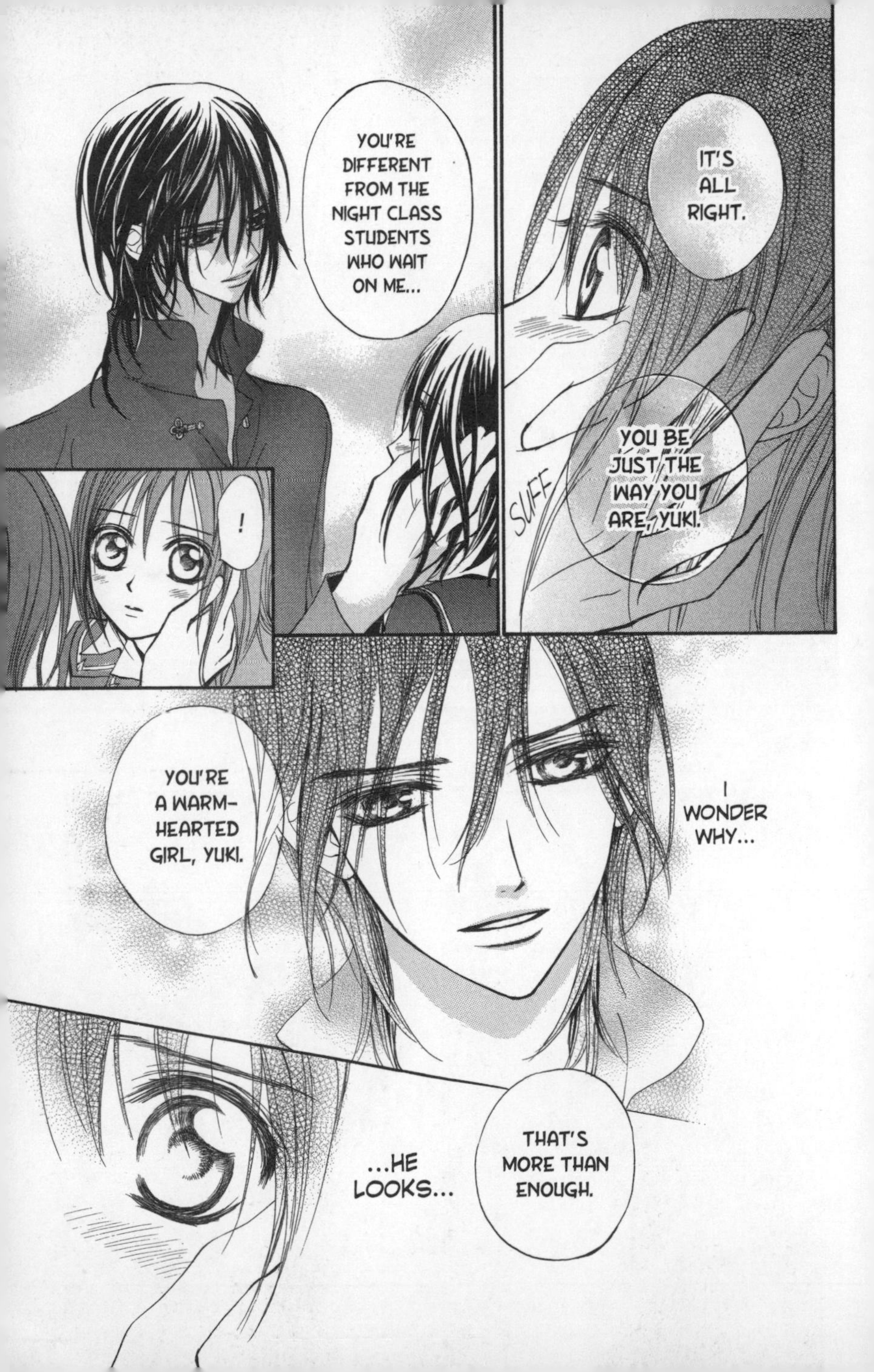
IT'S ALL RIGHT.
YOU BE JUST THE WAY YOU ARE, YUKI.
SUFF
YOU'RE DIFFERENT FROM THE NIGHT CLASS STUDENTS WHO WAIT ON ME...
!
I WONDER WHY...
YOU'RE A WARM-HEARTED GIRL, YUKI.
THAT'S MORE THAN ENOUGH.
...HE LOOKS...

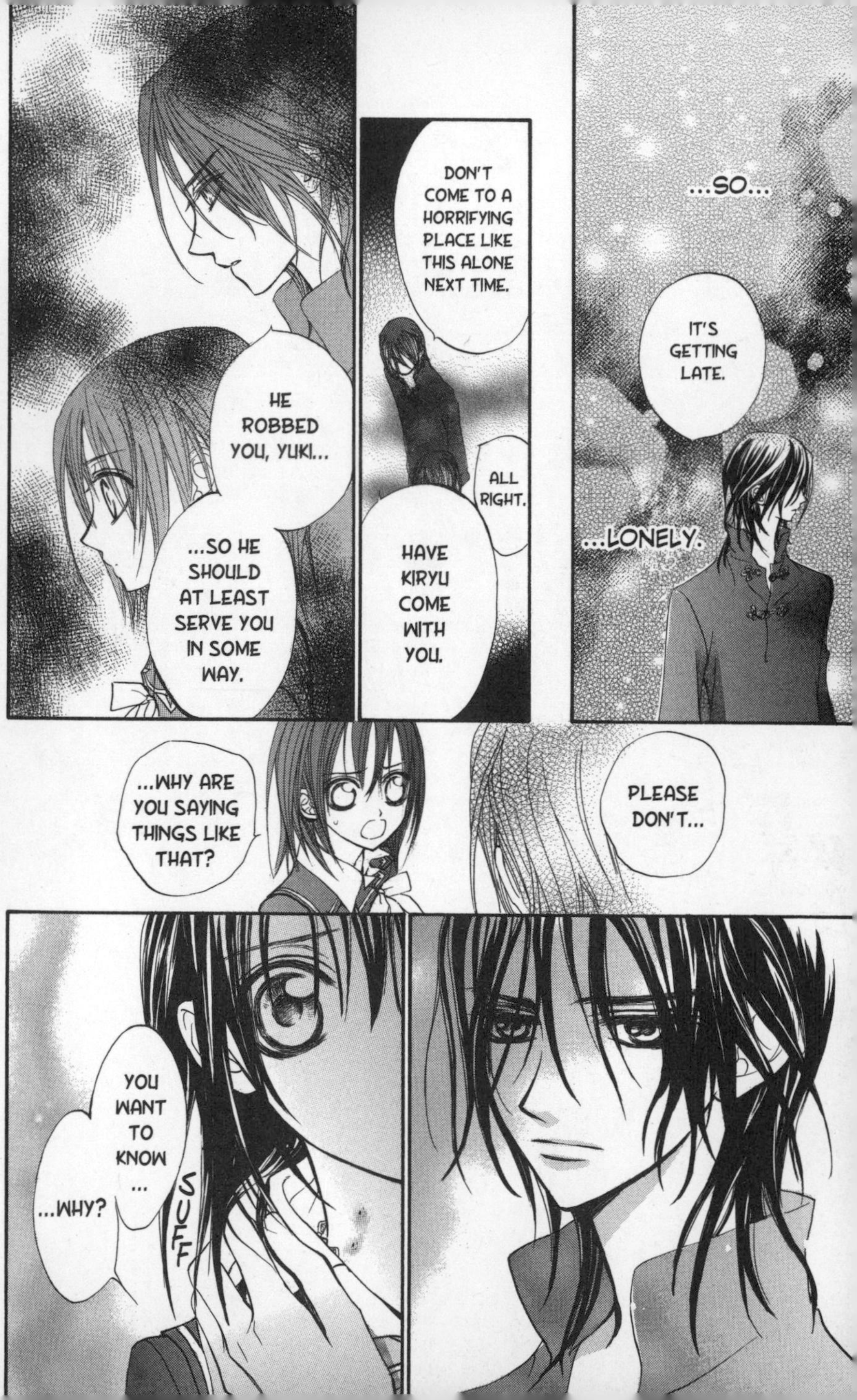
...SO...
IT'S GETTING LATE.
...LONELY.
DON'T COME TO A HORRIFYING PLACE LIKE THIS ALONE NEXT TIME.
ALL RIGHT.
HAVE KIRYU COME WITH YOU.
HE ROBBED YOU, YUKI...
...SO HE SHOULD AT LEAST SERVE YOU IN SOME WAY.
PLEASE DON'T...
...WHY ARE YOU SAYING THINGS LIKE THAT?
YOU WANT TO KNOW ...
...WHY?
SUFF

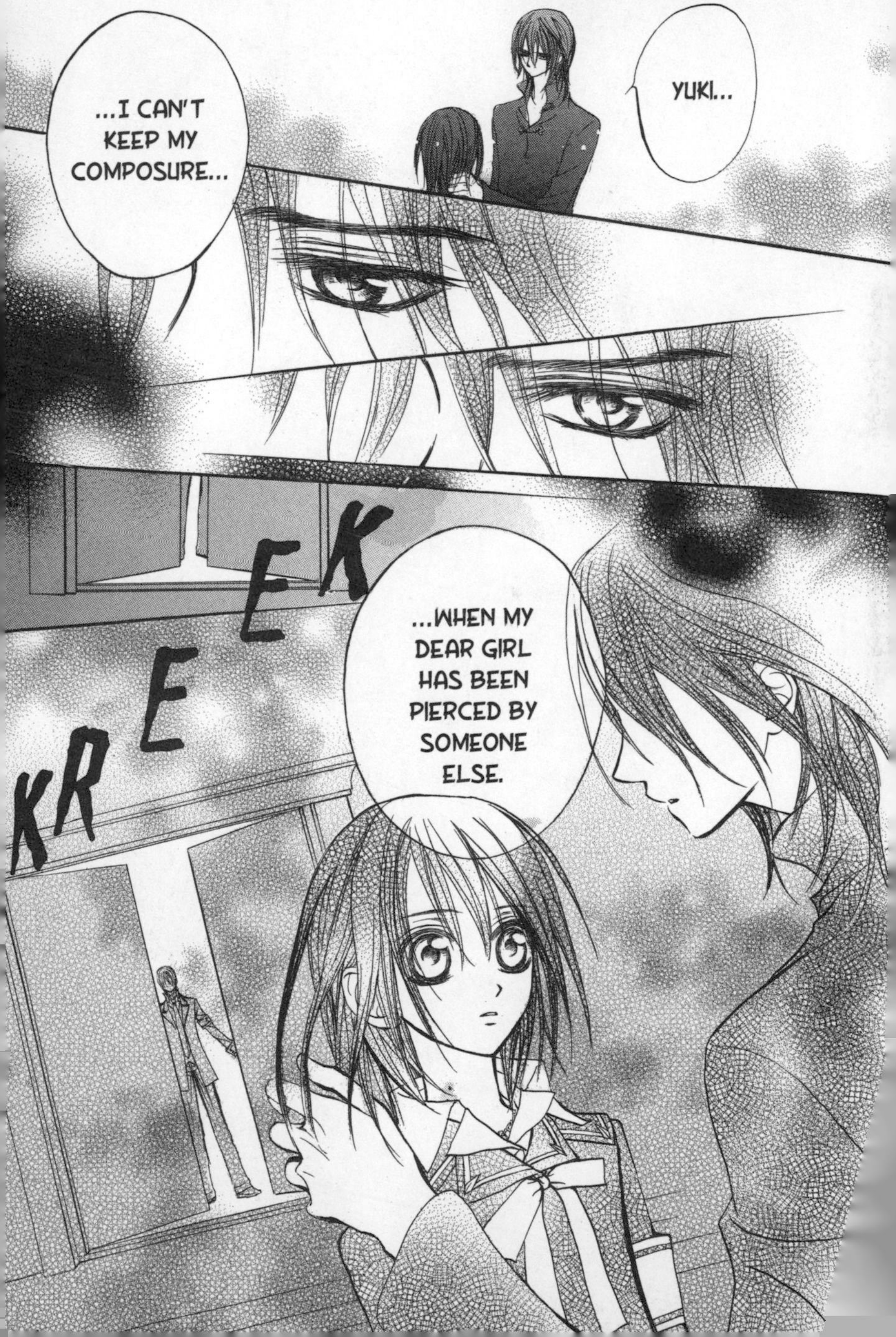
YUKI...
...I CAN'T KEEP MY COMPOSURE...
...WHEN MY DEAR GIRL HAS BEEN PIERCED BY SOMEONE ELSE.
KREEK

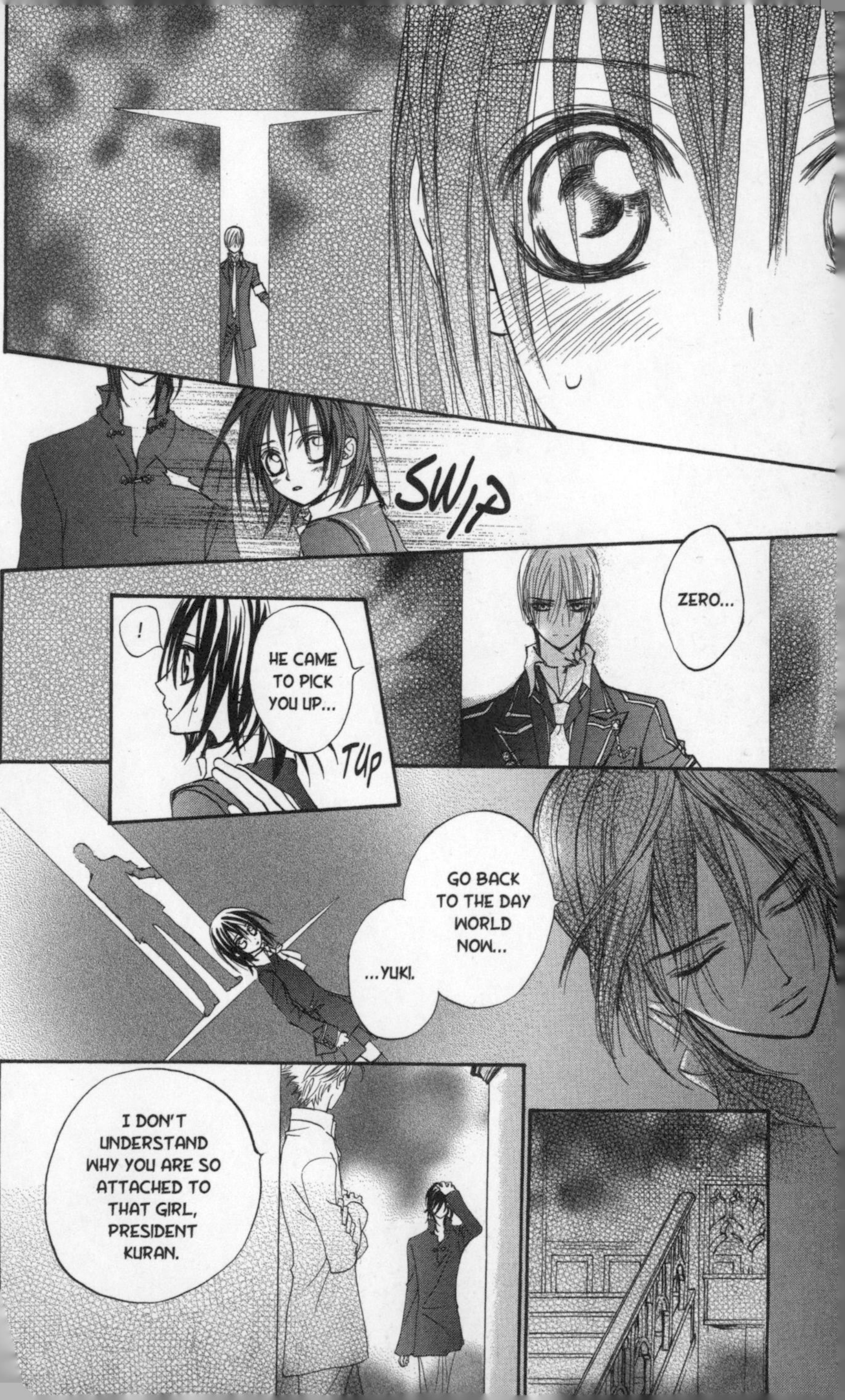
SWIP
ZERO...
!
HE CAME TO PICK YOU UP...
TUP
GO BACK TO THE DAY WORLD NOW...
...YUKI.
I DON'T UNDERSTAND WHY YOU ARE SO ATTACHED TO THAT GIRL, PRESIDENT KURAN.

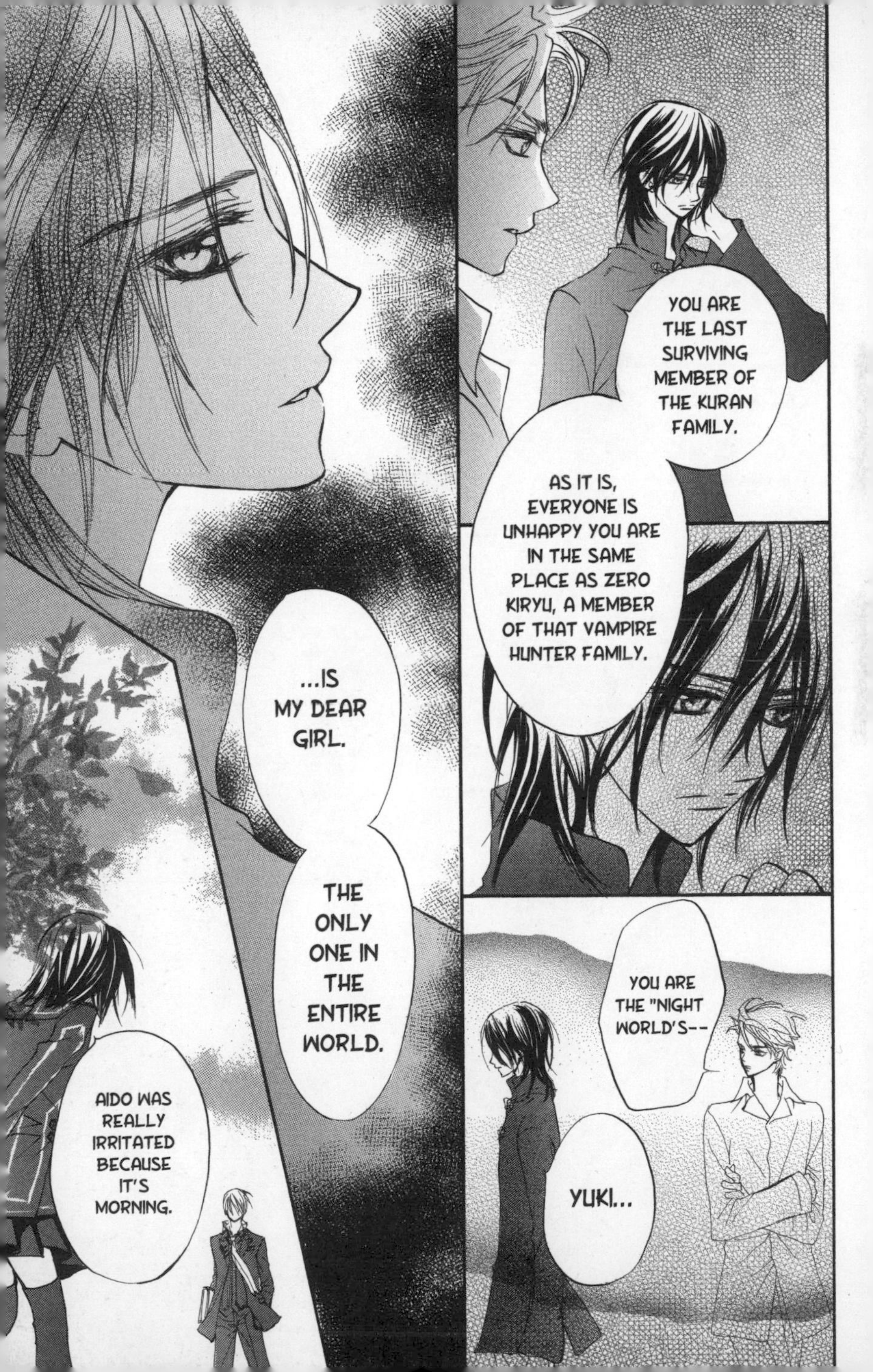
YOU ARE THE LAST SURVIVING MEMBER OF THE KURAN FAMILY.
AS IT IS, EVERYONE IS UNHAPPY YOU ARE IN THE SAME PLACE AS ZERO KIRYU, A MEMBER OF THAT VAMPIRE HUNTER FAMILY.
YOU ARE THE "NIGHT WORLD'S--
YUKI...
...IS MY DEAR GIRL.
THE ONLY ONE IN THE ENTIRE WORLD.
AIDO WAS REALLY IRRITATED BECAUSE IT'S MORNING.

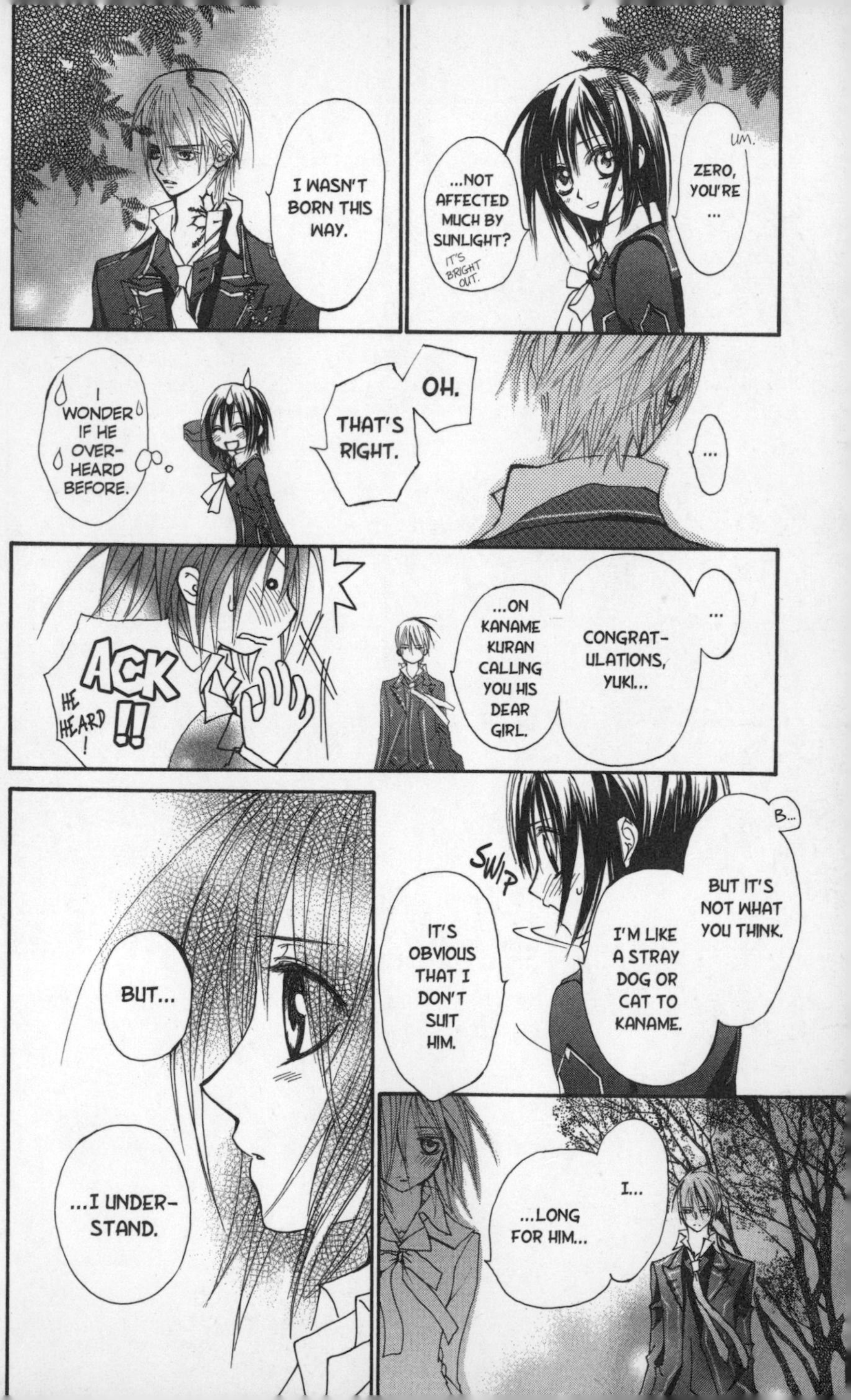
UM.
ZERO, YOU'RE ...
...NOT AFFECTED MUCH BY SUNLIGHT?
IT'S BRIGHT OUT.
I WASN'T BORN THIS WAY.
...
OH.
THAT'S RIGHT.
I WONDER IF HE OVER-HEARD BEFORE.
...
CONGRAT-ULATIONS, YUKI...
...ON KANAME KURAN CALLING YOU HIS DEAR GIRL.
ACK !!
HE HEARD!
B...
BUT IT'S NOT WHAT YOU THINK.
I'M LIKE A STRAY DOG OR CAT TO KANAME.
SWIP
IT'S OBVIOUS THAT I DON'T SUIT HIM.
I...
...LONG FOR HIM...
BUT...
...I UNDER-STAND.

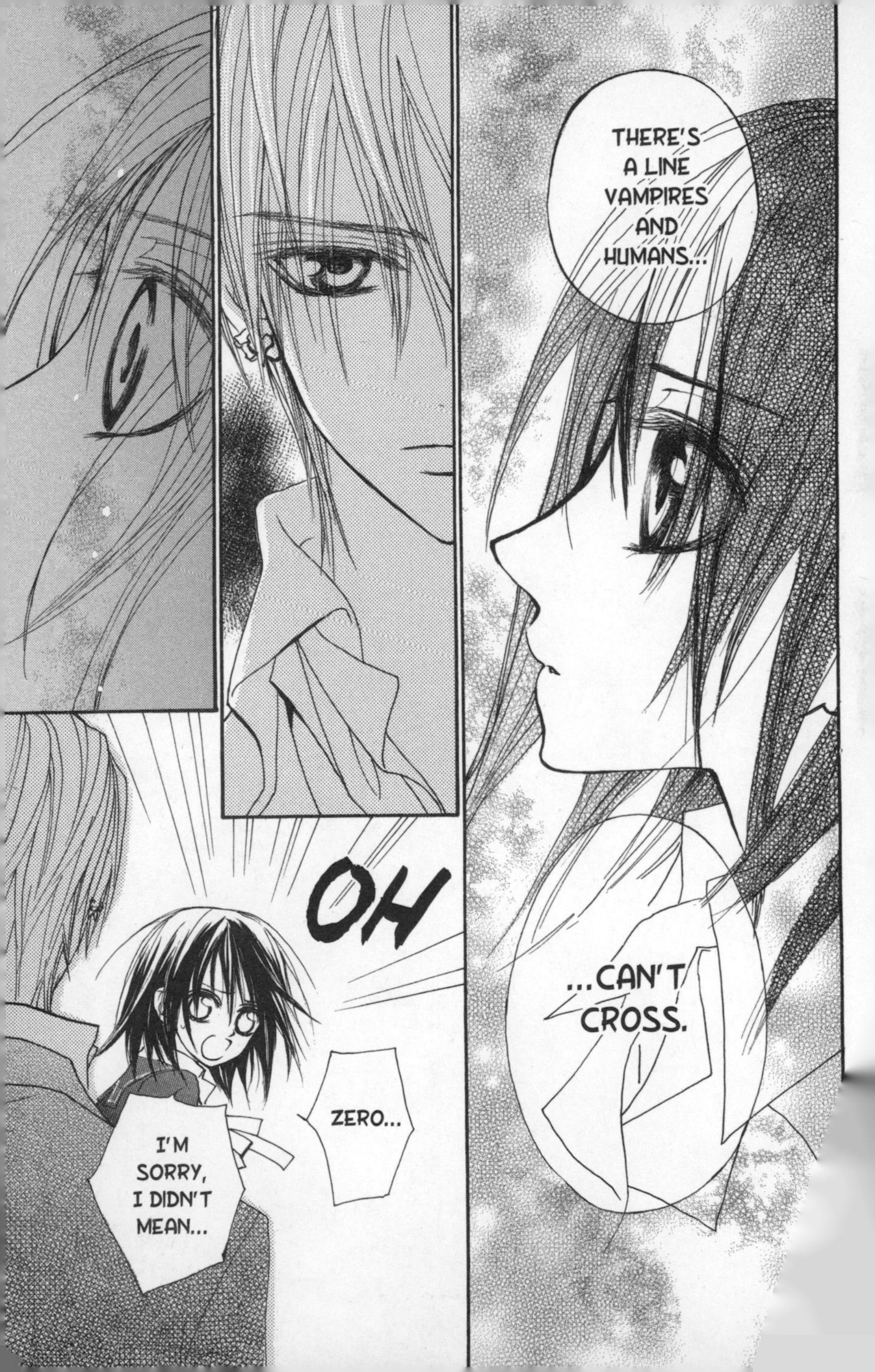
THERE'S A LINE VAMPIRES AND HUMANS...
...CAN'T CROSS.
OH
ZERO...
I'M SORRY, I DIDN'T MEAN...

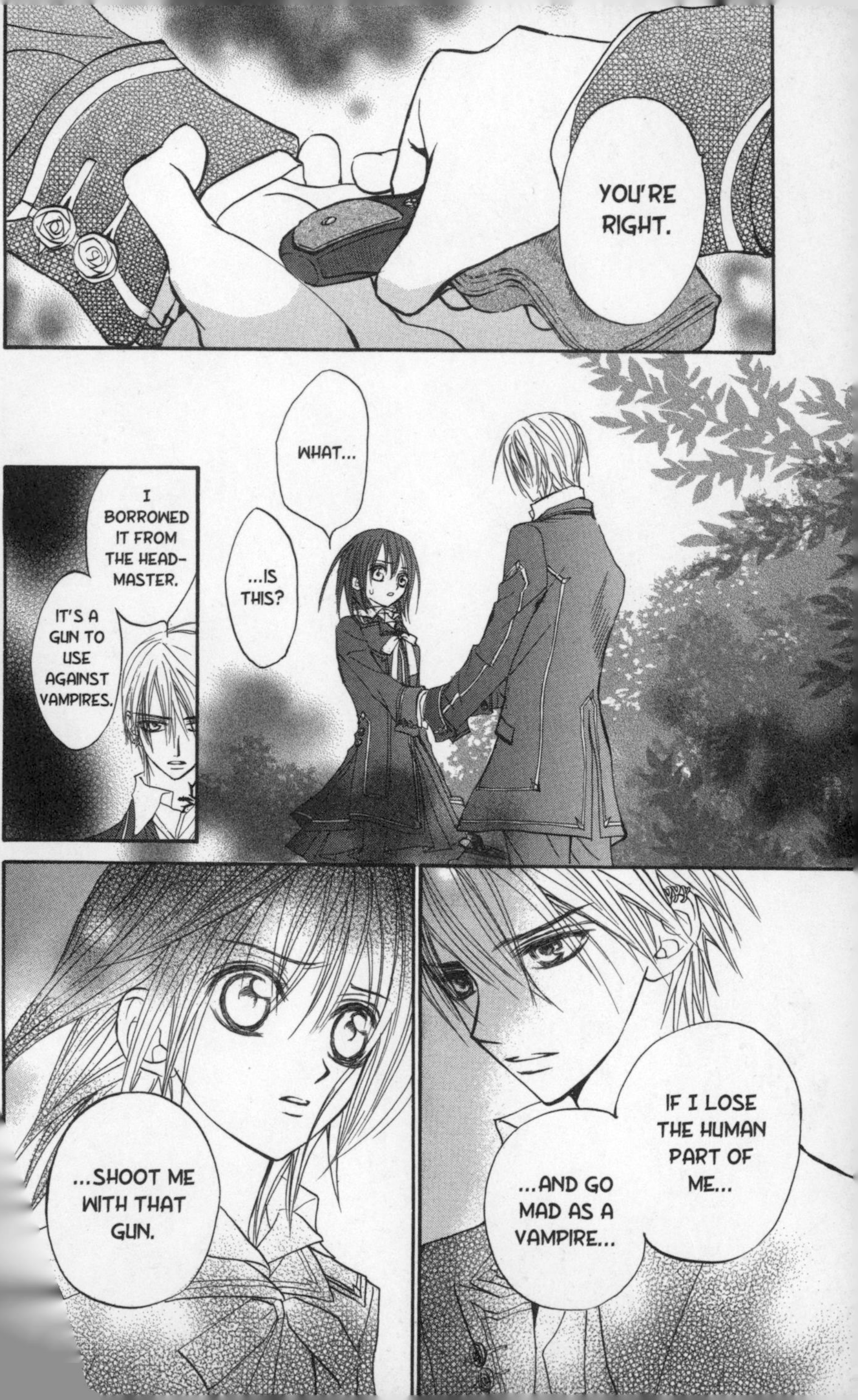
YOU'RE RIGHT.
WHAT...
...IS THIS?
I BORROWED IT FROM THE HEAD-MASTER.
IT'S A GUN TO USE AGAINST VAMPIRES.
IF I LOSE THE HUMAN PART OF ME...
...AND GO MAD AS A VAMPIRE...
...SHOOT ME WITH THAT GUN.

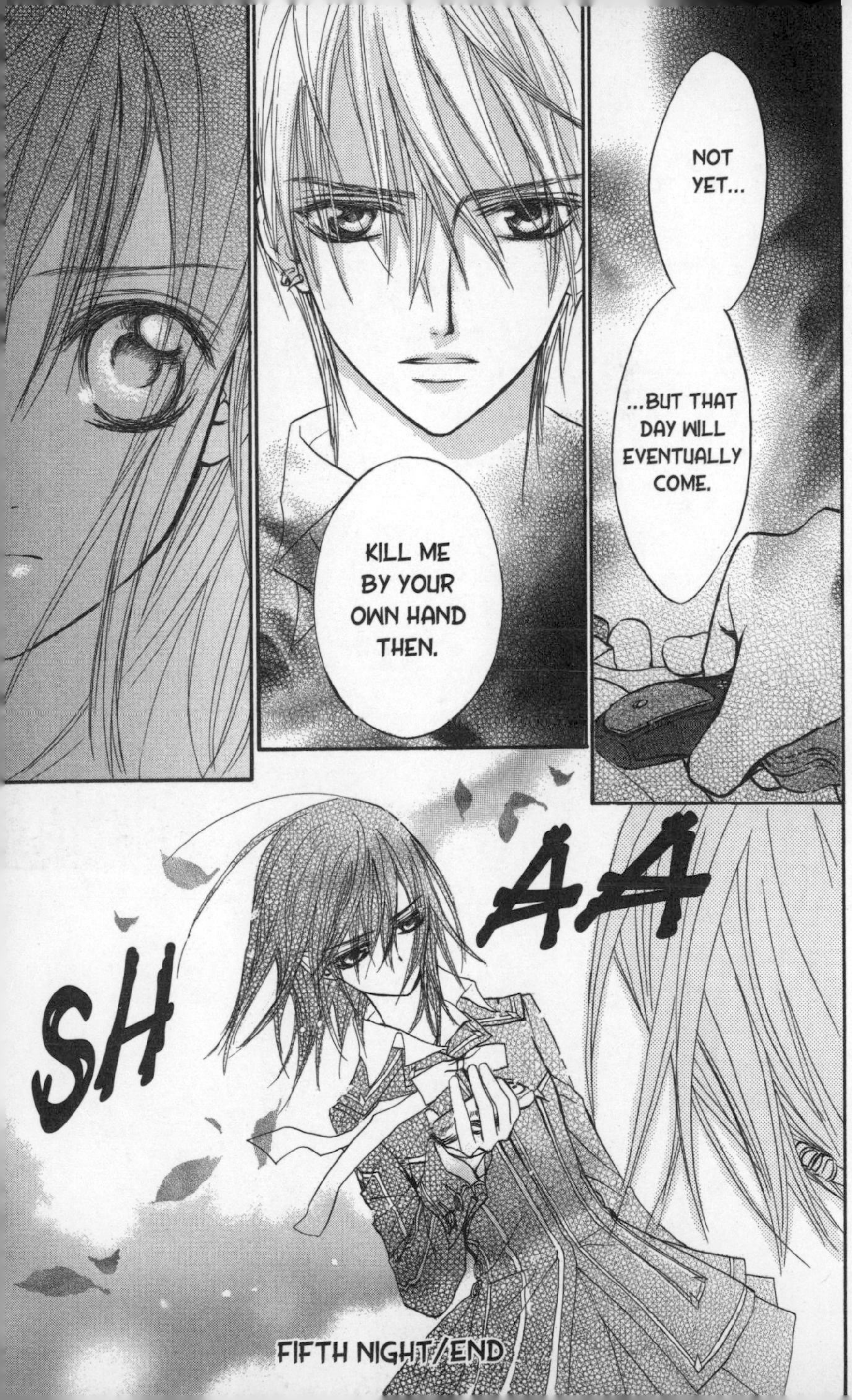
NOT YET...
...BUT THAT DAY WILL EVENTUALLY COME.
KILL ME BY YOUR OWN HAND THEN.
SH
FIFTH NIGHT/END

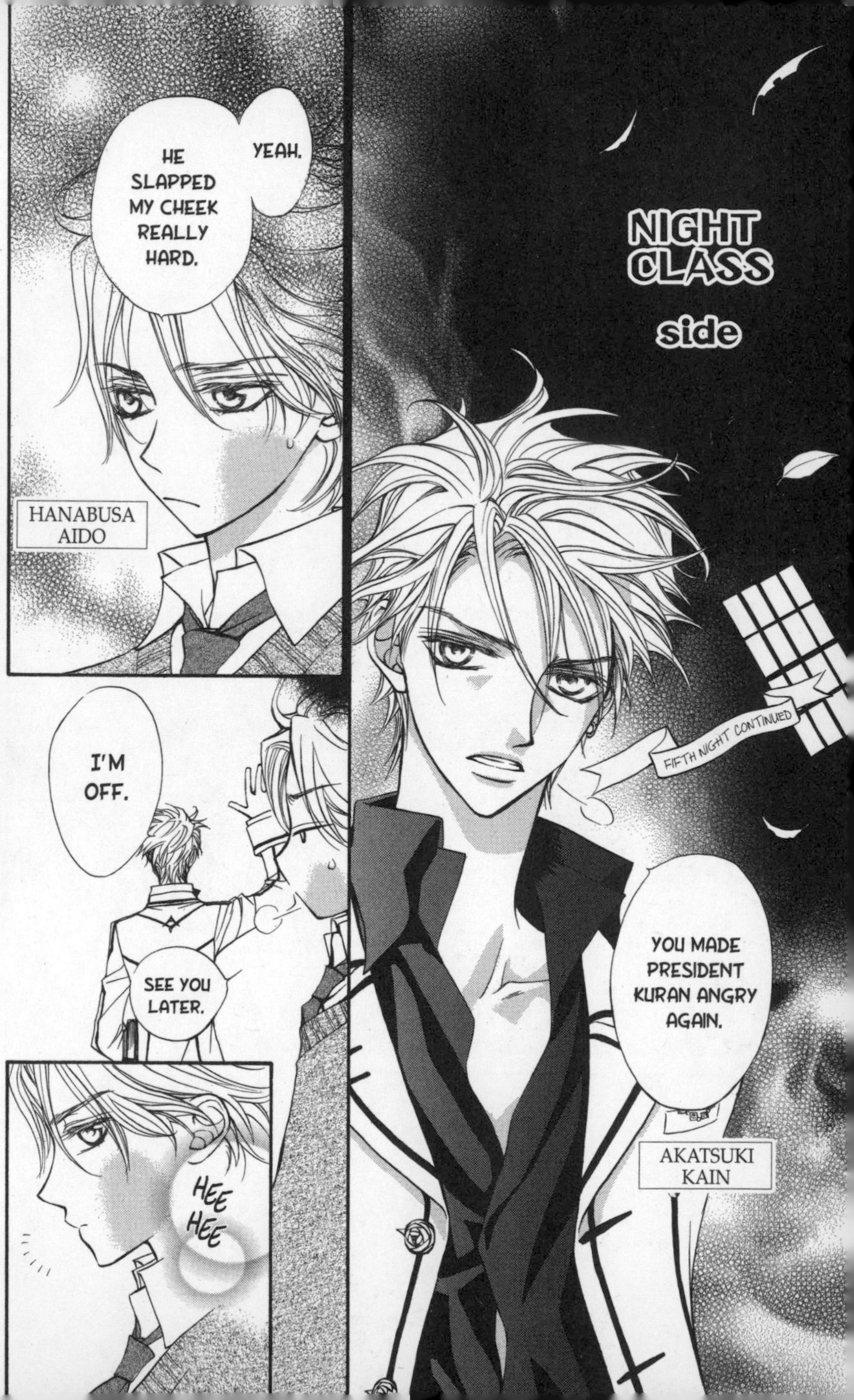
NIGHT CLASS
side
FIFTH NIGHT CONTINUED
YOU MADE PRESIDENT KURAN ANGRY AGAIN.
AKATSUKI KAIN
YEAH.
HE SLAPPED MY CHEEK REALLY HARD.
HANABUSA AIDO
I'M OFF.
SEE YOU LATER.
HEE HEE

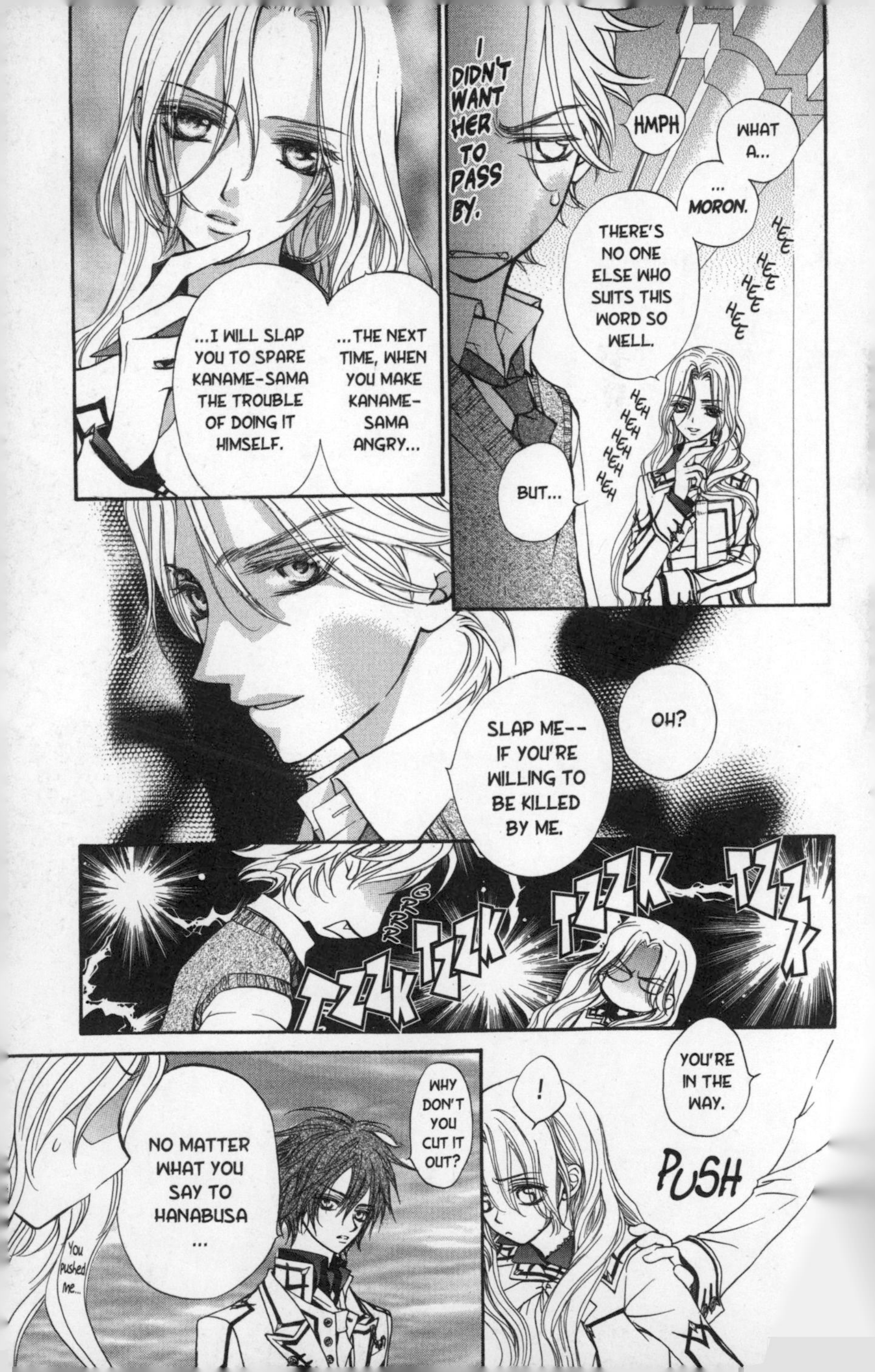
WHAT A...
HMPH
... MORON.
I DIDN'T WANT HER TO PASS BY.
THERE'S NO ONE ELSE WHO SUITS THIS WORD SO WELL.
HEE HEE HEE HEE
HEH HEH HEH HEH HEH
BUT...
...THE NEXT TIME, WHEN YOU MAKE KANAME-SAMA ANGRY...
...I WILL SLAP YOU TO SPARE KANAME-SAMA THE TROUBLE OF DOING IT HIMSELF.
OH?
SLAP ME-- IF YOU'RE WILLING TO BE KILLED BY ME.
TZZK
TZZK
TZZK
TZZK
GRRR
TZZK
YOU'RE IN THE WAY.
!
PUSH
WHY DON'T YOU CUT IT OUT?
NO MATTER WHAT YOU SAY TO HANABUSA ...
You pushed me...

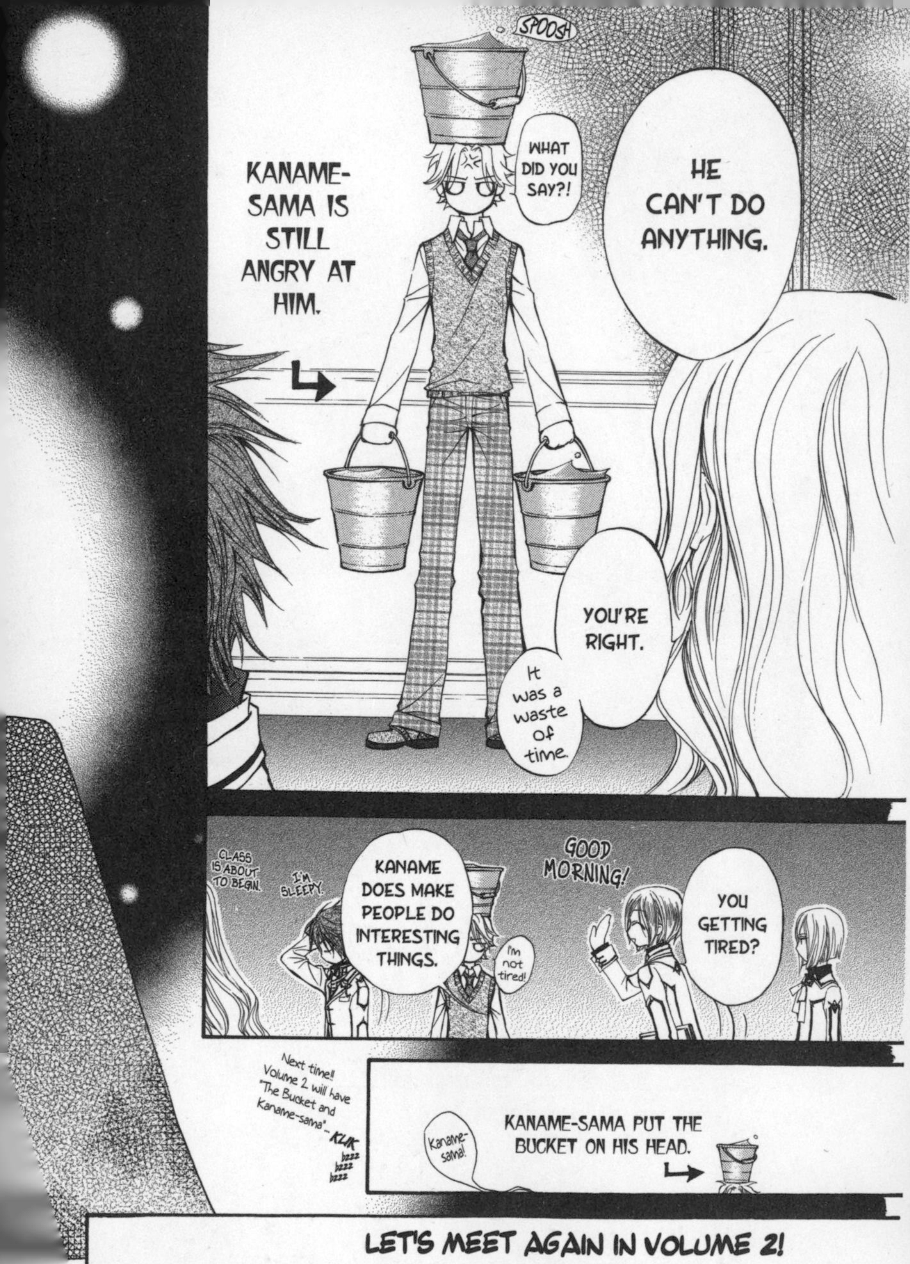
SPOOSH
HE CAN'T DO ANYTHING.
WHAT DID YOU SAY?!
KANAME-SAMA IS STILL ANGRY AT HIM.
YOU'RE RIGHT.
It was a waste of time.
YOU GETTING TIRED?
GOOD MORNING!
I'm not tired!
KANAME DOES MAKE PEOPLE DO INTERESTING THINGS.
I'M SLEEPY.
CLASS IS ABOUT TO BEGIN.
KANAME-SAMA PUT THE BUCKET ON HIS HEAD.
Kaname-sama!
Next time!! Volume 2 will have "The Bucket and Kaname-sama"-- KLIK
bzzz bzzz bzzz
LET'S MEET AGAIN IN VOLUME 2!

THANK YOU TO MY EDITOR, MY MOTHER, M. OKUDA-SAMA, I. AKAI-SAMA, U. SAWANOYU-SAMA, M. KIJIMA-SAMA, K. TANAKA-SAMA, K. MAKABE-SAMA, N. FUJIMINE-SAMA, H. TOTOBA-SAMA, AND MY DEAR READERS. ♡

NIGHT CLASS SIDE/END

樋野まつり
Matsuri Hino

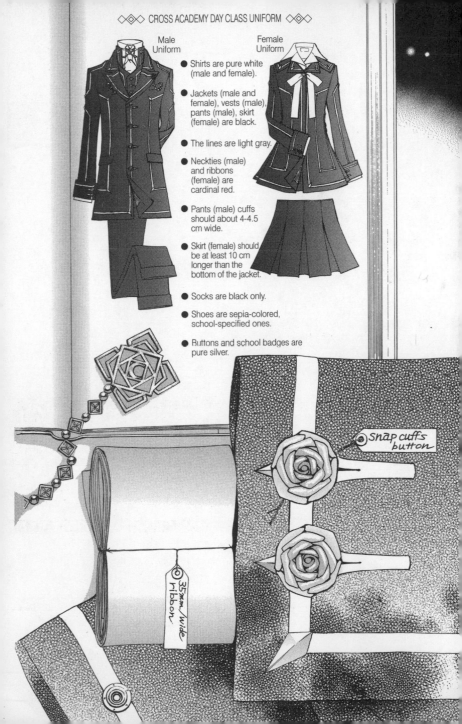

# CROSS ACADEMY DAY CLASS UNIFORM

Male Uniform

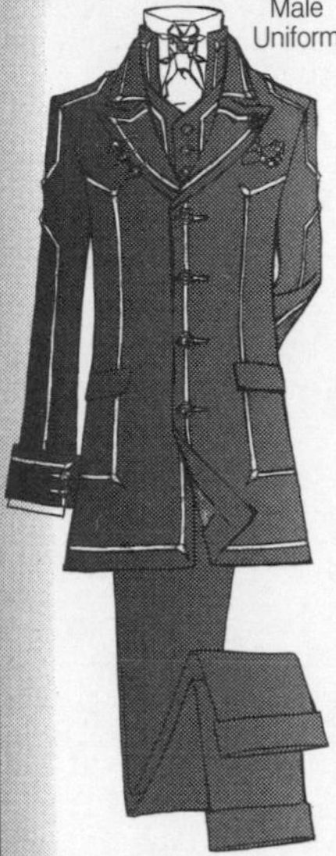

Female Uniform

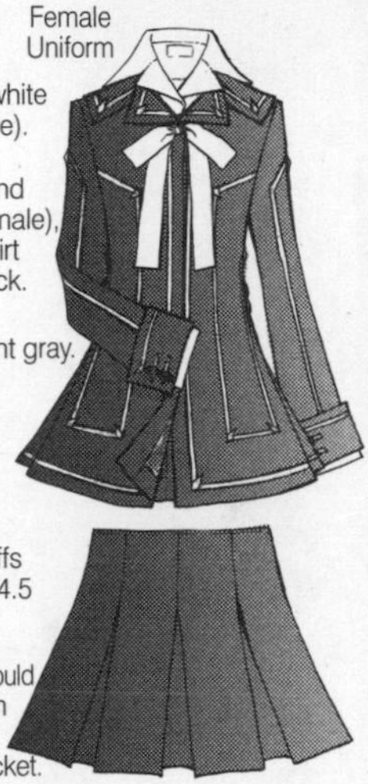

- Shirts are pure white (male and female).
- Jackets (male and female), vests (male), pants (male), skirt (female) are black.
- The lines are light gray.
- Neckties (male) and ribbons (female) are cardinal red.
- Pants (male) cuffs should about 4-4.5 cm wide.
- Skirt (female) should be at least 10 cm longer than the bottom of the jacket.
- Socks are black only.
- Shoes are sepia-colored, school-specified ones.
- Buttons and school badges are pure silver.

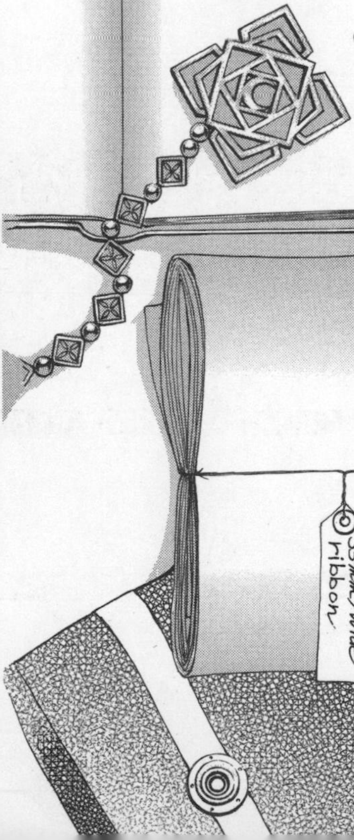

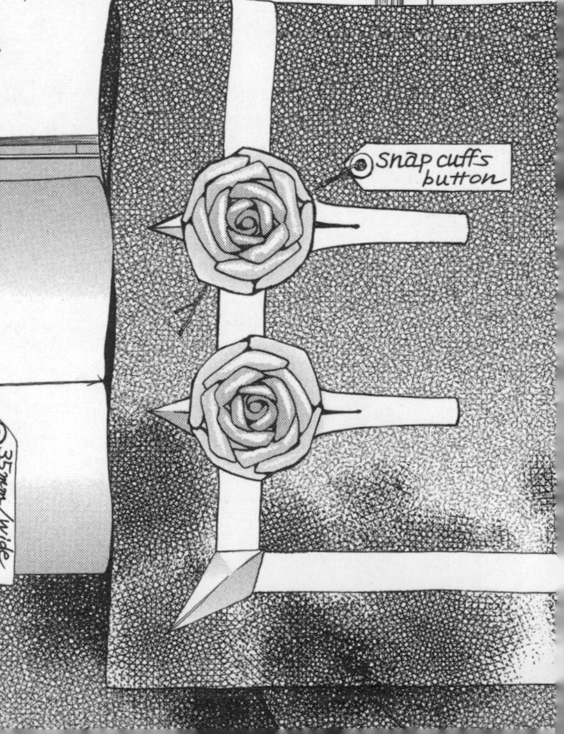
snap cuffs button
35mm/wide ribbon

# EDITOR'S NOTES

## Characters

Matsuri Hino puts careful thought into the names of her characters in *Vampire Knight*, so in each chapter of *Shojo Beat* magazine you'll find an explanation of the kanji for one character's name. Here is the collection of character names so far:

藍堂英

**Aido Hanabusa**
*Hanabusa* means "petals of a flower." *Aido* means "indigo temple." In Japanese, the pronunciation of *Aido* is very close to the pronunciation of the English word *idol*.

架院暁

**Kain Akatsuki**
*Akatsuki* means "dawn," or "day-break." In *Kain, ka* is a base or support, while *in* denotes a building that has high fences around it, such as a temple or school.

早園瑠佳

**Souen Ruka**
In *Ruka*, the *ru* means "lapis lazuli" while the *ka* means "good-looking," or "beautiful." The *sou* in Ruka's surname, *Souen*, means "early," but this kanji also has an obscure meaning of "strong fragrance." The *en* means "garden."

# 錐生零

**Kiryu Zero**

Zero's first name is the kanji for *rei*, meaning "zero." In his last name, *Kiryu*, the *ki* means "auger" or "drill," and the *ryu* means "life."

# 玖蘭枢

**Kuran Kaname**

*Kaname* means "hinge" or "door." The kanji for his last name is a combination of the old-fashioned way of writing *ku*, meaning "nine," and *ran*, meaning "orchid": "nine orchids."

## *Terms*

**-sama**: The suffix *sama* is used in formal address for someone who ranks higher in the social hierarchy. The vampires call their leader "Kaname-sama" only when they are among their own kind.

**Xocolatl**: Xocolatl, or "bitter water," is thought to be an early Aztec word for chocolate. In the world of *Vampire Knight*, St. Valentine's Day is called St. Xocolatl's Day.

Matsuri Hino burst onto the manga scene with her series *Kono Yume ga Sametara* (When This Dream Is Over), which was published in *LaLa DX* magazine. Hino was a manga artist a mere nine months after she decided to become one.

With the success of her popular series *Toraware no Minoue* (Captive Circumstance), and *MeruPuri*, Hino has established herself as a major player in the world of shojo manga. *Vampire Knight* is currently serialized in *LaLa* and *Shojo Beat* magazines.

Hino enjoys creative activities and has commented that she would have been either an architect or an apprentice to traditional Japanese craft masters if she had not become a manga artist.

# VAMPIRE KNIGHT
## Vol. 1
The Shojo Beat Manga Edition

This manga contains material that was originally published in English in *Shojo Beat* magazine, July–November 2006 issues.

**STORY AND ART BY**

MATSURI HINO

**Translation & English Adaptation**/Tomo Kimura
**Touch-up Art & Lettering**/Mark McMurray
**Graphic Design**/Amy Martin
**Editor**/Nancy Thistlethwaite

**Editor in Chief, Books**/Alvin Lu
**Editor in Chief, Magazines**/Marc Weidenbaum
**VP, Publishing Licensing**/Rika Inouye
**VP, Sales & Product Marketing**/Gonzalo Ferreyra
**VP, Creative**/Linda Espinosa
**Publisher**/Hyoe Narita

Printed in Canada

Published by VIZ Media, LLC
P.O. Box 77010
San Francisco, CA 94107

Shojo Beat Manga Edition
10 9 8 7 6
First printing, January 2007
Sixth printing, September 2008

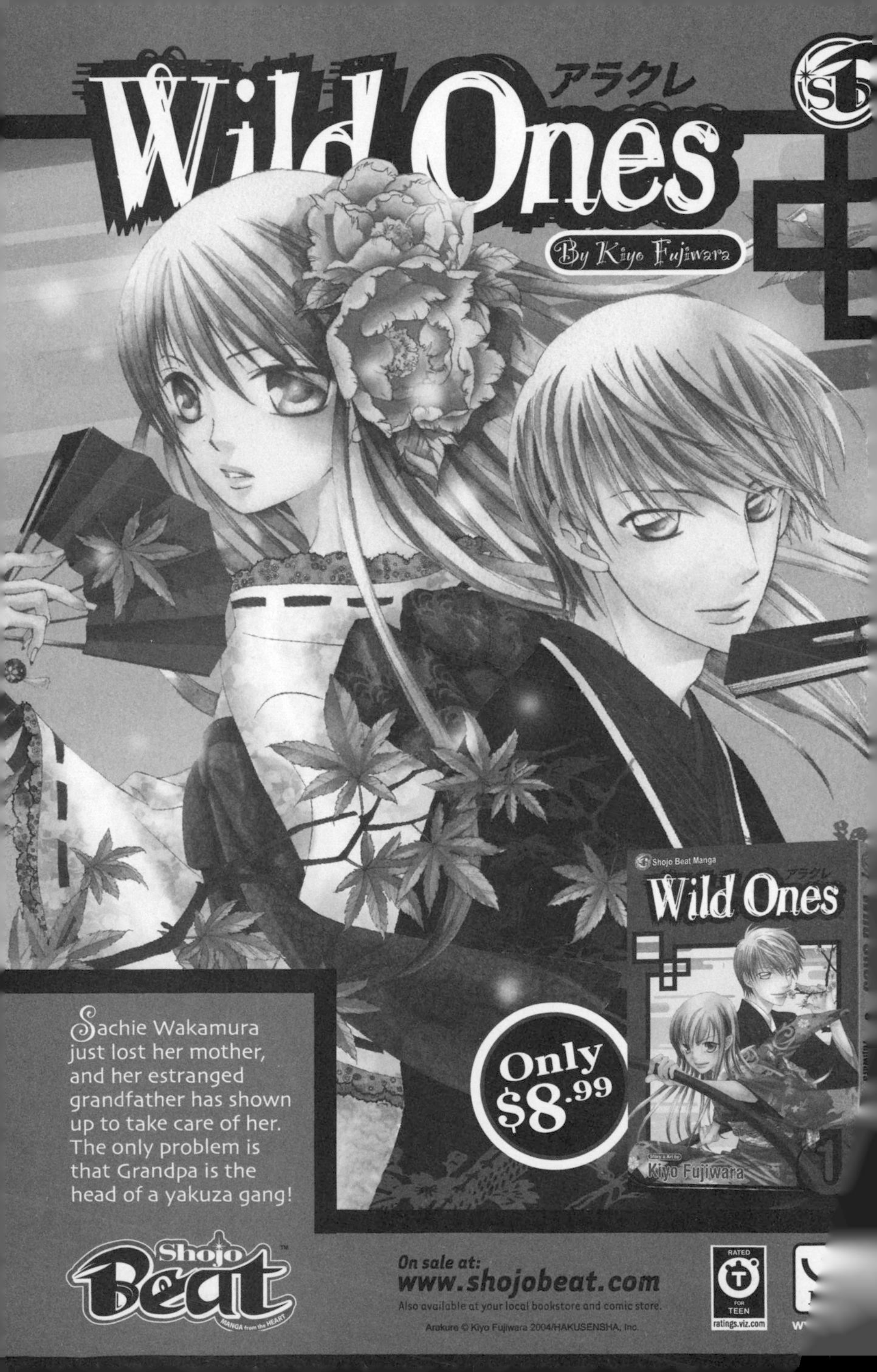
Wild Ones
アラクレ
By Kiyo Fujiwara
Shojo Beat Manga
Wild Ones
アラクレ
Kiyo Fujiwara
1
Only $8.99
Sachie Wakamura just lost her mother, and her estranged grandfather has shown up to take care of her. The only problem is that Grandpa is the head of a yakuza gang!
Shojo Beat
MANGA from the HEART
On sale at:
www.shojobeat.com
Also available at your local bookstore and comic store.
RATED T FOR TEEN
ratings.viz.com
Arakure © Kiyo Fujiwara 2004/HAKUSENSHA, Inc.

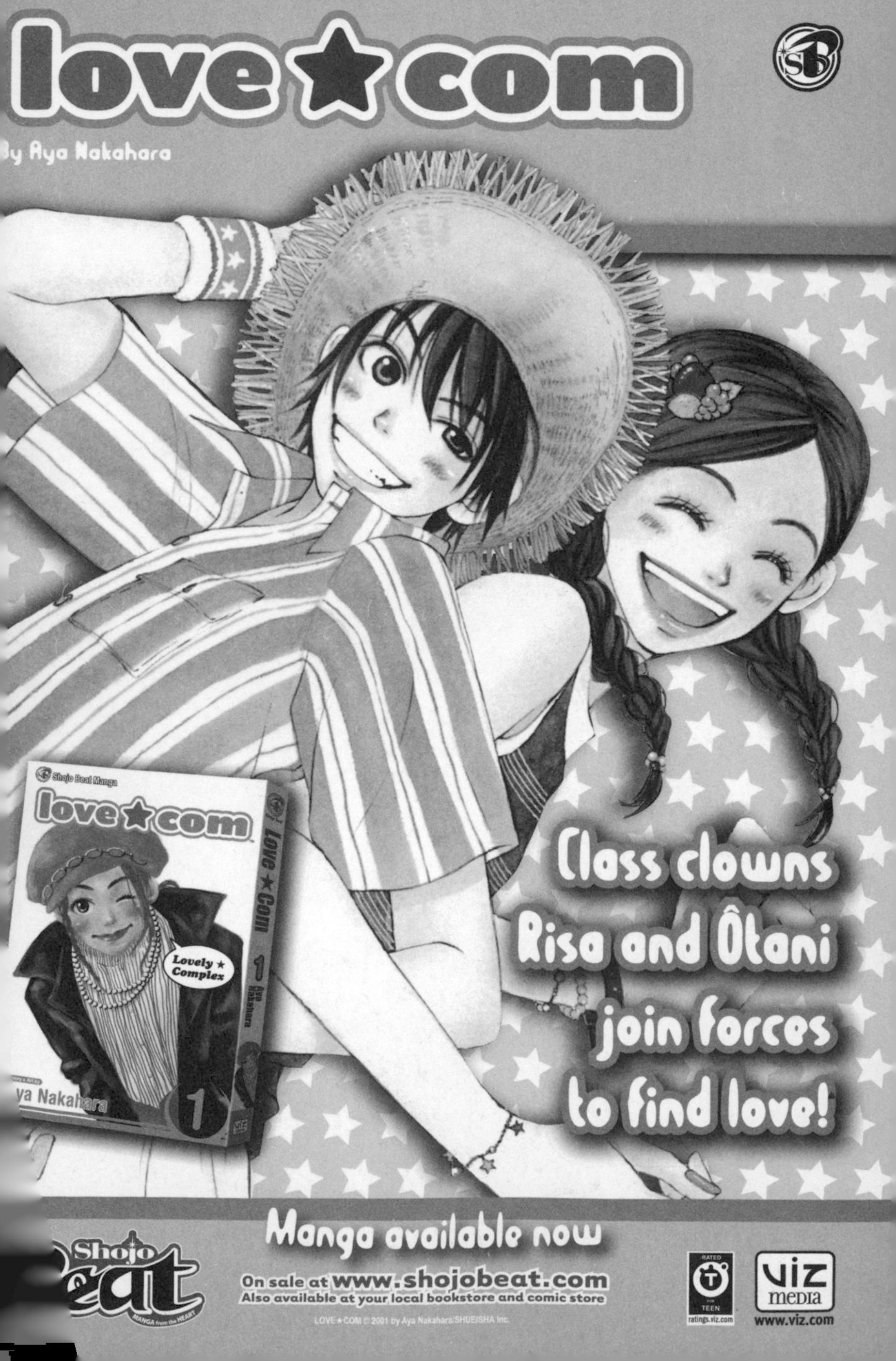
love★com
By Aya Nakahara
Shojo Beat Manga
love★com
Love★Com
1
Aya Nakahara
Lovely ★ Complex
Story & Art by
Aya Nakahara
1
Class clowns Risa and Ôtani join forces to find love!
Manga available now
Shojo Beat
MANGA from the HEART
On sale at www.shojobeat.com
Also available at your local bookstore and comic store
LOVE★COM © 2001 by Aya Nakahara/SHUEISHA Inc.
RATED T FOR TEEN
ratings.viz.com
VIZ media
www.viz.com

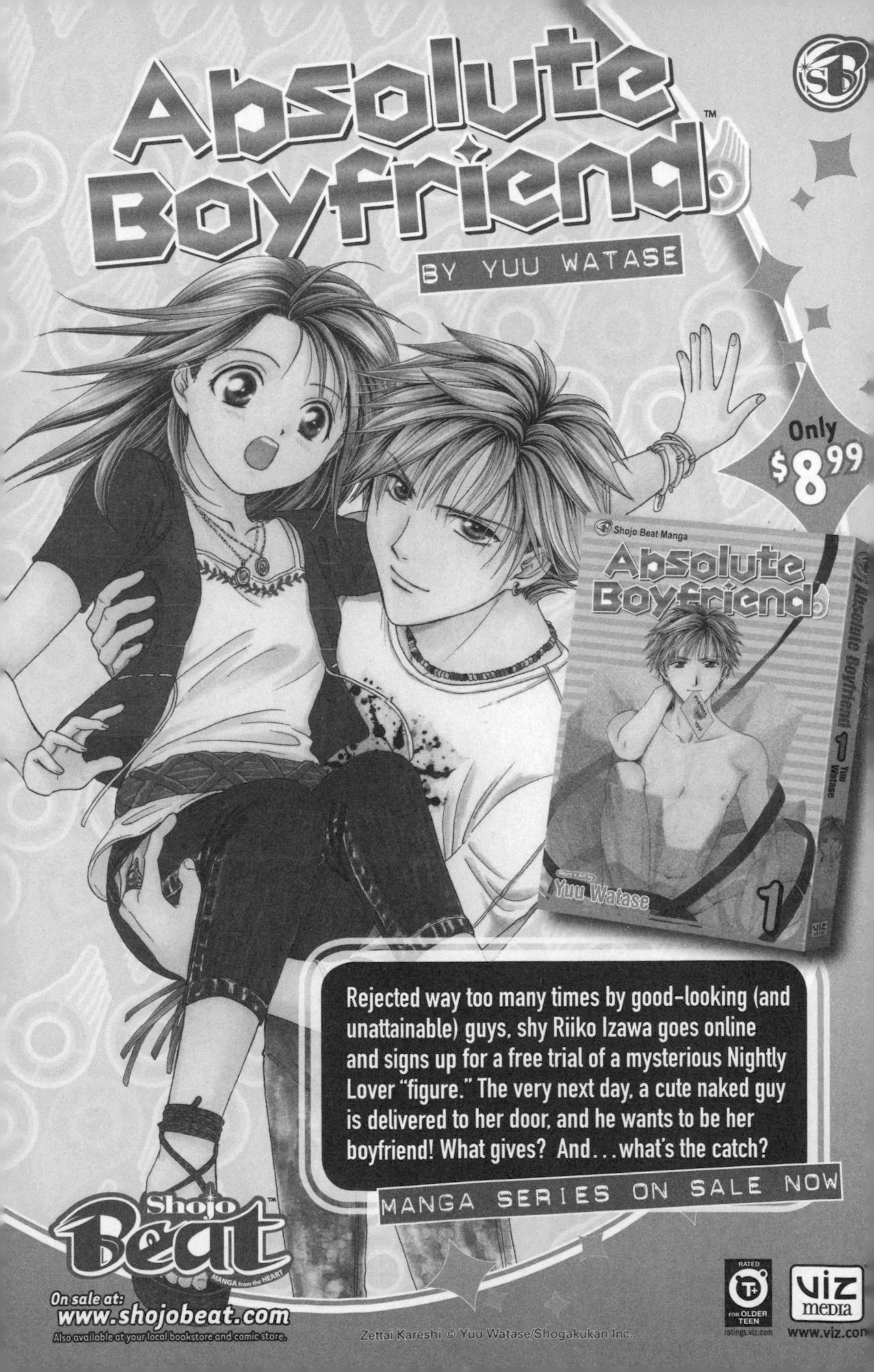

# Tell us what you think about Shojo Beat Manga!

Our survey is now available online. Go to:

**shojobeat.com/mangasurvey**

Help us make our product offerings better!